Hincmar of Laon and Carolingian Politics

Hincmar of Laon
and Carolingian Politics

Peter R. McKeon

UNIVERSITY OF ILLINOIS PRESS

Urbana   Chicago   London

Library of Congress Cataloging in Publication Data

McKeon, Peter R   1938-
   Hincmar of Laon and Carolingian politics.

   Bibliography: p.
   Includes index.
   1. France — Politics and government — To 987.
2. Hincmarus, Bp. of Laon, d. ca. 879.   I.   Title.
DC76.3.M3   944'.01'0924   78-12418
ISBN 0-252-00536-8

To Laura, J.G.L., and R.P.M.

Contents

Introduction   xi

I.   Dramatis Personae   3

II.   Bishop versus King, 868-69:   Property and Prosecution   17

III.   The Politics of Divorce and the Seizure of Lotharingia, 857-69   39

IV.   The Ordering and Tensions of the Ecclesiastical Hierarchy   57

V.   The Quarrel Matures   75

VI.   Bishop versus King, 870   99

VII.   The Conspiracy of Prince Carloman, 870-71   120

VIII.   The Bishop Falls: The Council of Douzy and Its Aftermath, 871-72   132

IX.   The Last Years, 871-79   156

Abbreviations   165

Appendix 1, Registrum Hincmari Laudunensis   169

Appendix 2, The Villa of Poilly   179

Notes   187

Bibliography   299

Index   319

Preface

The arduous task of reconstructing the past is eased by
the aid of comrades and colleagues. Of the many who
have helped me in various ways, I should like particularly to acknowledge several whose generous advice en-
abled me to complete this work. An early form of the
study was read and criticized by Professor David Jordan,
my friend and associate at the University of Illinois.
Discussions and conversations with Professors Shafer
Williams and Karl Morrison provided me with guidance and
illumination on various points. I am greatly indebted
to the criticism and advice of Professor Gerhart Ladner,
who read the manuscript, and whose encouragement and
example have long supported me. I owe no less a debt
to Prof.-Doc. Horst Fuhrmann, who not only read my work,
but kindly sent me not yet published portions of his
own monumental study of the Pseudo-Isidore. Again, it
would be hard to overstate the aid received from Professor Richard Sullivan, who read the manuscript twice,
and provided many valuable criticisms and suggestions.
Finally, I wish to express my thanks to my friend and
colleague Professor Leo Schelbert, whose help, support,
and counsel have been invaluable to me.

P. R. McK.
Chicago, July 1976

Introduction

The Carolingian era as a period in European history is
as significant as it was short. The three generations
that separate Charlemagne's imperial coronation in 800
from the liquidation of the Carolingian empire with the
deposition of Charles the Fat in 887 spanned years that
saw the emergence and elucidation of numerous historical
developments that have vital importance both of themselves and for the effects they would exert upon the
future. The unique character of this extraordinary century is expressed in as many ways as it is many-faceted.
The present work is founded upon two principles, both of
which to some extent contradict each other.

The first is that the ninth century, the era of Carolingian Europe, was an era of transition, a period of
increasing specificity in a society that was moving between the undifferentiated condition of the earlier
Frankish community and the complex distinctions of the
later medieval order. It is this character that in many
ways gives the era its importance. As men sought to
cope with immediate situations, they produced new formulations by utilizing old materials, and they laid the
groundwork for the differentiations--political, societal,
and intellectual--of the centuries to come. This age
saw the beginnings of the western European nations no
less than of the feudal order, and it witnessed the
origins of a sharp distinction between theology and canon
law and of the expression of important formulations in
both.

On the other hand, one ought not to interpret this
tendency too strongly; it is anachronistic to read back
into the ninth century sophisticated distinctions and
modes of thought that developed only gradually in the
course of centuries that followed. The Carolingian era

must be studied on its own terms as a period that still
remained, in many essential respects, unitary in culture
and society. This aspect of the age finds expression,
for example, in the unitary nature attributed to the
populus Dei, the Christian society that was conceived to
be an *ecclesia*, and more specifically in its institutions, in the broad agendas of the great councils and in
the wide range of activities characteristic of those who
attended them.

These two aspects, unity and differentiation, found
expression in various modes, through a succession of
perennial issues that reflected the efforts of an un-
stable society to resolve its tensions. Problems concerning rights of property, the ordering of the ecclesiastical organization, the assessment of spheres of
jurisdiction in such important matters as marriage or
the relationships between cleric and layman, the conduct of diplomacy and politics, and the nature of rule
and monarchy, all were vehicles through which various
elements in society--monarchs, popes, metropolitan and
suffragan bishops, and nobles--sought to assert their
respective interests. But these were problems rarely
to be found in isolation; the character of the times ordained their association.

No better example can be found of the manner in which
the personally oriented politics of ninth-century society dictated the combination of private and public in
the career of an influential figure into a dynamic and
nearly symbiotic whole than does the history of Hincmar,
bishop of Laon from 858 until 879, that is, during the
score of years that witnessed the start of the final
struggles and collapse of the Carolingian experiment.
Nephew and namesake of the extraordinary archbishop of
Reims who for so many years dominated the politics and
diplomacy of the western portion of the empire, which in
843 fell to the lot of King Charles the Bald, Hincmar of
Laon's associations with the Carolingian monarchs were
as close and complex as was his relationship to his
uncle and metropolitan.

Hincmar's career was a stormy one, marked by a succession of quarrels at once personal and public, through

the course of which he came to serve as catalyst and major spokesman for a number of questions of immediacy to the orders that dominated the society of his time. His name occurs in a variety of historical contexts. He is prominently mentioned in studies concerned with the fealty intended to cement the elements that composed the Christian empire. Students of the councils of the Church also find a rich mine in the records of those assemblies before which the affairs of Hincmar of Laon were aired. In the important debates regarding the property of the church and the nature and extent of episcopal administration in diocese and province, the evidence of his disputes provides the latest, fullest, and most paradigmatic of statements. And, in the course of argumentation that accompanied these and other developments in the bishop's life, Hincmar came to serve as the foremost advocate of the canonical principles expounded by the Pseudo-Isidore, while the antithetical ecclesiologies that he himself and the archbishop of Reims produced as a vehicle for their long and bitter quarrel represent the fullest of such statements made at that time and are pregnant with significance for later ages.

All of these histories are part of Bishop Hincmar's own. Further, the context of these discussions reveals the importance of Hincmar's particular situation, for his intimate connections with nearly every person, trend, and event of major political consequence meant that his activities were in themselves instrumental in defining the course of Frankish political history, in which he appears not only as a representative but as an actor as well. Between 860 and 868 he played a role in the diplomacy connected with the divorce of King Lothar and in the seizure of the Lotharingian realm after Lothar's premature death in 869. Again, in the course of his extraordinary conflicts regarding the regulation of his church, no one was more responsible than he for promoting the active involvement of the papacy in the affairs of the northern realms, an involvement with obvious ecclesiological and political ramifications at every stage of his career. Finally, the failure of his schemes ultimately alienated him from the establishment he had

sought to use and sent him into the camp of rebels whose
opposition to a dubious political settlement perhaps best
typifies the spirit that most truly guided the Carolingian *imperium christianum* during these years of failure.

   That spirit ultimately is the subject of the following pages. The line that separates biography and history is a fine one, while distinctions between aspects
of the history of an era necessarily sacrifice context
to subject-matter. The present work is not a study of
ecclesiology, though this is a theme that will appear
prominently; nor is it one that takes kingship, papacy,
or intellectual or ideological development as its central theme, though these too, in varying degrees, are
recurrent subjects. This work is, rather, a study of
some of the intricacies involved in the manipulation of
political power, as seen in terms of the interrelation-
ship between men who held great power and used it for a
variety of reasons.

Hincmar of Laon and Carolingian Politics

I

Dramatis Personae

1. King Charles the Bald

In the summer of 858, a fleet of Viking longboats entered the mouth of the river Seine. For years the Carolingian empire had been prey to pirate attacks,[1] but by the middle of the ninth century the Danish freebooters had established a more permanent stronghold on this richest of Frankish waterways. Now from a defensive camp on the island of Oscelle they could move with impunity against Rouen or Paris and any of the other wealthy towns and ecclesiastical foundations inland.[2] The threat could hardly be ignored. Raising an army, King Charles the Bald marched to beseige the fort, aided by his nephew, Lothar II. But, taking advantage of the distraction of his relatives, King Louis the German crossed Lotharingia and entered the western realm, where he proclaimed himself a liberator of the church.[3] Many of Charles's own *proceres* or nobility welcomed the invader, abandoning the fealty they had sworn to their monarch at the villa of Quierzy the previous March.[4] Charles broke off the seige and went to meet with his brother at Brienne, but discussion proved fruitless. His troops routed and dispersed, Charles fled to refuge in Burgundy.[5] By December, Louis was installed in the palace of Attigny, and he prepared to legitimize his victory by assuming the royal title.[6]

The situation was hardly a novel one. For nearly thirty years intrafamilial warfare had been habitual among the descendents of Charlemagne, ever since Lothar, Pepin, and Louis, the eldest sons of the emperor Louis the Pious, had first risen against their father in 830 to protest his incompetent rule

and the blatant favoritism that he and his second
queen, Judith, showed to their young son Charles.[7]
Louis's death in 840 had afforded no alleviation of
the civil strife. Lothar, who succeeded to the
imperial title, was anxious to consolidate his rule.
He now found himself the target of attack by Louis
the German and Charles, both of whom were no less
eager to maintain their kingdoms autonomously. In
August 843 the de facto division of the empire was
recognized when the Treaty of Verdun apportioned
the Carolingian realm among the three surviving
brothers--Lothar, Charles, and Louis--the grandsons
of Charlemagne.[8] In the years that followed, an
effort was made to establish a principle of imperial rule based upon a concord between the fraternal monarchs, but implementation of this plan was
rarely successful, and with the death of Emperor
Lothar in 855, its failure became apparent, most
evidently in the rivalry between Louis the German
and Charles the Bald, which culminated three years
later in Louis's invasion.[9]

   King Charles, who was born on 13 June 823,[10] was
barely seventeen years of age at the time of his
father's death and, when the Treaty of Verdun
assigned him rule over the western portion of the
Carolingian empire, but a few months past his
twentieth birthday. In appearance he was well-
proportioned, though of only medium height.[11] As
the best educated member of his family, he would
later on make his court into something of a haven
for men of letters.[12] Intelligent and resourceful,
he had the capacity to be an excellent general,
always prepared to take rapid advantage of his
opportunities. But even with the best will possible,
no one could have found the task that confronted
the young king an easy one.

   Lothar had the lands between the rivers
   Rhine and Scheldt up to the sea, and down
   to the Cambresis, Hainault, and the
   territories of Lomme and Mezières; below,
   the counties adjoining the Meuse [on the
   left bank] up until the intersection of

the Rhône and the Saône, then the length
of the Rhône to the sea, including the
counties on both banks of the river.
Beyond these boundaries he held only [the
abbey of Saint-Vaast of] Arras, his
through the love of his brother Charles.[13]

Thus Prudentius, the author of the middle section
of the almost official *Annales Bertiniani*, described the northern region that went to the new
emperor after months of consultations which culminated at Verdun. Hence, the areas east of the
Rhine fell to King Louis the German; and all
territories west of the rough frontier--with the
exception of Saint-Vaast--including the western
portions of the Lyonnais, the Viennois, the
Vivarais, the Uzège, and the county of Châlons,
went to Charles.[14]

The land Charles received was not a homogeneous
one, but rather one where centuries of immigration,
colonization, and conquest had produced a disparate
population with differences that were enhanced by
the geographic separations provided by the great
French waterways and the mountainous regions ex-
tending from the Pyrenees up to the northeast.
Thus, in Aquitaine the traditions of the old Iberian
and Gothic inhabitants had long stymied Carolingian
efforts to impose control, and by the ninth century,
the "inconstancy" and "faithlessness" of its inhabitants had become proverbial among the Franks.[15]
Louis the German's invasion was inspired, at least
in part, by the appeal of the Aquitanians for a new
king.[16] In Brittany, too, the Carolingian rulers
had long been distracted and hindered in the
imposition of their rule by a widespread desire of
the populace to remain independent.[17]

To such internal difficulties, the incursions of
the Vikings added in no small measure. As early as
the year 800, Charlemagne had found it necessary to
construct a fleet for the defense of Aquitaine
against Danish attack,[18] and some fifty years of
nearly constant terror began with the civil wars

of Louis the Pious's reign. Although the whole empire
suffered, the western kingdom sustained the brunt by far.
Geography accounts in part for this: the west was the
logical direction for ships sailing from Jutland and
the Scandinavian peninsula west of the Keel mountains;
the great French rivers were easy of access; and the popu-
lous regions along the Seine, Loire, and Garonne were
filled with wealthy churches and cities that made easy
prey. That the monarchy was so little able to contain
these attacks showed inability less than it reflected the
divided condition of society. In addition to regional
differences, Charles the Bald was plagued with a noble
class that was at once powerful and eager to assert its
autonomy against any efforts to centralize political control.[19] Charles was often unable to raise an army from
among the *fideles*, who did not hesitate to betray him,
and he was frequently forced to follow the precedent established by Lothar I of imposing upon his subjects a
tax, called the Danegeld, by which the pirates might be
bought.[20]

In these circumstances, with so tenuous a hold upon
his realm, King Charles sought and found his firmest support in the church.

*   *   *

Late in 858, his invasion apparently a success, Louis
the German turned to the episcopacy of the western realm
to convey to him the crown and title of king; from Attigny he summoned the prelates of the western realm to
convene for his coronation.[21] But now, at last, he was
to be frustrated. The bishops from the provinces of Reims
and Rouen, at a meeting at the **villa** of Quierzy, announced their support of King Charles in a letter to the
German monarch that admonished him for his attempt to
appear as their benefactor.[22] Having failed to gain
episcopal support, Louis's cause rapidly lost momentum,
while his brother regained his strength. Charles's re-
grouped forces surprised him shortly afterward, when
they attacked him at Jouy, forcing him to retreat into
his own lands.[23] By January 859 the threat had passed.
Charles's bishops, the saviors of their monarch's throne,
had once more shown the importance of their order in

Carolingian society and politics.[24]

In his reestablishment of the ecclesiastical
organization, which was a shambles after years of
Merovingian anarchy, Charlemagne took as his base
the fourth-century *Notitia provinciarum*,[25] and by
the year 794 he had organized seventeen provinces,
each headed by a metropolitan bishop.[26] By 843 the
empire north of Italy had a total of eighteen provinces, of which the Treaty of Verdun gave two metropolitan sees to Louis the German, eight to Lothar I,
and eight to Charles. But in long-evangelized Gaul,
the church was naturally far more highly developed.
The turbulent years of the reign of Louis the Pious
had seen the Frankish episcopate emerge as a viable
force in politics.[27] Particularly in the west, the
bishops continued in this role, identifying their
interests with those of the central authority to the
extent that the leaders of the church played a part
in virtually every activity or formulation of policy
attempted by the monarchy. Though control of the
province of Tours was felt necessary for the maintenance of authority in the northwest,[28] and though
Charles would later say that peace in Aquitaine depended on the timely appointment of a capable archbishop at Bourges,[29] the greatest role in Frankish
politics was played by the prelates of the three
Neustrian provinces of Rouen, Sens, and Reims, who
composed the bulk of ecclesiastical attendance at
nearly every great council and assembly and provided
the most active workers and advisors to the royal
court. And throughout the reign of Charles the Bald
one man--Archbishop Hincmar of Reims--unquestionably
played the most important part in Frankish politics.

2. Archbishop Hincmar of Reims

Toward the end of the fourth century B.C., a
migration of Celtic peoples settled in the area north
of the rivers Seine and Marne, giving their names to
the regions in which they established themselves.[30]
For all their common background, they made up an

aggregate bound together only tenuously, in which
rival tribes fought for supremacy. The first tribe
to dominate was the Remes, who settled in the region
around the Mont-de-Berrn and in the valleys of the
rivers Suippe, Aisne, and Vesle; but by the time the
legions under Caesar penetrated the area, their position of dominance had passed to their western neighbors, the Suessiones.[31] This presumably influenced
the Remes in forming an alliance with Caesar, as a
result of which the tribe emerged in Roman favor and
thus extended its sphere of influence to include the
region between the Ardennes and the Marne and from
Fismes to the Argonne.[32] The political center of
this area was called Durocorter.

Here the Romans, too, established headquarters.
Adopting the old name, they called their *oppidum*
Durocortorum,[33] and this area (the site of the future
city of Reims) became the core of the Roman province
of Belgica. The place thrived under Roman rule; and,
fortunate as it was in land and water routes that
made it a convenient point of access from the south
and west to both Germany and Britain, it soom became
a *civitas*.[34] By the first century A.D., Durocortorum
was the largest city of the province; and in the centuries that followed, its prosperity increased, as the
city became a provincial capital and the point of
intersection for no less than six roads.[35]

The reform of Diocletian divided the province of
Belgica into two parts; and, by the mid-fourth century,
Trier, the capital of Belgica I, had far outstripped
her rival in Belgica II. Still Reims, as Durocortorum
comes increasingly to be called--the city that some
said had been founded by Romulus's brother Remus--
continued to prosper as the head of a province that by
the fourth century contained twelve *civitates*. Near
one of these, Thérouanne, the Franks established themselves in Gaul in the first half of the fifth century.[36]

Legend ascribes the evangelization of Belgica II
to saints Valerian, Crispin, and Lucian, the disciples
of the martyred Saint Denis, who died in the Decian

persecutions of 249–251.[37] The church of Reims itself
appears to have been founded between 230 and 240;
Bishop Imbetausius, whose name figures among the
prelates attending the council of Arles in 314, is
fourth in the episcopal catalog of the city.[38] It
seems reasonable to believe that by the end of the
fourth century an episcopal see existed in each of
the other eleven cities of the province: Soissons,
Châlons-sur-Marne, Noyon, Arras, Cambrai, Tournai,
Senlis, Beauvais, Amiens, Thérouanne, and Boulogne.[39]
At Reims itself, a cathedral was built in about the
year 400, during the episcopate of Saint Nicasius.[40]
In the fifth century an oratory was erected and
dedicated to Saint Christopher, which later became a
great shrine. This oratory, it was alleged, was the
burial place of Remi, the apostle of the Franks, who
in 496 baptised King Clovis and thus set the seal on
Frankish fortunes no less than on those of his city.[41]

During the failure of the Roman empire and in the
centuries of Merovingian rule, the physiognomy of the
province was altered, as shifts of population and
divisions of the realm brought about the collapse of
the see of Arras into that of Cambrai, the elimination
of the see of Boulogne, and the creation of the see of
Laon.[42] But, in spite of these changes, the significance of Reims and of its bishops persisted. By the
early ninth century, the church of Reims stood among
the most important of all in the Carolingian Empire,
associated with the very beginnings of Frankish
Christianity, head of one of the most prominent provinces, and based in a city ranked among the first in
the realm. Within the borders of its province were
such great monasteries as Saint-Vaast, Saint-Omer,
Saint-Riquier, and Corbie; and such favorite Carolingian residences as Compiègne, Samoussy, Servais,
Attigny, Verberie, Quierzy, and Ponthion. To this
great metropolitan see the emperor Louis the Pious in
816 appointed Ebbo, his lifelong friend.[43]

Ebbo of Reims is one of a rare type in the Carolingian empire who derived from servile origins and
attained to one of the highest posts in the empire.
His mother was Louis's nurse, and the very close quasi-

fraternal relationship thus established provided an
opportunity for the development and exercise of the
youth's intelligence. A gifted student and later
widely known for his learning, he served as royal
librarian at Louis's court in Aquitaine, and assumed
a like post at Aachen in 814. He was well known as a
patron of scholarship and art, as an evangelist, and
as a great builder of churches.

In 833 Ebbo cast his lot with those who supported
Lothar against Louis, and his consequent deposition
in 835 ushered in an evil decade for Reims. Neither
he nor Lothar had recognized the unique circumstances
of his resignation that for a long time prevented the
naming of a substitute; as a consequence, the vacant
see fell prey to the depradations that affected so many
churches of the empire during the years of fraternal
warfare.[44] Only in 844, after the Treaty of Verdun had
been signed and the realm in which Reims would lie had
been determined, did Charles the Bald accede to requests of the people and prelates and agree to appoint
a new bishop.[45] Then, at Beauvais in 845, Hincmar, a
monk of Saint-Denis, was consecrated archbishop of
Reims and began his extraordinary career.[46]

The lifetime of Hincmar of Reims nearly corresponds
with the duration of the empire he ultimately affected
so profoundly. As he lay dying in 882-just five years
before the deposition of the emperor Charles the Fat-
he might have recalled the days long before when as a
child he had seen the first emperor, Charlemagne, at
Aachen.

Hincmar was born in about 806, one of several
children in a noble family, and had at least two
sisters and a brother.[47] In spite of his long association and many ties of friendship with the inhabitants
of Reims, he himself did not originate from that province.[48] Instead, he grew up at the monastery of
Saint-Denis, where he was placed at an early age.[49]
There his intelligence soon merited distinction, and
he became a favorite pupil of the abbot Hilduin.[50]
When Hilduin succeeded his uncle Hildebold as archchaplain at Aachen, Hincmar accompanied him to the imperial

court.[51] He would never forget his old monastery, however and it would be the recipient of his favors in the
distant years to come.[52]

   At the imperial palace from 822 to 830, Hincmar was
present throughout the prelude to the rebellion.[53] But
far from being involved with the opponents of the
emperor, he became a close and faithful supporter of
Louis and of his youngest son, Charles. In 831, when
Hilduin was suspected of complicity in the events of
the previous year and as a result was exiled, Hincmar of
his own volition accompanied his mentor to Paderborn,
and it was his influence with the emperor that brought
Hilduin back to Saint-Denis.[54] Both Hincmar and
Hilduin saw Louis surrender to the rebels at Colmar in
833, and both were among the few who remained faithful
to him in spite of his defeat.[55]

   Two years later the young monk was on hand to see
Ebbo deposed at Thionville.[56] His lifelong fidelity to
Charles was manifested at the death of Louis in 840,
when Hilduin deserted the young king to side with the
emperor Lothar. Hincmar, who was no imperialist, nevertheless was a strong believer in the importance of
personal obligation, and he sought, even in defeat, to
employ his considerable talents in the service of the
monarch whose prosperity he identified with his own.
Although he was in many respects a narrow man and a
stringent taskmaster, his ambitions for himself and for
his king led him to employ his great knowledge of canon
law in remarkably innovative ways to justify his
actions and plans in directing the policies of the
western realm.

   He was not yet a bishop when he was with Charles in
844, but that year he played a part in the issuance of
the *capitula* by which the council held at Meaux sought
to assert the rights of the churches against the op-
pressions of the nobility.[57] Hincmar continued to
fight this battle throughout his life with increasing
intensity and sophistication, just as his self-asser-
tiveness likewise led him to compose works--political,
pastoral, theological, and ecclesiological--directed to
particular situations but simultaneously developing

arguments and statements that would be used as common-
places for centuries to come. Hardly the least among
the many services for his monarch was rendered late in
858, when he organized the episcopal opposition to Louis
the German and wrote the letter that rejected his pretensions to the throne of Charles.[58] The archbishop's
own nephew and namesake carried a copy of that letter to
King Charles.[59]

3. Bishop Hincmar of Laon

In March 858 the prelates and nobles of Charles's
realm assembled at the villa of Quierzy to renew their
fealty to the king.[60] Among them was Bishop Hincmar,
only recently ordained by his uncle to preside over the
see of Laon, who there makes his first public appearance
in the sources.[61] The bishop was already a favorite
with King Charles at the time of his retreat into
Burgundy,[62] and only upon the failure of Louis the
German in January 859 did Hincmar return to his see.

Laon alone among the episcopal sees of the ninth-
century province of Reims does not figure in the list
of cities of the *Notitia provinciarum*. Under the Romans
it possessed the status of a *castrum*, a fortified
military center, and it was made a *civitas* only during
the sixth century.[63] Laon is a rare example of a city
originally so designated for a religious rather than
civic cause. The *pagus* of Laon was initially a part of
the civic area of Reims; but at the death of King
Clovis, it was separated from the mother city, falling
into the kingdom of Clothair I of Soissons, while Reims
went to the Austrasian dominion of Theodoric I. The
ecclesiastical boundaries of the two regions remained
intact, however,[64] and to accommodate the needs of this
detached portion of his flock, Remi of Reims, between
511 and 535, constituted Laon a diocesan center.[65] In
549 the new *civitas* was represented in council at
Orléans by Bishop Gennobaudis;[66] and twelve years later,
at the death of King Clothair, Laon was reintegrated
into Austrasia but retained its civil and episcopal
status.[67]

Laon was a favorite residential area for the
Carolingians, who maintained several villas and palaces
in the *pagus Laudunensis*. During the ninth century it
became noted as an intellectual center, where Irish
refugees from the Vikings established a school that
became associated with such men as John the Scot and
Heiric of Auxerre. When Laon emerged in the twelfth
century as one of Europe's great centers of learning,
her bent toward Greek and theology reflected traditions
that were already deeply ingrained.[68]

Though long separated from the mother church at
Reims, some twenty-eight miles to the southeast, the
church of Laon through the years maintained excep-
tionally close ties with the metropolitan see, at first
exchanging clergy, and then, by the mid-ninth century,
also manuscripts and scribes from the important
scriptoria connected with the two cathedrals.[69] Even
before Hincmar of Reims, who was related to the counts
of Tardenois, ascended the episcopal throne at Reims
in 845, he had long-established roots in the Laonnais.[70]

When Bishop Simeon, who held the see of Laon at the
time of Hincmar's elevation to the see of Reims, died
in 847, the new archbishop had his second opportunity
to fill an episcopal vacancy.[71] His choice to serve as
Simeon's successor was his closest friend, Pardulus, who
was a deacon in the church of Reims[72] and the youngest
son in a family prominent at Laon since at least the
time of Charlemagne.[73] The archbishop always relied
upon the comfort of unquestioned loyalty from a small
circle of intimates to balance off the dislike and lack
of trust that characterized so many of his relationships, and Pardulus met that need admirably. For a
decade he was Hincmar's faithful aide and confidante,
facilitating the handling of innumerable difficulties
for the archbishop during many trying times.

When Pardulus died in 857,[74] his replacement was a
matter of exceptional importance to Hincmar, who sought
to fill a vacancy that was both episcopal and personal
with someone who would be a loyal friend and helper as
well as colleague. His choice now fell upon his
closest relative.[75]

The younger Hincmar, who was born near Boulogne[76] probably between 835 and 838,[77] was one of at least two children.[78] With the early death of his mother, he came to Reims,[79] where he was placed in the care of his uncle the archbishop. He grew up there and at Laon, destined for orders and in constant contact with the clerics who staffed the cathedrals of the two cities. Though these men and others associated with the intellectual life of the region must have been his regular tutors, the archbishop himself took great interest and pleasure in supervising his nephew's education and upbringing.[80] The youth was intelligent,[81] and even though the course of his career as a scholar was somewhat haphazard,[82] he was apparently well liked by his many "nutritors."[83]

When it became necessary to find someone who might appropriately succeed Bishop Pardulus, young Hincmar appears to have been the choice not only of his uncle but also, says Archbishop Hincmar, of the many people in Laon who had both respect for the archbishop and a long acquaintance with his nephew.[84] With his appointment favored by his future flock and readily permitted by King Charles, the bishop-elect might well have anticipated a long and successful career.

Hincmar's episcopal career began on a Saturday, perhaps in the early months of 858,[85] when the bishops of the province of Reims assembled in the cathedral of Laon[86] to affirm their belief that the *electus* possessed the canonical qualifications requisite for the episcopal office and to witness his examination in doctrine and the ministry administered by the archbishop of Reims,[87] who, having received the oath of obedience required by the metropolitan from each new suffragan,[88] presented his nephew with two books, a copy of the *Regula pastoralis* of Pope Gregory I and a convenient collection of canon law that Hincmar of Reims compiled for the occasion, to help the new bishop in his administration.[89]

The actual ceremony of consecration was held the following day before a great crowd, which saw the young Hincmar, dressed in pontifical robes, led to the altar,

before which stood the assembled bishops. The archbishops having intoned the opening prayers of the mass
and one appropriate to the ceremony, the prelates all
bowed, then rose while the clergy sang the *Agnus Dei*,
leaving the bishop-elect alone on his knees. Two
bishops, one on either side, held the open volume of
Scriptures over his neck and back, while the archbishop
recited further prayers. The infusion of the Holy
Spirit was sealed by anointment, the Scriptures were
raised and the *anulum* placed upon the third finger of
his right hand by the archbishop. Having received the
baculum, the staff symbolic of the bishop's rule, the
new prelate exchanged with his senior colleagues the
kiss of peace that marked his perfected fellowship in
their order; then he took his seat among them, last in
order of ordination. The ceremony completed, he received documents signed by all the attending prelates
testifying to the canonicity of his elevation and left
the cathedral over which he now presided.[90]

*   *   *

The aid that the bishop of Laon provided his monarch
in 858 went far beyond mere messenger service. In this
time of crisis, when King Charles desperately needed to
raise troops, Bishop Hincmar placed at the royal service
many of the lands belonging to his church, taking in
commendation a large number of royal vassals--so large
a number, in fact, as to tax carrying on the more regular functions of his office.[91] In appreciation for
the bishop's help, Charles in 860 restored to the
church of Laon a number of properties lost to it in
previous years.[92] During the next years, Hincmar of
Laon was held in high esteem by his monarch, who used
him as a *missus*[93] and relied upon him to bring needed
contingents of vassals, many holding lands belonging to
the church, to serve in the armed host.[94]

Hincmar was regularly present at the councils and
assemblies of the realm[95] and was a great frequenter of
the royal court; which, indeed, was often to be found
in the Laonnais, at palaces and villas like Samoussy or
Servais.[96] There the bishop encountered such great men
as the lords Conrad and Rudolf--the Welf brothers of

Empress Judith and uncles and valued councillors of
Charles.[97]   Hincmar met other prelates as well, like
Bishop Aeneas of Paris, who was ordained two years before him and was among the king's closest aides, and
Archbishop Wenilon of Rouen, who was the other metropolitan bishop to join with Hincmar of Reims in 858 in
his opposition to Louis the German.[98]   Bishop Hincmar's
court life and the location of his see also brought him
into touch with scholars, like John the Scot, whom the
king supported.[99]   As he became increasingly popular
with Charles and his attendants, the king provided him
with the perquisites of royal favor, granting him a
palatine office.[100]

By 867 Bishop Hincmar had emerged as one of the
important figures near King Charles, active in the
politics and diplomacy of the realm.   But success engendered abuse.   While the archbishop of Reims looked
on in shocked disappointment at what he saw to be a
display of pride and avarice,[101] the ever more greedy
bishop grew irascible with his subordinates and with
the tenants of his church lands.   It was said that he
became a simonist to satisfy his needs and the demands
of his followers,[102] and that he would require gifts
from his clergy, while exacting payment from his flock
for the performance of his ministry, in violation of
the canons.[103]   That he himself had no wealth was a
constant torment,[104] which according to rumor led him
to make use of the properties of his church for personal gain.[105]   He granted lands in benefice only to
those able to pay the price and dispossessed tenants of
long standing so that the properties they held might
go to his favorites instead.[106]   For many years, it
seems, he was able to behave in this way with impunity,
secure in the position of favor he held with King
Charles.   But finally his insatiable need, uncontrolled
by respect for either law or propriety, was to bring
an end to the privileged position he had so long en-
joyed.

II

Bishop versus King, 868-69:
Property and Prosecution

Among the perennial problems that confronted Carolingian society, none is more typical or significant than
that which concerned the status of landed property
owned by the individual churches and monastic institutions of the empire.[1] In the course of the sixth and
seventh centuries, the Frankish church had emerged as
the largest landowner in the realm, as monarchs and
nobles sought to express piety or allay guilt by making
donations to favorite ecclesiastical foundations. But
as the Merovingian monarchy foundered, and with the
introduction of vassal benefice, the Carolingian mayors
of the palace, now more and more de facto rulers, had
to seek new ways to obtain land in amounts adequate to
provide for the support of their armed forces. Pepin
of Herstal and Charles Martel found this supply in the
lands of the church, which they expropriated in large
quantities to grant in benefice to royal vassals. By
768, when Charlemagne came to the throne, the amount of
land controlled by the Frankish church had been greatly
diminished both by royal seizure and by the usurpations
of powerful magnates who over the years had taken advantage of the anarchy resulting from the absence of
effective governmental control to profit at the expense
of the defenseless churches of the realm.

One immediate result of the advent of Carolingian
rule and its notions of government was to raise the
question of these lost lands with greatly increased
force, for not only did the reform of the church permit
prelates to voice with far greater strength their
demands for restitution of church property and for its
protection by the monarchy thereafter, the very essence
of the Carolingian monarchy made the expropriation of
church lands so contradictory as to be particularly
unjustifiable.

The early Carolingian monarchs, who were themselves
truly religious, had no desire to justify or continue
the practices of their predecessors. They wished to
restore to the church the lands of which she had been
deprived, but they found the barriers to this insuper-
able. On the one hand, in this as in other matters,
the aristocracy formed a powerful and potentially
dangerous counterpoise to the assertion and maintenance
of the new dynasty; on the other, the exigencies remained that had brought the mayors of the palace to
lend royal sanction to the abstraction of church lands.
Faced with the practical impossibility of restoring
lands previously granted to and presently held by
laymen who would hardly embrace principles that demanded they resign much of their wealth and power, and
given the equal impracticability of themselves abandoning the practice of using church lands to support their
armies and their rule, the Carolingians were forced to
seek compromise. Several measures were undertaken by
Pepin the Short and Charlemagne, as they sought to
give definition to their status as defenders of the
church. Outright usurpation by private individuals was
condemned in legislation that also commanded the immediate restitution of property so acquired.[2] As to
the land required by the monarchy itself, various forms
of recompense and regulations were instituted, which
sought to use the royal authority to guarantee the
title of a church to its property held by royal vassals.
In 744 Pepin associated such benefices with a precarial
tenure to be secured by royal sanction, according to
which the royal vassal beneficed with ecclesiastical
lands was acknowledged to hold these lands from the
church as well. This form of benefice, which required
by law that the vassal pay a regular rent to the church,
was at least partially intended to preserve the church's
right to ownership of the land.[3] After 751, when war
and a still tenuous hold upon a newly acquired throne
required that Pepin increase the number of grants made
to his lay followers, the king enacted a principle of
division, by which in time of need those portions of
church land over and above the quantity necessary for
everyday support of the church were to be placed at
the disposition of the monarch for the duration of the

emergency. As compensation, payment of a tithe was
made compulsory for all subjects; and later the holders
of church property were held responsible for contribu-
ting to the maintenance of the church.[4] Under Charlemagne these measures were continued and refined, and
when the precarial rent was altered, a second tithe was
instituted, owed by the property holder and payable
directly to the despoiled church.[5]

The very multiplicity of these regulations is itself
some indication of the difficulties involved in the
problem. The monarchy possessed neither power nor
machinery to guarantee the enacted provisions, and
rents were disregarded, while the tithe itself tended
to become yet another opportunity for corrupt nobles
and clerics to profit at the expense of church and
realm. The need for a better system was even more
evident in the case of property that had been taken
without royal sanction: not only did magnates seek
to avoid following the restoration laws, but the
question of actual ownership was often difficult to
resolve, particularly when a disputed piece of land had
been held for many years. Such problems were among
the most basic that the emperor Louis the Pious confronted in his attempted reorganization of the imperial
government. The emperor, whose conception of the imperial power was strongly influenced by the arguments
of his prelates, sought to eliminate the incongruity
of monarchic expropriation by suppressing the principle
of division of church lands. That principle had, at
any rate, been vitiated by the ambiguity attendant upon
determining what was an emergency and when it had
ended.[6] To what extent Louis might have succeeded had
his reign been less tumultuous is a matter for speculation. As it was, the years of civil war negated the
gains he had already made and, in addition, gave impetus to another tendency implicit in the emperor's
renunciation of the *divisio*, which, according to many
members of the increasingly powerful and vocal episcopate, conceived the role of the monarch to be one of
defense alone, without any rights with regard to church
lands, which lay at the exclusive disposition of the
bishop.[7]

The long period of civil war beginning in the last
years of Louis's reign gave rise to a new rush of
abuses, and Louis's sons--Charles the Bald especially--
were among the worst culprits.[8] A few months after the
Treaty of Verdun had been signed, the bishops of the
western realm began a series of insistent petitions to
the king, which called upon him to restore the properties he had seized since 840 or at least to guarantee
the churches against further alienations. At Yütz[9] and
Ver[10] in 844, demands for the restitution of expropriated property were given formal statement. At Beauvais
the following year, Hincmar made his acceptance of the
see of Reims conditional upon Charles's restoration of
property lost to it in previous years.[11] By the
council of Meaux-Paris, held during 845-46, the earlier
demands were incorporated and extended, and were given
the status of law, effective pending approval by the
aristocracy.[12] There, the desires of the churchmen met
with steadfast opposition, for the great lords were
unwilling to give this sanction. The national assembly,
which met at Épernay in June 846, accepted only nine-
teen of the *capitula* and thus put a halt to the move-
ment.[13]

In succeeding years, the clergy looked increasingly
to other means of insuring the integrity of church
property. As it became more and more evident that the
royal power was inadequate of itself to afford protection either to the lands of the church or to her per-
sonnel and dependents, churchmen tended to use their
particular skills and their ministry to supplement
monarchic authority. Among the means at their dis-
posal were the fabrication of property titles, the
confection of ostensibly ancient laws that asserted the
rights of ecclesiastical persons, and the composition
of sermon literature in which the infringement of
church prerogatives was made a theological concern.[14]
Meanwhile, efforts at legislation continued, for a
time, it appeared, with greater success. In the
council held at Soissons in April 853, the bishops
obtained passage of a number of the provisions previously rejected at Épernay, as well as other regulations concerned with the question of church property.
In the capitulary there issued to his *missi*, Charles

instructed the royal officials to ascertain precisely
the status of payments owed on precarial holdings.[15]
In affirmation of a conciliar decision, he announced
that laymen would no longer receive royal precepts
authorizing the holding of ecclesiastical benefices,
even if the request were made by a bishop or by the
abbot of a monastery.[16] Hereafter, according to law,
the king might not on his own initiative support his
vassals through benefice of church lands held in
precarial tenure; the disposition of these properties
should pertain wholly to the bishop. Necessity might
make impossible the immediate return of lands already
so held, even as it might dictate that churches be
requested to support the defense of the realm by taking
as vassals men whose aid in royal campaigns was
essential. Now, however, these were to be men who
held their benefice from a bishop rather than from the
king, who might grant in benefice only lands belonging
to the royal fisc. But such success as there was in
the implementation of these regulations, no less than
those various earlier measures they were intended to
supersede, was slow and erratic at best.

By the 860s the successive accretion of legislative
enactments itself formed a problem; the multiplicity
of legislation required harmonization and theoretic
statement. It was generally conceded that the rights
of churches had been infringed and that it was the
monarch's task to correct these abuses; and it was also
acknowledged that the churches must materially assist
the king in their defense. But within these termini
there arose many questions, the significance of which
extended into complex issues of social, ecclesiological,
and legal import. What precisely were the obligations
of ruler and clergy? Under whose jurisdiction and by
what means might disputes regarding the ownership of
property be resolved? How did questions regarding the
various modes of property tenure evolved over many
years relate to questions concerning the relationships
of the people involved in such transactions?

Few churches did not have any of these problems;
Laon, under Bishop Hincmar, faced them all. The bishop
had, indeed, begun at a disadvantage. As has been

noted, during the crisis of 858, Hincmar took on as
episcopal vassals a large number of men required by
King Charles for his armed force--so large a number,
the bishop later alleged, that the cost to his church
was more than could be borne.[17] As a result, and no
doubt in recognition of his service, Charles promised
in 860 to restore not only these lands but also others
long before seized from the church of Laon.[18] Among the
latter was the villa of Poilly, expropriated by
monarchic authority many years before and currently
possessed as a royal benefice by Count Nortmannus.[19]
Initially, the count and bishop had been friends, but
in the years following Hincmar's ordination their
friendship grew strained, as the bishop's desire for
land in his control increased and his repeated requests
that Charles honor his promise went unheeded.[20]   Indeed,
this was by no means the only sort of quarrel that
arose from Hincmar's administration of the properties
of his church. The bishop, thinking himself secure in
royal favor, appears to have taken little heed of
either law or propriety. Complaints regarding his
activities came to the king, who admonished restraint,
but as Hincmar paid no attention to his admonitions,
Charles's patience grew ever more strained. In 868 the
king's forbearance at last reached its limit, and a
long, tangled history of controversy over property
began that provides a leitmotiv for the bishop's career
which, always expanding in scope, came to involve
persons and problems of every order and level of
society.

During the first half of 868, Ariulfus and Amalbertus, two vassals of the bishop of Laon, complained
before the king that Hincmar had treated them unjustly;[21]
Amalbertus in particular alleged that he had held a benefice from the bishop which Hincmar had entered upon and
seized without justification.[22] The king referred the
matter for episcopal hearing under Hincmar of Reims as
metropolitan bishop,[23] but the case had not yet been
terminated when the growing tension between king and
bishop finally erupted in an explosion that cast Bishop
Hincmar from his position in royal favor.

The problem that caused the rupture concerned the son

of one Liudo, who appeared before Charles and his
fideles to complain that the bishop had without reason
taken from him a benefice from the church of Laon that
had formerly been held by his father, with which he in
turn had been enfeoffed by Hincmar of Laon in return, he
alleged, for payment. Perhaps stimulated by the bishop's
presence and perhaps affected by absence of the re-
straining influence that might have been exercised had
Archbishop Hincmar been in attendance, the angry monarch
publicly upbraided Bishop Hincmar, an act that the
episcopacy could not condone.[24] Nor was this all.
Determined to put a curb upon the bishop's thus far
uncontrollable behavior, the king commanded him to
appear with his *advocatus*, in person or by delegate,
before the royal court.[25] Hincmar sent a written reply
to the king, in which he alleged that the summons was
illegal and requested that he be excused from appearing.[26] The court convened, however, with neither he
nor any representative of his present, and judgment was
given to his accusers. Charles interpreted Hincmar's
failure to appear as contumacy, and he sought to force
the bishop's presence by issuing what amounted to a
confiscation order, commanding the local viscount to
place under ban all goods of the church of Laon except
the episcopal house, the cloisters of the cathedral
clergy, and the cathedral building itself, and commanding the *vicedominus* and the provost of the church of
Laon to prevent Hincmar from receiving either the
service of his men or income from his church.[27] In an
endeavor to avoid this penalty, the bishop turned to
Hincmar of Reims and informed him that the king had
sequestered the properties of his church. The archbishop, always zealous to guard the rights of the
church, wrote several times to remonstrate with Charles
for his actions.[28] Then, late in August 868, he and
his nephew set out to confront the king in person at
the royal *villa* of Pîtres, near Senlis, before a
placitum held on the occasion of Charles's receipt of
the annual gift owed him by his vassals and *fideles*.[29]

On their arrival at Pîtres, the two took counsel
with other prelates who were in regular contact with
Charles and hence were able to inform them of the king's
disposition so that their tactics might be worked out.

The news was not encouraging. Hincmar of Laon's
accusers were already on their way to Pîtres to lay
their charges before the receptive monarch, whose
anger, it was said, might be allayed only if the bishop
apologized for his disobedience.[30] The situation was
one that affected far more than Bishop Hincmar alone;
defiance of Charles could not only cause great personal
trouble, it might also, by stimulating royal action,
lead to a precedent most harmful to the whole episcopal
order. Hincmar of Laon bowed before the royal power
and avuncular wisdom, and he beat a retreat.

On 30 August 868, a group of ten prelates heard
Bishop Hincmar make his statement of explanation and
defense.[31] He reiterated arguments contained in the
Codex Africanus that oppose a cleric's appearance
before a secular court[32] and declared the right of a
bishop to be tried by the proper tribunal, that of his
metropolitan in a synod of his province, with the
prerogative of appeal to Rome. He would gladly, he
stated, recognize his faults, but as a preliminary to
any proper disposition of the case, the king in turn
must desist from his own actions and permit the canon
law free operation, by restoring the goods of which
the bishop had been unjustly despoiled.[33]

This mixture of admission of personal fault coupled
with assertion of royal impropriety was but part of
the effort made by Hincmar of Reims to turn his
nephew's situation to the advantage of the church. To
this end, the archbishop had composed a treatise for
presentation to Charles, in which the laws relevant to
the immediate issue were given exposition as a theoretic statement governing a whole complex of questions
connected with the present case.[34] To the archbishop,
the question of Hincmar of Laon's guilt or justification with regard to the charges against him was wholly
subordinate to the problems arising from the manner in
which Charles had handled the situation. The elder
Hincmar was concerned not merely with aiding his
nephew, but also with firmly establishing principles
to govern the trial of clerics and regulate the use of
ecclesiastical property by laymen.[35]

In the treatise, Hincmar of Reims accused Charles
of responsibility for a novel injury, which went
against laws secular and ecclesiastical, ancient and
new, as they applied to the church.[36] Indeed, he
claimed that Charles had violated his own laws and
oaths; for, although he had pledged himself to protect
the church, he had called Hincmar of Laon before a
secular tribunal and had kept the goods of his church
from his control.[37] He advised that a bishop might be
judged only by his peers and that he is, in fact,
specifically enjoined, at the risk of loss of his
office, from appearing before a lay court.[38]

As to the problem of benefices, the archbishop said,
the law held that to the bishop falls the charge of all
the goods of his church, which he has the duty to dis-
pense properly and not to diminish.[39] The necessity of
defense did indeed require that military benefices be
given, but the holders of these should be the men of
the church, with obligations to the church.[40] If such
a vassal felt that he had been unjustly deprived of
his benefice, he should attempt to gain the support of
the neighboring bishops, who might admonish his lord
and correct him. If this should prove insufficient,
the vassal might make complaint before the king himself;
but the matter must not go to public judges, and the
king was under obligation to recall that he was the
defender of church property.[41] In the present case
many regulations had been abused: the bishop had not
been accused before his metropolitan or called before
a synod; he was not present at the judgment, where, indeed, improper witnesses and accusers had been admitted; not did he have an opportunity to answer the
charges; and the goods of his church had been withdrawn.[42] These infractions, the archbishop stated,
were an injury not to Hincmar of Laon alone, but to the
whole body of the church;[43] and in them, Charles, by
his deviation from the old laws, had endangered himself
as well.[44]

Archbishop Hincmar's statement constituted no mere
trial brief. It was rather a treatise of major importance; for, in addition to providing a summary history
of Carolingian legislation regarding rights over

ecclesiastical property and jurisdiction over clerics, it presented a clear announcement of the archbishop's views regarding the obligations of the church to aid in its own defense and the proper solution of problems concerning the fair transmission of lands held in benefice. The work is ample evidence of that sensitivity to political circumstances which Hincmar of Reims possessed to so great a degree. No less striking is the inadvertent forecast the archbishop made; his points should be recalled during the exposition of successive stages in his nephew's career. Perhaps, as Hincmar of Reims would imply, the bishop paid too little attention to this treatise; perhaps, though, he studied it quite well.

In any event, Charles refused to receive the piece. Hincmar of Reims attributed this to its excessive length;[45] and, perhaps at Pîtres, he composed another shorter defense, in which he alleged much the same rules might be read.[46] Yet this statement is hardly true, for the shorter treatise omits a number of citations present in the larger work, and in other respects also indicates a certain change of tenor. This new work seems almost a compromise, as though written after Archbishop Hincmar had arrived and had had second thoughts about the problems involved.[47] It is essentially a manual of procedure, beginning with the question of jurisdiction, and reiterating the regulations of councils, emperors, and popes forbidding the hearing of civil and criminal cases involving the clergy by a lay tribunal.[48] As to judicial forum, the archbishop says, the canons are clear that the province within which the alleged act occurred is the proper location for the case to be heard.[49] The sentence should be given either in synod or by *judices electi*;[50] if by the latter, the judges should be chosen by the parties themselves or appointed by the primate of the province.[51] If there is a civil case between a cleric and a layman, it is up to the lay authority to force attendance of the laymen involved, to have judges present, and to guard the decision as final. If a bishop, properly summoned, cannot appear, he must send a representative empowered to choose his judges, so that the case may proceed to completion.[52] But the king

must make certain that his judges are above reproach
and are concerned with justice rather than with money
or relationship,[53] and he must have a cleric judged not
in a public court but by bishops met in synod or as
determined by the primate.[54]

   Absent from this brief are all references to the
character of Bishop Hincmar's accusers; gone, too, are
the Pseudo-Isidorian citations calling for the penalty
of anathema against violators of church property. What
remains is a short collection of canons that tend to
establish the role of the metropolitan in ecclesiastical judicial decisions, in a work no longer oriented
to the property questions that had elicited the king's
wrath, but rather concerned with a more general request
that Charles respect the rules of the church and of his
predecessors. The reasons for this shift in emphasis
lie in the realm of speculation, but evidence suggests
that certain possibilities, either separately or in
combination, are more likely than others. First, the
archbishop may simply have considered this more ab-
stract approach as likelier to win Charles over and
hence to save Hincmar of Laon; a similar tactic may
appear in the bishop's statement, a work clearly influenced by his uncle. Again, once the archbishop had
arrived at Pîtres, he may have found the situation more
awkward than he had been led to think. He may have
felt that perhaps Hincmar of Laon did not stand on as
firm ground as he had indicated, or that perhaps he was
involved in other still more peculiar dealings that
Hincmar of Reims wished to inspect at greater length.[55]
Finally, as previously suggested, the king's attitude--
his great anger against the bishop--may have suggested
to Archbishop Hincmar that a dangerous precedent was in
the offing, and that, with a direct royal confrontation
threatening, the issues of accusation and of benefice
had better be deferred.[56]

   The shorter treatise was presented to Charles,
probably in a session of the *placitum*, together with
an oral statement in which the archbishop of Reims
reminded the king of Charlemagne's capitularies regarding ecclesiastical property[57] and of the vows he himself had taken to preserve those laws and guard the

church in its good condition, safe from secular interference.[58] To Hincmar of Reims, at least, the outcome
appears to have been satisfactory. Charles ordered
restitution of the banned properties[59] and ruled that
the question should be handled by a synod meeting in
the province of Reims.[60] This assembly convened,
apparently during September 868, appointed *judices
electi*, and the elder Hincmar informed the king that
the matter was settled as far as it pertained to episcopal affairs.[61] With regard to the question of contumacy, he added that another end was awaited, and he
counseled the king to moderation.[62]

But to Bishop Hincmar the resolution had been anything but sufficient; and the following December, when
his next confrontation with the king came about, he
was prepared. In July, even before he had enlisted the
aid of the archbishop of Reims, Hincmar had secretly
dispatched a messenger, Celsanus, to Rome, bearing a
complaint addressed to Pope Hadrian II against Count
Nortmannus, who, the bishop said, had possession of
the villa of Poilly, a property that belonged to the
church of Laon, which he continued to hold in spite of
Hincmar's complaints.[63] What ensued as a result of
this tactic presents a strange and tangled series of
events that is complicated further by the contradic-
tions of tendentious sources.

In the first days of December 868, a number of prelates of the province of Reims, Hincmar of Laon among
them, assembled at the royal villa of Quierzy for the
ordination of the priest Willebert as bishop of
Châlons-sur-Marne.[64] Meeting thereafter with other
fideles in Charles's presence, the group witnessed
another stormy scene between Bishop Hincmar and the
king, which culminated when Hincmar produced the papal
responses to his complaint, addressed to Charles and
Hincmar of Reims, that Celsanus had carried north on
his return from Rome.[65] In these the pope announced
his summons to the bishop of Laon, whom he commanded to
appear at Rome by the following 1 August, to place before him his charges against Nortmannus, the clear
predator of estates belonging to the church of Laon.[66]
The pope chided Charles the Bald as one devoted to the

church more in word than in deed, and he assigned to
king and archbishop the task of guarding the properties
of Hincmar's church during the bishop's absence.
Nortmannus was commanded, under threat of excommunication, to restore the despoiled property immediately,
the execution of the sentence being given to the charge
of the archbishop of Reims.[67]

The affair seems to have come as a surprise to
Hincmar of Reims.[68] For some time his relationship with
his nephew had not been close; and he, often ill, had
been generally out of touch with events.[69] Turning in
accusation to Nortmannus, he received the count's reply
that the case had been misrepresented. Nortmannus
begged not to be excommunicated and asserted that he
had done no wrong but rather held Poilly in benefice
from the king himself.[70] Charles in turn was furious,
and his rage increased as it was found that Bishop
Hincmar had returned to Laon unannounced after the
king's initial outburst.[71] The monarch's commands that
the bishop return to Quierzy met with rejection.[72]
Then Charles sent his *missi* to Laon with a summons to
the bishop, stating that since he refused to appear
himself, the free men of Laon should attend the king
at the palace of Compiègne, where Charles had gone to
spend Christmas.[73] Again the response was unsatisfactory; although some of the men came, others, it was
later said, were prevented from following the royal
order.[74] Still more angry, the king sent the bishops
Odo of Beauvais and newly ordained Willebert of Châlons
with yet another summons to Hincmar. He sent with them an
armed force charged to bring, under duress if necessary,
the bishop and the men remaining with him. But Bishop
Hincmar, hearing of the approach of the company, assembled with his clergy and several other bishops in
the cathedral, where they issued an order placing the
diocese under a general excommunication directed
against the intruders, and Hincmar himself refused to
obey the orders brought by Odo and Willebert. The
defense was effective. Unable to accomplish their
mission, Charles's company had to content themselves
with obtaining from Bishop Hincmar's men a renewal of
their oath of fealty to the king; then they returned.[75]

Meanwhile, during December and January, Hincmar of
Reims worked to mediate the quarrel and appease Charles's
rage, hoping to prevent the king's committing so serious an offense as injuring the person or status of a
bishop. Prior to Odo's journey to Laon, the archbishop
had written him to request that he counsel Bishop
Hincmar.[76] A second letter to Odo asked that he use
his influence with the king to quiet Charles's rage
against Hincmar and Celsanus, not for Bishop Hincmar's
sake but for Charles's sake and for the church, lest
the king act with violence toward a churchman.[77] With
this letter he sent another addressed to Charles himself, in which he asked that the monarch curb his
wrath.[78] The mediation was successful. Charles
abandoned the tactics of force and commanded that a
council of all the bishops of the realm be held, to
convene on 24 April at the villa of Verberie, north of
Senlis; then he rushed off to Cosne,[79] where he remained until the end of January, when he returned
north, to spend Easter at Saint-Denis.[80] Meanwhile,
in the latter part of January 869, Hincmar of Reims,
as metropolitan, summoned his nephew to the council.
Perhaps surprisingly, the bishop agreed, asserting that
at Verberie God would give him words to speak.[81]

The immediate crisis seemed then to have passed in
January, for Bishop Hincmar, too, intended to defer
matters until the meeting of the council. Should he
not be able to gain satisfaction there, he would appeal,
he said, from the council to Rome, as already prescribed by Hadrian.[82] But the bishop, less sanguine
regarding his chances at Verberie than he acknowledged,
suspected the possibility of a trap, and he took pre-
cautions. On 19 April, five days before the council
was to convene, he summoned the Laon clergy to a
diocesan synod. He explained his past troubles to them
and placed the diocese under a provisional interdict,
which was to go into effect if he should be detained or
forbidden to journey to the pope; in such event none of
the priests of his diocese might exercise any minister-
ial functions until either he had given his permission
viva voce or they had received his letter from Rome.[83]
With that the bishop left for Verberie.

Hincmar had good reason to be wary, for the council gave him little hope of a fair hearing. At Verberie he found twenty or thirty bishops assembled,[84] less to hear him than to accuse him, and he discovered that the anathema he had issued in January to prevent his capture was now contrued as an illicit penalty levied with neither cause nor jurisdiction upon men subject not to him but to other prelates at the council.[85] The meeting, which was under the control of the king and Hincmar of Reims, refused to hear the bishop's own complaints until after this charge had been resolved, and it alleged that thus his appeal was irregular, because judgment in the court of first instance had not preceded.[86]

Still more trouble threatened the bishop at the *placitum* also held to Charles, before which he appeared as well.[87] Having at last gained Hincmar's appearance, King Charles was inclined to permit his lay opponents to place their charges against the bishop, but the archbishop of Reims could not permit this. In a turbulent session he reiterated before the court the principles he had expounded at Pîtres the year before and was thus able to prevent the hearing and to avert immediate trouble.[88]

Hincmar of Reim's concern now was for the church and for canon law rather than for his nephew. Like Charles, he saw a chance to avoid reenactment of the events of the previous winter should Bishop Hincmar be dissatisfied, and he too had planned ahead. Verberie, he had written to Odo of Beauvais, was the opportunity to capture the indomitable unicorn;[89] and in another letter to Charles, he had advised the king to keep in readiness at nearby Senlis a number of men sufficient to restrain the wild beast.[90] But the beast still had friends, and word of the possibility of trouble came to Bishop Hincmar. Before the council terminated, he had again exited secretly. He returned to Laon, perhaps by a circuitous route, arriving there at some time during the first half of May.[91]

Though he remained at liberty, the bishop knew well that his freedom was tenuous, and he sought to regain

the offensive.   Once again at Laon, he sent another
secret mission to Rome, in the persons of his vassals
Walco and Berno, who left bearing a letter in which the
bishop attacked both Charles and Hincmar of Reims.[92]
The king, he told Pope Hadrian, was no more than a
tyrant, an oppressor of the church, and an invader of
her property;[93] and the archbishop had failed both in
his duty to protect the church and in his obligation to
aid his nephew.[94]   Then, with the messengers away,
toward mid-month the bishop wrote to Charles, reiterating his request to go to Rome.[95]   Charles immediately
forwarded the letter to Reims, ordering the archbishop
to prepare a response, which should be delivered to him
at the palace of Servais near Laon; the king himself
left at once for the Laonnais.[96]   At Servais, he found
the archbishop not yet present, for in his haste he had
neglected to specify a date for his appearance.   A
second letter, written during the third week of May,
also lacked a date, but Archbishop Hincmar responded
that he would hasten to Servais and should be with
Charles on 2 June.[97]   When he arrived, he found his
nephew there as well, imprisoned.

On 27 May, Charles had taken matters into his own
hands and had sent men to Laon, as he had done the
previous January, to bring Bishop Hincmar before him by
any means necessary.[98]   This time the bishop made no
effort to avoid his removal and accompanied the royal
missi to Servais, bringing with him two of his clerics,
the priest Clarentius and the deacon Teutlandus.[99]   At
the palace he encountered Charles and throughout a
tumultuous interview remained obdurate.   Charles,
unable to exact his obedience, commanded that he be
constrained to remain at Servais for safekeeping.[100]
Once again, however, the bishop had made provision for
trouble.   Enroute to Servais he had instructed his
clerics that, should he be detained, the interdict provisionally levied on 19 April should go into effect
now.[101]   Thus, on 28 May, Clarentius and Teutlandus,
upon their return to Laon, announced the imprisonment
of their bishop and the consequent prohibition of all
holy offices in the diocese of Laon.[102]

Word of the sentence only increased the royal anger.

On 30 May, when Charles wrote his second summons to
Hincmar of Reims, he informed him of what Bishop
Hincmar had done and ordered the archbishop to include
a statement regarding the interdict in the response he
had already requested.[103]   But Hincmar of Reims had
already heard of his nephew's action.   Many of the
people and clergy of Laon were no less close to him
than to their bishop.   Teutlandus in particular seems
to have been a personal acquaintance.[104]   The events of
the last month seem, further, to have given the Laon
clergy grave doubts about the bishop's activities, and
the stringency of the sentence caused them misgivings,
for Bishop Hincmar had commanded that during the period
of his detention no children might be baptized, no
masses celebrated, no viaticum administered, and no
Christian burial performed.[105]   Thus, on 30 May, the
day Charles had written to the archbishop, a meeting
of the Laon clergy had determined to send a delegation
to Reims to tell the elder Hincmar what had occurred and
to ask his advice about what they should do.[106]   On 31
May, the delegation arrived at Reims and presented the
petition.[107]   The next day the archbishop set out for
Servais.

There he found the king in his sun-room overlooking
the river Suippe, with Count Eiricus and two palace
clerics, Ottolfus and Hildeboldus, and presented him
with the requested reply.   Hincmar of Laon was brought
before them.   Still adamant, he was given the night in
which to consider the charges that had been informally
made against him,[108] but the delay availed nothing.
Convinced that both Charles and his uncle were conspiring against him, he refused to acknowledge the allegations made against him and was returned to his imprisonment.[109]   The deadlock was complete: Charles had no
intention of releasing him without new guarantees of
his obedience in the form of a renewal of his fealty,
Bishop Hincmar was equally decided in his refusal to
accede to the pressure imposed by what he considered
the king's illegal action and the archbishop's betrayal.

The interdict, then, remained in force, much to the
concern of Hincmar of Reims.   Not only did he feel that
the ban on services imposed great hardship upon the

faithful of Laon, he was also personally rankled by his
nephew's refusal to respect his admonitions.   Immediately upon his return home, the archbishop of Reims
dispatched letters regarding the interdict to the
clergy and people of Laon, to his nephew, and to the
king.[110]   In the letter to Laon, he announced his
receipt of their petition.[111]   It grieved him deeply,
he said, that brother Hincmar, unlike any bishop before
him, contrary to all law or decency, had seen fit to
use his office to redress personal grievances.[112]   It
is fortunate, he said, that the clerics had turned to
him, since he as metropolitan was directly charged with
the care of the entire province.   The canons do, indeed,
give bishops the power to ordain and judge priests and
deacons, but the judgment meant here pertained specifically to each cleric and not to all, while ordination
did not mean exordination.   Further, concern with
general matters involved the metropolitan bishop of a
province, and the severity of the interdict placed the
present affair in that category.[113]   Hence, he said, he
had sent a letter to Hincmar of Laon in which he had
called for a raising of the interdict and had warned
the bishop that if he did not obey, he would be in
grave violation of the canons.   Meanwhile, the archbishop declared the sentence null and instructed the
clergy that, should their bishop disagree, those injured should bring their case either to himself as
metropolitan or to a provincial council.[114]

    The bases for the archbishop's act and for his
interpretation of the situation are made plainer in the
letter written to the bishop of Laon.[115]   In the view
of the elder Hincmar, the sentence had been issued less
with regard to Charles than against the unoffending
clergy.   The public significance of the sentence, which
of course formed its whole context, was minimized, and
the bishop's act was presented as an excommunication of
his priests without either accusations against them or
any of the procedural benefits required by canon law.
Hincmar of Reims sought to prove this by compiling for
Charles and for his nephew a brief treatise on the
significance and importance of the prohibited sacra-
ments, including the legislation he felt appropriate to
the case, and he stressed the injury Hincmar of Laon

might have inflicted by his unconsidered and illegal use of ecclesiastical sanction to revenge private injuries.[116]   Rather than violate his ministry in this manner, the archbishop felt Bishop Hincmar should have waited patiently until his metropolitan, with other provincial bishops and with royal clemency, had made a just resolution of the complaints he had alleged against Charles. This, said Archbishop Hincmar, was precisely the place of the metropolitan, the reason why the canons had established his office;[117] these laws made clear the nature of the metropolitan function, which was one pertaining to all general matters, among which the baptism of children was surely included.[118] Thus, the archbishop concluded, it was plain that the bishop had acted contrary to the rules governing the church, and that he should raise the sentence to avoid serious trouble.[119]

To understand the nature and purposes of the arch- bishop's arguments, it must be recognized that in the ninth century no real distinction was yet made between excommunication per se and interdict, and that the penalty of excommunication thus levied signified an inability otherwise to gain redress for a continuing infringement of ecclesiastical rules.[120] The placing of an interdict had by the ninth century acquired a long and respectable tradition of use in precisely such circumstances as those pertaining in the situation of Hincmar of Laon, and the question of the legality of the sentence was intimately involved with the reasons for which it had been levied. Clearly, it was directed against the king, in that it was an effort to bring to bear a pressure sufficient to effect Charles's abandon- ment of his opposition and to force him to release Hincmar and accede to his demand that he be permitted either a fair hearing or the right to appeal to Rome. On the contrary, the interpretation of Hincmar of Reims placed all emphasis upon the sentence itself, removed from consideration of its context, and the question at issue became instead one concerning the delimitation of general and particular areas of authority and of canoni- cal regulations governing the imposition of ecclesias- tical sanction; the archbishop construed the interdict as an excommunication directed for personal reasons

against the bishop's clergy and its placement by
Hincmar of Laon as a violation of the canons, which
ignored the responsibilities of his ministry by imposing sentence upon his clerics, who were unjudged, and
by usurping a jurisdiction that was not his in any case.

It is not surprising that Hincmar of Laon now saw
his uncle in the role of an oppressor. As the archbishop continued to support his detention by Charles,
the bishop became increasingly obdurate, refusing to
recognize either the assertions of metropolitan authority now presented to him by the elder Hincmar or the
arguments directed to him by the archbishop at Servais.
While to Archbishop Hincmar the questions of imprisonment and interdict were separate, to his nephew they
were inextricably joined. Thus, to the groups of *missi*
sent by his uncle, he replied only that Hincmar of
Reims ought not to urge him to respond or judge him
while he was in prison and deprived of his clergy.[121]
The archbishop, he continued, should comply with the
command given him by Pope Hadrian and permit him to
go to Rome; his appeal had been voiced at Verberie.[122]
On 24 June, Hincmar of Reims wrote an angry letter of
response.[123] The bishop, he said, had been warned at
Verberie about his excommunications, which were both
illegal and a general scandal, yet he had immediately
perpetrated an offense that even surpassed his previous
offenses.[124] On this account, the archbishop had sent
him letters of remonstrance, but his nephew had not
even deigned to read them. Nor would he release his
clerics from the excommunication with which he had
bound them in an act so unbefitting a bishop, who ought
rather to provide consolation and encouragement to his
helpers in their difficult work.[125] As to himself, the
archbishop said, even if Hincmar of Laon should despise
him, nonetheless a bishop was bound by oath to obey his
metropolitan. Thus he again warned the bishop, by
virtue of his metropolitan office, to unbind what he
had wrongly bound.[126] Concerning the replies that
Bishop Hincmar had sent through Hincmar of Reim's *missi*,
the archbishop continued, it was precisely for making
a judgment so that a wrongful situation in his province
might be put right that the office of metropolitan was
instituted; and, in insisting that his clergy be present

at his response, the bishop showed only his misunderstanding of the canons. Further, he said, the pope's letter to him made no mention of an obligation to provide that Hincmar of Laon be permitted to go to Rome; and the prelates at Verberie knew full well that the bishop had made no regular appeal.[127]

A short time later, perhaps about 28 June,[128] Hincmar of Reims wrote to Laon, announcing that he had raised the interdict. He instructed the clergy in their proper functions during the absence of their bishop, who, he said, would not be with them until an episcopal decision had been made concerning his continuing contumacy and its bearing on the further course of diocesan affairs.[129]

The episcopal council to which the archbishop implicitly referred was imminent. Charles had sent notice to his *fideles* that the annual assembly would once again be held at Pîtres late in June, and when Hincmar of Reims wrote the bishop of Laon on 24 June, he was himself about to leave to attend the meeting.[130] There he encountered his nephew under quite unexpected circumstances, for during his weeks at Servais, Hincmar of Laon had yielded to the advice of his friends, Bishops Aeneas of Paris and Wenilon of Rouen; and without his uncle's knowledge had come to terms with Charles. He had left the province of Reims, met with the king, and finally sworn the oath of fealty so long demanded of him.[131] Apparently bishop and king had arrived privately at an accommodation agreeable to both of them: Charles would restore the disputed villa of Poilly in return for Hincmar's renewed oath.[132]

But what reasons can account for this sudden reversal? Several immediately suggest themselves. By the summer of 869, Hincmar of Laon had come to feel that it was essentially his uncle against whom he should direct his anger as the real author of his troubles, and it was natural then for him to mend his relationship with the king. Charles, on the other hand, may have recognized that a degree of public sympathy supported Bishop Hincmar and opposed the archbishop of Reims. By means of their agreement, the king might

avoid a possibly embarrassing scene at a national
council and, more important, render moot the bishop's
appeal to Rome, for the 1 August deadline scheduled by
Pope Hadrian for Hincmar's appearance was rapidly
drawing near. In July 869, neither king nor bishop was
anxious to involve Rome in his affairs; a far more significant purpose loomed over them.

The extant records concerning Bishop Hincmar's disobedience to his king are to no small degree at variance with one another, and they raise a number of
questions regarding the full context of the events just
recounted. The extent of royal anger and the measures
taken by King Charles to bring the bishop to heel seem
disproportionate to his alleged offenses; on the other
hand, Bishop Hincmar's imprisonment, the renewal of
his fealty and that of his men in Laon, and the sending
of troops against him argue that Charles did see the
bishop as presenting a threat. In fact, it was less
property than treason that concerned the king, for
Hincmar of Laon possessed information that it was imperative be kept a closely guarded secret. What moved
King Charles against the bishop was Hincmar's complaint
to Rome and, in connection with it, his threat to enter
the service of Charles's nephew, King Lothar II, for
these contacts affected what had become the most vital
issue in the politics and diplomacy of the realm.

III

The Politics of Divorce and the
Seizure of Lotharingia, 857-69

In the early months of the year 858, a crowd composed
of *proceres* and prelates of the kingdom of Lotharingia
assembled at the palace of Aachen to witness the judgment of God. There a woman accused of adultery and
incest was defended by a champion who thrust his arm
into a caldron of boiling water and withdrew a sub-
merged stone in an attempt to prove her innocence.[1]
Such methods of proof, which were finally outlawed by
the church about three and a half centuries later,
during the ninth century, in spite of considerable
criticism, continued to be an influential and presumably unimpeachable means of ascertaining the truth of
unsupported testimony.[2] At some later time, the champion's wounded arm would be examined, and if it was
found to have healed properly, it might well have been
assumed that the woman's innocence had been proved.

This ordeal in actual fact marked only the beginning
of a trial that was endured by Theutberga, the queen of
Lotharingia,[3] whose royal status reflected neither her
own choice nor that of her husband, Lothar II. This
dramatic event grew out of a tangled mesh of political
circumstances that proved to be of great consequence to
a large segment of Carolingian society, including even
Hincmar of Laon.

When the emperor Lothar I died in September 855, he
left three sons, among whom his realm was divided.[4]
The difficult task of ruling Italy, a land torn by civil
strife and perpetually threatened by Arab attack, fell
to the capable Louis II, who had been king of Italy
since 851 and now succeeded to his father's imperial
title.[5] In the north, however, the ability of Lothar's
descendants to continue his family's rule was from the

start more problematical. The newly created kingdom of
Provence, under the nominal rule of the epileptic child-
King Charles, Lothar's youngest son, fell prey almost at
once to the depredations of his relatives. Only the
administration capably undertaken by Count Gerard of
Vienne and Archbishop Remi of Lyons, both faithful ser-
vants of Lothar's dynasty, permitted its continued existence.[6] Unfortunately, no similar resource existed in
the third and northernmost segment of the emperor's
realm. The region stretching from the Jura mountains
in the south to Frisia and the North Sea, including
Burgundy and *Francia Media*, became a kingdom that
ultimately took its name, Lotharingia, from its first
monarch, Lothar II.[7] Lothar found, on the one hand,
that his title was largely dependent upon his success
in satisfying the desires of a venal and opportunistic
nobility and, on the other, that his strongest, if not
wisest, support rested with the episcopate. The influence of these two forces upon this young and not
overly intelligent monarch was to color the whole picture of Carolingian diplomacy and politics.

Even before his father's death, Prince Lothar had
contracted a liaison with Waldrada, the daughter of a
noble Alsatian family.[8] But by the start of his own
reign, he was faced with the immediate problem of ap-
peasing a far more powerful family than Waldrada's--
that of Count Boso, which possessed great resources on
both sides of the Alps. In the north Lothar II himself
may very likely have been an architect of the fortunes
of this family, when, fearing attack from his brother
Louis, he created a large duchy, comprising the greater
part of modern Switzerland, and granted it to Boso's son
Hubert.[9] Hubert, who is known principally in the
sources for his excoriation by Pope Benedict III,[10] had
sufficient power and influence that Lothar sought to
bind him closer still by rejecting Waldrada in favor of
the duke's sister Theutberga. Toward the end of 855,
Lothar married Theutberga and made her queen of
Lotharingia.[11]

From the start, the situation seems to have pleased
neither Lothar nor Waldrada, and the royal displeasure
assumed greater immediacy as it emerged that Theutberga

was unable to bear children. As early as 857, dissolution of the marriage became the question that most pre-occupied the king and his advisers.[12] It was a problem not easily resolved, for the growing influence of the Frankish church during the past century had introduced norms of canon law into consciousness and had left the rules governing marriage in a yet unresolved state. The old Frankish civil law permitted divorce and the subsequent remarriage of the male spouse. The canons, on the other hand, opposed divorce and denied the validity of any subsequent marriage so long as both original partners remained alive. However, the law of the church did permit the annulment of a union found to have been in fact invalid, and it was upon this rule and upon the reputation of Duke Hubert that Lothar and his primary adviser, Archbishop Gunthar of Cologne, based their strategy.[13] Theutberga was accused of having had incestuous relations with her brother, an accusation which, if proven, would present a bar to her contracting any marriage.[14]

But the accusation merely served to place Lothar in a more difficult situation than before, for Theutberga's champion was successful and exonerated the queen, and Duke Hubert reacted to the accusation with rebellion.[15] During the next years the problem remained dormant, as Lothar sought to support his tenuous position by gaining the approbation of his uncles, Louis the German and Charles the Bald, for whom he sought to serve as mediator in the quarrel that arose from Louis's invasion of the western realm.[16] Meanwhile, Archbishop Gunthar matured a new plan. As confessor to the queen, he possessed both the access and the influence to persuade her to admit to having committed grievous offenses with Hubert, thus circumventing her previous exculpation; and by moving the case from a lay to an ecclesiastical tribunal, Lothar was able simultaneously to increase his own influence and diminish that of Hubert's partisans. Even so, Lothar was unable to gain his ends. On 9 January 860, a small council held at Aachen heard testimony regarding Theutberga's offense and her request to enter a nunnery, but it issued no decision.[17] A second council, which included two bishops from the west and was held at the same palace in mid-February,

had little more effect. The bishops heard Theutberga's
confession and imposed public penance upon her but
deferred any decision regarding annulment of the
marriage until they might consult with absent colleagues.[18]

The fact that Lothar could not muster sufficient
support even among the prelates of his own realm
augured poorly for the success of his plan, which by
860 had become an international cause célèbre. Thrust
into a greater arena, Lothar and his partisans had to
seek the support of influential opinion outside of
their kingdom. In 860 no voice in Carolingian affairs
carried more weight than did that of Archbishop Hincmar
of Reims. The archbishop of Reims, after his trium-
phant vindication of his monarch's rights against Louis
the German, was entering a five-year period in which he
would function as the primary force shaping the politics and diplomacy undertaken by King Charles the Bald,
a role to which he brought the full measure of his
expertise in the canon law. His influence was recognized by Lothar's men, who, in an attempt to enlist his
support, relied first upon his nephew. Early in 860
Bishop Adventius of Metz visited Reims, accompanied by
Hincmar of Laon. They tried to persuade the archbishop
to attend the second council at Aachen, but were disap-
pointed.[19] In the months that followed, Archbishop
Hincmar emerged as an implacable foe of the divorce.
His treatise *De divortio Hlotharii regis et Tetbergae
reginae*, written at the request of dissident Lotharingian bishops, effectively destroyed the position advocated by Lothar's supporters.[20] According to the archbishop, the case should never have arisen; but since
it had, it must go before a general council.[21]

Even at this point one may assume that political no
less than moral or legal concerns determined the archbishop's position.[22] To Hincmar of Reims it must have
been immediately apparent that for a policy less devoted to scrupulous than to practical ends the affirmation and continuation of Lothar's union with Theutberga
were profitable. If King Lothar failed to produce an
heir, his realm, and ultimately the whole inheritance
of Lothar I, including the imperial title, would

eventually fall to his uncles or their heirs, for
Lothar II appeared to be the sole hope of his line.
Perpetually ill, survival itself presented a challenge
to Charles of Provence while the emperor Louis, near
the age of forty, himself lacked male offspring.[23] The
influence of the tough and self-serving diplomacy es-
poused by Hincmar of Reims is immediately apparent in
the aggressive activity that characterized Charles the
Bald during the years following 860, when the efforts
of his nephew to gain his support were persistently
rebuffed.[24] In his western kingdom, Charles gave sanc-
tuary to Theutberga, bestowed the abbey of Saint Martin
of Tours upon Hubert, and late in 861 plotted to invade
Provence.[25] The acerbity between the two monarchs grew
as Lothar, in retaliation, received Charles's fugitive
daughter Judith and condoned the hostilities that had
arisen between the archbishops Gunthar and Hincmar.[26]

Rejected in the west, Lothar sought support from
other sources. In 861 he reestablished his alliance
with King Louis the German, perhaps promising to cede
to the German monarch the succession in Alsace in return for his support.[27] Relying overmuch upon the connection, Lothar summoned a new council to the palace
at Aachen, where on 29 April 862 it was ruled that
Theutberga's incest did indeed render invalid her subsequent marriage, thus opening the way for the king's
union with Waldrada.[28] But the inadequacy of this
assembly was patent. Only eight bishops were present,
and two of these opposed the decision.[29] In these circumstances, Lothar sought the support of Rome.

*   *   *

The advent of the Carolingian dynasty and the pro-
grams instituted by the Frankish rulers in the eighth
and ninth centuries had greatly reinforced the prestige
of the bishop of Rome and had opened the possibility
that a capable and ambitious pope might attempt to
assert the prerogatives of the Roman see to an active
role of immediate leadership in the administration and
government of the Christian world.[30] Such a man came
to the papal throne in 858, and he found the ambitions
he entertained for his office aided by the quarrels in
which the Frankish rulers were embroiled. Nicholas I,

who was elected pope ostensibly because his previous
relations with the emperor Louis II ensured his docile
conduct, soon disabused his patron of any notions that
he would subsume papal rule to imperial purposes.[31]   To
Nicholas the primacy of Rome signified an obligation to
preserve and guarantee the unity of the Church Universal
through direct papal regulation of an indefinite range
of situations.   The Roman see for him was not merely the
head of all other churches but their source as well; all
authority in Christian society ultimately originated in
Rome, which guaranteed the regular administration of
the church and to which all questions must ultimately
be referred.[32]   The assertion of these ideas would bring
Nicholas into conflict with a variety of elements in
society, among them Hincmar of Reims.   Nicholas strenu-
ously opposed Hincmar's opinions regarding ecclesiastical government; but on the issue of Lothar's divorce,
the two stood in agreement.

  Even prior to 862, both parties to the divorce had
appealed to the pope, a device resorted to with increasing frequency in the years following the mid-ninth
century.[33]   Now, in the face of Charles the Bald's
unyielding opposition, Lothar decided to renew his
request for papal intervention, to avoid the danger and
humiliation of having to submit to the judgment of
hostile forces in the north.[34]   Actually, the king was
less than truthful in making his request.   His appeal
for papal mediation concealed the fact that on the basis
of the decision rendered at Aachen in 862 he had proceeded to marry Waldrada.   To counter papal opposition
to annulment, the story was invented that the pair had
really been married even before the death of Lothar I.[35]
In November 862, Nicholas commanded the convocation of
a council in the city of Metz, to be held under his
legates to examine the questions raised by the alleged
previous marriage;[36] when, some months later, he heard
of the events of 862, he threatened Lothar with excommunication.   It should have been clear to Lothar that
no support would be gained from papal involvement.
Nicholas permitted no grounds for annulling a marriage,
while asserting that the general significance of the
question required papal decision.[37]

  In the early months of 863, the cardinal-bishops

Radoaldus of Porto and John of Cervia left Rome for the
north, bearing papal letters authorizing them to preside as Nicholas's representatives over a council to be
summoned to Metz.[38] But the death of Charles of Provence on 24 January and the dislocations attending his
succession delayed the meeting.[39] It was only toward
mid-June 863 that the council convened. Meanwhile,
Lothar and his supporters, now aware of the papal mood,
were moved to desperate actions; during their journey,
the legates were intercepted and their pontifical
letters taken.[40] But relations between Lothar and the
delegates sent by Nicholas became even more bizarre, as
the papal legation, apparently approached with a bribe,
succumbed to the temptation. When the council met, its
conclusion was forgone. On the basis of Lothar's allegations regarding Theutberga's incest and his own
previous marriage, the assembly approved the annulment
of the one relationship and confirmed the propriety of
the other.[41] Radoaldus and John left to the Lotharing-
ians the task of communicating the decision to Rome,
which task fell to the archbishops Gunthar of Cologne
and Theutgard of Trier, who arrived there during the
first weeks of fall 863.[42]

    In these circumstances, the full strength of
Nicholas' will and personality were evident. Nicholas,
now confronted with the fact of the divorce and under
heavy pressure from the emperor to accept the result,
repudiated his legates. Furious at the crass attempt
to circumvent his orders and manipulate papal authority,
he declared the conciliar judgment null, announced the
deposition of Gunthar and Theutgard from their archiepiscopal offices, and threatened anathema against any
who should resist the decrees of the Holy See.[43] He
was in fact, however, on very precarious ground: not
only did he incur the anger of the emperor Louis, the
sentence he imposed against the two archbishops also
had no legal precedent. Yet his steadfastness seemed
to overcome these obstacles. An imperial army sent to
coerce papal obedience had to withdraw without success,[44] and efforts to rally support in the church for
the deposed prelates had as little effect.[45] In the
year that followed, the Lotharingian bishops and the
king himself submitted to Nicholas, who planned the

convocation of a general council to affirm his orders
and make a final resolution of the marriage issue.[46]

   The force of Nicholas's assertions of papal right to
supervise the functioning of the church, and the coin-
cidence of these notions with other current ecclesiological sympathies, led to alterations in the policy and
control of power in the north.[47] To Charles the Bald,
the precedent of a pope ruling upon the deposition of a
monarch was not a welcome one, and the king hurried to
blunt the edge of the papal thrust by assuring that
Nicholas's demands were met.[48] Negotiations with Louis
the German led to a meeting in February 865 at the
villa of Tusey, where the two monarchs adopted the pos-
ture of defenders of the church and its head, and committed themselves to securing their nephew's obedience,
while avoiding convocation of the papal council.[49] In
these circumstances Nicholas, too, adjusted his tactics.
In April 865, Arsenius of Orta was sent north as papal
legate, and the following summer, under his aegis,
Lothar received Theutberga, who was crowned anew, and
was reconciled with his uncle King Charles.[50]

   The papal triumph was, in fact, a fragile thing, the
main effects of which were to cause a realignment of
directions in the north and to blur the sharp outlines
of the assertive diplomacy propounded by Hincmar of
Reims. King Lothar, who had initially feared that
Charles intended to oppose him with violence, soon
resumed his plans to abandon Theutberga for Waldrada,
as his relations with his uncle seemed to improve,
while Charles and Louis carried on a desultory wait-and-
see policy.[51] Nicholas, who realized that the information he received from the north was frequently less
than truthful, refused any compromise, even when
Lothar's pleas were seconded by the German king.[52] To
Lothar's requests that he be permitted to appeal at
Rome against his accusers, Nicholas responded that the
young monarch would never be allowed to wed Waldrada
with papal sanction, even if Theutberga should die.[53]
To the king's appeals for the pardon and restoration
of Gunthar and Theutgard, the papal refusal was no less
flat. Nicholas commanded Lothar to proceed to the
election of their replacements and threatened to annul

any appointment in which the influence of the deposed prelates might be evident.[54] He remained unyielding to the end. His last letter to Lothar is dated 7 October 867;[55] hardly a month later, on 13 November, the pope died.[56]

Nicholas I, by the strength of his self-assurance and the force of his personality, was able successfully to assert the authority of his office in a way that was hitherto unknown and to establish extraordinary precedents for successful Roman intervention in the affairs of kings and churchmen. His death was like the removal of the essential mortar in a dam, which released a variety of tensions that had built up around the uncompromising barrier of his position, and the energies of other forces, blocked and frustrated for years, now surged forth to undermine the structure he had sought to erect. These forces broke upon a man who was very different from his predecessor. Far less assertive than Nicholas, and perhaps more humane, Pope Hadrian II was susceptible to pressure, and his elevation once again raised the hopes of Lothar and his brother Louis.[57] Encouraged, the king renewed his appeals, and the pope was not unresponsive. The excommunication of Waldrada was raised, and Lothar himself was given permission to come to Rome, so that the question of his marriage might be considered by a papal council.[58]

The immediate problem now was to gain the neutrality, if not the support, of Charles the Bald and Louis the German, a problem whose difficulty both Lothar and the emperor knew full well. Consequently, having received the papal invitation, Lothar's first preparations for his journey included two meetings with his uncles, the business of which is not known.[59] Although the particulars of the meetings remain unclear, the fact that Lothar hesitated in embarking and did not go to Rome immediately is some indication that even now he and his partisans were suspicious of Charles and Louis. The two monarchs had profited greatly from the involvement of Pope Nicholas, who had assumed the burden of opposing the divorce from a position far stronger than any they alone could have discovered. They, as papal champions, could avoid the onus of personal interest

while waiting assuredly for the rewards of papal policy
to fall to them. Hadrian's attitude seemed to change
all this and to open the way once more for an active
policy of the sort previously advocated by Hincmar of
Reims. In June 868, during the absence of King Lothar,
a secret meeting was held between Charles the Bald and
Louis the German at Metz in Lotharingia. It was under
the aegis of Bishop Adventius and had few attendants.
Adventius, who was an unwavering champion of the principle of self-interest, had initially been a supporter of
the divorce but had, since 863, drawn ever closer to
Charles the Bald. At the meeting the brother monarchs
exchanged promises of mutual assistance and agreed that
should God present them with the kingdoms of their
nephews they would make a fair division of these lands
between themselves.[60]

The tenor of this document seems almost to force its
interpretation and, further, to provide a context for
the relations between Charles the Bald and Hincmar of
Laon in the months that followed. It is unlikely,
though of course not impossible, that Charles and Louis
anticipated Lothar's imminent demise. It seems far
more probable that they themselves intended in some way
to forestall the possibility that the receptiveness of
the new pope to Lothar's requests might rob them of
eventual benefits. Thus the royal brothers may well
have been placing themselves in the ranks of those
others who championed the integrity of the positions
assumed by Nicholas I, interpreting the actions of
Hadrian and Lothar as an illicit contravention of the
inviolable decisions of Nicholas, an interpretation that
would impose upon them as champions of church and papacy
the obligation to invade Lothar's realm during his absence, to seize it, and thereby rescue its inhabitants
and its church, and incidentally render nugatory any
papal action that might provide Lothar with an heir.

That King Lothar suspected something of the sort
might ensue appears from his great reluctance to leave
the north without having received specific guarantees
from his uncles. In January 869, although still lacking
the guarantees he sought, Lothar left for Rome, but
when well under way he turned back and returned to

Lotharingia.[61] Whether he had any grounds for more
than suspicion or whether he could have learned of the
meeting at Metz is difficult to judge. But it may be
noted that at precisely this time Charles sent his
troops against Hincmar of Laon, having received the
bishop's threat to desert him for Lothar, and that the
bishop was among those most close to the king and privy
to his secrets; he is one of the attendants at Metz.[62]

During June 869, while Bishop Hincmar languished at
Servais, Lothar II went to Italy at last.[63] The journey was as risky as it was necessary. While Lothar and
his supporters, including the emperor Louis, seem to
have had fears about what might happen during his absence, a growing opposition was already being formed,
spearheaded by men in league with Lothar's uncles and
by others who opposed what they felt would be a derogation of either the papacy or Nicholas himself should
Hadrian reverse his predecessor's judgments. Seeking
to gain support, Lothar went in June to Benevento, where
his brother was engaged in battle with the Arabs. But
Louis could give no immediate help. Unable in any event
to leave his post, he feared the effect of Lothar's
remaining too long in Italy, and advised him to return
at once to the north. Lothar had little choice but to
comply. The influence of the empress Engilberga had
brought about some renewal of encouragement from the
pope, but even here the situation was plainly a difficult one.[64]

In July a council held at the monastery of Monte
Cassino indicated the extent of the opposition to a reversal of Nicholas's penalty against the deposed archbishop Gunthar. Here Hadrian decreed that Gunthar be
restored to lay communion; but in this measure, which
was really preliminary to the greater question of
Lothar's divorce, he received strong dissent from a fac-
tion that denied the propriety or legality of his dis-
allowing the earlier sentence. The pope was not able to
rule on Lothar's case, but he promised that a future
council would meet at Rome the following March to take up
the matter.[65] With that Lothar took the road homeward.

It seems not unlikely that the advice of the emperor

Louis was wise, perhaps even that he had had some word
of the things afoot in the north. Louis the German was
presently immobilized by action in the east,[66] and
thus was out of the picture. But this was all the more
to the advantage of Charles the Bald, who had earlier
commanded the presence of his most trusted *fideles* at
Attigny, near the border between his realm and Lotharingia.[67] If he had not been planning an invasion, he
was at any rate well prepared when, during the third
week of August, word reached him at Senlis that Lothar
had taken ill some days before and had died on 8 August
in the north Italian city of Plaisance.[68]

By 23 August Hincmar of Reims had received orders
from Charles to prepare immediately to journey.[69] A
deputation from Louis the German to his brother requesting a moratorium on any action was ignored, as Charles
and his followers arranged to reap the benefits of
rapid action and moved into Lotharingia.[70] On 1 September the king was at Verdun, and four days later he
arrived at Metz, just as the pope, hundreds of miles to
the south, was sending letters to him, ordering that he
respect the emperor's right of succession.[71] At Metz,
on 9 September, he was elected to succeed Lothar as king
of the middle realm, and was crowned and anointed by
Hincmar of Reims, as senior ecclesiastic and the only
metropolitan among the six bishops--three from the west
and three from Lotharingia--who were present.[72]

Hincmar of Laon was among the prelates present at
this coronation,[73] possibly because Charles sought his
support for the difficult time ahead, for the coronation
itself would be merely an empty ceremony if three
sources of real opposition could not be removed. These
were the complaints of the pope and the emperor Louis
II, the possibility of an armed contest over succession
with Louis the German, and the need to gain the adherence of those who were formerly in Lothar's service.
On the assumption that these three forces did not com-
bine, the Italian threat carried the least weight, and
Charles, forced to seek a rapid settlement in the north,
deferred consideration of the papal and imperial protest.

In November 869, Charles convened an assembly at the

villa of Gondreville, near the Lotharingian town of
Toul, primarily to receive the oaths of his new subjects
in Provence and High Burgundy.[74] In the course of the
meeting, legates from the emperor Louis and the pope
arrived. The papal emissaries bore several letters
dated 5 September directed to Charles the Bald, the western nobles and bishops, and Hincmar of Reims. These
concerned the possibility of Charles's occupation of
Lotharingia and threatened Charles with excommunication
if the lands were not left to the rightful heir, Louis
II. Hincmar of Reims was instructed to stand as protector of the integrity of the territories.[75] On his
own testimony, Archbishop Hincmar communicated the substance of the letters, except his own, to the assembly.[76] The receipt of the warning sent by Hadrian and
Louis II made resolution of the situation in the north
all the more pressing, for while neither pope nor emperor was himself in a position to actively assert the
emperor's right of succession, the protests of both
could well provide a solid foundation for opposition to
Charles by hostile elements within Lotharingia or by
Louis the German, who during the later months of 869
was well on his way toward recovery from the illness
that conveniently had seemed likely to carry him off.[77]

Charles's acceptance, even in Lotharingia proper, in
spite of an immediate appearance of success, was by no
means assured; on the contrary, it was opposed by many.[78]
In the Jurane and Provençal regions, which Lothar had
gained on the death of his brother, King Charles of
Provence, were even stronger opposition and desire for
either autonomy or the succession of Louis II, led by
such men as Count Gerard of Vienne, formerly protector
of Charles of Provence and unyielding in his adherence
to the family of the emperor Lothar.[79]

Charles the Bald sought to gain support by issuing
privileges to the laity and prelates[80] and by seeking
to fill episcopal vacancies with men favorable to or
dependent upon him. He saw his best and probably most
immediate chance of success through the episcopacy.
Gondreville counted among its attendants such important
prelates as the archbishops Remi of Lyons and Hardwic of
Besançon;[81] and the relation of Ado of Vienne to Pope

Nicholas and his previous connections with Charles make
his attendance at the Gondreville assembly not unlikely.[82]

Early in 870 Charles turned his attention to the
long-vacant sees of Cologne and Trier. At Cologne he
attempted to gain the support of the still-powerful
Gunthar by appointing his nephew as his successor--that
same Hilduin who in 862-63 had been denied the see of
Cambrai and had been in Charles's service since 866.[83]
Trier, whose former archbishop, Theutgard, had died in
868, was presented to Bertulfus as a reward for the
long service of his uncle, Bishop Adventius of Metz.[84]
Both Hilduin and Bertulfus were ordained in January
870.[85]

In that same month Charles attempted to secure the
support of Theutberga and her powerful family.
Charles's queen, Ermintrude, had been ill for some time;
and with his entrance into Lotharingia, he also entered
into a relationship with Theutberga's niece Richilde.[86]
When his queen died on 6 October 869,[87] he was able to
remarry, and on 22 January 870 Richilde became his
second wife.[88]

But the complaints of Louis the German were becoming
rapidly more importunate, and when Hilduin arrived at
Cologne in February to assume his archiepiscopal see,
he found the priest Willibert, the opposition candidate
supported by the German king, already installed there.[89]
A short time later, Bertulfus encountered like opposition at Trier from the monk Waltonus.[90] In general,
Charles's earlier successes among the Lotharingian prelates had failed to lead to any widespread acceptance
of his rule by either clerical or lay elements of the
population. In February 870, Louis the German threatened war if Charles did not leave the Lotharingian
realm,[91] and it was apparent that for any occupation to
succeed some form of accommodation had to be made by the
two kings. From Aachen, where he had been since his
marriage, Charles now answered his brother.[92] Arrangements were made, culminating on 6 March in a meeting at
Aachen, at which four representatives of Louis the
German and three representatives of Charles the Bald

reaffirmed, as a preliminary to the difficult task of arranging an equal division of Lothar's realm, the agreement made by the two kings nearly two years earlier at Metz.[93]

About the second week of March, Charles left Aachen for Compiègne, where he spent Easter,[94] and during April he was at Compiègne and Saint-Denis.[95] Now that the first preliminaries of an accord had been drawn between him and his brother, Charles felt it essential that the provisional agreement be converted into a permanent treaty. Such negotiations required the support of his followers. On 1 May Charles was at Attigny[96] for a *placitum* he had summoned, which was also attended by twelve delegates sent by Louis the German.[97] The arduous process of negotiation continued through weeks of trying meetings until late in June, when a settlement satisfactory to the western delegation was reached and the eastern delegation, accompanied by a party including Bishop Odo of Beauvais, went to Frankfurt to seek the approval of the German monarch.[98] On his return toward mid-July, Odo could report success, and late in that month Charles left for the villa of Meersen, near the east bank of the river Meuse not far from Aachen.

At Meersen, on 8 August 870, a treaty was concluded, by which the former realm of Lothar II was divided into two parts by a border that roughly descended south from the mouth of the Rhine, along the Meuse and east of the Saône, and finally joined the Rhône at about Valence. Charles received the lands to the west of the border, Louis those to the east.[99] Thus, in addition to his other gains, Charles now was recognized by Louis the German as ruler of the territories formerly held by King Charles of Provence; and he had thus acquired the archbishoprics of Lyons, Vienne, and Besançon, while the see of Cambrai in the north, for so long a torment to Hincmar of Reims, who bemoaned that his province had been divided between two rulers,[100] now came at last into the western kingdom.

It was left to the archbishop of Reims to deal with the complaints of pope and emperor, complaints that the concessions to Louis the German and the fait accompli

of Meersen had robbed of much of their force. At
Gondreville the archbishop had circulated a synopsis of
certain of the letters sent by Hadrian on 5 September
869.[101] The visit of the delegates from Louis the
German at Attigny offered Hincmar an opportunity for a
more public presentation that could now expect combined
support. With the territorial negotiations at least in
part completed, on 15 June 870 the archbishop presided
over a session of the assembly before which the papal
missives were read, along with a commentary written by
Hincmar himself. The archbishop explained the significance of the dangers threatened by the pope for disobedience to his orders: deposition for prelates and
anathema for anyone who invaded the lands Hadrian considered the rightful inheritance of Louis II. Some
months later Hincmar said that, in answer to the papal
threats, the assembly responded that the so-called
"invasion" was in fact most necessary; for, were no
strong authority immediately placed over Lothar's realm,
sedition must surely have followed. He said the
assembly was in full agreement with his view that
Hadrian had overstepped the bounds of his legitimate
authority; that, not only was legality on the side of
the king, but his authority and his presence were supported and, indeed, had been requested by the inhabitants of Lotharingia themselves.[102] Though this statement hardly reflected the truth, the agreement with
Louis the German had increasingly involved the German
king in the invasion and had permitted Hincmar and the
westerners to ignore and oppose papal censure, and to do
so with impunity. Though Louis II was a warrior whom
his uncles might well fear with reason, it was unlikely
that this "emperor of Italy," as Hincmar would refer to
him, would be able to undertake an armed defense of his
claims. The signing of Meersen at last made possible a
direct response to the pope, and the occasion upon which
the response was made was the important delegation sent
north by Hadrian in the late summer of 870.

This delegation arrived at Saint-Denis in October
870, bearing letters dated 27 June and addressed to the
western archbishops and *proceres*, as well as to Charles
the Bald and to Archbishop Hincmar in particular.[103]
All chastised the parties involved for having invaded the

Lotharingian territories in spite of the pope's express
prohibition, but the letter addressed to Hincmar of Reims
was by far the harshest. The pope expressed amazement
that the archbishop had abused his trust and had not
responded to his previous letter. This failure, the
pope said, revealed Hincmar as the true instigator of
the whole policy, and he ordered that the archbishop now
exercise his authority to bring Charles to leave Lotharingia immediately, on threat of excommunication. If
necessary, he said, he would make a personal visit to
Francia.[104] This letter was discussed by the archbishop
of Reims, in the company of king, legates, and a number
of prelates, in the days following 19 October, and a
response was drafted, to be sent with the legates on
their return to Rome.[105]

In his response Hincmar asserted that, as he had
earlier promised the legates, he had acceded to the
papal orders as far as he possibly could and had on two
occasions transmitted these orders to the episcopate.[106]
He had had, he alleged, no part in the agreement made
between the two kings, but indeed many in Lotharingia
had warned that if such a settlement were not made,[107]
establishing there a king who could defend them, civil
war must follow. As to an oath granting succession in
Lotharingia to Louis II, which Hadrian had asserted to
have been given by Charles, the king denied having taken
it. On the contrary, Charles held that both right of
inheritance and prior oath favored his own succession.
Said Hincmar, no legal process had disproved Charles's
claim, and he could then hardly condemn him.[108] Again,
to accuse him, the archbishop of Reims, of instigating
the invasion was wrong and unheard of. The demand that
he excommunicate Charles should he invade the middle
kingdom was one that both bishops and lay lords, whom
Hincmar had queried, had found to be totally novel. The
task was given to him alone, when many others were close
to the king, many of these, indeed, not eager, as he
was, to fulfill the papal commands.[109] Even in the case
of Lothar II, who was a known malefactor, Nicholas I
had not imposed such a demand upon any single bishop,
whereas Charles, on the contrary, had had no fault
proved of him. In fact, the archbishop said, it was
upon the plea of the inhabitants of Lotharingia that the

king had entered into and brought order and defense to
their land, a deed beyond the spiritual forces of popes
and bishops. Thus had those whom he had confronted with
the papal warnings replied to him, and they had added
that a pope should not obtrude himself into the affairs
of an earthly government that did not concern him, and
he should not attempt to impose upon a people a ruler
who lived at such a distance that his inability to
defend them would leave them open to pagan attack and
would hence result in the exchange of their status as
Franks for that of slaves.[110]

Archbishop Hincmar's letter marked the first official
acknowledgment of the several papal and imperial protests directed against the invasion of Lotharingia, and
through it ran three constant themes: exculpation of
Charles the Bald; assertion that Hincmar of Reims had
been obedient to papal commands; and allegation that
widespread sentiment in the north considered Pope
Hadrian to be misinformed, mistaken, and misguided in
having called for remedies that were both detrimental
and widely disapproved of. But in other respects, too,
the responses sent to Rome with the legatine party in
October 870 marked a significant point: they reflected
the beginnings of a concerted effort by the archbishop
of Reims to regain the ideological ground he had lost
during the pontificate of Hadrian's powerful predecessor
and of a repudiation of papal interference in the
conduct of Frankish politics.

IV

The Ordering and Tensions of the Ecclesiastical Hierarchy

1. The Cases of Rothad and Wulfad, 858-67

That King Charles had been able to assume the crown in Lotharingia was testimony to the hard-line diplomacy so persistently advocated by Hincmar of Reims, who in late 870 played the most important role in the formulation of royal policy. But this triumph constituted for the archbishop not a continuation of power but a return to it after a period of eclipse. Archbishop Hincmar's most lasting influence was surely in his achievement as canonist and in ecclesiology, but he was less a theorist than a controversialist. His personality and circumstances underlay his role as the most ardent advocate of metropolitan authority in church government and his opposition to the ideas of papal hegemony as propounded by Pope Nicholas I and of episcopal autonomy under papal supervision as formulated by the Pseudo-Isidore. All of these positions evolved in the course of political combat, and in its early stages the archbishop of Reims was dealt a firm defeat.

Ordained in the year 832, Bishop Rothad II of Soissons proved himself an adept tactician throughout the crisis of his metropolitan Ebbo of Reims, and in 845 was present at Archbishop Hincmar's ordination.[1] But within a few years Hincmar became dissatisfied with his administration and obedience[2] and, perhaps as early as 857, decided to depose him.[3] King Charles provided the final impetus for such action. For some time complaints had been coming to the monarch from priests who had found their congregations depleted as a result of the erection of private chapels by laymen with permission obtained from local bishops.[4] To remedy this situation, Charles requested that Hincmar of Reims prepare a statement of governing principles. The request

permitted the archbishop to promote his notions of
metropolitan supremacy while condemning the practices
of corrupt bishops; his treatise *De ecclesiis et
capellis* was presented at the council of Quierzy in
March 858.[5]

Rothad was one of the bishops most frequently the
subject of the complaints made to King Charles, and his
priest Adeloldus successfully presented such a complaint
before the council at Quierzy. When the bishop of
Soissons refused to acknowledge this synodal action, a
provincial council was held in 861, which found him
guilty of disobedience and passed a provisional sentence
of excommunication against him.[6] The next year, before
a large council meeting at the villa of Pîtres, Archbishop Hincmar began proceedings to depose the unrepen-
tant prelate. At this point Rothad invoked the
authority of the Pseudo-Isidorian decretals, appealing
his case to Rome and arguing that his plea demanded the
immediate suspension of the local proceedings. Rothad's
argument was initially accepted by the council, but
Hincmar of Reims, who construed one of the bishop's
letters to signify abandonment of his appeal and a
request for synodal judgment, appointed judges, who
pronounced Rothad guilty of contumacy and of illegally
sentencing Adeloldus, and declared him deposed from his
see.[7]

In late 862 Rothad wrote to the prelates of Lotharingia and informed them of his circumstances.[8] Most of
the prelates of Lothar's realm supported the divorce of
their king and felt anything but friendly toward the
archbishop of Reims. In addition, Gunthar of Cologne
had a particular grievance. The treaty of Verdun had
divided the diocese of Cambrai, which, with the city
itself, belonged to the ecclesiastical province of Reims,
although most of its area was in the realm of Lothar.
When Bishop Theodore had died in 862, Hincmar of Reims
had opposed Gunthar's desire to have the vacant see go
to his nephew Hilduin, and the memory of this grievance
contributed to Gunthar's championship of the deposed
bishop. Under Gunthar's leadership, the Lotharingian
prelates informed Pope Nicholas of Rothad's plea and
encouraged the deposed bishop to renew his appeal.[9]

Early in 863 King Charles and Archbishop Hincmar received papal letters commanding that Rothad be restored. Pope Nicholas based his complaint against the deposition largely upon what he viewed as a violation of the Sardican appeal canons. He stated that he objected to so wanton a disregard of the law and of the Roman privilege by which the proper ordering of the church was assured, and threatened excommunication against all who consented to contravention of the papal order.[10] Bishop Odo of Beauvais was sent to Rome to present the other side of the case, but he returned unsuccessful; for the pope refused to confirm the deposition. The pope had said that, not only were the arguments presented insufficient to counter the charges of Rothad's defenders, but that furthermore the two sides required by the canons for proper judgment had been lacking. It was to Rome that all major cases must be referred, he continued, and the judgment of a bishop belonged in that category. Indeed, he said, the very conciliar *acta* brought to him by Odo revealed the injury done to the Roman privilege by the deposition of Rothad in spite of his appeal; but even if Rothad had never raised an appeal, the obligation lay with the council to honor the memory of Saint Peter by initiating a review. The bishops should now recall Rothad, restore his see, and permit him to come to Rome; and they themselves should send vicars to represent their side, should they still oppose him.[11]

Nicholas was intent upon asserting the prerogative of his office in all aspects of ecclesiastical administration. In this he quite readily recognized the archbishop of Reims as his primary adversary and the Frankish episcopate as a potential ally.[12] He sought to establish himself as the champion of episcopal rights against the dominance of the metropolitan bishops, and he hoped to undermine Hincmar's position by singling him out and by making the suffragan prelates aware that Rothad's case might later be their own.[13] The papal reaction had immediate effect. At first Hincmar sought further delay, while he enlisted the support of Charles and Queen Ermintrude and undertook to persuade the pope of the propriety of what had been done.[14] But Nicholas was determined to pursue the matter, and he was seconded

by the bishops of Lothar's realm. Hincmar sought some
form of compromise. A council, which met in October 863
at the villa of Verberie, decided that Rothad should be
allowed to go to Rome, but unrestored, thus shifting the
burden of his reinstatement and having it seem a matter
of extraordinary papal fiat.[15]

After considerable delay, Rothad arrived in Rome
about June 864, and he remained there for half a year,
ostensibly awaiting the arrival of his adversaries.[16]
Finally, as Christmas approached, Nicholas held a
council, before which he declared the bishop to be restored. In a sermon delivered to the clergy and people,
the pope censured the techniques by which, he said, the
Frankish bishops had sought to derogate the Roman privilege, and he announced that, as no accusers had arrived
during so many months to present a case against Rothad,
the only possible conclusion must be that he was really
innocent and had been wrongly judged. Hence, the pope
said, he had decided that Rothad should be restored and
that all the possessions of which he had been despoiled
should be returned under penalty of anathema.[17] In the
spring the bishop set out for the north as a member of
the papal delegation led by Arsenius.[18]

The papal letters announcing the restoration of
Rothad were presented by Arsenius at Attigny in July
865. In these letters Nicholas intended to make the
assertion of papal supremacy more palatable by casting
Hincmar of Reims in the role of violator of Christian
order.[19] The spread of Christianity, he said, had given
rise to many churches, yet all still remained parts of
one church, whose proper functioning depended upon
obedience to the hierarchic ordering that united the
many, and in this hierarchy Rome was the major element.
Nicholas stated that although the bishops had admitted
papal primacy, they had misconstrued it in denying
Rothad's appeal and the major status of his case; and
their action had endangered the unity of the church,
which, like any living body, was organized in relation
to its head. They had opposed Nicholas's interpretation
of appeal on the grounds that the decretals upon which
it was based did not appear in the standard canonical
collections; this, he said was merely an argument of

convenience, one obviously not in accord with the pro-
mouncements of Popes Leo and Gelasius regarding the
importance of attaching due veneration to the decretals.
The proper regulation of the church rested upon a
general care exercised by Rome over all; hence, no
appeal was even necessary. Now, relying upon the
authority that was his by God, Saints Peter and Paul,
his predecessors in the papal see, and the council of
Nicaea, he had restored the bishop of Soissons. The
bishops should obey, rather than assert the privileges
of their own churches and deny the supreme primacy of
Rome, a privilege established by Christ Himself.[20]

Rothad's reacceptance by the Frankish church and,
more important, the acknowledgement of Nicholas's action
by King Charles constituted a great rejection for
Hincmar of Reims, both for the ecclesiological theories
he advocated and for the influence he exerted at the
royal court. In 865 the vigorous papalism asserted by
Nicholas supported the role of champion of the church
that had been assumed by Charles in connection with the
question of King Lothar's divorce, particularly since
papal doctrine coincided with widespread feeling in the
north, most clearly visible in the Pseudo-Isidorian
decretals, that opposed the pretensions of the archbishop
of Reims.[21] But in turning away from the archbishop,
Charles had other reasons as well; behind the case of
Rothad loomed another situation, one more personally
threatening to Hincmar of Reims.

The archbishop of Reims had long been aware of this
threat. When Bishop Odo was sent to Rome in 863, he
bore with him two documents that had earlier been confirmed by Pope Benedict III, which the archbishop sought
to have reaffirmed by his successor.[22] Hincmar of Reims
himself, then, looked to Rome for support and justification. When the still-accommodating Nicholas agreed to
his request, the archbishop seemed to have denied his
enemies access to a danger with origins that even antedated his pontificate.[23]

In 840, at the start of the fraternal wars that
followed the death of the emperor Louis the Pious, his
eldest son Lothar briefly seized the city of Reims, which

had been designated a part of Charles's inheritance, and
immediately arranged for the restoration of Archbishop
Ebbo, who had been deposed five years earlier. The old
man's tenure was short, however, for within two years
King Charles had gained the city and both Ebbo and his
champion were in flight.[24] But in the interim Ebbo had
ordained a number of clerics,[25] and in 852 several of
these men applied to Hincmar of Reims for a clarifica-
tion and adjudication of their status. The danger that
such a request presented to Hincmar is readily apparent:
if the clerics were legitimately in orders, by implication Ebbo's deposition had not been effective and
Hincmar's own ordination must consequently be in question. In April 853 the clerics presented their case
before a synod held at Soissons. Under the influence
of Archbishop Hincmar and King Charles, the attending
prelates declared the clerics improperly in orders and
forbade them to seek high ecclesiastical status thereafter.[26] Hincmar, in an attempt to place the security
of his office upon as assured a foundation as possible,
turned to the papacy. The *acta* of the council were
sent to Pope Leo IV, and they were ultimately confirmed,
along with Hincmar's metropolitan privilege, by Pope
Benedict.[27]

Among the clerics created by Ebbo but absent from the
synod at Soissons was a man named Wulfad. With Ebbo's
departure, he too had left Reims, but he had returned
by 849, and held the cathedral post of *oeconomus*.[28]
Wulfad, who was a man of learning and ability,[29] was
drawn into increasingly close contact with King Charles
in the years that followed the Soissons proceedings.
In 857 Charles attempted to promote him to the see of
Langres, but the archbishop of Reims was successful in
opposing what amounted to a direct contravention of the
conciliar judgment.[30] But Wulfad, who since 854 had been
tutor to Charles's son Carloman,[31] received other royal
favors. In 855 he was made abbot of Montier-en-Der, in
858 of Saint-Médard, and in 860 the monastery of
Reisbach was added to his holdings.[32] By this time
Wulfad was one of the men of influence at court, a
minister regularly present at councils and meetings.[33]
Only high ecclesiastical office eluded him, and now Pope

Nicholas's rebuff of Archibshop Hincmar provided Charles
with a precedent for overcoming this disadvantage.

On 3 April 866 Nicholas addressed a letter to Hincmar
of Reims, in which he informed the archbishop that the
case of the clerics was to be reopened. He announced
that upon his reexamination of the materials relating
both to Ebbo and to the clerics he had found them an
insufficient basis for a decision to be made concerning the propriety of the council held at Soissons
thirteen years earlier. Nicholas gave Hincmar two
choices: either reinstate the clerics or call a new
council to review their case.[34] Quite clearly the pope
intended to make this the opportunity for a really
definitive assertion of papal authority by forcing the
archbishop to openly acknowledge obedience to his
commands. Nicholas anticipated possible objections.
Time, he said, presented no bar to the clerics' appeal;
furthermore, the records disclosed that the men had in
fact appealed immediately after the decision was made
against them. Nor might Hincmar object that papal confirmation of his metropolitan privilege implied Roman
acceptance of that decision, for the privilege had been
issued with the explicit proviso that it depend upon
the obedience of its recipient. This, the pope said,
was what he now required.[35]

This time the archbishop of Reims could not call
upon royal support. Indeed, Charles considered Wulfad's
status a matter of vital importance, for he wished to
have him made archbishop of Bourges. Wulfad was engaged
in tutoring the young King Charles of Aquitaine, whose
tenuous rule depended upon the influence of the presti-
gious archbishop Rudolf of Bourges.[36] But Rudolf lay
near death, and Charles felt that only Wulfad possessed
the qualities necessary to succeed him and quell inci-
pient revolt in this perpetually troubled province.[37]
As time passed and Hincmar of Reims did not summon the
council, the king's impatience increased, while the
situation in Aquitaine deteriorated. By late July
Rudolf was dead, and Charles the Younger had been
seriously injured in a drunken fall.[38] By now King
Charles was able to inform Nicholas that the council
had been called; and, to expedite affairs, he asked the

pope to allow him to have Wulfad ordained before
Nicholas had received and confirmed the council's surely
favorable decision.[39]   But the papal plan did not permit
such a violation of Nicholas's notion of proper procedure.[40]

In fact, the Frankish prelates, for all that they may
have desired relief from metropolitan hegemony, were not
eager to conform so fully to papal dictates, and Hincmar
of Reims was again able to gain compromise when the
council met.[41]   The bishops who assembled at Soissons in
August 866 decided that, although they approved of
Wulfad, his restoration must be based upon direct papal
action rather than upon their own alteration of a previous synodal decision.[42]   The pope was furious and
commanded that the prelates reconvene to redo the work
that they had mishandled.[43]   Hincmar of Reims in particular he accused of falsifying the accounts of Ebbo's
deposition, of having manipulated the council in 853,
and of tampering with the very privilege he had
received from Rome.[44]   Though Wulfad had long since been
consecrated archbishop,[45] the greater issue of the
ordering of ecclesiastical regulation remained, its
solution to elude Nicholas.   Late in October 867, a
council met in the city of Troyes and reaffirmed the
policy of accommodation and compromise.[46]   Noting that
of the bishops who had been present at Ebbo's deposition
in 835 but one remained, the synod asserted that the
affair was moot. It laid all the onus upon Ebbo and
absolved Wulfad of any complicity in uncanonical
actions.[47]   In a separate letter to the pope, King
Charles corroborated the decision.[48]   But Nicholas, who
died on 13 November,[49] never saw this further rejection
of his orders, and his successor confirmed the action of
the council.[50]

2. Archbishop vs. Bishop.
The Quarrel Opens, 860-69

The period during which Hincmar of Reims saw his
power diminish also witnessed a growing estrangement
between him and his nephew.   Perhaps it was inevitable
that the two should fall out, for Hincmar of Reims was

intolerant of either opposition or independence.
Throughout his career he had been careful in the choice
of episcopal appointments for his province, selecting
men whose affection or dependence guaranteed subser-
vience, and he had been remarkably successful.[51] That
he should have erred in the case of his nephew is not
surprising. To the archbishop it seemed wholly natural
that Bishop Hincmar should be his most dedicated fol-
lower, thus manifesting the appropriate gratitude toward
one who had taken in a penniless boy, raised and educated him, and been responsible for his promotion to
high ecclesiastical office. But to Hincmar of Laon, his
position meant rather different things: independence
from tutelage and the ability to lead the life of a
courtier. Secure in his monarch's favor, he resented
the rebukes that his uncle constantly directed at him.

The disagreement between the two came out into the
open as early as the year 860, when Hincmar of Laon
appeared as an advocate for the cause of Lothar II.[52]
Although he seems to have eventually abandoned this
position, Bishop Hincmar does appear to have had close
relationships with the Lotharingian prelates, and it
has been suggested that he may have aided in the reconciliation between Charles and Lothar in 865.[53] To
Hincmar of Reims, the activities of his nephew at court
were at least questionable, and that Charles had granted
the bishop a palatine office piqued him greatly.[54] The
office had been presented during the archbishop's absence from the kingdom, and upon his return he confronted Bishop Hincmar in the presence of the king and made
him resign the post, on the grounds that he, the metropolitan bishop, had not first been consulted regarding the appointment.[55] But Charles later acceded to
requests of the bishop's friends at court and restored
the office, adding to it the control and revenues of a
monastery outside the province of Reims.[56]

Relations between the two prelates also deteriorated
in matters pertaining more immediately to the administration of the church, as Hincmar of Laon generalized
a habit of disobedience into advocacy of an episcopal
ecclesiology diametrically in opposition to the
theories enunciated by the archbishop, and ultimately
emerged as the foremost champion of the Pseudo-
Isidore. According to Hincmar of Laon, he had opposed

his uncle even in 862 by refusing to sign the deposition of Bishop Rothad prior to papal hearing;[57] but the archbishop denied this.[58] The first certain dispute between the two Hincmars regarding the spheres of their respective authority arose over the villa of Aguilcourt, which took its name from Attolus, a seventh-century bishop of Laon.[59]

When Bishop Attolus died, his property--among it at least part of the villa of Aguilcourt, upon which he had erected a private chapel--went to the church he had ruled. Both the villa and the chapel stood within the limits of the diocese of Reims.[60] In the eighth century, Aguilcourt and the neighboring villa of Jouvincourt, which also belonged to the church of Reims, were among the many properties expropriated by the monarchy for the support of the army.[61] Granted out as one benefice, the two villas remained withdrawn from their ecclesiastical owners until well into the ninth century, when Bishop Pardulus of Laon obtained from King Charles restoration of the lands and chapel at Aguilcourt that belonged to his church.[62]

Over many years the chapel had ceased to function, as the inhabitants of Aguilcourt joined those attending services at the newer chapel at Jouvincourt, where they also paid their tithes.[63] This situation continued throughout Pardulus's pontificate and during the first years of the pontificate of Hincmar of Laon. Then, in 865, while his uncle was absent, Bishop Hincmar determined to assert his church's proprietary right at Aguilcourt, and he sent his provost Bertharius to demand that the dues of the faithful there should be paid to their rightful recipient.[64] The move was momentarily successful. A short time later, however, the news reached Ausoldus, the priest to whom Hincmar of Reims had entrusted the administration of diocesan affairs in his absence, who responded by levying an interdict upon the villa until the tithe was once more paid to the priest at Jouvincourt.

The sentence had the desired effect. Hincmar of Laon, expectably, protested to his uncle, drawing up a collection of the canon law that he felt supported his

claims.[65] The archbishop countered by asserting that
the long period during which the Aguilcourt chapel had
not received the tithe had extinguished its right of
greater antiquity in favor of the church at Jouvincourt. He and his power of sanction prevailed,[66] but
the incident rankled Bishop Hincmar, and in later years
he was to recall and seek to avenge it.

In 866 came the question of Amalbertus, a resident of
the diocese of Reims who had married a woman from Laon.
Now, however, his wife complained through mandate to
Bishop Hincmar that her husband did not sleep with her.
On the basis of this testimony, Hincmar of Laon excommunicated Amalbertus. The archbishop of Reims was
drawn into the matter and three times requested that the
sentence be raised, but the bishop refused.[67] Unfortunately, all that is left concerning this incident is the
archbishop's report; and, while he seems to have opposed
the action because the procedure involved was uncanonical, one suspects that here, as happened so frequently,
he has concealed his feelings behind his legalisms.
Here, indeed, Archbishop Hincmar appears to have had
reason for his anger, though the affront to himself
seems to have galled him more than did the situation in
which Amalbertus had been placed.

That same year saw still another clash--one that
seemed in many ways to place the bishop of Laon directly
in the camp of his uncle's enemies. In spite of Pope
Nicholas's command that there be a free and canonical
election to the see of Cambrai, the vacancy there remained until after the visit of the legate Arsenius and
the improvement of relations between Charles the Bald
and Lothar II.[68] At last, in June 866, Hincmar of Reims
was able to summon his suffragans to the ordination of
the priest John as bishop of Cambrai, which he scheduled
to take place on 7 July. On the assigned day the bishop
of Laon neither appeared nor sent any messenger or representative.[69] The rite was postponed for two weeks,
and on 13 July the archbishop sent another call to his
nephew. Again, to the indignation of all present, we
are told, Hincmar of Laon failed to appear; but the
ceremony took place.[70] A special emissary was sent to
Laon but could obtain no response from the bishop.[71]

By this time Hincmar of Laon had become an open associate of Bishop Rothad and of Wulfad and his company.
These associations suggest that he may also have been
involved in other activities in which he might have made
use of the close relationship between himself and
Hincmar of Reims, and between the churches over which
they presided, to undermine his uncle in a more surrep-
titious fashion. In 866 and again the following year,
the archbishop of Reims complained to Pope Nicholas that
false and malicious charges had been delivered by his
enemies to him and to the king, and he alleged that his
correspondence and a set of documents he had sent to
Rome in his defense had been tampered with.[72] The pope
agreed that something was amiss, and he warned the
archbishop that he had in fact received a letter that
purported to be from him but lacked the archbishop's
seal.[73] In July 867 a letter to the archbishop from
Nicholas was diverted to the royal palace. The archbishop later charged that the bishop of Laon was responsible, a charge that receives at least some circumstantial support from the fact that, when he went to receive the communication at the palace of Samoussy, he
found there, not only the king, but also a group composed of Hincmar of Laon, Rothad, and Wulfad and his
collegium.[74] One final circumstantial observation may
be made regarding the letters and documents of defense,
which were intended for very select eyes. They are
still extant, in the form of a virtual dossier compiled
by Hincmar of Reims, which records the difficulties he
experienced in his relationships with the pope during
866 and 867, and includes not only copies of the letters
he had drafted to Nicholas but also private instructions
regarding the issues at hand. These included tactical
directions concerning the topics to be raised before the
pope as the best means for presenting the archbishop's
case at Rome, clearly intended to be seen only by
Archbishop Egilo of Sens, Hincmar's representative to
Nicholas. All are contained in a manuscript that ori-
ginates from the abbey of Notre-Dame de Laon and was
almost certainly executed during the pontificate of
Bishop Hincmar.[75]

*   *   *

Thus, when Hincmar of Laon appealed to his uncle in

868, during the bishop's quarrel with King Charles, it
was a call behind which lay an acerbic history. In the
following year, after Bishop Hincmar's release from
royal confinement, the antipathy between the two prelates rapidly gained public notice. In the course of
his weeks of detention at Servais, Hincmar's animus
against the archbishop of Reims increased, as the elder
Hincmar raised the Laon interdict and lifted the excommunication long ago imposed upon Amalbertus.[76] Upon
his reconciliation with King Charles, the bishop made
haste to return to Laon, remaining at Pîtres barely long
enough to provide Hincmar of Reims with some foretaste
of what was to come.[77] By 8 July he was back at his
episcopal see, where he embarked upon a campaign of
revenge directed against the archbishop. This took the
form not only of personal attack for the injuries he
felt he had received from Hincmar of Reims but also of
a concerted criticism aimed at the archbishop's alleged
misuse of his metropolitan office. Confident now that
in the king he had regained a champion, the bishop began
to attack his uncle at every opportunity, first through
written polemic and then through action.

The confrontation between nephew and uncle assumed
the form of a rivalry expressed through canon law. The
bishop selected a group of extracts from a large canonical collection he had prepared, and promulgated them
before the clergy of Laon on 8 July.[78] In a farrago of
Roman law and canonical sources, containing among often
contradictory maxims[79] such assertions as the total
immunity of bishops from earthly judgment, coupled with
the admonition of the council of Antioch that cases
against a bishop must be heard by all bishops of the
province,[80] the younger Hincmar took aim at what he
considered the unjust treatment he had been subjected
to in recent months. The collection concluded with an
**axiom against informers, and an extract from a letter of
Leo I to the bishops of Gaul, in which the pope threat-**
ened excommunication against any who transgressed the
ordinances of his letter. There followed the signature
of the bishop of Laon, with the statement that all who
felt as he did regarding these matters might be at peace
with him, while others who did not wish to share this
unity were not part of his communion.[81] To this

libellus he commanded and attached the signatures of his clergy as evidence of their adherence.[82]

It is clear, as the archbishop suggested later, that the target of this document, particularly in the references to informers, was Hincmar of Reims himself,[83] and the whole work bears witness to the extraordinary hostility that the bishop felt toward his uncle for his real or imagined betrayal, an anger which, developing into an idée fixe, became a ruling passion in the young Hincmar's life. Similar feelings are indicated in various other legal collections he compiled during the summer and fall of 869. All basically concern the relationship between a metropolitan and other bishops as manifested particularly in the problems connected with the Laon interdict and the excommunication of Amalbertus.[84] All explicitly or implicitly attacked Hincmar of Reims for misuse of his office.

Once again on close terms with the king, the bishop of Laon was, perhaps, among the few who were with Charles when he received news of King Lothar's death.[85] He accompanied the royal party that entered Lotharingia, and was in attendance when Charles was crowned at Metz.[86] Late in the year he was with the king at Aachen, and in January 870 he was present at the ordination of Bertulfus as archbishop of Trier.[88] Bolstered by the renewed favor of his monarch, his slights and attacks against the archbishop of Reims became bolder and harsher, until they reached a peak in a public confrontation at the assembly held at Gondreville in November 869.[89]

At such ceremonial meetings, it was customary for the younger bishops to exchange the kiss of peace with their seniors. Hence, one may imagine the impact when Hincmar of Laon, clearly acting on the lines suggested by his subscription of the past July, brought the quarrel between his uncle and himself into the open by refusing to give the kiss of peace to his metropolitan and by refusing to even speak with him at all.[90] When Archbishop Wenilon of Rouen asked him why he behaved in this way, the bishop of Laon replied that he would be willing to be at peace with his uncle if the latter would publicly burn and declare null the writings he had directed to

his nephew in opposition to the Laon interdict.[91]
Furthermore, the young bishop said, what he had done
at Laon had been no more than what the archbishop had
done in the case of Aguilcourt.[92]

Wenilon conveyed this message to Hincmar of Reims,
and the archbishop responded that he would like to see
proof of this assertion.[93] Then, reflecting that he had
heard from colleagues that bishop Hincmar had spoken of
a number of works, including a canonical collection
drawn from letters of the popes, another document that
he himself and his clergy had signed, and finally a work
that the bishop declared to show the invalidity of all
the arguments posed by the archbishop against the interdict, Archbishop Hincmar requested that Wenilon return
to his nephew and ask that these materials and the
letters written by the archbishop be submitted to the
assembly, so that the issues might be discussed and a
fair resolution and peace emerge. The archbishop of
Rouen conveyed this message and returned with the reply
that Hincmar of Laon did not have these works with him,
but that he would send them soon to his uncle. Meanwhile, Wenilon brought the archbishop another canonical
collection, which his nephew had compiled for King
Charles.[94]

This collection, the most famous and widely circulated of the bishop's many canonical works, soon acquired the name *Pittaciolus*, the word by which its
author described it in the dedicatory verses appended
to it.[95] As even Bishop Hincmar admitted, it is a
confused mixture, which includes selections from the
Pseudo-Isidorian decretals, from the *Capitula Angilramni,*
and from the genuine letters of several popes.[96] Some
of the confusion may be accounted for on the assumption
that the compilation was made not only in haste but
also at different times and for a variety of purposes.

The contents of the collection deal essentially with
four categories of questions. The first relates to
proper accusation and the qualifications necessary for
accusers, the right of appeal to Rome, and the necessity that a metropolitan hear charges against bishops
in his province only with all the other bishops present

and that sentence be given by judges chosen by the accused bishop himself.[97]   The second places its main emphasis upon the inability of any metropolitan to act outside his own *parochia* without the consent of the local bishop, upon the right of an accused bishop to transfer his case to Rome if he suspects that his metropolitan is prejudiced against him, and upon the absolute preeminence of the pope in the determination of episcopal cases and in providing authorization for any synodal activity.[98]   The third category contains decretals that relate to the *exceptio spolii*.[99]   The fourth type of selection, which consists mainly of admonitions against the voiding of sentences of another bishop and the refusal to follow the decretals of the popes,[100] is buttressed by a long extract drawn from Pope Nicholas I regarding the unretractable nature of papal judgments, the status of decretals, the nature of appeal, and the necessity of episcopal *causae* receiving definition by the pope.[101]   A poem of dedication to Charles the Bald headed the work, suggesting that the bishop may have originally brought the collection to Gondreville to present it to the king.[102]

The archbishop of Reims responded on the following day with a short evaluation of the work[103] which he had delivered to his nephew through Wenilon of Rouen, so as, he said later, to avoid the possibility of rebuff.[104] The letter, written in a mild and patronizing tone, chided Hincmar of Laon for tendentious citation of the laws. Hincmar of Reims informed his nephew that these rules had been known to him--and known in their integrity--since before his birth.[105] As metropolitan he counseled his suffragan to undertake a more careful study of the canons and the decretals, so that he would be able not merely to read in them what he wished, but also to understand the intent of their framers, and in so doing avoid the danger of schism.

Hincmar of Laon persistently refused to acknowledge his uncle during the course of the assembly.[106] It is easy to understand the hurt this must have caused the elder Hincmar, who, for all his ferocity, deeply felt the need for love and loyalty, as both his correspondence and actions show. It is not surprising then that

the archbishop was so sensitive about derogation of the
principles through which he expressed his feelings. In
867 he had complained bitterly about King Charles's
forgetfulness of his past services.[107] Then, as now
with his nephew, the wound was deep, and Hincmar of
Reims reacted as always by using his pen.

In the days that followed delivery of the *Pittaciolus*, Hincmar of Laon failed to send the promised
treatises, and his uncle remonstrated with him on the
unfairness of not permitting him to reply publicly to
the charges raised against him, which he said in fact
amounted to slanders delivered unsubstantiated to his
colleagues.[108] In another letter, similar in intent
but directed specifically against the charges relating
to Aguilcourt, he reproached the bishop for his mendacious account of the circumstances, which Hincmar of
Reims stated he was willing to refute in either informal or synodal meeting.[109] In addition, he said,
several points might be noted regarding the bishop's
arguments. First, the Laon interdict was in fact a
closed issue, since in analogizing it to Aguilcourt the
bishop had by implication admitted a guilty act. But
he continued, in comparing the two situations of Laon
and Aguilcourt, Bishop Hincmar had obscured the fact
that they were by no means the same. And the worst harm
he had done, the archbishop said, was having used his
tongue as a sword, to spread lies and false accusations.[110] In yet another message, of uncertain date,
the archbishop chided his nephew for demanding that he
burn his writings. To do so, he said, would amount to
destroying the Scriptures and canons; this would, as
Hincmar of Laon knew, make the archbishop guilty of
sacrilege and worthy of anathema and deposition.[111]

Such matters hardly bothered Hincmar of Laon. For
him the Aguilcourt affair, like the raising of the
interdict, had been an unwarranted intrusion, a clear
case of illicit interference by a metropolitan in the
affairs of another bishop. In the tradition of Rothad
of Soissons, he expounded a doctrine of episcopal
autonomy and championed the principles of the Pseudo-
Isidore. But the bishop did know that his uncle too had
struggled over these same questions for many years.

Thus, even as the principles at issue emerged with
increasing clarity, one may surmise that he had clear
insight into what his uncle's reaction must be, and
one is perhaps not far wrong in imagining that the archbishop's anguish was not simply the by-product of a
quarrel motivated by an opposition of principle but
also an end in itself, a well-calculated revenge for
the alleged betrayals of Verberie and Servais.

V

The Quarrel Matures

1. From Gondreville to Attigny, 869-70

On 13 February 870 Hincmar of Reims addressed a letter
of admonition to his nephew.[1] The subject was a man
named Nivinus, a vassal of the church of Reims, who
some months earlier had been smitten by the charms of
a young woman and had determined to seduce her. It
developed that his passion was reciprocated, and the
two arranged for an assignation, neither being dis-
couraged, apparently, by the fact that the woman was a
nun. Choosing a time when the archbishop of Reims was
away, the pair arranged for the aid of a sympathetic
doorkeeper; at the given time, the woman left her convent and was escorted by two of Nivinus's followers to
a house in the city, where the lovers remained together for several days and nights. Of course, the scandal
could not be contained, and the woman was severly chastised upon her return.[2]

The subject of nuns and virgins and their inviola-
bility seems to have loomed large in the consciousness
of Hincmar of Reims,[3] and perhaps it was fear of his imminent return as much as desire that led the woman once
more to flee the convent. Lacking a friendly helper
this time, Nivinus's men scaled the walls and returned
to their master with their prize. Men sent in pursuit
arrived at the benefice Nivinus held from the church of
Reims only to find that their prey had absconded.[4]

Upon his return, the archbishop said, he conferred
with his clergy and with the noble laymen of the city
concerning the course of action he should follow, and
on their advice he issued several warnings calling
upon Nivinus to attend the episcopal court and there
either purge himself of guilt or confess his sin.
When he did not appear, he was excommunicated in an

attempt to force his attendance.[5] Then, the archbishop
said, he heard that Nivinus had found a protector in
Bishop Hincmar, who not only received the excommunicate,
but doubly offended the law by giving him a benefice of
lands that belonged to the church of Laon in exchange
for other properties he had held.[6] Hincmar of Reims advised his nephew to reconsider his ill-conceived deeds
and also warned him against Nivinus's brother Bertricus,
who, he said, had been ejected from Reims as a notorious
adulterer and a practitioner of incest.[7]

In late February or early March, the cleric Heddo
arrived at Reims bearing the bishop's response.[8] Nivinus's account of what had happened was quite different,
he said. The whole story, according to the vassal, was
based upon lies and unfounded rumor; for when he had
learned that the archbishop had summoned him, he had
responded--even though he lay under no formal accusa-
tion--and had gone with twelve oath-helpers to clear
his name. It was in fact Hincmar of Reims himself who
had failed to appear. Indeed, the vassal said, he had
sought on yet another occasion to purge himself; but
the archbishop had been prejudiced against him by the
lies of his enemies and had commanded that because he
had been contumacious Nivinus must now either confess
or have his men submit to the ordeal by water. Finding neither alternative acceptable, he had been forbidden to remain more than one night in the diocese of
Reims.[9]

As to the archbishop's allegation that he, Hincmar,
had granted church lands not freely but in profitable
exchange, this too was a lie, the bishop said, and one
that his uncle could quite easily have discovered. The
truth was that when Nivinus had come to him and offered
what was in fact an exchange of convenience, his request had been seconded by Eutramnus and Humerus, both
of whom were the archbishop's own men, and he had resisted their advice. Nivinus then had received his
land quite freely.[10]

It is impossible to separate fact from fiction in
this extraordinary story, but the facts here are not so

important as what the interchange reveals of the personalities of the two prelates and the form and style
their confrontation was assuming. This is apparent in
the bishop's questions regarding Bertricus. The archbishop's warning concerning him was unclear, the younger Hincmar said. Should he consider Bertricus excommunicated, although he was not from the province of
Reims--as Hincmar of Reims had acknowledged--and thus
the archbishop could not legally sentence him? Or if
Bertricus was not an excommunicate, was it illegal for
him to remain in anyone's diocese? Further, Bishop
Hincmar continued with regard to the crimes of Bertricus, how had his capture come about, how had the investigation been conducted, and how had his punishment
been assessed?[11] These are all relevant questions,
particularly when asked of a man who exercised enor-
mous power in the name of respect for the law and for
proper procedure. But, in addition, the parallels to
be drawn between Bishop Hincmar's presentation of the
case and his own detention at Servais are hardly subtle.
Theory and legalism had become the vehicle through which
the feelings and personalities of the two Hincmars were
expressed. This is evident in the bishop's generalized
response to the question of Nivinus's benefice. Never
before, he said, had Hincmar of Reims accused him of releasing church property for compensation,[12] and he continued that the canons demanded a public evaluation of
such charges; and the canons, as the archbishop knew,
were particularly stringent regarding anonymous and un-
charitable accusations against a cleric[13] and did not
permit a metropolitan to judge a bishop without synodal
hearing.[14]

Yet another incident reveals the state of tension
between the two prelates and the manner in which their
quarrel was taking shape. About the beginning of March,
the priest Clarentius arrived at Reims to inform the
archbishop of his nephew's action regarding Hadulfus,[15]
a priest whom both Hincmars knew well. His service to
the church of Laon predated Bishop Hincmar's ordination,
and he had been one of the bishop's early mentors.[16]
Now the two had fallen out. The cause, Hincmar of Laon
said, was Hadulfus's disobedience. He had been ordered

to undertake a journey to Bishop Witgarius of Augsburg, from whom Bishop Hincmar wanted a book, but the priest had persistently refused to go. Finally Hincmar had punished his contumacy by forbidding Hadulfus to communicate in the diocese. Even then the priest refused to hear the sentence, stuffing his fingers into his ears.[17]

While Clarentius was making his report, Hadulfus himself appeared and, the archbishop said, gave a somewhat different version. Though he had indeed refused the mission, Hadulfus said, he neither had any knowledge of his excommunication, nor had he been contumacious. He now repented his mistake and begged to be allowed to return to Laon. The archbishop permitted him to send a servant with Clarentius upon his return. The man subsequently reported that Hadulfus's church had indeed been closed and that neither his house nor its contents were accessible. The priest begged Hincmar of Reims to intervene on his behalf, promising that should Bishop Hincmar lift the sentence, he would forever be faithful to him. On 20 March the archbishop sent his nephew a temperate letter, in which he noted the approach of Easter and counseled mercy.[18]

The reply came eight days later. Hincmar of Laon accused the priest of being a liar, and he promised to explain the facts at the proper time. Why, he asked, had Hincmar of Reims listened only to Hadulfus, rather than finding out what had really happened? Out of honor for his uncle's request, the bishop agreed to permit Hadulfus the house and to let others communicate with him if they wished. He himself would not do so until either satisfaction or formal judgment should conclude the matter.[19] The outcome of the case is not known, but Hadulfus meanwhile remained at Reims,[20] where he became a scapegoat in the third, and in some ways most bizarre, of the encounters between uncle and nephew during the first half of 870.

*   *   *

The list of properties restored by Charles the Bald

to the church of Reims on 10 October 845[21] contains no
mention of Follembray, although this villa near the town
of Coucy in the Laonnais was well known to have belonged
to that church for as long as a century.[22] Perhaps Archbishop Hincmar's forebearance in this case owed to the
fact that for many years Follembray had formed part of a
royal benefice held by the family of Pardulus, the archbishop's closest friend. Between 748 and 762 Pardulus's
grandfather, Rodolfus, had been granted lands in the
Laonnais by Pepin the Short, lands of which the **villa** of
Follembray was a part.[23] In previous times the inhabitants of the villa had attended the parish church in
Coucy, but under Rodolfus a private church was built on
the villa, and its priest, according to the law, approved
and ordained by the bishop of Laon.[24]

About the year 798, a vacancy occurred at Follembray,
and Bishop Wenilon ordained the priest Ottericus to fill
it.[25] In the years since the lords of Follembray had obtained the villa, they had established three new villas--
Landrica curte, Noviante, and Broeris--on adjacent land
held by them, and the care of the chapels built on these
villas went to Ottericus as well. Ottericus, in serving
his flocks here for nearly sixty years, outlived not
merely several of the lords of Follembray but their entire line. Last in the line of succession was Odelharius,
who was a nephew of Bishop Pardulus; and when he died,
Follembray finally returned to the church of Reims, to be
let in benefice by Hincmar of Reims to a man named
Osverus.[26]

At the death of Ottericus, Osverus and the men of
Follembray proposed one Wulfgerius as his successor, and
Bishop Pardulus was about to proceed with the ordination
when he himself followed Ottericus to the grave.[27] Without either a bishop to look to or an incumbent priest to
span the gap in episcopal authority, and perhaps given
the political crisis of the years 858 to 860, the community lost its continuity. In 858 or 859 Haimeradus,
who was then the parish priest at Coucy, asserted that
the chapel at Follembray properly fell under his spiritual administration; an investigation undertaken by Hincmar of Laon at this time disproved his claim.[28] In the

meantime, about 859, Broeris, one of the three villas created adjoining Follembray and like it made destitute of a priest by the death of Ottericus, received Bertfridus as his successor upon the appointment of Hincmar of Laon, and this man continued to conduct services at Follembray as well.[29]   Then, about 864, Bertfridus was removed, and for a time the residents of Follembray worshipped at Coucy.[30]

The archbishop of Reims had become directly involved with Follembray with the repossession of that villa. Even before the removal of Bertfridus, Osverus, the new holder of the villa, had died, and about 865 Hincmar of Reims gave the property to Sigebertus, the archbishop's great-nephew.[31]   In 866 or 867 Sigebertus requested that services be restored at Follembray. To minister to the congregation, Hincmar of Reims sent his *mancipium* Senatus, a cleric of Reims still in minor orders, whom Hincmar of Laon ordained an acolyte, and pending his ordination to the priesthood, services at Follembray were conducted by temporary vicars who were appointed by the bishop of Laon from among his own cathedral clergy.[32]

It will be evident that the complicated nexus of relationships that evolved around the villa of Follembray contained the seeds of possible discord. Such situations were, of course, hardly rare. They might be settled through accommodation or, as in the case of bishops such as Rothad of Soissons, they might engender disputes that reflected far wider issues of ecclesiastical authority.[33] Follembray presented a perfect stage for continuation of the quarrel between the two Hincmars, upon which personal feelings might readily be merged with statements of principle and legal interpretation.

Although Hincmar of Laon did ordain Senatus an acolyte, he apparently had never been receptive to the idea of renewing services at Follembray. Obviously, such a course of action would have meant the loss of a portion of the congregation and tithes of his church.[34] Senatus's elevation to the priesthood was delayed over the years, and priests from Laon continued to act as vicars at Follembray. Eventually the men of Follembray protested that

they still lacked a priest of their own. When on one
occasion a group of them made their complaint in public
before the archbishop, they received from the bishop of
Laon only a curt response that the villa had no need of
a priest. Hincmar of Reims misunderstood his nephew's
meaning and, wishing to smooth over the response, explained to the petitioners that the bishop had meant that
no priest was needed because Senatus would in time assume
the position. His nephew apparently did not contradict
him, and the situation at Follembray continued as before.[35]

Then, on 4 February 870, Haimericus, the priest who
was currently serving as vicar for Senatus, placed an
interdict upon the church at Follembray.[36] The residents
immediately complained to the archbishop of Reims, who
sent his *missi* to Laon to inquire into the matter.[37] It
became clear at once that Hincmar of Laon intended to
make Follembray a part of the feud with his uncle, for
the bishop's only response to the delegation was that he
was doing nothing that Hincmar of Reims had not previously done at Aguilcourt.[38] When Bishop Hincmar gave reasons for his action, he said Haimeradus had renewed his
claim that the chapel at Follembray was in fact subject
to his church at Coucy and had, on this basis, charged
Senatus, the holder of the chapel, with illegally de-
taining church property. As a consequence, the bishop
said, he had reopened the investigation into the relationship between the two churches and had summoned Senatus to his diocesan synod to answer the charge of expropriation. When Senatus did not appear, it was ordered
that he should exercise no functions at Follembray until
the case had been settled. Meanwhile, Bishop Hincmar
said he had talked with Sigebertus and had remonstrated
with him for having violated the law by introducing a
cleric at Follembray without having first obtained episcopal consent. In fact, he told Sigebertus that he would
have been willing to overlook this infraction if Haimeradus had withdrawn his claim, but the priest's adamant
refusal had given the bishop no choice but to follow the
path of reason and authority. Thus, he had summoned the
contending parties and had told Sigebertus to make an
immediate provisional restoration to Haimeradus of the
property of which he claimed to have been despoiled.[39]

On 27 April Hincmar of Reims sent the bishop a de-
tailed argument in support of Senatus and of the autonomy
of the chapel at Follembray from the church of Coucy.[40]
In his argument the archbishop assessed the villa and its
church in their relationship to one another, to the
bishops of Laon and Reims, and to the priest of Coucy.
Clearly, Follembray is independent, he said, and that it
had long been so is one indication of that fact.[41] Further, he said, the canons guarantee a bishop the right to
build a church and appoint its priest anywhere, even outside of his own diocese, with the local prelate holding
the rights of dedication and ordination.[42] Hincmar of
Laon should follow these rules, as had his predecessors
and others in cases where the see of Reims possessed
churches beyond its immediate limits.

As to Senatus, laws issued by Charlemagne himself oppose the expulsion of a priest without consent of the
bishop and, indeed, deny the legitimacy of expulsion under any circumstances if the priest has served well.
These laws, the archbishop observed, had recently been
confirmed by Charles the Bald.[43] Thus Hincmar of Laon
had only two proper courses to follow. If Senatus had
proven himself capable, the bishop should request that
Hincmar of Reims, to whose church the cleric belonged,
give him *libertas ecclesiae*, and he should then proceed
with his ordination.[44] If, on the contrary, Senatus had
not proved adequate (although the archbishop noted that
Hincmar of Laon had ordained him acolyte), then he should
so inform the archbishop, who would send another candidate. In any case, he continued, the canons must be followed, as well as the old customs of the province, which
here go back a century without interruption. To suppress
the church at Follembray was illegal. Just as it was unlawful for a bishop to divide parishes at will, so too it
was unlawful for him to confound them.[45]

As to the bishop's synodal summons and the penalty
that threatened Senatus for nonattendance, these also
were illegal, for the cleric had the church by proper
authority and so need hardly attend a synod to explain a
charge of expropriation for holding it. In fact, the
archbishop said, since Senatus was a *mancipium* of the

church of Reims, the bishop of Laon could not so summon
him in any case; he rather should have gone to Hincmar of
Reims, who would have sent his *missi* to the synod.[46]
Hincmar of Reims concluded that it was Hincmar of Laon
who could himself be brought before a provincial council
on the charge of illicit ordination, for it was he who
had ordained Senatus an acolyte without the archbishop
having first granted the man liberty to receive this
rank.[47]

   As the bishop of Laon had noted, the cases of Follembray and Aquilcourt had many points of similarity;[48] and,
indeed, albeit the questions were complex, neither in
terms of the situation of the properties nor of the issues of episcopal jurisdiction raised in their connection
were such circumstances rare. What is significant, again,
is the manner in which currently topical questions became
a mechanism through which the two Hincmars continued their
personal quarrel. It is difficult to assess fault in the
immediate situation. Clearly Hincmar of Laon sought to
provoke his uncle by insult and harassment, and to demonstrate superiority by showing up his uncle in his interpretation of the law. On the other hand, the archbishop's
use of his expertise in the law as a club, to be wielded
at will to gain his ends, was an unjustifiable practice
that many besides the bishop of Laon found both enraging
and frustrating.

   These emotions are revealed in a letter by means of
which Hincmar of Laon responded on 1 May to his uncle's
arguments.[49] He began by recalling that it was then almost the anniversary of his "*traditio*" at Servais,[50] and
stated that he was undertaking an investigation of the
status of Follembray and Coucy, so that the question
might be decided at the diocesan synod he had called for
the fifteenth of the month. In fact, he said, among those
witnesses who should be present at the synod was Hadulfus;
and Bishop Hincmar expressed surprise that the archbishop
had not long since sent him back. His uncle, he said, had
alleged that he had consented to the placement of Senatus
at Follembray; but this, he said, the archbishop could
neither know nor prove and hence should refrain from
making such an accusation. Indeed, he said, the law

stated that one who presented a charge which he cannot
prove should no longer be considered a credible witness.[51]
In fact, he said, Sigebertus had told him that the consent had been given by his clergy; and on being asked by
whom in particular, he had named Hadulfus.[52]   As to the
archbishop's citation of Charlemagne as an authority
against the despoliation of a priest, he continued, actually it was Haimeradus who had been despoiled. He again
alleged that with regard to Senatus's ordination, his
uncle had spoken without knowing what had occurred; and
he stated, furthermore, that his uncle had misunderstood
the law he had invoked. Charlemagne's capitulary, he
said, actually held that an unfree person who is elevated
to clerical office must be deposed.[53]   All of this,
Bishop Hincmar continued, should be taken up in the proper place and at the proper time, instead of the archbishop serving as both accuser and judge, without the proper legal forms of council, interrogation, and the rest.[54]
He himself intended to do what was just, so he had called
Senatus to the synod, because Haimeradus had accused him.
Now that the issue of Senatus's ordination as acolyte had
arisen, the bishop said he awaited enlightenment by his
metropolitan and was full ready to hear proof of the cleric's status. Finally, as to his having summoned Senatus
when the cleric had been despoiled, not only was Senatus
himself the real despoiler, but Hincmar of Laon bade his
uncle recall the treatment he himself had received the
year before.[55]

   The angry archbishop sent a long response on 11 May;
and here, too, the case at hand receded into the background, while questions personal and theoretical came to
the fore.[56]   In fact, Hincmar of Reims said little about
the immediate matter; he responded to his nephew's arguments mainly with accusations of lying.[57]   Clearly, the
archbishop said, Hadulfus was not contumacious; rather,
he had been driven to the breaking point by Bishop Hincmar. Again, he said, the arguments put forth regarding
Follembray and Senatus were puerile and senseless, not to
be believed.[58]   He was perverting the canons, the archbishop stated, as he had done before; and this seemed like
but another attempt to win a battle.[59]

On this score the archbishop was quite correct, and
indeed a public confrontation between the two prelates
was at hand. For months both men had asserted that their
differences should be aired before a council; and, when
on 15 June the prelates from ten provinces gathered at
the palace of Attigny,[60] each came prepared to present
his respective case. The issues at stake were far greater than a simple resolution of dispute between two churchmen; they involved questions of immediate interest to all
the bishops present. For Hincmar of Reims, Attigny represented an opportunity **to diminish papal authority in** support of the ecclesiology that had so suffered under Pope
Nicholas I. For Hincmar of Laon, on the other hand, it
presented an opportunity to support papal authority and
champion the ecclesiology of the Pseudo-Isidore. It is
likely that Bishop Hincmar came to the council expecting
the support, not only of those prelates who either liked
him or disliked the archbishop, but also of all those
bishops who were interested in the assertion of episcopal
independence from metropolitan rule.

The tone of the confrontation was immediately apparent, to judge by the words of Hincmar of Laon, even before
the council had opened. When the bishop approached to
enter the door of the hall, he found himself confronted
by Hincmar of Reims, who demanded that he take an oath in
recognition of the privilege of his metropolitan see. To
this the young Hincmar demurred, and finally the council
opened without fulfillment of the demand.[61] But in the
events that followed, the archbishop of Reims was never
forced to yield the advantage or retreat from his aggressive stand. The particulars of this session are recorded
by only one source, which is anonymous, but which was probably written much later by Hincmar of Reims, perhaps to
form part of a dossier intended specifically as an apologia for himself, a fact that must be considered in the
lines that follow.[62] But Hincmar of Laon's own failure
to provide a more favorable relation, as well as his
other actions at and after Attigny, lend at least some
verisimilitude to the record.

In the hall, before the assembled prelates, the archbishop presented his nephew with a massive treatise of

fifty-five chapters, which he informed the bishop was directed against the complaints made at Gondreville and was
in response to the decretal collection Hincmar of Laon had
sent him there through Archbishop Wenilon of Rouen.[63]   He
warned the bishop about the need to correct actions that
were not appropriate to his episcopal station and, in addition, issued a stern pronouncement. He had heard other
things concerning the bishop, he said. He admonished his
nephew that if these were true he should immediately desist, and if not, he should beware.[64]

     This cryptic statement seems to have made no appre-
ciable impression upon Hincmar of Laon. The bishop only
responded that he, too, had certain complaints against his
metropolitan that he wished to place before the council.
He then produced material relating to the chapel at Aguilcourt (which Hincmar of Reims later referred to as a
"*rotula prolixissima*"), another *rotula* pertaining to Haimeradus and the dispute over Follembray, and the statement,
issued in 869, signed by himself and his clerics, the intention of which was to show that Hincmar of Reims, in
raising the interdict imposed by the bishop, had most seriously overstepped his office and endangered the episcopacy.[65]   The case of Haimeradus was deferred in the
priest's absence, but the basic quarrel between the two
Hincmars, which had developed into a trial of metropolitan privilege, was submitted, with the consent of both
parties, to be adjudicated by the assembly.

     The archbishop's response to his nephew's somewhat
frenetic display was presented in a low key, deferential
and inspiring sympathetic consideration. When he rose to
speak to the assembly, he said he wished he were able to
reply to the charges made by his suffragan, but the pains
of rheumatism made this impossible. He would instead of-
fer the council a schedule, not by way of accusation, but
with the intention of seeking their advice--should they
think right to be on his side--as to how they might be
able to admonish the bishop, toward which end he himself,
albeit he had tried, had been unable to accomplish anything of profit.[66]

     He then proceeded to read a brief account of the Laon

interdict. Having heard of its imposition, he said, he
was horrified at such a deed, unheard of and opposed to
every scriptural and canonical authority. He had written
immediately to the bishop, had explained precisely the
nature and seriousness of what had been done, and had begged him to raise the ban. But Hincmar of Laon had remained obstinate, and remained so even to this day, refusing
to heed all warnings to correct his behavior and recognize his obligations toward his metropolitan. Upon the
archbishop's request, the letters he had sent to Hincmar
of Laon before raising the interdict were read to the
council.

Finally, the prelates responded with the opinion that
Hincmar of Reims had written and acted in accordance with
the Scriptures and with papal and canonical authority, and
that his nephew's consistent disregard for the precepts
expressed by the archbishop constituted an invitation to
schism.[67] Hincmar of Laon's case, so long nurtured and
so assuredly advertised, was dashed to pieces. He had
overestimated his strength and had erred in his tactics.

So subdued by his setback was the bishop, says Hincmar
of Reims, that at the session's end he yielded to the
persuasion of certain of his episcopal colleagues, and
agreed to sign the oath of fidelity earlier demanded
from him. The archbishop of Reims relates the incident
evocatively. The time was evening, and a number of
the bishops remained in conversation in the synodal hall.
As he stood beside a window with his friend Bishop Odo,
Archbishop Hincmar was approached by two of his nephew's
comrades, Aeneas of Paris and Frotarius of Bordeaux,
who bore the news that the young Hincmar now wished to
profess his obedience, and to be there after with his
uncle as son to father. Overjoyed, Hincmar of Reims
agreed. The bishop of Laon now revealed to him that
his previous reservations concerned not his uncle, but
rather the uses to which his statement might be put by
future occupants of the see of Reims. Together, uncle
and nephew drew up an oath, which the archbishop then
sought to consign to Bishop Odo, so that it might be
prepared for presentation at the synodal session the

next day. But at this Hincmar of Laon demurred; the
progress of a fever, he said, made it imperative that all
be settled immediately, so that he might leave Attigny
and receive treatment. But eventually, says Archbishop
Hincmar, the advice of his friends again prevailed. The
following day, 17 June, Bishop Hincmar swore and subscribed the oath before the assembled bishops; his triumph
complete, Hincmar of Reims adjourned the synodal meeting.[68]

The issue of the council of Attigny was a complex pro-
duct composed of many factors, and it held an importance
far beyond the personal confrontation of the two major con-
tenders there. Among the elements that found expression
at the council was the question of administrative and
governmental authority in the ecclesiastical hierarchy.
By now Nicholas I had been dead for over two years, and
in the interim different parties had attempted in a variety of ways to take the measure of his successor. To
Hincmar of Reims this involved, not only the invasion of
Lotharingia, but also the opportunity to raise once again
those principles of metropolitan supremacy that had suffered so disastrous a setback at Nicholas's hands. The
council of Attigny had offered the first opportunity since
the great pontiff's death for a public confrontation between the principles formulated by Hincmar of Reims and
those expressed by the Pseudo-Isidore; and in the ecclesiological positions debated by the two prelates, this
contention manifested its most public form.

2.   Some Ecclesiological Issues

The restoration of the hierarchy and its erection to
a position of great political importance under Charlemagne
and his successors engendered a succession of theoriza-
tions, often under controversial circumstances, that were
intended to elucidate the proper ordering of authority in
the church. Hincmar of Reims and Hincmar of Laon, in
their personal confrontation, worked within the terms of a
broad ecclesiological context, of which, indeed, they provide the fullest exposition. The writings of the two prelates and of others who became involved in their contention, and the actual progression of that argument, are
inextricably bound up with the most basic ecclesiological

issues of the time. The quarrel between metropolitan and
bishop, between a metropolitan monarchy posited by the
Frankish archbishops and a papal monarchy asserted by the
Pseudo-Isidore, was not one in which the poles of contention were sharply defined.[69] It was, rather, a spectrum
upon which various positions assumed fine shades of meaning.[70]

The Frankish episcopate, in its practical concern
with the problem of principles that should regulate the
church in its institutional aspect, could draw upon several great traditions, all of which had been current in
the north since the Carolingian rulers of the eighth century had first revived serious interest in the government
of the ecclesiastical hierarchy. The first centuries of
Christianity had seen the evolution of a monarchic episcopate, composed of autonomous bishops, each of whom possessed complete authority within diocesan limits that the
church tended to follow even as a persecuted, illegal religion.[71] In the early church, the lower clergy exercised a wholly derivative authority, with the priesthood
subject to episcopal supervision and discipline exercised
by the bishop through periodic visitations and meetings
of his diocesan synod. Above the bishop, the head of the
Christian community, the early church knew no similar
rule; supradiocesan matters were dealt with either
through informal consultation or by irregular meetings of
the bishops in councils that convened for the resolution
of particular problems of doctrine and discipline considered to affect the whole church.[72] These bodies derived their authority from the meeting itself, from the
unanimity of the attending prelates, which manifested
Divine presence and hence precluded reversal of its decisions by any other person.[73]

When, in the fourth century, the newly legalized
Christian religion was incorporated into the framework of
the imperial government, it became necessary to refine
the machinery of ecclesiastical government and to complete its juxtaposition with that of the older offices of
the imperial administration.[74] In the imperial church,
the great councils were readily assimilated to the senate,
the procedures of which the Christian episcopate had long
since imitated, and they took on a specifically ecumenical

character that derived from the empire itself and from the authority of the emperor. From the fourth century, legislation sought to stabilize and institutionalize the framework of ecclesiastical administration, and the regulations issued by the great councils of the fourth and fifth centuries formed the basis of a growing body of canon law that mirrored the evolution of an increasingly articulated hierarchy.

In theory at least, the administration of this church emphasized the provincial college, which was governed by synodal meetings of the bishops in each province. These synods, unlike the great councils, were to convene regularly to consider, not a unique and pressing concern, but a specific agenda of the perennial problems constantly arising in the course of the normal functioning of a diocese. The competence of the provincial council, established initially as a court of review and appeal,[75] was gradually extended and to some degree assimilated to other activities that required the presence of more than one prelate, such as episcopal ordination. The convocation of these meetings and the presidency of the sessions was the task of the bishop of the metropolitan city in each province.[76]

This system lapsed during the centuries of imperial failure and Germanic occupation of the territories of the western empire, as the institution of kingdoms subject to no real imperial control gave to the church a national character that operated in a much vaguer context and the rudimentary government of the German monarchies sought to adapt to new circumstances by making use of the structures of the church whose religion they had so recently embraced. Meanwhile, a papal ideology had been developing that strove to extend the preeminence of the bishop of Rome as the final arbiter of appeals and doctrine, conceded during the fourth and fifth centuries, into a general regulatory supervision to replace and perpetuate the imperial authority then lost in the west.

Thus it eventuated that the Carolingians, who sought to utilize an ecclesiastical authority that derived from Rome to assure the success of their rule and dynasty, revived and brought to currency several notions of eccle-

siastical administration whose centuries of development
demanded assimilation and working into a coherent and acceptable system of regulation. Faced with the need to
standardize forms of worship and discipline in the cor-
rupted Frankish church, Charlemagne continued the ten-
dencies introduced by the Bonifacian reforms, importing
authoritative canonical and patristic sources.[77] The immediate results were an amalgam of traditions and an
ecclesiastical organization that tended to stress the
significance of the metropolitan office, even as the needs
of the time and the orientation of the imperial government tended to stress the episcopate in all aspects of
imperial administration.[78]

But there was no time for a controlled assimilation
of the various currents of thought thus brought to renewed consciousness. During the first half of the ninth
century, the importance of the episcopacy increased; and
as more emphasis continued to be placed upon the governmental *ecclesia* of the bishops, questions regarding the
nature and composition of the episcopal *synodus* became
increasingly immediate.[79] Provincial regulation tended
to enhance the role of the metropolitan bishop, but it
left unresolved such issues as whether his function was
to coordinate supradiocesan activity and his authority
derivative, or to operate as an autonomous supervisor,
exercising an authority inherent in his metropolitan
position over suffragan bishops owing their creation to
him.

It was natural that contentions between bishop and
metropolitan, through which the ninth century church
sought to resolve the still unsettled problem of relationships between members of the ecclesiastical hierarchy,
should arise in the realm of Charles the Bald and appear
in the context of debates concerned with unitative and
conciliar forms of authority. It was during the course
of the pontificate of Hincmar of Reims and largely due
to the extraordinary influence he wielded that these debates took place, and if the cases of Rothad and Wulfad
greatly stimulated episcopal reliance upon Rome and upon
the forged decretals, it was Hincmar of Laon who became
the most ardent defender of episcopal rights founded upon

Roman privilege.[80] As he and his uncle played out their
personal dispute, they simultaneously provided the fullest exposition of a complex rivalry between still in-
choate ecclesiological statements, a rivalry that on each
side sought to use the many available authorities to construct a system that would define the nature of governmental and administrative authority in the church, its
source, location, and proper exercise.[81]

The notion, prominent in the ninth century, that the
church as an institution was essentially an episcopal
body[82] found support in the canons and assured the continuity of a prominent conciliar ideology; for the administrative function that reflected the purpose of the
episcopal *collegium* might only be expressed in council.[83]
In a society regulated in such a large part by an episcopacy, so cognizant of the importance of ancient norms,
and so anxious to further the restoration of those norms,
it is hardly surprising that the episcopal council should
prove a central factor in ecclesiology and ecclesiastical
regulation. But beyond that point agreement ceased.

The theoretic conflict between the two positions represented by Hincmar of Reims and Hincmar of Laon re-
volved around the definition of synodal identity. To
Hincmar of Reims the metropolitan function meant the regulation of any business within the province that was not
strictly and solely related to local diocesan affairs.[84]
He viewed the whole province as his parochia,[85] and, to a
great extent, the suffragan bishops, whom he had created,
as his agents.[86] The canons, he felt, provided for the
metropolitan privilege precisely as they enunciated pri-
matial precedence ("metropolitan" is, in fact, the western
equivalent of "primate");[87] and these laws, by calling
for a show of honor and reverence on the part of the provincial bishops, clearly indicated the true, supervisory
nature of the metropolitan office.[88]

Nor, in the archbishop's interpretation, did the association of metropolitan and provincial council imply any
restriction to the circumstances of a formal meeting;
rather, it indicated the continuous operation of the metropolitan prerogative within the province, a prerogative
often most conveniently exercised in a formal assembly.

But the provincial council itself did no more than provide this convenient synodal expression; the assemblies
met for convenience, rather than for mutuality or for the
limitation of the metropolitan's activities.[89] Thus, in
any case where a bishop has committed an offense, the
metropolitan should and, in fact, must correct the situation,[90] always using the canons as his guide; to Hincmar
of Reims, at least, it was his interpretation of the intention of the canons that was determinative.[91] So, too,
it followed that within the synodal unit all authority and
all capacity to issue binding decisions flowed from the
metropolitan:[92] he is the source of episcopal ordination,
he is the recipient of episcopal oaths of obedience, and
he is in fact the governmental (as opposed to sacramental)
unit of the province.[93] As to extradiocesan and extra-
provincial activities, no prelate might undertake any
action beyond his diocese without the express permission
of his metropolitan.[94] Infractions that could not be substantiated prima facie (which, hence, required close assessment of testimony) or that were not specifically
covered by the canons were to be taken up in the provincial council, to be handled according to strict procedural
rules.[95] But here, too, the metropolitan need not proceed by full consultation, for the canons also provided
that a case might be heard by a smaller number of officials
chosen either by the metropolitan alone or, at his discretion, by himself and the parties involved, and from the
finding of these judges there could be no appeal.[96]

Clearly, such an interpretation provided great leeway
for the metropolitan, and Archbishop Hincmar applied it,
for example, to justify his raising of the Laon interdict,
which, he said, though it affected no one beyond the diocesan boundaries, was of general concern because of its
provisions and its severity.[97] On the other hand, Hincmar of Laon and the Pseudo-Isidore, with whom he had so
close an affinity, denied the propriety of any metropolitan dominance or interference with the activities of
the other prelates in the province.[98] Within the diocese,
according to his view, all regulation pertained to the
bishop, to whom the property of the church and the foundation of churches, no less than the souls of the faithful,
were charged.[99] At no time, he asserted, might the metropolitan bishop intrude into the affairs of his "com-

provincials";[100] complaints regarding episcopal conduct
had as their proper forum the provincial council,[101]
which body was a meeting of equals and not a stage for
metropolitan pronouncements.[102]

The question of appeal from local judgment was hotly
contended between the two Hincmars; in this also they reflected positions vociferously argued by others. Here it
was the metropolitan who drew upon the conciliar tradition
and regarded any conciliar determination as being unsus-
ceptible of change, unless by unanimous vote of the assembly.[103] This was the principle that Hincmar of Reims
had enunciated in 866 and that the prelates gathered at
Soissons had accepted.[104] But for the archbishop of
Reims the identity of the governing entity was metropolitan rather than collegial, and the circumscription was
provincial rather than determined by the number of bishops
in attendance. In these circumstances his espousal of
this principle of finality on the basis of ancient regulations might well seem inappropriate and unfair; yet it
was, for Hincmar of Reims, the rule. In his view, a local
decision was final, and in the normal condition of ecclesiastical administration, such decision permitted no appeal to any group or person outside the province.[105]
Where Hincmar of Laon sought to identify the sacramental
and governmental jurisdiction of the bishop, Hincmar of
Reims distinguished these functions sharply. By ordination, all are equal, he said, but the government of the
church on earth proceeds from the canons, and these establish not an autonomous and monarchic episcopate, but
rather a government whose entity is the province, a unit
that has no existence without the metropolitan.[106] Within
his province, his area of authority, no one may interfere,[107] nor he in the province of any other metropolitan.
The term "comprovincial" then referred not to the other
bishops in a province but to the peers of the metropolitan.[108] Clearly, the canons that enunciated the metropolitan privilege did not permit a right to demand a
change of venue, for such a right would ipso facto des-
troy the privilege.[109]

In the face of these assertions, opponents of the

metropolitan privilege had two tactics available: they
might place their reliance upon the canons as did their
adversaries, or they might assert the existence of a
higher authority that possessed the right to act as a
court of first instance in certain cases. Each assumption had a long history. The Council of Sardica, in the
context of Athanasius's appeal to the bishop of Rome, had
issued rules asserting and regularizing the process of appeal from local decision to the Roman pontiff,[110] while
popes from the time of Innocent I had asserted exclusive
papal jurisdiction over all major cases, in particular
over cases that involved episcopal deposition.[111] Clearly implicit in such claims--whether they were made by the
episcopate or by the bishop of Rome--were the most fundamental questions concerning the nature of the church and
the papacy; and in answer to such episcopal statements,
the metropolitan asserted the essentially derivative nature of the papal authority itself. Nicaea, the council
in which the universal church was first able to express
its will, had laid down certain rules. As the declaration
of the *assensus ecclesiae*, its decisions took precedence
over those of a lesser council, and they were binding
upon the popes as well.[112]

The antimetropolitan position was elaborated by the
Pseudo-Isidore, who combined appeal to popes and to canons
and gave to the papal decretals an authority equivalent
to that of the canons.[113] The argument was strong, following the episcopal ecclesiology, for only the bishops,
and they all alike, had a Divine origin; the exception
was the pope, who alone had precedence, since in the person of Peter he had received the keys of the kingdom of
heaven from Christ Himself.[114] In governmental terms,
this meant that all authority flowed from Rome by Divine
designation and that the validity of any decision and the
synodal status of any meeting depended upon no human regulation but, rather, upon a specific and particular authorization and review by the Roman bishop.[115] Thus, whereas
the metropolitans sought to establish the canons as a form
of ecclesiastical constitution, the bishops in effect opposed the notion of an established and regular supradiocesan government, viewing all such regulation as basically

ad hoc promulgation, which is ultimately dependent upon
the one head of the church. In this view, even the ecumenical council derived its authority from the pope; or,
otherwise stated, all councils shared with the ecumenical
the character of irregular and nongovernmental bodies,
operating not upon fixed constitutional principles but
upon the specific authorization of the pope. Only the
neglect of canon law has made men unaware of such proper
norms, says the Pseudo-Isidore, as he announces his intent to remedy this defect by a more complete compilation.[116]

The forged papal letters of the Pseudo-Isidore form
the principal arsenal from which Hincmar of Laon drew for
his polemical collections of ecclesiastical law,[117] and
against them Hincmar of Reims posited theory based upon a
conciliarism of quite another sort. Whereas Hincmar of
Laon and the Pseudo-Isidore sought to find the Divine institution of the church in the Petrine donation applied
to the popes as the heirs of Peter, and to deny a universal governable church by equating the councils through the
generalized requirement that all alike have express papal
command and ratification, Hincmar of Reims sharply distinguished the governmental, provincial synod from the
great constitutive bodies responsible for the establishment of universal regulation on a provincial scale. There
are he says, many general councils; but only a few are
general in the fullest sense, in that they have issued regulations binding upon all.[118] There are, in fact, but
six, of which Nicaea was the first.[119]

But, the archbishop says, it is not antiquity that
gives so vast an authority to the pronouncements of that
council, nor is it either numbers or manner of convocation. In effect, just as it is a mistake to interpret
Matthew 16:18-19 as a reference either to ecclesiastical
government or to the bishop of Rome alone, so also is it
erroneous to consider any man or collection of men to be
the source of authority in the church.[120] The key
scriptural passage, it would appear, is rather Matthew
18:15-20,[121] for *assensus ecclesiae*[122] reflects, not
numbers and not only the agreement of the episcopal *collegium* (both of which are characteristics that can be
possessed by a heretical or schismatic group),[123] but pri-

marily the Divine inspiration of this agreement. This is
the true link between the mundane institution and the
heavenly; antiquity cannot provide the evidence of Divine
inspiration--and no more can the *paradosis* of a particular church--so well as can the direct imparting of this
inspiration to the deliberations of the great councils.
This is recognized by the popes themselves; thus, Gregory
I stated that he revered the great councils as he did the
Gospels.[124] The proper association, then, does not equate
these councils with human institutions and judge them according to criteria appropriate to mundane establishments,
for they are, rather, the complement and extension of
Holy Writ, and their canons may be said to have been enacted by the Holy Spirit.[125] To allege that the "two or
three" in Matthew 18:20 provides the foundation for a
deliberative body is to understand but poorly, for the
primary significance of the passage lies in the mystical
presence of the Divine at a gathering that by its propriety is privileged to receive such inspiration. The
Divine presence attaches to the meeting itself; thus it
is that Nicaea, which so evidences that presence, is
called "mystical."[126] So, too, in a lesser degree, may
other councils and even individuals share in this mystical presence; and the test of this participation is a
simple one, requiring only faithful adherence to the
canons of the great and inspired councils.[127]

Hence, once again it is clearly these canons that provide the foundation for all ecclesiastical authority; and
just as a lesser council that operates according to them
can produce decrees which possess a universal significance, so too a pope who disregards them endangers the
church and can be deposed.[128] Far from possessing equal
or superior status, the papal decretals in fact have validity only insofar as they, like the decrees of the lesser
council, reflect the canons;[129] the decretals are not law
but rather only commentary on law, says Hincmar of Reims,
for the pope too is under the canons.[130] The pope does
indeed possess a primacy in the universal church, but to
confuse this function with his metropolitan status in his
own province is erroneous.[131] He does not rule the church
universal, for to do so would be to go against the canons;
he, like other prelates, cannot authorize or deny activities and functions unless his actions are firmly based

upon these rules. His office is one of guardianship, and
his proper characteristic *aequitas*.[132] For these reasons
he has certain privileges, which are to be exercised in
extraordinary circumstances. He should be consulted on
matters of doctrine and general discipline; he should, if
necessary, convoke general councils (although the function is not limited to him); and he may on occasion review
the judgments of local assemblies.[133] But these privileges are closely restricted by canonical norms, which
it is his duty to follow; and his decisions are restricted by *aequitas*, the basis of his privilege.[134]

Thus the papal prerogatives contain no implication of
any right to interfere, no more than any metropolitan may
interfere with another. The papal privilege is not analo-
gous to that of a metropolitan. And to posit the pope as
a court of first instance on the basis of the canons; for
Sardica is once again to misinterpret the canons of
Sardica, whether ecumenical or not,[135] established a right
of appeal, that is, a right at papal discretion to a new
hearing of a completed case.[136] No canons, not even those
of Sardica itself, provide any foundation either for a
papal jurisdiction in the first instance or for a suspension of local proceedings.[137]

VI

Bishop versus King, 870

The success achieved by the archbishop of Reims and the shattering failure sustained by Hincmar of Laon at Attigny cannot, of course, be construed simply as a victory for one set of principles over another; rather, they must be understood in terms of the context of events in which the opposing principles were presented. This context was, indeed, fundamental to the archbishop's triumph, for Hincmar of Reims, who was a consummate politician, well understood that the forces and motives governing the operation of events are not static and do not function in a vacuum, but are determined by a whole complex of circumstances that can be manipulated although not controlled. Hincmar of Laon did not possess this subtlety and insight. The direction of his actions was so dominated by immediate gratification that he was largely incapable of attributing to others any drives that bore no relationship to himself and his own desires. He saw people as being essentially monolithic, devoid of will and life until so endowed by his attention. Thus, the support he sought from king, colleagues, friends, archbishop, and pope, and the arguments upon which he based his assertion or rejection of influence, were for him basically indifferent, neither participating in nor manifesting any principle other than their advantage to himself. They could be exchanged at will or as needed, and after an interim of no relationship, he could return to find that they had remained unaltered, ready to hand for his use.

After his release from captivity and his return to the king's good graces, Bishop Hincmar no longer had any compelling reason to pursue his appeal to the pope, and the deadline of 1 August 869 set by Hadrian for his appearance at Rome saw the bishop still in Francia.[1] But Hincmar again seems to have interpreted royal favor as conveying license for unreasonable behavior, and the months that witnessed the deterioration of his relation-

ship with the archbishop of Reims saw also a renewal of
his policy of manipulating the tenants and property of
his church to the advantage of his own particular followers. Thus, now that the king had agreed to the restoration of Poilly, Bishop Hincmar proceeded to take it
by force, violently ejecting Nortmannus and his family.[2]
With regard to his own vassals, too, he resumed the same
sort of arbitrary treatment that had first brought him
to grief in 868. Apparently now he felt as secure in
Charles's confidence as he believed himself to be in his
contentions with his uncle.

But again the bishop deluded himself. On 1 May 870,
King Charles arrived at Attigny, where, in the days preceding the council, he held a *placitum*.[3] One Ansgarius,
a royal vassal to whom Charles had given in benefice
certain lands that bordered upon Poilly, appeared before
this tribunal.[4] He complained that Bishop Hincmar, in
seizing the **villa**, had taken as well the five *mansi* that
comprised his own holding--lands which he alleged belonged not to the church of Laon but to the royal fisc.[5]
The bishop was firm in his denial of the charge. He had
taken nothing, he said, beyond what pertained to the
villa, and he could prove this by the royal precept,
which he had at Laon. The king, according to his own
subsequent recollection, decided that Hincmar might
provisionally hold Poilly and any other properties mentioned in this document, but that Ansgarius should retain his benefice pending an investigation of its status,
and that should the investigation disclose that these
lands too belonged to the church of Laon, he would
gladly restore them as well.[6] But Bishop Hincmar had a
different impression of Charles's decision. Finding
that the five *mansi* were in fact among those mentioned
in the precept, he decided that there was no need to
return them to Ansgarius; and at the opening of the
council at Attigny in mid-June, the lands were in the
possession of Teduinus, the bishop's own vassal.[7]

Bishop Hincmar, who was busily engaged in both his
public life and his private quarrels with his uncle,
seems to have forgotten that this council represented
also an opportunity for other aspects of his conduct to
receive scrutiny and for those injured by him to bring

their grievances to public hearing.[8] In his report of
what happened at the synod, Hincmar of Reims omits any
mention of the various influences at work there and con-
veys only a simple tale of the triumph of principle and
propriety, whereas Hincmar of Laon provides a broader
context of the synodal debacle. His account of events
and that of the archbishop differ in a number of important respects.

The bishop attributed his defeat in no small measure
to his uncle's having undermined his position with the
king by sowing seeds of doubt and enlisting royal pressure against him.[9] He said it was Charles's newborn
hostility that drove him to subscribe the oath before
the council, and this oath had been still further
vitiated by the archbishop's duplicity. On the first
morning of the council, the bishop said, he had gone to
the hall and there, at the entrance, had been confronted
by his uncle, who had demanded that he renew his oath of
obedience to him. At first he had refused to do this;
then King Charles had come up and supported the archbishop's order, saying that the lack of such an oath
would be seriously prejudicial to the bishop. Only the
day before, Hincmar said, he and the king had met quite
amicably, but in the intervening time Charles's mind had
been poisoned against him.[10] On this account, then, the
archbishop's triumph occurred against the background of
an ambiguous royal threat.

Charles's words and the absence of support from his
episcopal colleagues seem to have shaken Bishop Hincmar
and to have led him to reconsider his refusal. According to his recital, on the evening following the first
session of the council, he had spoken with Archbishop
Frotarius of Bordeaux and had explained to him that his
reluctance to swear an oath of obedience to his uncle
was due to fear that a later archbishop might use it as
a precedent to infringe upon the rights of the bishop's
own successors at Laon. This threat, he felt, could
only be averted if Hincmar of Reims would give him a
complementary guarantee. Frotarius could see no harm in
such a request; and, according to the bishop, his uncle
too had readily agreed.[11] The elder Hincmar consigned
the oath he had demanded, clearly prepared in advance,

to the bishop, who took it back to his quarters in the
house occupied by Archbishop Hardwic of Besançon. There,
he edited it and prepared his own counterpart, which was
delivered to Hincmar of Reims by Hardwic's priest
Fredigisus, who gave it directly to the archbishop. But
on the next day Archbishop Hincmar repudiated his promise, and only the bishop swore an oath.[12]

    The archbishop of Reims did not deny having received
the complementary oath; he alleged that when it was given
to him he did not know what it was. By his account, as he
journeyed back to his residence after the second session
of the council, he recalled that a slip of paper had been
handed him that morning by Archbishop Hardwic, as he was
entering the synod. The poor light had prevented his
reading it at the time, he said, and he had thrust it
aside, to discover it much later.[13] But, he stated in
addition, the very notion of such a demand being made by
a bishop upon his metropolitan was abhorrent and insuf-
ferable.[14]

    By the bishop's account, his decision to take the
oath had depended upon the promise of **mutuality; conse-**
quently, his signature had been obtained under false pre-
tenses.[15] Though we cannot know the truth with any
degree of certainty, the archbishop's statement regarding the counter-oath is in character. Furthermore,
though it is by no means unthinkable, it is unlikely
that Hincmar of Reims would have acted with such blatant
deceit as his nephew alleged. And, finally, the archbishop was in a position of overwhelming strength; he had
no need to compromise himself by the false promise of a
distasteful bargain. The truth, then, is likely much as
Hincmar of Reims would say later, in different words and
context, that the Bishop of Laon, feeling the threat of
charges made by Charles and by his vassals and failing
to gain the support of his colleagues at the synod, had
seen the walls closing in and had taken his oath in an
effort to escape the pressure.[16]

    But the bishop's troubles had in fact just **begun.**
The following day, 17 June, King Charles informed the
archbishop and his nephew that he intended to proceed
with the investigation of several charges of expropria-

tion that had been brought against the bishop by certain
of his men, and he requested that Hincmar of Reims name
several prelates of the province to be present at the
hearing. Hincmar of Laon immediately protested that the
necessary witnesses were not available, for during the
previous days all of his men, both clerics and laymen,
had been kept at the palace under the king's ban, and
only one cleric and three laymen were at present with
him. Charles persisted, however; and, when the bishop
eventually informed the king that two of his four attendants were cognizant of the events at issue, the king
insisted that the cases be heard the next day. The
bishop then conceded, he tells us, lest he appear to be
causing willful delay, and Hincmar of Reims appointed
the bishops Actard, Rainelmus of Noyon, and John of
Cambrai to attend the trial.[17]

Thus, on 18 June, Hincmar of Laon confronted his accusers before the royal tribunal. The first complain-
ant was his man Ragenardus, who charged the bishop with
having unjustly and without reason seized the benefice
he had held. Bishop Hincmar did not deny the fact, but
in response accused his tenant of continual contumacy.
During a royal mission into Gothia, he said, Ragenardus
had returned home without leave. In the course of the
next three years he had failed to perform any services
for his benefice or to attend any of the *placita* held
by the bishop, and during this time Hincmar had not even
seen him. More recently, when the bishop had led his
men in armed service for the king, they had passed near
the town of Mouzon, where, although the benefice of
Ragenardus was quite near, he had neither joined them
nor sent excuses. Neither had they seen his son, whom
Ragenardus had commended to Hincmar and to whom the
bishop had granted lands in the same area. In fact, the
bishop said, he had subsequently learned that the son
had, without informing him, entered the service of Bishop Rothad of Soissons. Finally, Bishop Hincmar said,
Ragenardus himself had virtually destroyed the property
and church on his benefice. The lay judges ruled that
the bishop substantiate his charges by oath, and when
he refused, the court reached a verdict in favor of
Ragenardus.[18]

The second accuser was a man named Grivo, who years before had exchanged his vassal status under Bishop Pardulus, Hincmar's predecessor of Laon, to enter the service of the archbishop of Reims. He had returned after Bishop Hincmar's ordination, Grivo said, and at his father's death had received in benefice not only the land he had held but also twelve *mansi* more, all of which the bishop had now taken from him without cause.[19]

Bishop Hincmar made an effort to avoid having to respond to these charges by reiterating his complaint that the men who knew the real situation, whose testimony would support him, were not present; but the king remained unmoved and ordered him to reply. Once again the bishop alleged that his adversary's charges were untrue and that, in fact, it was he who had been the victim of a disobedient and destructive man, who had himself spurned the land he now claimed.

Hincmar said that he had ordered Grivo and his friend Beraldus to carry to Rome letters in which he explained to the pope the reasons for his delay in arriving there,[20] but that when he had seen Grivo later on, the man had refused to take the letters until his friend too was present. When Hincmar responded that he had no objection to this and suggested that the pair return on the following Friday, Grivo fell upon his knees, excusing his conduct and explaining that he had been told the bishop bore a grudge against him. In response Hincmar said he too had heard rumors, to the effect that Grivo had stated to others that he had been called upon to undertake this arduous journey only so that he would pay a bribe to avoid it. Hincmar said that Grivo's denial was received graciously.

But, he continued, he had also received word that his vassal had destroyed part of a wood that his father had grown on the benefice. This, too, the man denied, asserting that the damage had been done in his absence.[21] The two had parted on friendly terms, the bishop said; but before the following Friday had come, he had been informed that Grivo had told his neighbors to take whatever timber they wanted, for he would no longer be holding the property; and, as a consequence, the wood had

been stripped bare. When Friday passed without the
man's appearance, Hincmar said, he had sent out a party,
which discovered not only the wood gone but also the
entire benefice in ruin. Other *missi* found Grivo armed,
with a number of his relatives, and a skirmish ensued,
from which the bishop's party emerged victorious. Grivo
thereupon pledged to repair the damage he had caused and
to remain obediently in Hincmar's service, but by the
next day he had changed his mind once again and announced that he rejected both the bishop's land and his service.[22]

In his response, Grivo denied all but his nonappearance on the designated Friday, which he said had been
unavoidable; and, in this case too, the court ultimately
passed judgment against the bishop of Laon for failure
to prove his case. Since Grivo had not destroyed the
wood, Charles said, he should not have lost his benefice.
Bishop Hincmar protested.

Finally Charles realized that the hearings could not
be completed in one day, so he called a recess. He
warned the bishop to return with witnesses on 28 June.
Then he left Attigny for the city of Senlis.[23]

In the interim Bishop Hincmar seems to have realized
the full gravity of his situation and of the manifold
defeat he had suffered at Attigny; he seems to have
realized, too, that Charles's return would hardly prove
more favorable to him. Thus, once again, he sought to
invoke a powerful authority as his champion.

The year before, after his failure at Verberie, he
had written to the pope a second time, to complain
against both his king and his uncle, and Hadrian had
sent two letters in response.[24] The pope had instructed
that Bishop Hincmar give one of these to the archbishop
of Reims, who, he said, should deliver it to Charles and
plead with the king on his nephew's behalf. In the
letter itself he castigated Charles and Nortmannus, and
charged the king with having lied in his accusations
against the bishop, whose attendance at Rome he again
demanded.[25] By the time these letters had reached
Bishop Hincmar, his circumstances had, of course, altered

completely, and he had not delivered the message, but
had prudently kept it. Now, determined to avoid judgment by renewing his appeal to Rome, he brought it with
him on his return to Attigny.

Once there, however, the bishop found that his
plight posed even more of an immediate threat. Count
Nortmannus, he knew, had already prevailed upon the king
to place his men under royal ban, to await synodal consideration of the serious charge that the count and his
family had been subjected to violent treatment at
Poilly.[26] Now one of the bishop's followers learned, in
a conversation with a vassal of the count, that Charles
had already decided, even before the hearings had reconvened, that some of the properties, the possession of
which was to be adjudicated, would in fact go to another
of the vassals of Nortmannus.[27] With so clear an indication of royal hostility, the realization that Charles
questioned not only his veracity but his loyalty as
well,[28] and the recollection of his imprisonment the
year before, Bishop Hincmar's nerve failed him.[29] He
turned the papal letter over to the archbishops Hardwic
and Remi, fled Attigny, and returned to his episcopal
city.[30]

Though it can hardly be said that the bishop's fear
of imprisonment was without basis, his flight has at
least some of the aspects of a hysterical reaction. It
was both irrational and self-destructive, and was in itself a violation of the renewed oath he had just taken.
He was a man made distraught by the host of setbacks he
had encountered and, as the archbishop of Reims observed, by the apparent impossibility of his situation.[31] But one feels that the archbishop, in accusing
his nephew of intentional duplicity, was less close to
the mark; such a moral category does not seem to define
the sources or the form of his conduct. The bishop's
intention was to gain time and relief, but even now he
does not seem to have consciously believed that he had
done any wrong. Rather, he felt that his rights were
being infringed by unscrupulous men.[32] His uncle informs us, in another passage, that young Hincmar was
unable to admit a wrong and instead always sought to
justify his behavior.[33] This seems to have been the

case; and, indeed, the bishop appears to have been, to a
great extent, unable to admit his shortcomings even to
himself. Hence he sought to account for his actions
through outward show, and perhaps it is the nature of
these displays that reveals something of his unacknow-
ledged feelings. Thus, while the imprisonment at Servais had become a ridinghorse for numerous charges
directed against his metropolitan, it may as well have
been for Bishop Hincmar a reminder of what in some way
he felt to have been a well-deserved punishment.[34]

In fact, there is no indication that during the following weeks either Charles or Hincmar of Reims bore
the bishop any implacable illwill. On the eve of the
signing of the Meersen treaty, having apparently vindi-
cated with great success the acquisitive diplomacy so
long pursued, the two men seem almost good-natured, if
condescending, in their messages to the absent bishop.[35]
Both seem to have retained some measure of good feeling
toward the bishop; and, having publicly exposed and de-
feated him, both might well have felt indulgent toward
him. But condescension was unacceptable to the bishop;
and Hincmar of Laon appears willy-nilly to have been
intent upon proving himself both right and important at
whatever cost, even if this could only be done by con-
verting indulgence into wrath.

From Laon, Bishop Hincmar wrote to notify his uncle
of his exit,[36] which hardly came as news to the archbishop, who had already reconvened the synod in his
nephew's absence.[37] The surprise came when Archbishops
Remi and Hardwic presented Hadrian's letter to the king.
The archbishop of Reims, who was the designated recipient of the papal missive, was furious, particularly
at the slight to himself. He wrote to his nephew immediately, castigating him for this manifest violation
of his newly sworn obedience and pointing out that he
had now in fact twice neglected papal calls.[38] The
argument that an appeal to Rome had been implicitly
abandoned, which Hincmar of Reims had used in questionable circumstances against Rothad of Soissons,[39] was
clearly a strong one here; and the archbishop's assertion that his nephew looked to Rome only when in dire

straits seems to carry much force.[40] Furthermore, the
advantage of the Pseudo-Isidorian appeal lay, not only
in the possibility of obtaining a fair hearing and in
the fact that it delayed proceedings, but also in its
requirement that immediate provisional restoration be
made of all honors and possessions.[41] It seems apparent
that once again Hincmar of Laon had made a tactical mis-
judgment in invoking assertiveness and belligerence
where his ends might have been better served by a conciliatory attitude and the avoidance of antagonism.

But admissions of this sort were foreign to the bishop, who answered his uncle on 2 July by reiterating his
demands, less with tact than with threats. He denied
the archbishop's charges and stated that he had followed the dictates of the pope precisely. He criticized
the archbishop for alleging that he had declined two
calls to Rome; the truth was, he said, that each time
he had been prevented from making the journey. Thus,
he declared, in renewing his request now, he wished to
remind his uncle of the importance of not obstructing
papal commands. His actions should not be construed as
a matter of disobedience to the archbishop, but rather
as the effect of an obligation that he had to an even
higher authority.[42]

Hincmar of Reims made no response to these declara-
tions, hoping, he said later, that his nephew might
return to reason and abandon disobedience.[43] But only
days afterward the bishop sent his cleric Bertharius
with a still more pathetic self-justification to King
Charles, whose command that he return to Attigny he had
just ignored.[44] Now Bishop Hincmar explained that he
had departed because of a return of his fever, and he
denied that he had intended any disobedience toward the
king. He said that he hoped no serious consideration
would be given to those who attempted in secret to im-
pugn his fidelity (for no one would dare to make such
accusations in public), and that now, because he was
bound by the canons, he was seeking license from Charles
to attend the papal summons.[45] The king, even though
not unfriendly, was hardly about to accept such an argument. He replied to Bertharius that he found it surprising that Hincmar's illness, though sufficiently

severe to prevent his appearance before himself, was at
the same time mild enough to allow a journey to Rome.
Charles advised that if Hincmar were to appear before
him, he would find him not unreasonable with regard to
a trip to the pope.[46]

Presumably Charles was aware that Bishop Hincmar
really had as little desire to appear before Pope
Hadrian as he had to return to Attigny. He surely knew
what had elicited this sad and desperate request; for
with the bishop's failure to appear before the royal
tribunal, the hearing of charges against him had continued in spite of the appeal interposed by Remi and
Hardwic. The king had commanded that the lands
Ansgarius claimed should go to him, and he had received
the pledge of Hincmar's men that they would not try to
impede the royal *missi* from executing this order.[47]
With regard to the claims made by the bishop's own
vassals, it had been decided, not only that their holdings should be restored to them in the cases already
dealt with, but also that the lands disputed in the
cases still pending should be turned over to the accusers pending final disposition.[48] Early in July the
missus Flotharius was sent to Laon to begin implementation of these decisions by seeing to the restoration of
the five *mansi* claimed by Ansgarius.[49]

The arrival of the royal official at last induced the
bishop to send Charles the precept he had requested so
many weeks before.[50] This document seems to have represented to Hincmar of Laon an all-inclusive justification
for his behavior, and his account of its reception at
Attigny projects this attitude upon the king. Relying
upon the report brought him by Bertharius, the bishop
later alleged that Charles, having discovered that the
disputed lands were indeed mentioned in the precept, had
acknowledged before the assembly that he had been misinformed, and had now decided not to permit Ansgarius
possession of the five *mansi* adjoining Poilly.[50] But
this story is hardly credible. There is no indication
that the king recalled Flotharius, and it is most unlikely that he would have openly violated so public a
statement. Furthermore, by any interpretation of
Charles's remarks of the previous May, Bishop Hincmar

and his vassal were to have abandoned the property in
question pending investigation of the conflicting claims.
The bishop's actions seem increasingly to reveal panic
and, at this point, an inability to operate within a
reasonable frame of reference.

This immediate threat, then, provides the context
for the request relayed to Charles by Bertharius, but
upon his return the deacon bore only news of further
dispositions the king had made in the bishop's absence,
notably a royal command that Hincmar should restore the
benefice he had taken from his vassal Eligius, who soon
appeared in person with a formal notice to this effect.[51]   At this point a number of the bishop's other
men seem to have decided that they no longer needed to
regard his authority with any seriousness. Seeking to
gain time, Hincmar had ordered that they appear on 16
July to discuss their grievances with him, but none
bothered to come. Eligius, who was instructed to return on the following day so that the restoration of his
benefice might be discussed in the presence of the bishop's *fideles*, said that he had no obligation to do so,
since the king had restored his land. He then proceeded
to enter the benefice, apparently unopposed.[52]

On 18 July the bishop's provost, Heddo, bearing a
schedule and a somewhat hysterical message, appeared at
Ponthion, where Charles and his advisers awaited the
return of the delegation sent to King Louis the German
at Frankfurt.[54]   He informed the archbishop of Reims of
what was occurring at Laon and stated that it was the
bishop's plea that he, his uncle and metropolitan,
should intercede with the king to allow Bishop Hincmar
to order and govern the affairs of his church without
interference, rather than overturning all his dispositions. Should he do this, the bishop of Laon would
gladly obey his uncle and consult with him; and he assured the archbishop that he had not given out the property of his church on account of relationship or
friendship, or for bribes, but rather as best he knew
how. On the other hand, Heddo said, should Hincmar of
Reims be unable to prevail with the king, the bishop in
turn would be unable to obey Charles, to provide him
with service, or to refrain--as he had for so long--from

making further appeal to Rome. Before he did this, however, it would be necessary for him to follow the papal
command that he first exercise his ministry, that is,
that he himself excommunicate those who infringed his
rights.[55]

A number of other prelates were also present at
Ponthion, among them Remi of Lyons and Hardwic of
Besançon, as well as the recently returned Odo of
Beauvais. Hincmar of Reims, in responding to his nephew
toward the end of the month, said that, upon hearing
Heddo's recitation, he had assembled the bishops,[56] and
the group had gone before the king, who had told them
the real nature of his command regarding Ansgarius.[57]
The archbishop added that, with respect to his own men,
Hincmar of Laon himself was responsible, for he had
committed the breach of having left the assembly prior
to determination of the judgments, in spite of the fact
that he had himself requested the appointment of judges.
These, indeed, **had** completed some of the cases before
the intermission, and had left the rest, to be defined
later.[58]

With this the archbishop turned to the schedule that
Heddo had delivered along with the verbal message, which
Hincmar of Laon had enclosed as conciliar justification
for the intended "exercise of his ministry." It consisted of five *capitula* under the title of a council
held at the **villa** of Tusey in the year 860, and it con-
tributes still another bizarre aspect to this peculiar
history.[59] The regulations provided, Bishop Hincmar
said, not only a basis for his proposed means of dealing with the men who were presently taking the lands of
his church *"regia potestate,"*[60] but also support for a
number of his earlier actions and positions. In assertion of the powers and prerogatives of the episcopal
order, the *capitula* held that anyone taking things belonging to a church without permission of the bishop or
his representative must restore them, submit to a penance imposed by the injured prelate, and compensate for
the damage done by a triple or quadruple payment; failing this, any culprits involved should be held anathema
and be denied Christian burial.[61] Another provision, a
more general sanction opposing crimes committed against

the church, called once more for excommunication and
ordered that news of the sentence be transmitted to
other bishops, so all might know not to communicate
with the malefactor.[62]   The rules of Tusey provided an
implicit threat to both Charles and Hincmar of Reims and
a strong support indeed for the bishop of Laon, support
that was made even stronger by the great size of the
council--the name list of which counted fifty-seven
bishops.[63]

   Archbishop Hincmar's reaction to the Tusey regulations was as striking as it was simple; he denied their
existence. Neither he nor the others at Ponthion had
ever before seen these rules, he said, although several
of them, including himself, had been present at the
council.[64]   Why, he asked, should Hincmar of Laon have
done so mendacious a thing as to send false *capitula*
rather than the true synodal definition, which was in
congruence with the sacred rules and, being so, was
followed by Hincmar of Reims, his primate? Hincmar of
Laon, he said, should know that even were the *capitula*
valid, justice and equity are best served through
proper procedure. He counseled patience in dealing
with the problems of which the bishop had spoken, and
he called upon him to await the next provincial council,
where matters might be handled judiciously and properly,
thereby avoiding the chance of such a mistake as he,
alone and unadvised, might make and, in so doing, fail
to fulfill the apostolic mandate.[65]

   The incident of the Tusey *capitula*, observed from any
aspect, is a mystifying one. To accept the account of
the archbishop of Reims is to place his nephew in the
extraordinary position of having intentionally sought
to pass off as genuine a set of forged rules supposedly
issued by a council at which he, the archbishop, and
other prelates had been present. The bishop's response
to his uncle's criticism, in a letter sent the following
November,[66] only heightens the mystery. His great surprise on reading what his uncle had written was all the
greater, Bishop Hincmar said, since it was from Archbishop Hardwic himself, one of those at Ponthion, that
he had received the *capitula*.[67]   The transcription had
been made by two deacons, Teutlandus and Hartgarius,

who the bishop knew could not conceivably alter an
apostolic or synodal letter; nor had he started them
along this path, having never had such presumption.
Furthermore, he would like to see the definition that
his uncle had called "authentic," for he too had been
present at Tusey, and he well remembered subscribing
his name to the succinct definitions drawn from the
statement presented there by his uncle, which the council had considered too long.[68] As to the alleged deviation of the *capitula* from the canon law, he could
neither see this nor understand that his reliance upon
these rules was in any way a derogation of metropolitan
authority, for, as quotations showed, the *capitula* were
clearly based upon the letter read at Tusey. Thus it
was obvious, he said, that Archbishop Hincmar's remark
to Bertharius was unjustified and that a sentence given
on the basis of these rules would in fact be valid.[69]

The questions raised in connection with the *capitula*
of Tusey were never really to be answered;[70] indeed, by
the time the bishop responded to his uncle's criticisms,
the issue had lost its immediacy. By the end of August,
after having been stymied at every turn and with his
resources apparently drained, Bishop Hincmar was forced
to concede, and he managed to effect a compromise with
the enemy he least disliked. About 1 September he went
before the king at Servais.[71] Hincmar of Reims provides
the little information we possess regarding this incident, which is never alluded to by his nephew. According to the archbishop, Hincmar of Laon requested and was
granted three new judges, and managed to gain, not only
a revision of the provisional judgments rendered at
Attigny in his absence, but also an alteration in the
cases previously defined. Further action was now to
await discovery of the necessary witnesses; and, in the
meanwhile, the bishop was to hold, not only the property
assigned to his accusers following his flight, but also
that which had been adjudicated at Attigny.[72]

The archbishop's report is tinged with both rage and
amazement. Without even the vestige of an appeal to
Rome, his nephew had reversed himself, to the detriment
of his order.[73] By requesting lay adjudication, he had
violated the canons that required the presence of metropolitan and other bishops at an episcopal *causa*,[74] as

well as those that ordained a loss of office as the
penalty for a prelate who appealed to a lay tribunal
from a judgment rendered by episcopal judges.[75] The
anger is understandable, but, by his eagerness to condemn Bishop Hincmar, the archbishop seems, in his argument, to have distorted what had occurred. The cases
that had been on the agenda at Attigny did not require
synodal definition, and at that assembly had come before
a lay court.[76] What the bishop had done now really
amounted to a long overdue response to the royal summons.[77] It may be noted that the three prelates referred to as *judices* by Hincmar of Reims are designated
cognitores by his nephew, that is, perhaps, witnesses
whose presence is not juridically essential.[78]

The precise dispositions of the court remain largely
a matter for speculation,[79] but probably one price the
bishop paid was to agree to a compromise by which the
question of Poilly, the case which far more than any
other had received embarrassing public notice, might be
quietly resolved. Thus it is likely that at this time
Hincmar of Laon consented to take only half of the property into his direct control and to permit Nortmannus's
son to hold the rest as a benefice, not from the king,
but from the bishop himself.[80] In this way Charles
might erase the charge that he was despoiling the church,
which Pope Hadrian had posed against him.

For it was only a few weeks later, in October of 870,
that the papal legation visited Saint-Denis and Reims,
and that Hincmar of Reims formulated the first response
he and Charles made to Hadrian's recriminations over
the invasion of Lotharingia.[81] Another prominent subject of the legatine mission was Bishop Hincmar of Laon,
who, in the dire straits of the previous summer, had
again written to the pope.[82] Now, in answering Hadrian's
accusations regarding the larger and less justifiable
question, the archbishop was able to draw for support
upon the analogy of the lesser and more defensible one;
by associating the two cases, Archbishop Hincmar could
convert apologia into attack. That he did so appears
from the fact that, while he sent a letter specifically
concerned with the bishop of Laon,[83] he also worked his
nephew's case into the greater one of Lotharingia.

The archbishop acknowledged that he had received two
papal letters concerned with the bishop of Laon. The
first of these, he said, had ordered him to excommunicate Count Nortmannus as an expropriator of church property; yet the sequel to the accusation had shown the
charge levied against him to be untrue. He had, rather,
occupied land he had received from the king, to whom
Bishop Hincmar himself had conceded its use for that
very purpose. This truth, he continued, the bishop had
confessed in writing, and it was widely known. The
archbishop expressed his hopes that thereafter the
pope would ascertain the veracity of rumors delivered
to him and not command a metropolitan to impose an
excommunication that ought not to be levied.[84] Hincmar
continued that the pope had chastised him, in the
second letter, for failing to aid his nephew in the
latter's time of need[85] and for prohibiting his going
to Rome, and he charged once again that whoever had told
the pope these stories was a liar. During all these
past years, as many knew, he had actually worked hard
at the thankless task of providing just such aid; and,
as anyone knew and letters could prove, he had never
attempted to prohibit Bishop Hincmar's attendance at
Rome. But, he said, he could do only what was within
his power; and, as he had explained to the papal legates,
he could not send any bishop to Rome or anywhere without
the permission of the king.[86]

The connection between the two aspects of the letter
is apparent; in both cases--Lotharingia and the bishop--
the criticism is that Hadrian's uninformed commands had
nearly led to grievous injustice, while attempts made
by Hincmar of Reims to fulfill the intent of the papal
orders were hindered by circumstances and lies. The
case of Hincmar of Laon served to strengthen justification for the invasion: just as the pope, by uncritical
belief of lies and unenlightened injunctions in the
question of Bishop Hincmar, had unfairly impugned the
archbishop of Reims and caused great harm, so, too, it
would eventuate with regard to Lotharingia if the pope
did not examine the real situation with greater care.

This is not, however, to deprecate the importance of
his nephew's actions as the archbishop saw them. No

small part of the art of this letter consists in the
manner in which archbishop Hincmar combined the expression of undeserved long-suffering with righteous indignation, and both emotions ring true with regard to the
bishop of Laon, even if they smack of hypocrisy in the
matter of Lotharingia. It is as though the archbishop's
intense feelings of anger, sadness, and frustration at
being unable to "correct" Bishop Hincmar (with all the
ramifications that word possesses) had welled up with
his nephew's latest rejection. Throughout the numerous
references to the pain he suffered with regard to the
bishop, in almost all cases it is a pain caused by some
deed ungratefully perpetrated by his nephew to the archbishop's injury and in disregard of the trouble taken
on his behalf. Yet from behind these repeated formulas
there seems to peer forth a more real expression of
anguish felt by a man who in his way cared deeply and
who found a rebuff of his feelings intolerable--doubly
intolerable, in fact; for the bishop had not only, as in
868, turned to Rome but had also spurned his uncle and
preferred King Charles to him.

The tone of the elder Hincmar's correspondence and
contact with his nephew changed now forever. Hereafter
the archbishop, with a turn striking in its suddenness,
averted his face, and in his dealings with the bishop
no longer argued, cajoled, or expressed hope of reconciliation, but breathed ice.

Toward the middle of November, Hincmar of Reims
received, from the hands of the priest Clarentius, a
long letter written by his nephew in response to the
arguments of the treatise in fifty-five chapters and to
questions that had been raised regarding his behavior at
and after Attigny.[87] Beginning with the latter, Bishop
Hincmar explained the situations of Nortmannus and his
own men, described the circumstances of his flight, and
defended the authenticity of the Tusey *capitula*.[88]
Then he moved on to attack, in his second section, the
huge work presented to him at Attigny, concentrating on
the subjects of appeal and papal primacy, excommunication, and episcopal autonomy.[89]

The question of appeal was argued, first on the principles enunciated by Hincmar of Reims, and this argument turned on the issue of the number of canons published by the first Council of Nicaea. To the archbishop's contention that that council did not promulgate more than twenty canons, Bishop Hincmar responded that even the fathers of the African church had been unable to find the others; he gave as his authorities for a greater number Pope Sylvester and the tradition of the Roman church.[90] In his criticism of the letters ascribed to Popes Julius and Felix, Hincmar of Reims noted, not only that their lists of Nicene canons differed in number, containing twenty-four and twenty respectively, but also that the lists themselves did not match. Hincmar of Laon responded that neither pope was giving a complete list, but merely a list of certain canons as the occasion demanded; this, he said, they had clearly indicated.[91] Finally, the bishop asserted that he could marshall three popes as witnesses, for Mark, Julius, and Felix all agreed that Nicaea had produced more than twenty canons. Thus, the bishop said, he stood in the Scriptural tradition, which held that credibility might be established by two or three witnesses.[92]

Nor did the alleged dissonance of the Julian canons indicate a selection and collection from many sources, Hincmar continued, since any synod would produce varied rules to handle a variety of situations.[93] The main issue, of course, concerned the inclusion of the Pseudo-Isidorian appeal canons in the Julian list, for if these were in fact Nicene (or rather were accepted to be so), then by Hincmar of Reims's own well-advertised encomia of that council, appeal according to Pseudo-Isidorian principles must stand. The archbishop had argued that had appeal been established at Nicaea, it would not have been considered at Sardica.[94] The bishop alleged the contrary, noting differences in the language used by Hosius of Cordova, the president at Sardica, who at times initiated a statement with the phrase *"placuit autem"* and provided no formal termination to his declaration, while at other times no *"placuit"* appeared, and the canon concluded with a question as to the disposition of the bishops, to which they answered *"placet."* The latter were new canons, the bishop said, the former repeated from Nicaea. Even so, he said, according to

Pope Boniface, Nicaea did nothing that was above the
Roman see; and due to the merit of Rome, no institution
or person is able to confer any privilege upon it.
Hence, even if no specific appeal canon had been enacted
at Nicaea, the papal decrees, which consistently call
for the right of appeal, must be followed.[95]

   As to the matter of his excommunications, which
Hincmar of Reims had raised again at Attigny, the bishop contended that this question should go to Rome.[96]
The issue ultimately turned, particularly, upon the interpretation of a forged letter attributed to Pope
Calixtus regarding relationships between bishops. To a
passage in this letter denying the right of a metropolitan bishop to act alone in the territory pertaining to
another prelate,[97] the archbishop had stated that this
was a reference, not to metropolitans and suffragans,
but to relationships between metropolitans; and the same
construction had been given to a passage relating to a
metropolitan's entrance into another's *parochia*.[98]   But,
the bishop said, this passage thus construed not only
made no sense but also detracted greatly from the archiepiscopal status, since on this interpretation a general meeting must be called even for infra-provincial
decisions. The true relationship, Bishop Hincmar said,
might be found expressed, for example, in the decretals
of Calixtus (properly understood), Lucius, and Anicius,[99]
for whom the canons provided further support, in holding
that the autonomous sphere of a metropolitan bishop is
limited to his own *parochia* and that he required the
presence and advice of the provincial bishops in the
hearing of any other case. Furthermore, these rules
recognized episcopal autonomy and the requirement that a
priest receive the consent of his bishop before appeal;
and they held that a person under sentence of excommunication should not be received, or his sentence raised,
unless through conciliar decision. This, the bishop
said, was precisely the reason for the establishment of
provincial councils.[100] As to the role of the metropolitan bishop, it was properly to serve as guide and
protector to his colleagues in the province.[101]

   The archbishop sent a response to this disseration
probably near the end of November,[102] its tenor dictated

primarily by the intense frustration he felt at seeing
his nephew once again refuse to come around. This response contains a history of iniquities familiar from the
Opusculum 55 capitulorum but personalized to include an
account of how the archbishop had raised and nurtured
his nephew, and had made him a bishop only to be deserted and mistreated thereafter. While the charges and
offenses are familiar, the emphasis here is more upon
the injustice done to Hincmar the doting uncle than to
Hincmar the archbishop, a shift that marks the end of a
stage.[103]

One may speculate that this shift was in part responsible for the letter, which is a catalog of irreme-
diable injuries. The new step is indicated, too, by a
tone of heightened hostility and of loss of desire to
reach any agreement (or, as it were, to consider his
nephew as salvageable). No acknowledgement is given
either to the bishop's arguments or to his attempt,
albeit late, to initiate a relationship tolerable to
both men.[104] Hincmar of Reims could no longer conceive
of this, and with this letter he terminated their dialogue. From this point on, he awaited only a chance to
humble the younger prelate.

VII

The Conspiracy of Prince Carloman, 870-71

Though Hincmar of Reims took great pains to present Pope Hadrian with a picture of Lotharingia at peace and content with the accession of Charles the Bald, the facts were quite different. The Treaty of Meersen may have brought an accomodation, however temporary, between Charles and his brother Louis; but to others living in the central realm, it was hardly a satisfactory solution. Among these was Hugh, the bastard son of Lothar II and Waldrada, who desired to throw off the yoke of foreign domination, and in this was seconded by many great lords who resented the imposition of strictures upon their autonomy.[1] There was no dearth of sympathy with their aims in Charles's own realm; for, in addition to the problem of pacifying his new domains, the king was troubled by revolt within his own family.

Six years after his marriage in 843, King Charles might well have felt that his succession was secure, for Queen Ermintrude had given him five healthy children, four of them males.[2] But this good fortune was only apparent. The eldest son, Louis, soon revealed himself to be stupid almost to the point of incapacity, and his two nearest siblings, Charles and Lothar, both died at an early age.[3] In 866, at the great council called to the city of Soissons, solemn ceremonies were held and Queen Ermintrude was crowned and anointed anew in the explicit hope that God would see fit to grant to the royal couple progeny worthy of ruling the kingdom.[4]

The ceremony implied rejection, not only of Prince Louis, but also of the king's youngest son, Prince Carloman, who was born about 848,[5] and was destined early for an ecclesiastical career. He was tonsured in 854, made a deacon by Bishop Hildegarius of Meaux six years later,[6] and during the next decade was established as abbot of several monasteries, among them Saint-Médard of Soissons, Saint-Germain of Auxerre, Saint-Amand,

Saint-Riquier, Lobbes, Saint-Arnoul, and Réome.[7] That
he was intelligent seems indicated by the fact that
Wulfad, his tutor, was a close friend of John the Scot.[8]
Accounts of his character are conflicting: the monks of
Saint-Médard complained of his treatment of them,[9] but
among those at Saint-Riquier he was apparently well-
liked.[10] It seems clear, however, that he was not
suited for the cloistered life, preferring, as did many
another unwilling cleric, the career of noble warrior.[11]
It is not farfetched, perhaps, to assume that, as the
years went by without God's granting to Charles and
Ermintrude the heir they so desired, Carloman may have
seen the possibility emerge that he himself might be
called upon to rule, a chance that was made all the more
likely when Ermintrude died on 6 October 869. The
prince's thoughts and motives remain matter for speculation, but it seems clear that King Charles had no intention of promoting the political career of his youngest
son. In January 870, Charles married Richilde, with
whom, for some time, he had had a liaison.[12] In the
months that followed, Carloman plotted rebellion.

The sources provide us with little information concerning the plot, perhaps because it was so great an
embarrassment to Charles's aims and pretensions. Those
witnesses who do give a glimpse of these events portray
the prince as a bloodthirsty scoundrel, a self-seeking
bandit at the head of a ravaging pack of thugs.[13] But
it is difficult to accept this characterization, for it
would appear that Carloman had many sympathizers and
supporters, among them a number of prelates and such a
nobleman as County Baldwin of Flanders.[14] Indeed, it
was in Lotharingia that the prince later found his
safest retreat, and it is not unreasonable that his own
revolt was connected to the opposition that was favored
by so many there.

Secure in the belief that his plans remained a well-
guarded secret, Carloman appears to have continued his
ordinary activities, and in June 870 attended the
council held at Attigny. In the meantime, however,
Charles had been informed of his danger, and during the
council the prince was surprised and captured.[15] On 17
June the assembled prelates heard the charges against

him and pronounced his deposition; and the following day
he was escorted by Charles himself to imprisonment in
the city of Senlis.[16]

On 9 October the papal legates Peter and John arrived
at Saint-Denis to present King Charles with the letters
in which Pope Hadrian decried the seizure of Lotharingia.[17] In the interim, word of Carloman's plight had
reached the pope, and Hadrian had decided to champion
the young prince against the monarch whom the pope now
considered capable of any vile deed. The supplications
conveyed by the legates had their effect; and Charles,
anxious to minimize hostile contact with Rome, released
his son from imprisonment.[18] Carloman was one of the
royal and legatine party that arrived at Reims probably
on 19 October, when Archbishop Hincmar received Hadrian's messages concerning his part in the taking of
Lotharingia and in the troubles of his nephew.[19]

Many others were at Reims as well; for Charles, who
was now embarking upon an effort to eliminate opposition to his rule in Lotharingia, had summoned the army
to assemble.[20] Hostility to the monarch, which was
present throughout the middle kingdom, was perhaps best
organized in the south.[21] There Charles had, for some
time and with some success, sought to cultivate the
support of the great prelates. Archbishop Ado of Vienne
had long favored him,[22] and, more recently, he had won
over such powerful figures as the archbishops Hardwic
of Besançon and Remi of Lyons, the latter in earlier
times archchaplain to both Lothar I and Charles of
Provence.[23] But implacable opposition remained in the
person of Count Gerard of Vienne. The count was among
the oldest allies of the family of Lothar, whose cause
he had adopted as long ago as 840, when he had abandoned Charles and had relinquished his office as count
of Paris to follow the new emperor. Now he prepared to
hold out in his fortified city, presumably hoping either
to spearhead local opposition to Charles or to endure
until help might arrive from the emperor Louis II.[24]

At that time Louis was engaged in the siege of Bari,
which was in Arab hands, and he consequently was unable
to defend his claims in the north.[25] The time, then,

was ripe for Charles to move against Gerard, so on 26
October he led his army out of Reims toward Vienne.
Accompanying his party were the papal legates and
Ansegis, the abbot and archbishop-elect, who was serving
as envoy to the pope for Charles and Hincmar of Reims.[26]
Carloman, too, was present, probably less a member of
the royal entourage than a prisoner. At Lyons his
guards were distracted and he escaped to safety in
Flanders, where he assembled a band of followers.[27] In
spite of this threat, Charles was unwilling to disrupt
his original plan, and he could do nothing at the time
to deter the prince. By November 24 the army arrived
before Vienne, which was held by Bertha, the wife of
Count Gerard, who was himself ensconced in a neighboring
stronghold.[28] The city was betrayed, however, con-
siderably shortening the intended siege, and on December 24 the gates were opened to King Charles, who celebrated Christmas there, while Count Gerard prepared to
flee into Italy.[29]

The King was now able to turn his attention to the
problem of his son. He had already written to Hincmar
of Reims, instructing him to assemble a council to pro-
nounce ecclesiastical sentence against Carloman.[30] The
archbishop considered such action premature, favoring
rather the more private measure of mediation. In December he wrote to the counts Engelramnus, Goslinus, and
Adelelmus, enclosing a copy of Charles's command, but
informing them that, as the prince was under the ecclesiastical jurisdiction of another province, he himself
could neither proceed against him nor, of course, on his
own initiative summon together the bishops of other provinces. Indeed, he said, the lateness of the year made
even the convention of a provincial council impossible.
He questioned the efficacy of episcopal sanction to halt
Carloman and asked the counts to intervene and use their
influence with the prince to convince him that peace was
a course to be favored over the many dangers to body
and soul imminent in a course that continued to arouse
the wrath of both his father and the priesthood.[31] The
archbishop sent other letters as well, to Carloman himself and to various members of the nobility, calling on
the rebels to reconsider, to take advice, and to come
to terms.[32]

Before King Charles returned north from Vienne, a conference to be held between him and his son was arranged;[33] but, when the meeting took place near Laon in January 871, the prince, lacking faith in the intentions of the peacemakers, was absent. In his stead he sent four *missi*, among them Count Baldwin of Flanders.[34] The delegates received a blessing from the archbishop of Reims, but little of value was accomplished. Charles detained two of the messengers and sent the others back, admonishing Carloman to present himself. Instead, the prince sent more delegates to convey the terms under which he would make peace. When these were rejected, it was apparent that mediation would give way to more forceful action.[35]

Late in January, while Carloman's forces harassed the region around Toul, an episcopal council met under Hincmar of Reims at the palace of Compiègne. The bishops issued a provisional major excommunication against those of the rebels who fell under the jurisdiction of the province of Reims, forbidding the others to communicate in Reims or with its inhabitants. The sentence was to become effective on 11 March, unless the malefactors had come to terms by that date; and it was otherwise to be tempered only in the case of imminent death.[36] Notification of the decree was sent to other archbishops in the realm, and those prelates of the province of Reims absent from the council were instructed to signify their accord.[37]

Among the absent was Hincmar of Laon, for although he had been at Compiègne, he had adhered to his old habits and had made an unannounced departure.[38] On 31 January the archbishop wrote to his nephew, announcing the decision and requesting that the bishop send his *missus* forthwith, bearing his *consensus*, so that the general announcement might be made before the evil deeds of Carloman and his followers increased further.[39] On 1 February Heddo, the provost of Laon, came to Compiègne, but without the requested letter of consent, and was sent back with sharp orders that Hincmar of Laon send his endorsement.[40] For more than a month no more was heard. Finally, at the beginning of March, Hincmar of Reims sent another letter; the bishop, he said, should

send his consent, as those more distant than he had already done, or he should explain the reason for his delay.[41]   To this the bishop responded that, as Heddo had
explained to Hincmar of Reims, certain changes in the
sentence would be necessary before he could give his
agreement. He had been awaiting the archbishop's revised letter so that he might see if these alterations
had in fact been made.[42]   Hincmar of Reims wrote again
on 19 April, saying that Heddo had conveyed no such
demand, and that none of the other absent bishops had
reacted in that way. If Hincmar of Laon would state in
comprehensible terms what it was that he found objec-
tionable, the archbishop would be willing to review the
matter and, perhaps, stand corrected. But he warned his
nephew against attempting yet again to undermine his
metropolitan authority. He must remember, the archbishop said, that while all prelates are equal by election,
they do not hold a common dignity. On 5 May another
request for signature of affirmation was delivered, this
time orally, through the cleric Teutlandus, who had come
to see the archbishop for personal reasons. When Hincmar of Reims received no answer to this, he sent a sixth
and final admonition.[43]

In this final communication Hincmar of Reims attributed his nephew's intransigence to a continuation of
their quarrel over the relationship between bishop and
metropolitan;[44] and it is clear that the substance of
the bishop's objections did reflect the events of his
own history. In justification of his refusal to sign
the Compiègne sentence, Hincmar of Laon complained that
his uncle had illegally interfered in his diocese by
giving his benediction to Carloman's representatives;
and he demanded that the sanction be changed to bar the
viaticum to the excommunicates.[45]   As the archbishop
observed, this request reflected the situation of the
Laon interdict two years before, and it is likely true
that Bishop Hincmar at first was reluctant to subscribe
an implicit admission of error.[46]   As time passed, however, the bishop's excuses became more petty; his uncle
had acted without previous synodal consultation; he had
infringed Bishop Hincmar's rights by conveying an oral
rebuke through the bishop's cleric.[47]

As counterpoise to this determined policy of delay, Archbishop Hincmar's own continued insistence is no less remarkable, and it raises some questions about the council and its circumstances. Why should Hincmar of Reims have demanded his nephew's adherence to the conciliar sentence no less than six times? Preparation of a case against the bishop's disobedience seems hardly a sufficient reason, while the absence of one name could not hinder the efficacy of the condemnation; and the archbishop states that, but for his nephew, support would have been unanimous.[48] This was, in fact, not true. In spite of royal backing, the hastily summoned council had represented only the province of Reims, and the sentence had been issued by no more than eight bishops, Hincmar of Reims and at most seven of his suffragans.[49]

In these circumstances, it may be wondered whether opposition to Prince Carloman was in fact as universal as the sources indicate and whether his activity was simply that of a brigand. Clearly, Charles and his archiepiscopal adviser were concerned to gain as much support as possible for action against the rebel, and desired to act as rapidly as possible. The king's first efforts to end the uprising by force were unsuccessful; and when, on 1 March, Charles arrived at Saint-Denis, where he so often spent the Lenten season, Carloman remained at large.[50] During April, while Charles was at Senlis contemplating convocation of the army and of a larger council to include all bishops of the realm, the prince and his followers roamed the Transjurane at will and then moved into Provence.[51]

Delay was as advantageous for the prince and his company as haste was imperative for Charles, particularly since Carloman could count the pope among his champions. When in the first months of the year, word of the sanctions—ecclesiastical and military—threatening the rebel had been sent to Rome, it was clear, Hadrian felt, on which side right belonged.[52] On 13 July 871 the pope sent three letters: to Charles the Bald, to his archbishops, and to his nobles. He castigated the king for his actions against his son, commanded the archbishop that no sentence of excommunication be levied against

the rebel prince, and ordered that the nobles partici-
pate in no military activity against him.[53]

A tantalyzingly persistent thread links Carloman and
Hincmar of Laon at many points in their careers. Two
days before the prince was arrested at Attigny, Bishop
Hincmar was suddenly ordered to reaffirm his oath of
fealty to King Charles, and he heard his uncle allude
mysteriously to sinister rumors that were circulating.
Both the prince and the bishop were associated with conspiracy and with Lotharingia, and both were championed
by the pope. Both Hincmar and Carloman were the subject
of verbal instructions given by Hadrian to his legates,
and both were discussed by the **legates** in October 870.
Although no definite evidence joins them, it is most
tempting to associate them with each other and to see a
connection between their so similar fates, particularly
in view of the fact that, by the time the papal letters
forestalling further action against Carloman arrived,
the royal attention was centered upon Hincmar of Laon.

By this time, the long contention between bishop and
archbishop had reached its final stage. On 14 May Hincmar of Reims addressed a letter to his nephew, calling
him to a provincial council to be held at Servais the
following month. He added to the general summons the
information that the still unheard complaints brought
against him at Attigny would again be raised.[54] There
is no record that this assembly was actually held. Some
weeks later, on 10 June, the archbishop sent another
letter, in which he said word had reached him that Bishop Hincmar was holding his deacon Bertharius captive.
He commanded that his nephew permit the cleric to appeal
before an upcoming council;[55] but, unfortunately, all
we know of this affair is that Hincmar of Laon did not
obey. The archbishop also spoke of other concerns that
he intended to raise at this council, and it is clear
that Hincmar of Reims now meant to lodge against his
suffragan a whole series of complaints regarding the
conduct of his episcopal ministry as it pertained to
his consistent denial of obedience to his metropolitan.
In short, the scope of the summons issued on 14 May had
been both personalized and extended.

In the response to this summons, which the bishop
sent on 16 June, the answer to his uncle's charges was
so acerbic that it must be seen to reflect a still-con-
fident mind.[57] From his previous canonical collections
he selected a series of decretals that first illustrated
the principle that a metropolitan must work in coopera-
tion with the bishops of his province, and then dealt
with the matters of contumacy and the oath at Attigny.
He reminded his uncle that at Attigny they had had an
encounter prior to the synod, during which he had read
to the archbishop his papal summons and a letter of Pope
Felix II, which guaranteed episcopal appeal in cases
where a bishop felt his metropolitan was prejudiced
against him.[58] Unheedful of this injunction, the bishop
said, Hincmar of Reims had poisoned the king's mind
against him, and had used the royal threat to elicit his
oath. Even so, he had received his metropolitan's assurance of a complementary oath promising archiepiscopal
support in ecclesiastical matters; but, whereas he had
signed his oath, the archbishop had not signed his,
thereby adding to royal force his own fraud, as was soon
afterward made evident. For, contrary to the accusation
of Hincmar of Reims, the bishop said, he had not broken
his pledge; rather, the very example his uncle had cited
against him bore witness to his own treachery, since he
forbade the bishop to attend the papal summons. In the
matter of Carloman, he continued, the archbishop had
infringed in numerous ways upon the privilege of his
nephew's church, while letters that Hincmar of Reims
had written to Charles the Bald and to Bishop Odo of
Beauvais showed clearly that he had been responsible for
his nephew's imprisonment at Servais.[59] This, the bishop said, he knew to have been a matter of revenge, nurtured by his uncle for years, ever since the bishop had
opposed him in the matter of Rothad, when he had illegally attempted to install a new bishop at Soissons
before the pope had reviewed the case.[60] But opposition
to Rome, he said, was no rare thing for Archbishop Hincmar, who had again, in the case of Wulfad, disregarded
law and the express commands of Pope Nicholas I. It was
clear then, he stated, that the charges of oath violation and of contumacy attached not to the bishop but to
the metropolitan himself, who had, repeatedly from the
start, violated the promise he had made to his nephew at

Attigny, which was to have been a condition of his
oath.[61]

    The response of Hincmar of Reims (or that portion of
it which has been preserved) indicates that he was
deeply affected by this letter.[62] He said that, although Hincmar of Laon had never ceased to attack him
with tongue and poisoned writings, God would be his
guard against his nephew's malice and lies. Hincmar of
Laon had said that the archbishop's writings showed his
derogation of the apostolic see, but no sane person
would ever believe this, and neither could the bishop
prove it; whereas all were aware of Bishop Hincmar's
derogation of the metropolitan privilege and of the
violation of his oath, signed in the presence of an
assembly of prelates from ten provinces. As to the
charge that he had obstructed Nicholas I, it was a lie,
for with respect to both Rothad and Wulfad, far from
contradicting the pope, he had followed his orders precisely. With regard to the deposition of Rothad, Hincmar of Laon's own signature on the conciliar record disproved his statement that he had not consented to the
deposition, even as it demonstrated that in all the
archbishop did his nephew did just the same.[63] Archbishop Hincmar announced his prayer to God, to the Virgin
Mary, and to Saint Remi, whose privilege Hincmar of Laon
had disparaged, to help him in the tribulations caused
by his nephew's lies. To the bishop's comment that men
said of the archbishop, "What sort of uncle is he, who
can write thus to his nephew?" Hincmar of Reims replied
that men also say, "What sort of nephew, having received
so much from his uncle, would blaspheme him, and vitu-
perate his ministry? How can he do so much against the
one who raised and ordained him, and how much more does
he desire to do?"[64]

    This letter is the last we possess in the polemic
that had so long occupied the two prelates, for suddenly
the whole complexion of the quarrel was altered, as
Hincmar of Laon set forth upon the final road to ruin.
The first step was marked by the return of Ansegis from
his journey to Rome, undertaken so many months before.[65]
He bore two letters indicating that at last Pope Hadrian,
if he did not favor the archbishop of Reims, did finally

have his doubts about the sincerity of the bishop of
Laon. In his message to the young Hincmar, Hadrian
chastized him for his dilatory behavior regarding the
summons to Rome and reminded him that the metropolitan
privilege was established by the sacred canons. In
effect, the letter implied the inseparability of papal
and metropolitan obedience.[66] The second letter, addressed to Hincmar of Reims, advised him that the pope
was aware of his difficulties and suggested a synodal
affirmation of authority, lest the metropolitan privilege suffer further.[67] The clear tenor of Hadrian's
words was critical of the archbishop, but to Hincmar of
Reims they could be interpreted as support for the position he had constantly maintained. On 5 July 871 he
advised his nephew that he had received the papal
letters and, invoking apostolic authority, called upon
the bishop to attend a synod to be convened on the fifth
day of August at the **villa** of Douzy.[68]

When the council did in fact meet at last, questions
of ecclesiastical jurisdiction were distinctly secondary,
and the bishop's principal accuser was King Charles himself. Hincmar of Reims alleged that the king's involvement was part of a general anger that was felt by all at
young Hincmar's continuing offenses against both the
clergy and laity;[69] but while the conciliar records are
so constructed as to emphasize ecclesiological issues,
it is apparent that the royal anger had another source,
which was not of long standing; for as recently as the
preceding June, king and bishop had met without incident.[70] Thus, in the interim, Charles must have received information that was deeply prejudicial to Hincmar of Laon, or he must have otherwise become convinced
that the bishop was working against him. The facts are
not recorded, but it is clear that several questions
came to a head during the summer, and several sources
might have implicated Hincmar of Laon in a plot of rebellion.[71]

By June 871 the force of Carloman's revolt appears
to have been weakening; and the rebel, who had now moved
into the safer territory of eastern Lotharingia, appealed to his uncle, Louis the German, for aid against
his father.[72] We may believe that Louis's refusal owed

less to principle than to inability. In May or June his own sons, Charles and Louis, jealous of the favor shown their younger brother, had rebelled and fled west, where they requested the intervention of King Charles.[73] During July, Charles, in the role of mediator, met with his brother at Verdun, where preliminary discussions of the princes's grievances were held and arrangements were made for another meeting at Maestricht the following month, this one to include emissaries also from Prince Carloman.[74] Was Hincmar of Laon's name mentioned at Verdun? Or might Ansegis have brought to his king information, which was now to precipitate a crisis for the bishop? In any event, both the meeting at Verdun and the papal letters that forbade action against Carloman withdrew from the prince immediate attention, and left Hincmar of Laon as the sole defendant at Douzy.

VIII

The Bishop Falls: The Council of Douzy
and Its Aftermath, 871-72

The Carolingian era is a rich period for history of the
church councils. The extant records contain a great
variety of conciliar material that is of immense value
in the information it provides regarding matters of
contemporary significance and the operation of synodal
process.[1] Few councils of the ninth century have left
so complete a record as that held at Douzy in August
871; and few have dealt so directly and succinctly with
major issues of ecclesiastical administration, for that
council in many ways represents the ultimate metropolitan response to the assertions of the Pseudo-Isidore and
Pope Nicholas I.[2] At the same time, the very fullness
and precision of these records cast some doubt upon
their historicity, doubt that seems warranted on the
basis of internal criticism as well. Written under the
clear and immediate influence of Hincmar of Reims and
conceivably prepared by him at a later date to justify
his actions, the records of Douzy have much of the
character of a scenario.[3] The record of Hincmar of
Laon's fall must be suspected of being less history than
drama presented so as to exemplify principles of far
more than singular importance.

On 14 May 871 Hincmar of Reims had indicated to his
nephew that he intended to pursue the cases left un-
finished at Attigny,[4] and on 10 June the archbishop
allegedly disclosed a number of matters that he wished
to raise at the coming council--matters later stated to
be those contained in the polemical work read by Archbishop Hincmar at Douzy.[5] In fact, in spite of the
ecclesiological significance of the council and the
papal command that bolstered the archiepiscopal summons,
from the start it was royal imperative that provided
the greatest motive force of the council. According to
King Charles, when Hincmar of Laon received the summons
to appear at Douzy, he began to prepare to flee the

country, first taking in commendation a number of royal
subjects suspected of infidelity. Charles said that
when he heard of this he sent counts and *missi* to Laon
to guarantee that these men should remain. But Bishop
Hincmar prevented his emissaries from fulfilling their
task by placing every able bodied man around under arms
and threatening armed resistance. Then, as a ruse, the
bishop sent his own messenger to request that the king
provide him with an escort so he might journey safely to
the royal presence. The escort was sent the next day,
only to be told by the bishop that the offenders had
fled during the night. Clearly, the king said, the
bishop had told them to flee so the nature of their infidelity might not be found out.[6]

   Meanwhile, the conciliar *acta* recount that on 5
August--the day for the council to convene--Bishop Hincmar did not appear.[7] A final summons was issued to him
on the following day, and then Hincmar of Reims opened
the proceedings.[8] Although the actual attendance is
uncertain, the list of signatories to the council's
decisions and the evidence contained in the conciliar
records indicate that a total of twenty-nine prelates
were involved, twenty-one of whom signed the eventual
judgment or sentence.[9] The signatories represented eight
ecclesiastical provinces and included every archbishop
of the old western realm, with the exception of the
bishops of Auch and Narbonne. Apparently, then, a broad
spectrum of the episcopacy in the Frankish realm concur-
red with the actions and principles expressed at the
Council of Douzy. Closer inspection reveals, however,
that almost all of the eight metropolitans who appear as
signatories to the conciliar declaration had particularly close ties of dependence upon King Charles; and, of
the other prelates whose names appear, eight were suffragans of Hincmar of Reims, six of Ansegis of Sens, and
three of the province of Trier, where Charles's nominee
Bertulfus, the nephew of Bishop Adventius of Metz, was
contending for the see.[10] Political aspects and controls
are suggested, too, by the subsequent refusal of bishops
in the realm of Louis the German to sign the sentence
against Hincmar of Laon,[11] who clearly faced no impar-
tial tribunal.

In addition to the cases of Deacon Bertharius and
Count Nortmannus (neither of whom seems to have appeared
before the council), the ecclesiastical business that
Hincmar of Reims had allegedly warned his nephew to
expect included the affair of Haimeradus[12] (who also did
not appear) and matters that the archbishop is presented
as telling the prelates were contained in brief form in
the schedule he read to them.[13] Archbishop Hincmar here
evidences a typically peculiar notion of conciseness,
for the *Libellus expostulationis*, to which he refers, in
fact contains thirty-five chapters, which are bounded by
a preface and a conclusion.[14] This work was ostensibly
presented by the archbishop before the patient synod
between 6 and 9 August.[15]

The archbishop opens[16] by extolling the inspired wisdom of numbers; and he requests the aid of the assembled
bishops, as he had done before at Verberie, Gondreville,
and Attigny. He told the synod that his own efforts to
correct his suffragan had been fruitless, and now he
must look to them for help, particularly since the pope
himself had recently reproached him with negligence in
the administration of his province. In what follows he
says that he stands, not as an accuser or one making
charges on account of personal injuries, but as a defender of the canons, no less than of the papal decrees
promulgated from them, against one who holds them in
contempt and who exhibits disregard for the principles
that properly order the church, by calumnies against his
metropolitan, by disregard of his episcopal profession,
and, in general, by his attempts--even though only a
provincial bishop--to upset the metropolitan rule derived from the Nicene council.[17]

With the preface, then, Hincmar of Reims reaches for
his audience and generalizes his complaints. This is
no personal contention that the council is being asked
to mediate; rather it is a great threat, now also acknowledged by the pope, which only coincidentally relates to
Hincmar of Reims, who thus, of course, may legally assume the role of accuser. The archbishop holds that the
problem is really universal, in that it places in
jeopardy a principle that stands as the foundation of
the whole church. Immediately, we are in the presence

of material not contained in the announcement sent to
Hincmar of Laon on 10 June, at which time neither the
papal letter nor the general council had been anticipated in dealing with the bishop. Furthermore, the
archbishop has presented what was in reality a sharply
worded criticism of himself as a papal mandate for
synodal proceedings against Hincmar of Laon and thus,
in effect, as papal support or even demand for the
bishop's deposition. To what extent this desire derived
from Hincmar of Reims and to what extent from the king
is problematic. It is plain, however, that although
Hadrian had also criticized Hincmar of Laon and had
admonished him in strong terms to obey his metropolitan,
the main thrust of his letter to the younger Hincmar had
concerned itself with the bishop's failure to attend the
papal command at Rome.

The contents of the elder Hincmar's complaint are now
as familiar as they must have been by that time to the
long-suffering prelates who had assembled at the various
gatherings before which these matters had previously
been aired. The first twenty-four chapters constitute a
history of the wrongs committed by Hincmar of Laon, presented almost entirely from the standpoint of detrimental intent or of effect upon the metropolitan privilege. Beginning with the "illicitly" acquired abbey,
Hincmar of Reims proceeds to the letter delivered to him
on the previous 16 June, always accentuating his efforts to bring the bishop to proper behavior and the
equally regular efforts of Hincmar of Laon to avoid
correction and to continually violate his obligations
and oaths.[18] Chapters twenty-five to thirty-four turn
to a refutation of charges made by the bishop against
Hincmar of Reims, particularly the charges made orally
to Wenilon of Rouen at Gondreville and those contained
in the response to the *Opusculum 55 capitulorum* and,
recently, in the letter of 16 June.[19]

In his last chapter and conclusion, the archbishop
strives to eliminate any compunctions the members of his
audience might feel about ruling on the matter. The
bishop's absence presents no bar, he says; the great
councils have held that signed writings shown to be
mendacious are adequate for the conviction of a male-

factor on grounds of *reus falsitatis*, even in the absence of accuser or witnesses. Furthermore, Hincmar
of Laon's failure to appear, even after three calls
regulariter, is well-established grounds for deposition,
and such an absence in fact amounts to and falls under
the laws relating to contumacy. The personal nature
of the offenses related, the archbishop reiterates,
indicates no private cause, but shows rather the nature,
extent, and incorrigibility of Bishop Hincmar's crimes
against the metropolitan authority, so much the worse
because not done through ignorance.[20]

The question of whether the synod should act against
Hincmar of Laon or absolve him and leave the matter to
others is one whose answer the archbishop says he will
not dictate. He asserts that he does not intend to
influence the deliberations by reminding the participating prelates of the words of Pope Celestine concerning the dangers involved in letting a known evil increase or those of Leo I that in a situation where nothing is doubtful or obscure no new advice ought to be
awaited or new process begun.[21]   Indeed, he said, as the
bishops had just heard, the pope himself had called for
this council and had assailed metropolitans who permit
their office to be held in low esteem. Now, perhaps,
Hincmar of Laon, who had so often made irregular appeal
to Rome and failed to prosecute it, might be able at
last to make a correct appeal and thus properly honor
the apostolic see. The council, by the same stroke,
would no longer appear to merit reprimand, as being
responsible for any injury to the rules of ecclesiastical discipline.[22]

This clever peroration serves several functions. It
is designed to generalize, depersonalize, and authorize
the proceedings and the involvement of the metropolitan
prelates in particular. By his use of the papal letter,
the archbishop seeks to make the council appear as
though it were meeting and acting by specific papal
command and sanction, thus giving the appearance that
he is not a principal but, rather, a papal representative. He also removes himself by generalizing his complaint. This is no personal quarrel but a contention
over principle, he states, and he is not an accuser but

a prosecutor defending the canons. By this tactic the
other archbishops in particular are involved, the case
of the archbishop of Reims is made theirs, and their
participation concerns their duty and conscience as prelates who are sworn to defend the canons and the pope.
Hincmar of Reims assured the synod that no trouble could
follow from the bishop's absence and his failure to
defend himself, since he was properly summoned but did
not appear and since his writings and the testimony of
others proved him to be a liar.[23]

But it is with respect to the bishop's nonappearance
that the nature of the records constructed by Hincmar
of Reims are most clearly revealed. The charges made
by the archbishop are in fact found mentioned only
rarely and tangentially in the body of the *acta*.[24] The
real role of accuser is given to the king, who on 6
August delivered before the synod a complaint containing his grievances against Hincmar of Laon.[25] The short
work shows haste in composition, although it deals almost entirely with actions long past.

Charles began his accusations with the statement that
Bishop Hincmar had both given an oath to him and subscribed a profession of fidelity; then he brought up the
question of sedition. He proceeded that the bishop, in
violation of his oath, had taken land to which he had no
right. After having conceded to Charles the right to
rebenefice Nortmannus, he had made secret complaint to
Rome and, as the letters of the pope show, had impugned
Charles as a *distractor rerum ecclesiasticarum*. His
plots with Lothar II, of which his own letters were
proof, had led the king to obtain from the bishop's men
an oath that they would neither leave the kingdom without his permission nor carry messages in or out. But
the bishop had soon afterward persuaded two of his men
not only to violate their oath but, in so doing, to once
again calumniate Charles before the pope.[26]

The bishop had given yet another profession of obedience at Attigny but had immediately broken it by his
flight; and thereafter, although summoned, he had refused to attend the king, rather stating his wish to go
to Rome. Charles had made approval of such a journey

contingent upon Hincmar of Laon's fulfillment of his own
request that he first come to him; but, when Hincmar did
finally appear, and after that, upon four other occasions when he was with the king, he made no mention of
Rome, even though when he felt the need he did quite
readily flourish his appeal and his summons and complain
that Charles prevented his going.[27]   Finally, most recently, he had resisted the king's representatives by
armed force.[28]

His presentation completed, Charles noted that Hincmar of Laon had thus far declined to appear, and he
requested that the prelates collect and set down the
various laws governing his complaints, so that, if by
chance the bishop should come, the council might be able
to make a legal determination of the issues between
them.[29]

This list of charges presented by Charles against
Hincmar of Laon is in its way no less remarkable than
was the set of accusations that had been presented
against him by Hincmar of Reims in his own name. But,
whereas the archbishop had generalized his disputes in
ecclesiological terms, the king is shown specifying,
presenting as isolated and arbitrary incidents what were
really moments in a complex historical sequence in which
he had played a part at least as great as that played by
the bishop of Laon. Charles appears only secondarily and
passively in his own account, although, in general, his
involvement cannot really be separated from that of the
bishop. The same holds true for his particular charges,
regardless of the blame that might attach to Bishop
Hincmar. This is patent in the case of Poilly. The
letters written by Hincmar of Laon to Lothar (an example
of the written material used at Douzy to secure conviction of the absent bishop) do not on the surface reflect
an intent to desert, which intent Hincmar of Laon specifically denied (perhaps with little truth); but Charles,
of course, omitted any mention of why the threat so
alarmed him and of his own actions in December 868 and
January 869.

This technique is clearer still in the charge that
Hincmar had sent his men to Rome; for, as relevant as

the violation of his oath was in that affair, the most
evident reason for that offense was the bishop's illegal
imprisonment by the king. Finally, the allegation of
failure to heed the summons to Douzy, questions of
resistance or of possible intent to one side, was no
less false here than when alleged by Hincmar of Reims in
person, for in fact Bishop Hincmar was there, and was
imprisoned, as the *acta* reveal.

Charles's complaint was read on a Tuesday;[30] and,
still following the *acta*, on that day or the next, 7
August, a personal call from the synod was directed to
Hincmar of Laon.[31] Three ecclesiastics of different
orders--bishop, priest, and deacon--announced to the
bishop receipt of the papal letters and submission of
petitions to the council that required his response.
Their remarks elicited from Bishop Hincmar the presentation of a *rotula prolixa* and an announcement of
appeal to Rome. To this the answer of the delegation
was a calm but firm refusal and a reiteration of the
request that the bishop attend the synod. Afterward,
they said, appeal would surely be allowed; or, if not
necessary, he would be permitted to go to Rome anyway.
Finally they announced, by way of somewhat dubious
assurance, that this call came from the whole of the
synod; the bishops thus assured him that he would be
treated justly and without prejudice.[32] When Hincmar
did not respond to this call, a second delegation of
similar composition was sent out with a similar message,
followed by a third. Thereupon, the *acta* inform us,
Hincmar at last came before the council.

The strikingly rigid adherence to requisite synodal
procedure is intended to indicate here, as throughout,
that the synod had been punctilious in its actions; so
important an issue must be presented as tightly as
possible. Thus, to avoid the contention that new charges had been introduced, the *acta* reflect a new three-
fold summons following Charles the Bald's assumption of
the role of accuser; while, to sidestep the possibility
of Bishop Hincmar's avoiding the hearing by alleging
prejudice and creating a right to appeal directly to
Rome, the new call issues in the name of the bishops
present at the synod rather than Hincmar of Reims or

Charles.[33] One is led to ask whether it is likely that
if Hincmar of Laon did in fact understand the nature of
the charges against him contained in the royal petition
he would have proceeded quietly in answer to the new
summons. It is far more probable that the bishop appeared before this tribunal only under coercion, and
this indeed was the case.

The three oral summonses were actually delivered to
Hincmar while he stood under a form of house arrest.
King Charles informs us that he received news that his
unfaithful men had been loaded up with booty from the
church and were then sent off by the bishop, who intended to follow them with other items belonging to his
cathedral. The king said that he had sent out his
fidejussores to prevent this escape and yet leave the
bishop free to attend the synod if he desired.[34] But
Hincmar of Laon, after the death of Charles, would present another interpretation of what had occurred. He
said that he had in fact been on his way to the council
to which Hincmar of Reims had called him when he was
suddenly and violently taken from his men and brought to
the **villa**.[35]

Previous encounters have shown that the bishop's
testimony must be taken with care. It should be observed,
however, that the *acta* do not indicate where the messengers from the council found Hincmar of Laon; they
tend to create the impression that he had not yet come
to Douzy but had remained at Laon. The bishop's story
receives support from the rapidity with which these mis-
sions were sent and returned, for Douzy is over sixty
miles from Laon and such a series of journeys could
hardly take so short a time. The true account probably
contains elements of all versions. What most likely
happened is that Hincmar of Laon, while planning flight,
was seized and brought under arrest to Douzy.

On 9 August a for once laconic Hincmar of Laon finally appeared before the prelates gathered in the **villa,**
where the charges made by the king were again presented
to the synod, read in the presence of the accused bishop,
and a copy was given to him. The letter addressed to
him by Pope Hadrian was also read to him, "lest, as was

his custom, he be able to deny the things to be therein
which were in fact contained there." He was then granted a recess to prepare his responses to the particular
charges and returned to his quarters.[36]

On the following day, Saturday, the synod sent a trio
of ecclesiastics to request his response. Again Hincmar
of Laon tried to present them with the *rotula prolixa*,
but it was again declined, and the bishop was given an
extension until the next day. When yet another delegation of three, led by Bishop Rainelmus of Noyon, visited
Hincmar on 11 August he remained adamant in his refusal
to accept the jurisdiction of the synod. He was told
sternly that he had been informed of the council in
good time by calls from both metropolitan and king,
which had designated place and time and had provided
him with foreknowledge of the matters to be considered.
Then, finally, when he had answered the call of the
synod and attended, he had received the king's petition
and had been granted the favor of a delay so that he
could make his response. The *rotulae* he had attempted
to present, he was told, were out of order; for no
further business might be introduced before the synod
until after the charges already presented had been disposed of.[37]

In this account the *acta* may show Archbishop Hincmar's
conviction that legal argument is an adequate equivalent
to logical demonstration or dramatic verisimilitude.
However, the later complaint made by the bishop seems
convincing, for clearly he had not been forewarned of
the charges being presented against him by the king.[38]
Thus the time for response granted him had no relation
to the original summons and in actuality amounted to
but a few days, which were spent in at least relative
captivity. What is plain is that Hincmar of Laon was
then in the hands of men who were no longer disposed
toward friendly leniency but were instead implacably
hostile, and that legal niceties, whether their historicity is accepted as fact or rejected as fabricated
ex post facto justification, were wholly subordinate
to the royal desire to be relieved of Bishop Hincmar's
annoyances.[39] Nor could Charles afford great patience
in the exercise of proprieties, for the arrival of his

nephews Charles and Louis at Douzy, requesting his intercession on their behalf with their father, was soon
afterward followed by the reception of *missi* from Louis
the German himself, who was now in Lotharingia and was
prepared to attend the scheduled meeting on problems
connected with the rebellious offspring of both kings.[40]

King Charles had probably already received the episcopal response that his petition of 6 August had called
for,[41] which was to be a convenient compilation of the
laws relating to his charges against Bishop Hincmar.
Needless to say, even the request for relevant citations, made to prelates ostensibly assembled to render
synodal judgment with regard to a fellow bishop, must
raise serious questions in and of itself concerning the
neutrality of the meeting, regardless of the tenor of
the citations, or even if they formed only a totally
random and unbiased amalgam. Of course, if Charles had
any worry on this score (which one can easily doubt), he
was soon to be relieved, for the episcopal commission,
under the direction of the archbishop of Reims, had compiled in twelve chapters a series of citations--biblical,
patristic, and legal--that amounted to a prosecution
brief, which translated the complaints of the king into
specific charges.[42] With time pressing and charges formulated, there was neither a need for nor the possibility of delaying matters, and on 14 August Charles demanded that the grievances contained in his petition be
dealt with.[43]

The day of the bishop's downfall had finally come,[44]
and the *acta* render an extraordinary account of it.
Hincmar of Laon, accompanied by his priests and deacons,
was ushered into the presence of the synod, where he was
confronted by his uncle, who was acting in the role of
director of the proceedings. He was ordered to respond
to the charges brought against him by the king, and he
refused, citing the doctrine of *exceptio spolii*. He
then reached into his robes, extracted pages from his
ubiquitous canonical collection, and began to read the
letter of Pseudo-Felix to the Gallican bishops regarding
this rule and those held to govern appeal.[45] He was
quickly interrupted by the archbishop, who reminded him
that the canons of Sardica were familiar to the synod,

and they knew the rules governing appeals. What, he
asked, was the bishop reading? To Hincmar's reply, the
synod responded that treatment of the charges before the
council must precede any appeal.

Hincmar of Laon adamantly reasserted that, having
been despoiled of things belonging to his church, he
would not speak to the charges. The council consequently called upon the bishop to name the offender, and
Hincmar in turn, perhaps not wishing to give even this
negative recognition of the circumstances, called upon
his priest Fagenulfus to respond. The priest demurred,
stating that he had no power to deal with the malefactor. This led the king, his sensibilities apparently disturbed by the idea that injustice might be
perpetrated in his realm, to assuage the fears of the
priest. "Tell," he said, "what persons have been responsible for this act, and I shall render justice according to the laws." The priest, reassured, named the
king himself.[46]

Hearing this, Charles rose and, denying the truth of
the allegation, proceeded to explain the circumstances
immediately preceding the council. When Hincmar had at
last arrived at Douzy, he said, he had refused at first
to go to the quarters allocated him and to which the
cases containing the property in question had been removed. When the bishop did go to his assigned quarters,
he found his cases. The king took some pains to note
that they contained, among other things, a cross of
gold, encrusted with precious stones, which had been
presented to the church of Laon by Queen Ermintrude.
Witnesses could and did testify to this. In fact, the
acta go on to report that the contents of the cases
had been depleted only by Hincmar of Laon himself, who
after his arrival at Douzy had feared that their contents might be discovered and his own peculations be
found out.[47] He had caused the priest Irminonus to
take various things (a deed which Irminonus apparently
quickly confessed), while Hincmar himself took others,
including a cross of gold and wood that had been don-
ated by his predecessor, Bishop Pardulus.

Upon hearing this, the synod requested that the

bishop give up the cross, and Bishop Hincmar responded
that he would yield it to Hincmar of Reims's express
command. The archbishop, however, perhaps interpreting
this as a ploy to involve him in a charge of expropriation, stated that he would order only what the canons
called for. The twenty-fourth canon of the Council of
Antioch was read, asserting the position of the bishop
as administrator of the goods belonging to his church
and stating that a clear distinction should be made between this property and that owned by the bishop himself.[48] This led the king to remark that Hincmar of
Laon never had had anything of his own, from which it
followed that, in giving any property to his friends and
relatives, he had clearly violated the canonical injunctions against misappropriation of ecclesiastical property.[49] After an unpleasant interchange, which served
to publicize his poverty, Hincmar of Laon resigned the
point and removed the cross from its place in his capa-
cious robes.

It would seem that the records sought here to anticipate later criticism of the trial based upon Pseudo-
Isidorian principles; the council has considered the
bishop's charge, and converted it instead into yet another charge against him. Three closely related things
may be noted: first, this was an odd way to conceal a
theft; second, this episcopal donation, obviously a
piece of comparatively little value, sounds suspiciously
like a pectoral cross; third, the bishop's own charge
has been lost in the interchange.

The next stage of the dialogue is not dissimilar.
Once again Hincmar of Reims called upon the bishop to
respond, and now his nephew turned his charges against
the archbishop. He would neither obey his uncle's command nor accept his *judicium*, since he had a case
against the archbishop and hence was appealing to
Rome.[50] On the contrary, came the response, no such
case could delay the present proceedings, concerning
which the bishop had been long forewarned; neither could
such a countercharge permit avoidance of the archbishop's
judgment. The rules governing appeals are clear,
Hincmar of Reims said, and the present proceedings had
been specifically ordered by the pope in his letter to

the bishop of Laon, which commanded that he show obedience toward his metropolitan. But the younger Hincmar countered that the pope's letter called for his immediate attendance in Rome. No, the synod said, a proper reading of the letter, with the points taken in order, placed obedience to the metropolitan first.[51]

Hincmar of Laon, perhaps feeling stymied, then returned to his initial grievance: his uncle, he said, had caused the king to have him imprisoned at Servais two years earlier. Rather than reply himself the archbishop yielded to King Charles, who said that the truth was quite the contrary, that but for the intercession of Hincmar of Reims in his nephew's behalf, the bishop, whose insolence had driven Charles to distraction and the nobles to the point of murder, would still be at Servais. Witnesses then testified to the noninvolvement of Hincmar of Reims, and the archbishop was declared purged of guilt. It was held that by this accusation Hincmar of Laon had added yet another calumny to his list.[52]

Archbishop Hincmar then proceeded to interrogate his nephew concerning the accusations brought by King Charles: The answer to each question, when one was given, proved unsatisfactory. But, the *acta* say, a combination of the bishop's writings, his signatures, and the testimony of witnesses[53] demonstrated him to be an invader of royal property, a perjurer and calumniator, and a perpetrator of sedition and sacrilege. To these charges were added several others related to his contumacy toward his metropolitan.[54] Indeed, the *acta* recorded, as though in exemplification of his character, that throughout this proof the bishop had raised loud complaints which were taken to violate both episcopal propriety and Christian modesty. Hincmar of Reims, upon instruction of the synod, warned the accused three times, the record states, and when these metropolitan injunctions were not heeded, the synod took note that the sentence of contumacy was properly proferred against him.[55]

The proof completed, Hincmar of Reims, in his capacity as metropolitan of the accused and as president of the council, briefly recapitulated the course of the

trial, from its inception through the types of charges
and evidence brought against his suffragan, and then proceeded to call for the votes of the prelates.[56]   Twenty-
one prelates, in order of seniority from Hardwic of
Besançon, then each gave a reasoned *judicium* and recom-
mended a sentence.[57]   These statements are interesting as
indicative of the portion of the charges that each prelate found most applicable or advantageous; but they are
unexpected too, at least at first glance, for where with
one exception the archbishops speak only of the offenses
against the king,[58] the bishops tend far more to concen-
trate upon the strictly ecclesiastical counts, and a
number of them stress Hincmar of Laon's violation of
obedience toward his metropolitan.[59]   The judgments cannot be said to be unexpected in their unanimous call for
the bishop's deposition, *"salva per omnia apostolicae
sedis judicio."*[60]   The archbishop of Reims called for
and received the assurance of unanimous consent to his
pronouncement.   Then, having read the rules governing
appeal, he declared Hincmar of Laon to be deprived of
episcopal and priestly rank.[61]

Hincmar of Reims assumed the delicate task of communicating to Pope Hadrian the results of the Council of
Douzy.   The problem was complicated by Hadrian's long
association with the bishop of Laon and by the bishop's
connection with those events in Lotharingia in which pope
and emperor had so great an interest.   On the other hand,
the archbishop of Reims desired to subordinate the
Lotharingian issues to a reassertion of the principles
of metropolitan hegemony that had been so compromised by
Hadrian's great predecessor, whose papal championship of
episcopal autonomy from metropolitan strictures still
found wide support in the north.   Hincmar of Reims drafted three letters in early September 871.   These together form a succinct and significant statement of metropolitan dominance in exercise.   By them, the archbishop
hoped, in addition to eliciting papal acceptance of the
determination against Hincmar of Laon, to also establish
a more general recognition of the ecclesiology that
justified his deposition.[62]

The official synodal letter dated 6 September is a

mixture of mild explanation and polite but firm statement of principle.[63]   Under the names of the prelates
associated in the synodal judgment, the letter related
the benefits received by Bishop Hincmar from his early
days until finally, by election and royal favor, he was
raised to the episcopate.[64]   Then, the letter continued,
he commenced to commit injuries against both clergy and
laity, from which the appeals of neither king nor archbishop could recall him.   Neither were synodal warnings
successful; for Hincmar of Laon did not deign to heed
even the orders of the pope himself that he should be
properly subject to his metropolitan.[65]   He long had
failed to care properly for his church, and in addition
so infringed the activities of other bishops that his
iniquities could no longer be sustained.   Neither the
royal office nor the rest of the kingdom could any longer tolerate his disturbances,[66] and consequently a decision had been made to remove the bishop from the
priestly order.

   Following a brief synopsis of the charges proved
against the bishop, the letter requested that the assembly's judgment be confirmed by the pope.   Yet, it
continued, if by some doubtful chance Hadrian should see
fit, rather, to call for renewal of the *judicium*, in
accordance with the canons of Sardica, the bishops would
be willing, albeit not enthusiastically, to receive the
additional counsel of either bishops from the neighboring provinces or legates from Rome and would reconsider
their decision.[67]   But the canons must be followed;
hence there could be no question of Hincmar's being restored to sacerdotal communion prior to such a rehearing.
Such action would amount to a derogation of the church
in Gaul and Belgica and to a violation of the canons and
decretals, which assert the autonomy of a single metropolitan with regard to jurisdiction in and regulation of
his province, as well as the necessity for local judicial settlement.[68]

   The council, it was stated, fully desired to recognize the privilege of the apostolic see, but at the same
time insisted upon mutuality, for the law also called for
conservation of the privileges of local churches.[69]
They knew Hincmar of Laon and what he had done.   They

had tried to correct him; and when this proved impossible, they had necessarily given sentence of deposition, with God's guidance and in accordance with proper procedure. Hence, while the council acknowledged that the final definition of the case was in Hadrian's hands, they would accept no peremptory restitution of the bishop. If the pope should attempt such an act, they would nevertheless refuse their communion.[70]

In the second letter the archbishop humbly addressed the pope and sought to dissociate himself personally from the deposition. In it, in fact, he spoke of the deposition only in passing, as one item of information.[71] He began with a plea for papal sanction of the incardination of Bishop Actard to the see of Tours (an explicit recognition of papal privilege),[72] and then passed on to a quite personal history of his nephew's deeds as bishop of Laon. He presented a selective history that strongly emphasized the affair of Count Nortmannus, and he provided Hadrian with ample opportunity to remember the bishop's letters of accusation and the outcome of that matter.[73] The behavior of the bishop, he said, had been a cause of great scandal, to say nothing of embarrassment to himself, particularly as he had been falsely accused of nepotism.[74] Finally, he said, after endless attempts to correct his nephew he had come to realize that the bishop was incorrigible. But the pope must understand, he continued, that it was not himself alone who was aggrieved. Rather, Bishop Hincmar's offenses affected the whole church, the king, and indeed the whole kingdom.[75]

The letter closed with a report, requested by the pope, concerning the deposition of the priest Trisingus, who had made appeal to Hadrian.[76] Considering that in the case of Hincmar of Laon questions concerning the propriety and the efficacy of papal appeal were in so prominent evidence, the juxtaposition of the case of Trisingus is at least striking; for, not only was the procedure correct in the case of Trisingus (on report of the archbishop of Reims), but the history of his deeds and mischances made a rather vile story. The priest had become involved in an affair with the daughter-in-law of his sister, and had thereafter had a drunken alter-

cation with her uncle, Livulfus, during the course of
which he had sought to murder the man. But whereas he
had succeeded in striking a swordblow, he had merely
deprived his victim of four fingers. This, we must
think is no mere report. There could be no question
that the priest's behavior warranted deposition,[77] and
the seamy nature of the case lends subtle weight to the
archbishop's argument for local judicial action, exemp-
lifying as it does that in local determinations the pope
cannot possess sufficient facts to render proper judgment. In this case too, the archbishop indicated,
Hadrian had, in effect, been taken in. It should be
noted in fairness, however, that perhaps Hincmar of
Reims stated the case a bit strongly, since Livulfus and
the priest appear to have originally been friends, since
the priest had grabbed the swords from Livulfus's son,
and since this "intentional" attack on Livulfus was preceded by some cudgel work inflicted by him upon the head
of Trisingus.

The third letter was quite different, and was sent in
the name of Charles the Bald.[78] Redacted in the form of
a response to the papal letter of 869,[79] it announced to
the pope the bases of power that underlay the deposition
of the bishop of Laon, and also obliquely indicated the
royal intransigence on any other matters with respect to
which the pope should improperly attempt to obtrude himself into Frankish politics. Referring throughout to a
letter sent in Hadrian's name, which the king said could
not possibly have been written by the pope, challenge
appeared in the first sentence, with the reference to
Hadrian's plea for Hincmar of Laon, *"quondam episcopus;"*[80]
in other words, the deposition appears as a fait accompli, without deference to any final Roman definition,
however tenuous. The king continued, castigating Hadrian for believing the charges of evil people against
him, and condemning the pope's lack of respect toward a
king evidenced by his writing to him in terms not used
by Nicholas I even toward so flagrant a criminal as
Lothar II. Indeed, the king said, now Rome threatened
Charles with excommunication for no crime, but rather
for fulfilling his royal office.[81] It is not the place
of his office to function as *vicedominus* for a church or
to permit offenders and calumniators to escape punish-

ment because the pope requests it. As to the charge
made by the anonymous writer that Charles, in a letter to
the pope, was guilty of false and evil accusations concerning Hincmar of Laon, these accusations were in fact
not false, as both clergy and nobles, great and small,
were quite aware. It was by the bishop's own failure to
correct these iniquities that he brought his own fate
upon himself;[82] and he continued, had not a necessary
meeting with his brother called him away, judgment would
have been rendered on many other accusations as well.
Charles, he stated, expected that Hadrian too would
follow the canons; but that in any case the pope might
rest assured that during the king's lifetime Hincmar
would never again recover the see of Laon.[83] In conclusion, he requested that the pope refrain from sending,
either to him or to the bishops or nobles of his realm,
letters as offensive as those previously written over
his name.[84]

In this tirade, where the influence of Hincmar of
Reims is evident,[85] other currents underlying the particular issue are present. In effect, the strategy of
associating issues appears here in another form: what
is said with regard to Hincmar of Laon is intended also
to inform the pope concerning far greater matters. This
was the first direct response Charles had sent to Rome
in over two years, and the message clearly indicates that
the king would tolerate no interference in what he considered the concern of the royal government. Pope
Gelasius had spoken of the distinct roles of kings and
pontiffs, the king reminded Hadrian;[86] and in the king's
challenge to the threat of excommunication leveled
against him in the performance of his kingly duties, it
is neither difficult nor implausible to see, not only
the case of Hincmar of Laon and the men whom he had sent
to Rome in specific violation of their oath, but also
the cases of Lotharingia and his son Carloman.

The covering letters for the Council of Douzy, then,
served simultaneously as a broad statement of metropolitan privilege and jurisdiction as opposed to the Pseudo-
Isidorian and papal assertions of the pontificate of
Nicholas I and as an assertion opposing the policies of
supervision of and interference in secular affairs that

had also characterized the reign of Hadrian's great predecessor. Thus far, in spite of Hadrian's strong stand
regarding the rights of the emperor Louis and the prince
Carloman, he remained something of an enigma, his seem-
ing intransigence balanced by his modification of papal
policy with regard to the problems of Lothar II and by
the apparent credence he had given to Hincmar of Reims's
report concerning his nephew late in 870. There is some
chance that the references to another hand at work in
this correspondence were no mere rhetoric but, rather,
pointed criticisms of the influence exercised over the
ailing pontiff by the papal librarian Anastasius. The
sequel would seem to favor this possibility and to
validate the suspicions (if such they were) of Hincmar
of Reims and his estimate of Hadrian.[87]

But the test was yet to come. Bishop Actard undertook the mission of bearing the letters and synodal *acta*
to the pope.[88] Upon his return, he carried two letters
of response.[89] One, addressed to the Council of Douzy,
dated 26 December 871, refused confirmation of the synodal decision.[90] The pope said he awaited a further explanation, since the synod did not appear to have been
canonical: Hincmar of Laon having made appeal to have
the charges against him heard at Rome, no sentence of
condemnation should have been passed. The *acta* themselves, he noted, reserved the final decision to the
pope; hence, in no contentious spirit, but merely wishing to ascertain the facts of the case, he said, he must
summon Hincmar of Laon to Rome and with him a worthy
accuser, *"qui nulla possit auctoritate legitima respui."*
Thus the case might be heard by the pope and the Roman
chapter; for the *acta* sent by the council were not adequate, and Hadrian's knowledge was as yet insufficient
to judge the matter. This order must be construed not as
a vindication of the bishop or as a rejection of the
synodal judgment but as evidence of the pope's desire to
be certain that justice should be done. Meanwhile, of
course, no new bishop might be ordained to the see of
Laon.

The letter addressed to King Charles was by no means
so restrained.[91] Hadrian chided him for his unchari-
table and unwise attitude toward the papal admonitions;

he repeated the papal refusal to accept the synod; and
he added that, for as long as he lived, he would never
consent to the deposition without diligent examination
of the case at Rome.

When Actard reached the Frankish court, probably
about February 872, those to whom the papal messages
were directed were faced with the problem of pursuing
what now appeared to be another direct confrontation,
for the Roman missives seemed to leave little room for
compromise regarding either the principles so vital to
Hincmar of Reims and his party or the removal of the
bishop of Laon. Once again three messages were sent to
Rome, all exhibiting the importance of the case to those
involved in its prosecution while simultaneously reflecting the greater issues with which Bishop Hincmar's
affairs had become so closely identified. As much of the
episcopal response as remains is chiding.[92] Its author
expressed great surprise, stating that the incredulous
bishops had required that the letter be often reread.
Indeed, he said, Actard had informed them of the over-
burden of work at Rome, and they had assumed that the
person charged to write the papal letter had not read
the *acta* of the synod in full. In the matter of the
deposition and appeal, the synod had followed the example of Saint Peter, who in the face of challenge
supported his case by the testimony of six witnesses.
They knew that Hadrian, as Peter's successor, would wish
to follow his example. The writer then directed the
pope to the last portion of the *acta*, where the regulations calling for local hearings, even on appeal, are
stated.[93]

In addition to the episcopal letter, another stronger
message was sent in the name of the king. The apolo-
gists for the principles implicit in the deposition of
Hincmar of Laon had come beyond the point of return.
Here then stood a plain opposition between assertions
of centralization and autonomy in ecclesiastical government, as well as a compelling need to elucidate clearly
the bases of separation between the spheres of secular
and ecclesiastical rule. The king's response reflects a
joining of these two concerns in what amounts to a treatise on the origin and nature of kingship and its relation to papal authority.[94]

So amazing was the papal response to the full account of the synod, which the king in his desire to
maintain peaceful relations had sent to Rome with Bishop
Actard, the message states, that he must suppose the
pope himself was not responsible for it. As in the
earlier letters sent from Rome, in which Charles had
been unjustly accused of perjury, tyranny, and other
crimes, here too it would appear that Rome is attempting to assert an arbitrary dominance, wanting to be
followed in all cases, even in opposition to the canons.[95] The law requires that any who have been ordained
and commit a serious offense shall be deposed.[96] Accusations should not be willful but substantiated. Saint
Peter himself, when challenged, had responded with humi-
lity, not with a declaration that what he did must be
accepted ipso facto, and he had gained his point through
the persuasive testimony of witnesses rather than
through force of position.[97] No law forbids the degra-
dation of one who is proved to be a disturber of the
public peace. Hincmar of Laon had been shown to be such
an offender in three synods held prior to his deposition,
and this he remained, by all means possible, even now.[98]
The king is, by law, guardian of the church and of the
canons; and Bishop Hincmar, who was guilty even of the
alienation of property belonging to his own church, was,
by law, summoned and deposed. Thus, there was no basis
for condemnation of the king, who had followed the law
of the canons and the decretals, as well as of the Christian emperors, whereas the papal letter had sought to
overturn these very laws.[99] But, the letter continued,
the words of a pope, expressed as assertion of the papal
privilegium, are not to be accepted when his judgment is
not accompanied by *aequitas*. The sentence of Hincmar of
Laon thus stood in spite of the worthless threats of the
Roman author, for it contained no violation of the
Petrine privilege.[100] As to the demand for a worthy
accuser to accompany Bishop Hincmar to Rome, Charles
would willingly serve in that capacity when containment
of the Northmen and the consent of his nephew, the pope's
emperor, made it possible; and he would bring a quite
sufficient number of worthy witnesses in his company.[101]
But let the pope bear in mind in this regard that those
he thus called revered--as did Gregory I--the fifth ecumenical council.[102]

As though to emphasize the nature and significance of the rejoinder, a covering note was composed, which explicity acknowledged the extraordinary character of the long *mémoire* sent under royal seal and while asserting the utmost respect for the papal office, once again admonished the pope to refrain from offending the king.[103] Actard again left for Rome in February with these letters.[104]

This time the papal response must have been satisfactory to the northerners. From the firm position stated the previous December, Hadrian had now moved to a somewhat ambiguous position of mixed conciliation and partial retraction.[105] He disavowed the former hostile commands, which he alleged had been extorted from him or had even been added to his own words during his recent illness. He asserted his great surprise on reading of the offenses committed by the Bishop of Laon. But, he said that he could not judge the matter apart from the strictures of the canons and the decretals of his predecessors,[106] and hence it was necessary that Hincmar of Laon, if he wished to appeal, should come to Rome. The case would then be reviewed in the equal light of the synodal *acta* and the *libellus* of complaint presented by the clergy and people of Laon. And, should the appeal seem merited, its final disposition would take place not in Rome, but in the north, by judges in the province of Reims, without the bishop's first having been restored.[107]

Thus, Hadrian retreated from the position advocated by Nicholas I in regard to appeal to Rome and, in effect, acquiesced to Archbishop Hincmar's interpretation of the Sardican canons. Further, by his denial of the *exceptio spolii*, the pope dealt what would seem to be major blow to the Pseudo-Isidorian regulations, and to the efforts to move toward episcopal autonomy. The demand retained by Hadrian, that Hincmar of Laon be permitted to bring his appeal to Rome, must be seen as an effort to hold some measure of the papal position. But such motives had become far secondary to more pressing needs expressed by Pope Hadrian II in the same letter, circumstances that to the pope seemed to demand the good will of King Charles the Bald.

The pope prefixed to his message of compromise a long statement of the high regard that he felt toward the western king. Charles's wisdom and justice, he said, are related to him from many sources, as is also the news of his generosity toward the church, which is said to be so great that not a single bishopric or monastery in his kingdom had not been the recipient of royal gifts and restitutions. He thus wished to convey to Charles a message so secret that it should be communicated to none but the closest of his *fideles*: that should the emperor die, he, Hadrian, would not acquiesce in the bestowal of the imperial title upon any other than Charles himself.[108]

IX

The Last Years, 871-79

Hadrian's reference to the imperial title represented
more than a mere diplomatic turn, for during the summer
of 871 the question of imperial succession had assumed
great immediacy. For years the emperor Louis II had
been occupied in a constant effort to repulse Arab incursions in the south of Italy; and in February 871 he
gained a great success in driving the Saracens from
their stronghold at Bari, thereby relieving the perennial threat to the peninsula.[1] But it was clear that
such relief could be but temporary. The emperor Louis
was a fine soldier and devoted virtually all his abili-
ties to the defense of the realm; in his absence, where
might the pope and his church look to find a replacement?

On 13 August 871, while deliberations proceeded at
Douzy far to the north, the emperor Louis was taken captive by Duke Adalgis of Benevento, and news reached the
northern kingdoms that he and his entire family had per-
ished.[2] Charles the Bald, who was ever alert to opportunities for gain, raised an army at once and began the
march into Italy to lay claim to the imperial crown. The
news of the emperor's death proved to be false, however;
and at Besançon Charles received word that not only had
Louis not been killed but he had, in fact, secured his
own release from captivity on 17 September.[3]

Although Charles's actions had proved premature, his
abortive Italian campaign did result in the termination
of the career of his rebellious son. From Douzy, where
he met with *missi* sent to him by the sons of Louis the
German, King Charles and his attendants proceeded to
Maestricht for the scheduled meeting, to confer with his
brother and with the representatives sent by Prince
Carloman.[4] Although the situation in the north remained
tenuous for all concerned, and in spite of great efforts
expended during the meeting, the parties remained un-

yielding. Carloman refused to return to imprisonment; and eventually, in early September, King Charles left Maestricht to hunt near Orville.[5] But he apparently considered his rebellious son so serious a threat that he did not wish to leave the country while he remained at large. On the other hand, Carloman seems to have looked upon the assembled royal army as a threat to eliminate him by force; and, at the behest of his advisers, to avoid an all-out battle, he surrendered himself to his father at Besançon. He was placed under guard and was relegated to custody until Charles could find an opportunity to consult with his *fideles* regarding his fate.[6]

The opportunity arrived more quickly than anticipated, when Charles learned of the emperor Louis's safety, and the royal party returned from Besançon to the north, traveling through Ponthion and Attigny to Servais. There, in early December, a *placitum* heard the charges against Prince Carloman, and upon the advice of his *fideles*, King Charles commanded that his son be returned to the incarceration at Senlis from which papal intervention had released him a year earlier.[7] This time the prince would not be so fortunate. The influential parties in Italy who had once come to his aid were now confronted with new fears for the imperial succession and were seeking preferred candidates.

During the first months of 872, the empress Engilberga embarked upon a complex diplomatic mission, during which she interviewed both of the brother monarchs to the north. The net result of her efforts was ultimately of little consequence, even though the imperial family seems to have favored Louis the German.[8] The pope, on the other hand, had come to see in Charles the Bald the only possible successor to the vital role that had been played by the emperor Louis. Around June, as has been seen, even as Engilberga sought to deal with the two potential candidates, Pope Hadrian wrote and expressed his preference to Charles.[9] When Hadrian died toward the end of the year[10] and was succeeded by a new pontiff, John VIII, who was still more eager to gain Charles's aid and to promote him to the imperial throne, it was patently evident that Carloman no longer had a champion and that he was at the mercy of his enemies.[11]

The delicate negotiations that occupied Charles for
much of 872 took place against a background of activity
by Carloman's followers that to the king's mind (at
least so we are told) seemed to threaten even his own
title,[12] and the death of Pope Hadrian appears to have
offered an opportunity at last to deal with the rebel
once and for all. In the *Annales Bertiniani*, under the
year 873, the reader is informed that "since many await-
ted yet a renewal of Carloman's evil deeds," King
Charles commanded the convocation of an episcopal council at Senlis, where the prelates decreed the prince deposed from holy orders.[13] Then, on grounds that Carloman's altered status raised the possibility that he
might assert a claim to the throne, his eyes were put
out, and he was immured in the monastery of Corbie.[14]
Even yet he retained influential sympathizers and remained a threat. King Charles, while enroute to fight the
Normans at Angers, learned with alarm that the prince,
with the aid of his great-uncle Count Adalard, had escaped and been brought to the court of Louis the
German.[15] But Charles's fears were empty, for the
prince's active life was finished. Initially placed by
King Louis in the monastery of Saint Alban's near
Mainz,[16] Carloman was later made abbot at Echternach,
where he died a few years later, probably in 877.[17]

When on 12 August 875 the event anticipated four
years earlier--the death of the emperor Louis II--did in
fact occur, the Arabs were but a few miles from Rome itself, and his survivors were hard pressed to find a substitute champion. The empress still favored succession
by Louis the German, but Charles's readiness, supported
by papal favor, won out.[19] By 17 December Charles had
avoided the threatened opposition of Louis's sons Charles
and Carloman and was at Rome.[20] He received the imperial crown from John VIII on **Christmas** day.[21] For John
far more than for his predecessors the Saracen threat
was immediate and omnipresent, even to the degree that
the aged pontiff himself undertook to lead troops
against the invader;[22] and to him the bestowal of the
imperial title carried with it a demand that its recipient devote himself to the rescue of the Roman church.[23]
The reiterated plea that the new emperor fulfill his

obligations in Italy is easily the most constant topic
in John's voluminous correspondence.[24]

This papal expectation for the defense of Rome was
doomed, however, on several counts. In Italy itself
Engilberga's influence had so helped to divide the nobility that Charles was, until February 876, unable to
receive the title of king traditionally prerequisite to
the imperial coronation.[25] Meanwhile, the royal absence
from the north once more led to civil strife there.
Louis the German, who was disgruntled that the imperial
title had escaped his grasp, responded to the appeal of
a rebel party and repeated his invasion of 858. He
found no challenge in the forces left by Charles under
the command of Louis the Stammerer to guard against such
an eventuality, and he was in the palace at Attigny to
celebrate Christmas.[26] As before, his victory was ephe-
meral; for, even as the newly crowned emperor made his
way home in January 876, leaving behind his brother-in-
law Count Boso to serve as regent in Italy, the German
king had to retire to the east.[27] But Louis, who considered himself the rightful successor to the dead emperor, remained inimical, in spite of several efforts
made by the pope to mediate the dispute on his brother's
behalf.[28]

The hostility of Louis the German was also reflected
in Francia itself. The western realm was increasingly
buffeted by Viking raids, and opportunism meshed with
widespread recognition of royal irresponsibility to
drain away support from Charles.[29] In an effort to
counteract this, a great council was summoned to meet at
Ponthion under the auspices of a papal delegation. It
was planned that Charles would make his first public
appearance as emperor there, and it was hoped that the
papal authority might result in recognition and acceptance of the imperial status.[30] The success of this
poorly devised diplomacy is extremely dubious. In particular, John and Charles sought with scant return to impose a broad control over the northern church by reviv-
ing, in the person of Archbishop Ansegis of Sens, the
office of papal vicar. When Lothar I had attempted the
same tactic a generation earlier, it had been rejected
outright.[31]

The emperor did no better in the handling of his eastern relatives. A tentative step was taken toward a peaceful resolution of the quarrel when Charles dispatched an embassy, including two of the papal representatives, to treat with his brother monarch.[32] But on 28 August 876, the very day on which the delegation departed, Louis the German died.[33] Faced again with an opportunity for immediate gain through rapid conquest, Charles readily forgot the tenuousness of his own situation and invaded the Lotharingian territories that since 872 had been under the rule of Louis the Younger.[34] The forces of the two opposing monarchs met in battle on 8 October at Andernach on the Rhine. The invasion was repulsed in a struggle more bloody than any fought by Frankish troops since Charles and Louis the German had united thirty-five years earlier to oppose the emperor Lothar at Fontenoy.[35]

In the meantime, the spate of importunate letters from Rome to Charles continued, as Pope John found himself almost alone in opposing, not only Arab forces, but also a group of southern Italian nobles who made common cause against the pontiff and a group conspiring within the curia itself. The regent Boso provided no substantial assistance.[36] Finally, confronted with allegations of the duties that his imperial office imposed, Charles the Bald turned his attention from his no less pressing responsibilities at home to Rome. In early May he faced the Viking bands that threatened his realm, not with military force, but with the greatest monetary tribute yet levied upon the Frankish people.[37] In June he sought to gain support from the *proceres* for his Italian mission, to regulate the operation of the government in his absence, and to anticipate the possibility that he himself might not return alive to *Francia*.

A great assembly met at Quierzy in June; and the *capitula* issued by that body, with their strong emphasis upon the regency of the incompetent Louis the Stammerer and upon the modification of the rights of inheritance among royal officials, and with their implicit recognition of the likelihood of revolt, provide a revealingly and prophetically somber backdrop for the doomed campaign.[38] By September the Emperor Charles was in north-

ern Italy awaiting the arrival of additional troops from
the north. But the Frankish *proceres*, ostensibly angered by the unpopular Italian campaign, by the imposition of the Danegeld, and surely moved by the spirit of
opportunism perennially evident among the Carolingian
nobility, erupted in widespread rebellion.[39] Charles
immediately embarked upon his return. Enroute his already broken health collapsed, and on 6 October 877 he
died in the tiny Alpine village of Avrieux.[40]

Charles the Bald left the Frankish monarchy enfeebled
both as an institution and in the person of its incumbent. Louis the Stammerer, who had always been unpopular among the many who knew of his incapacity, came to
rule without even the benefit of having been crowned
during his father's lifetime.[41] Not until the following
December did Hincmar of Reims officiate at his coronation.[42] The new king, who was already in failing health
although only in his early thirties,[43] was totally unable to impose effective rule over the realm, much less
able to meet the demands of the pope.

In 878 Pope John was driven from Rome by conspiracy
in the curia, which was backed by the power of the
rebellious Italian dukes. He fled to the north in the
hope of gaining aid from one or another of the Carolingian monarchs.[44] To this end, on papal command, Louis
the Stammerer called a large council, which met in
August at the city of Troyes.[45] Here the prelates of
the north added their voices to the anathema that the
pope himself had previously pronounced against his enemies,[46] but this was the extent of the support he received. Of the Carolingian rulers, only Louis the Stammerer appeared at the council, and the state of his
health had made even his attendance seem unlikely.[47]
The council sat for a month and handled considerable
business; but when the pope returned to Italy, he bore
with him only vague promises of support.[48]

At this council, also, Hincmar of Laon makes his
final appearance in the sources. When the council of
Douzy had terminated seven years earlier, the deposed
bishop had gone into exile; but neither he nor his followers had ceased their activities.[49] In the aftermath

of Douzy, Hincmar alleged that his condemnation had resulted, not from the convictions of his fellow bishops,
but from their fear of King Charles;[50] and it is evident that the former prelate had considerable support
among the bishops in both the eastern and western
realms.[51] After Douzy, Hincmar had grown even more rad-
ical in his opposition to King Charles, siding openly
with Prince Carloman and other rebellious forces, among
them Hugh, the bastard son of Lothar II and Waldrada.[52]
Like Carloman, Hincmar seems to have inspired fear among
his enemies. He was captured in 873, was turned over to
the ministrations of Count Boso, and was imprisoned.[53]
Two years later, when Charles was planning his first
Italian journey and conspirators were plotting against
him, the count acted to insure that Hincmar should no
longer pose a threat. Like Carloman, he too was
blinded.[54]

But even in that condition and in spite of the un-
ceasing efforts of both Charles and Hincmar of Reims he
remained an influential force among the Frankish churchmen and nobility.

When the emperor set out on his journey into Italy,
the see of Laon had been vacant for more than four years.
The archbishop of Reims took advantage of his monarch's
absence to gain papal support for his nephew's replacement. On 5 January 876, as the newly crowned emperor
started on his return journey, Pope John dispatched a
letter to Hincmar of Reims. In it he said the emperor
had assured him that the deposition of the bishop of Laon
had been just, and so great a prince could not but speak
the truth. Hence, he was moved now, out of solicitude
for the church of Laon so long without a pastor, to command the election of a new bishop.[55]

The importance attached to the papal order is evidenced by the speed with which the letter was sent and
its command implemented. The bearer, Theodoricus, who
received the directive from the pope, turned it over to
the archbishop at Reims on 11 March, a full month before
Charles arrived at Saint-Denis,[56] and Hincmar of Reims
did not delay in communicating the letter to the elec-
tors. On 28 March the clergy and people of Laon an-

nounced to the archbishop as their selection the priest
Hedenulphus, whom they requested be ordained bishop.[57]

In the months that followed, however, Archbishop
Hincmar appears to have been unable to secure sufficient adherence to the new election from among his own
suffragans to permit the ceremony to take place. It is
not unlikely that the papal instructions were reiterated
by John's legates before the council held at Ponthion in
June and July 876 and that the matter was among the many
points of contention to hinder the plans of the new
emperor.[58] During this time Hincmar of Reims .called
upon Charles on several occasions for aid in implement-
ing the election,[59] but even the presence of the new
emperor was insufficient to compel the ordination. It
was not until March 877, on the eve of Charles's second
departure for Italy, that the archbishop, with seven
other prelates, was able to consecrate his new suffragan.[60] But the honor seems to have been an unwelcome
burden to Hedenulphus, and he soon sought to be rid of
it.

When the emperor died the following October, a tor-
rent of criticism long held in check broke out in reaction against the archbishop of Reims. In complaints
sent to Rome, Archbishop Hincmar was accused of refusing
to recognize the authority of the papal decretals and of
holding that his office was as high as that of the pope.
The charges centered specifically on the elder Hincmar's
role in the deposition of his nephew and in the affair
of Prince Carloman.[61] The opposition was likely manifest
in other action as well. When, during 878, Hedenulphus
announced his desire to relinquish his new position and
to enter a monastery, it is unlikely that the causes of
his request were in fact age and illness as he alleged.[62]
Evidently, influential opinion charged the deposition
of Hincmar of Laon with illegality and failure to permit
the prescribed Roman hearing, and so denied the canonicity of Hedenulphus's election in spite of Pope John's
confirmation of the deposition.[63]

Through all of this the blind man remained in prison,
but the efforts of his champions had their effect. At
the Council of Troyes held in August 878, Pope John com-

manded the appearance of the deposed bishop.[64]   Hincmar
was led before the assembly and at last fulfilled his
oft-asserted desire to present his case before the pope.
His appeal to John took the form of a declaration of innocence on his part and of accusation against his uncle.
In it he related the events of Douzy and of the intervening years, and he made a plea to the pontiff for an
equitable judgment.[65]

   Circumstances now favored the blind man's case.   On
10 September, the final day of the synod, King Louis the
Stammerer was crowned a second time, by the pope himself.
He then acceded to the request of a number of his *pri-
mores* that he intercede with the pope on Hincmar's behalf.   The king spoke privately with John at the papal
mansion, and then the two of them met with the bishops
in the adjoining chapel.   There John announced their
decision to the assembled prelates.[66]   Hedenulphus would
continue to hold the office of bishop of Laon, but a
portion of the income accruing thereto would go to the
former bishop Hincmar, who was restored to priestly
communion and was granted the right to say Mass again,
should he so desire.   Upon hearing this decision,
Hincmar's supporters, unbidden by the pope and to the
surprise of the other bishops present, led the blind man,
clothed in priestly robes, into the papal presence.   Then,
singing, they carried him into the church, where he gave
a sign of benediction to the people.[67]   A year later his
unhappy life ended.[68]

Abbreviations

Ann. Bert.	*Annales Bertiniani--Annales de Saint Bertin*, ed. F. Grat et al. (Paris, 1964).
BML	J. F. Böhmer and M. Mühlbacher, eds., *Die Regesten des Kaiserreichs unter den Karolingern, 751-918*, 2d rev. ed., ed. J. Lechner (Innsbruck, 1908).
Bouquet	M. Bouquet et al., eds., *Recueil des historiens des Gaules et de la France* (Paris, 1738-1904).
Cap. Ang.	P. Hinschius, ed., *Capitula Angilramni*, in *PI* (below), pp. 757-69.
CB	Charles the Bald
Flodoard	Flodoard, *Historia ecclesiae Remensis*, in MGH *SS* (below) 13. 409-599.
Hadrian	Hadrian II
Hadrian *Epp.*	Hadrian II, *Epistolae*, in MGH *Epp.* (below) 6. 691-765.
HL	Hincmar of Laon
HR	Hincmar of Reims
HR *Epp.*	Hincmar of Reims, *Epistolae*, in MGH *Epp.* (below) 8, pt. 1.
HR Libellus	Hincmar of Reims, *Libellus expostulationis*, in *PL* (below) 126. 566-634; and Reg. HL (below), (148).

HR Opusculum   Hincmar of Reims, *Opusculum 55 capitu-*
                    lorum, in *PL* (below) 126. 290-494; and
                    Reg. HL (below), (91).

JE   P. Jaffé et al., eds., *Regesta pontificum*
                    Romanorum, 1, 2d ed. (Leipzig, 1881).

Mansi   J. D. Mansi et al., eds., *Sacrorum con-*
                    ciliorum nova et amplissima collectio
                    (Florence and Venice, 1759-).

MGH   G. Pertz et al., eds., *Monumenta Ger-*
                    maniae historica (Hanover, 1826-).
                    Series frequently cited:

  AA   *Auctores antiquissimi*
  Cap.   *Capitularia regum Francorum*
  Conc.   *Concilia*
  Epp.   *Epistolae*
  Form.   *Formulae merovingici et karolini aevi*
  Poet. lat.   *Poetae latini*
  SS   *Scriptores*
  SS rer. merov. *Scriptores rerum merovingicarum*

Nicholas *Epp.*   Nicholas I, *Epistolae*, in MGH *Epp.* (above)
                    6. 257-690.

PL   J. P. Migne, ed., *Patrologiae Latinae*
                    cursus completus (Paris, 1844-).

Petitio   Charles the Bald, *Petitio proclamationis*,
                    in Mansi (above), 16. 578-81; and Reg.
                    HL (below), (147).

PI   P. Hinschius, ed., *Decretales Pseudo-*
                    Isidorianae et Capitula Angilramni
                    (Leipzig, 1863).

Rau   R. Rau, *Quellen zur Karolingischen*
                    Reichsgeschichte, 3 vols. (Darmstadt,
                    1955).

Reg. HL   *Registrum Hincmari Laudunensis*, appendix
                    1, below, pp. 169-78.

Reg. HR   *Registrum Hincmari [Remensis]*, in Schrörs,
                 Hinkmar, Erzbischof von Reims (Freiburg
                 im Breisgau, 1884), pp. 512-88.

Tessier   G. Tessier et al., eds., *Recueil des
                 actes de Charles II le Chauve* (Paris,
                 1943-).

Appendix I

Registrum Hincmari Laudunensis

(1) 858, early in   HR, letter to Rothad of Soissons, regarding the ordination of HL.[1] MGH *Epp.* 8[1], no. 109, p. 55.

(2) 858, before 21 Mar.   HL ordained; gives signed oath of obedience.[1]

(3) 858, before 21 Mar.   HR, canonical collection for HL.[1]

(4) 858, 21 Mar.   HL signs oath of fealty to CB at Quierzy assembly.[1]

(5) 858, first half of   HR, letter to HL, with instructions on administration of diocese.[2] Ibid., no. 119, p. 58.

(6) 858   HR, letter of warning and advice to HL.[2] Ibid., no. 123, p. 59.

(7) 860, early in   CB, precept restoring property to HL.[3]

(8) 863, Jan.   Lotharingian bishops, letter to HR.[4] *PL* 121. 381–82.

(9) c. 865   HL, canonical collection regarding Aguilcourt.[5]

(10) 866, June   HR, letter to HL, summons to Beauvais for ordination of John as bishop of Cambrai.[6] MGH *Epp.* 8[1], no. 182, p. 172.

(11) 866, 13 July   HR, second letter to HL regarding John; cf. (10).[6] Ibid., no. 183, p. 173.

(12) 866, Aug. – 870, June   HR, letters to HL, concerning ordination of John; cf. (10) and (11).[6]

(13) c. 866   HL, canonical collection regarding Amalbertus.[7]

(14) 867, July   HR, letter to Nicholas I.[8]
                                  Ibid., no. 198, pp. 205-17.
(15) 868, June   CB, summons to HL.[9]
(16) 868, June   HL, letter of excuse to CB.[9]
(17) 868, July   HL, letter to Hadrian regarding
                                  Poilly.[9]
(18) 868, July   HL, letter to HR regarding CB.[9]
(19) 868, c. July-Aug.   HR, letters of admonition to
                                  CB.[9]
(20) 868, Aug.   Hadrian, letter to CB for HL.[10]
                                  MGH *Epp.*, 6, no. 14, pp. 715-16
                                  (JE, 2911).
(21) 868, Aug.   Hadrian, letter to HR for HL.[10]
                                  Ibid., no. 15, pp. 716-17 (JE,
                                  2910).
(22) 868, Aug.   Hadrian, letter to HL.[10]
(23) 868, Aug.   Assembly at Pîtres.[11]
(24) 868, before 30 Aug. HL, *Schedula.*[11] *PL* 124. 1025-28;
                                  Mansi, 16. 779-80; Delalande,
                                  pp. 196-97.
(25) 868, July-Aug.   HR, *Pro ecclesiae libertatum
                                  defensione.*[11] *PL* 125. 1035-70;
                                  Mansi, 16. 755-84; first part at
                                  Delalande, pp. 186-96.
(26) 868, Sept.   HL, *Satisfactio* to CB.[11] *PL* 124.
                                  1027-28; Mansi, 16. 780; Dela-
                                  lande, p. 197.
(27) 868, Sept.   HR, letter to CB, regarding HL
                                  and benefices.[11] *PL* 126. 94-99;
                                  Mansi, 16. 785-88.
(28) 868, Sept. (?)   CB, letters (?) to HR, regar-
                                  ding HL.[12]
(29) 868, Nov.   HR, letter to Odo of Beauvais,
                                  regarding ordination of Wille-
                                  bert as Bishop of Châlons.[13]
                                  Flodoard, 3. 23. 529.
(30) 868, early Dec.   Meeting at Quierzy.[13]
(31) 868, Dec.   HR, letter to Odo of Beauvais,
                                  concerning Celsanus.[13] Flodoard,
                                  3. 23. 530.
(32) 868   HR, letter to Odo of Beauvias,
                                  concerning archbishop's inabi-
                                  lity to attend an assembly
                                  called by CB.[14] Ibid., pp.529-30.

(33) 868, late - CB, letters of summons to HL.[15]
     869, Jan.
(34) 869, Jan. HL, letters to CB and HR regarding Poilly, Nortmannus, and anathema.[13]
(35) 869, Jan. HR, letter to Odo of Beauvais, regarding HL.[13]
(36) 869, Jan. HR, letter to Odo of Beauvais, regarding HL.[13]
(37) 869, Jan. HR, letter to CB, regarding HL.[16]
(38) 869, latter half HR, letter to Odo of Beauvais, of Jan. regarding letters carried by Odo to CB for HL.[16] Flodoard, 3. 23. 530.
(39) 869, late Jan. HR, letter to HL, summoning him to assembly at Verberie.[17]
(40) 869, Feb.-Mar. HL, letter to HR, regarding Verberie.[17]
(41) 869, Mar.-Apr. HR, letter to Odo of Beauvais, regarding HL.[17]
(42) 869, 19 Apr. Laon diocesan synod.[17]
(43) 869, late Apr. Assembly at Verberie.[17]
(44) 869, 1-15 May HL, letter to Hadrian.[18]
(45) 869, c. mid-May HL, letter to CB.[16]
(46) 869, c. mid-May CB, letter to HR, requesting reply to (45).[16]
(47) 869, third week of CB, second letter to HR, concerning (45).[16]
     May
(48) 869, 22-31 May HR, letter in response to (46) and (47).[16]
(49) 869, 22-31 May HR, letter for HL.[16]
(50) 869, 30 May CB, letter to HR, complaining of Laon interdict.[19]
(51) 869, 30 May Laon church, letter to HR, regarding interdict.[19]
(52) 869, before late HR, letters to HL, concerning June excommunication of Amalbertus.[7]
(53) 869, May to c. 1 HR, letter to Odo of Beauvais, June regarding HL.[19]
(54) 869, after 3 June HR, letter to Laon church, concerning interdict.[19] *PL* 126. 511-14; Mansi, 16. 809-12.

(55)	869, after 3 June	HR, letter to HL, concerning interdict.[19] *PL* 126. 515-26.
(56)	869, after 3 June	HR, letter to CB, concerning interdict.[19]
(57)	869, 24 June	HR, letter to HL, concerning his diocese and appeal.[19] *PL* 126. 526-31; Mansi, 16. 822-26.
(58)	869, late June	HR, letter to CB, concerning HL.[19]
(59)	869, late June	HR, letter to Laon church.[19] *PL* 126. 531-33; Mansi, 16. 826-28.
(60)	869, late June – early July	HL, oath to CB.[20]
(61)	869, 8 July	HL, subscribed sentences.[21]
(62)	869, 8 July – before 23 Aug.	HL, signed canonical collection.[21]
(63)	869, June-July	Hadrian, letter to HR, for HL.[18]
(64)	869, June-July	Hadrian, letter to CB, for HL.[18]
(65)	869, June-July	Hadrian, letter to HL.[18]
(66)	869, July	Assembly at Pîtres.[20]
(67)	869, July-Aug.	CB, letter to Hadrian.[13]
(68)	869, July-Aug.	HL, letter to CB regarding Poilly.[21]
(69)	869, July-Aug.	HL, letter to HR regarding Poilly.[21]
(70)	869, 23 Aug.	HR, letter to HL, of remonstrance and announcement of impending journey.[22] *PL* 126. 533-34; Mansi, 16. 828-29.
(71)	869, c. 5 Sept.	Hadrian, letter to CB.[23]
(72)	869, c. 5 Sept.	Hadrian, letter to HL.[23]
(73)	869, 9 Sept.	Coronation of CB at Metz.[22]
(74)	869, Nov.	Assembly at Gondreville.[24]
(75)	869, July/Aug.– early Nov.	HL, *Pittaciolus*.[21]
(76)	869, after 11 Nov.	HR, letter to HL, regarding *Pittaciolus*.[21] *PL* 126. 534-37; Mansi, 16. 829-31.
(77)	869, Nov.-Dec.	HR, letter to HL, regarding the Laon interdict and the bishop's behavior.[24]

(78) 869, late -   HR, *indiculus* of letter of
     870, early   Hadrian to bishops.[24]

(79) 870, early   Ordination of Bertulfus as
          archbishop of Trier.[22]

(80) 870, 13 Feb.   HR, letter to HL, regarding
          Nivinus.[25] *PL* 126. 279-80.

(81) 870, Feb.-Mar.   HL, reply to (80).[25] *PL* 124.
          979-86.

(82) 870, 20 Mar.   HR, letter to HL, regarding
          Hadulfus.[25] *PL* 126. 280-81.

(83) 870, 28 March   HL, reply to (82).[25] *PL* 124.
          985-86.

(84) 870, Feb.-before   HL, letter concerning Follem-
     27 April   bray.[25]

(85) 870, 27 April   HR, letter to HL, regarding
          Follembray.[25] *PL* 126. 537-45;
          Mansi, 16. 832-38.

(86) 870, 1 May   HL, reply to (85).[25] *PL* 124.
          985-94.

(87) 870, 11 May   HR, reply to (86).[25] *PL* 126.
          545-66; Mansi, 16. 838-55.

(88) 869, Oct. -   CB, letter to HL, in support of
     870, May   HR.[26]

(89) 869, Nov. -   HR, letters to HL, concerning
     870, June   demand that archbishop burn his
          writings on Laon interdict.[24]

(90) 869, Nov. -   HR, letter to HL, requesting
     870, June   other collections mentioned at
          Gondreville.[24]

(91) 870, Jan.-June   HR Opusculum.[21] *PL* 126. 290-494.

(92) 870, c. Mar.-June   HL, *rotula* regarding Follembray
          and Haimeradus.[25]

(93) 870, c. Mar.-June   HL, letter regarding Nivinus, in
          reply to (86).[25]

(94) 870, before June   HR, *schedula* regarding excom-
          munication imposed by HL.[27]

(95) 870, before 15 June   HL, Attigny appeal collection
          (?)[21]

(96) 870, c. 15 June-   Assembly at Attigny.[27]
     16 July

(97) 870, 16 June   HL, oath to CB and HR sub-
          scribed in synod.[27]

(98) 870, 17 June   HL, oath written for HR.[27]

(99) 870, last week in   HL, letter to HR, explaining
       June   flight.[27]

(100) 870, last week in   HR, letter to HL.[27]
        June

(101) 870, last week in   HR, letter to HL, regarding con-
        June   signment of papal letters to
                          Rémi and Hardwic.[27]

(102) 870, after 28 June CB, letter to HL, ordering ex-
                          planation and return.[28]

(103) 870, 2 July   HL, letter to HR, requesting
                          help for trip to Rome.[27]

(104) 870, after 2 July- HL, letter to CB, requesting
        before 15   permission for trip to Rome, and
        July   explaining flight.[28]

(105) 870, c. 15 July   CB, letter or message to HL, in
                          reply to (104).[28]

(106) 870, c. 16 July   CB, *indiculus* for Eligius.[28]

(107) 870, 18 July   HL, message to HR, complaining
                          of property reconsignment by
                          Frotharius, and enclosing *capi-*
                          tula of Council of Tusey
                          (860).[29]

(108) 870, June-July   HL, letter to Hadrian.[30]

(109) 870, c. 28 July - HR, letter to HL, in reply to
        early Aug.   (107).[29] *PL* 126. 494-98.

(110) 870, July-Aug.   Hadrian, letter to HR.[30]

(111) 870, c. 1 Sept.   Secular hearing at Servais.[31]

(112) 870, c. 19-24 Oct. HR. letter to HL, on letters
                          received from Hadrian, requiring
                          episcopal consultation.[32]
                          Flodoard, 3. 22. 519.

(113) 870, before 25   HL, true Poilly *rotulae*, sent
        Oct.   to CB and HR (2) (?)[13]

(114) 870, 20-25 Oct.   HR, letter to Hadrian.[30] *PL*
                          126. 174-86.

(115) 870, 20-25 Oct.   HR, letter to Hadrian, regarding
                          HL.[30]

(116) 870, 13 Nov.   HL, letter to HR, in response to
                          (91) and other charges raised at
                          and since Attigny.[21] *PL* 124.
                          1027-70.

(117) 870, c. late Nov. HR, letter to HL, in response to
                          (116).[21] *PL* 126. 498-509.

(118) 870, first half   CB, letter to HR commanding
       of Dec.   call of council for action
                        against Carloman.[33] Flodoard,
                        3. 23. 530.

(119) 870, end of   HR, letter to Odo of Beauvais,
                        regarding Carloman.[33] Ibid.

(120) 870, end of   HR, letter to Engelramnus et
                        al., regarding Carloman.[33]
                        Ibid., 26. 543.

(121) 870, end of   HR, letter to CB, regarding
                        Carloman.[33] Ibid., 18. 508.

(122) 863-870   HR, letter to Adventius of Metz,
                        regarding HL.[32] Ibid., 23. 528.

(123) 870, end of -   HR, letter to Carloman.[33] Ibid.,
       871, beginning of   18. 508-9.

(124) 870, end of -   HR, letter to Carloman, concern-
       871, beginning of   ing meeting with CB.[33] Ibid.,
                        26. 543.

(125) 870, end of -   HR, letter to Engelramnus et
       871, beginning of   al.[33] Ibid.

(126) 870, end of -   HR, letter to Harduinus, regar-
       871, beginning of   ding Carloman.[33] Ibid., p. 544.

(127) 871, late Jan. -   Council at Compiègne.[33]
       early Feb.

(128) 871, 31 Jan.   HR, letter to HL, regarding
                        penalties imposed upon Carloman
                        and his followers.[33] Mansi, 16.
                        606b; Delalande, p. 203.

(129) 871, Feb.   HR, letter to Rémi of Lyon etc.,
                        regarding sentence against Carl-
                        oman and his followers.[33] *PL*
                        126. 277-80; ending at Mansi,
                        16. 605-6; Delalande, pp. 204-5.

(130) 871, early Mar.   HR, letter to HL, again reques-
                        ting consent to provisional sen-
                        tence of Compiègne.[33]

(131) 871, 25 Mar.   Hadrian, letter to HR.[34] MGH
                        Epp. 6, no. 29, p. 734 (JE,
                        2936).

(132) 871, 25 Mar.   Hadrian, letter to HL.[34] Ibid.,
                        no. 30, p. 735 (JE, 2938).

(133) 871, c. Mar. -   HL, letter to HR, explaining re-
       mid-Apr.   lunctance to consent to sentence
                        of Compiègne.[33] *PL* 124. 1069-72.

(134) 871, 19 Apr.　　　　HR, letter to HL, concerning
　　　　　　　　　　　　　sentence and bishop's con-
　　　　　　　　　　　　　tumacy.[33]

(135) 871, after 5 May -　HR, letter to HL, concerning
　　　before 14 May　　　　sentence.[33]

(136) 871, 14 May　　　　　HR, letter to HL, calling him
　　　　　　　　　　　　　to a synod.[35] *PL* 126. 566-67.

(137) 871, c. mid -　　　　HR, letter to Adventius of
　　　　　　　　　　　　　Metz, regarding sentence of
　　　　　　　　　　　　　Compiègne.[35]　Flodoard, 3. 23.
　　　　　　　　　　　　　528.

(138) 871, after 14 May-　Bertharius, petition to HR.[36]
　　　10 June

(139) 871, 10 June　　　　 HR, letter to HL, regarding
　　　　　　　　　　　　　Bertharius.[36] Ibid., 22. 519-20.

(140) 871, 16 June　　　　 HL, collection sent to HR.[37]

(141) 871, 5 July　　　　　HR, letter to HL, calling him
　　　　　　　　　　　　　to the Council of Douzy.[38]
　　　　　　　　　　　　　Ibid., p. 520.

(142) 871, after 5 July　 HL, reply to (141). (?)[38]

(143) 871, after 5 July　 HR, reply to (142).[38] *PL* 126.
　　　　　　　　　　　　　509-11.

(144) 871, after 5 July　 CB, letter to HL, calling him
　　　　　　　　　　　　　to Douzy.[38]

(145) 871, after 5 July-　Third call to Douzy sent to
　　　before 6 Aug.　　　　HL.[38]

(146) 871, 5 Aug.-　　　　 Assembly at Douzy.[38]
　　　c. 6 Sept.

(147) 871, before 6 Aug.　CB, *Petitio*.[38]　Mansi, 16. 578-
　　　　　　　　　　　　　81; Delalande, pp. 206-8.

(148) 871, c. June -　　　 HR Libellus.[38]　*PL* 126. 566-
　　　9 Aug.　　　　　　　 634; Mansi, 16. 581-643; Dela-
　　　　　　　　　　　　　lande, pp. 208-41.

(149) 871, c. 6 July -　　 HL, *rotula* regarding appeal to
　　　11 Aug.　　　　　　　Rome.[38]

(150) 871, 6-13 Aug.　　　 *Responsa episcoporum ad libel-*
　　　　　　　　　　　　　lum proclamationis Caroli
　　　　　　　　　　　　　regis.[38]　Mansi, 16. 643-58;
　　　　　　　　　　　　　Delalande, pp. 241-48.

(151) 871, 10-13 Aug.　　 HL, collection prepared at
　　　　　　　　　　　　　Douzy(?)[38]

(152) 871, before 14 Aug.Nortmannus, petition against
　　　　　　　　　　　　　HL.[38]

(153) 871, 14 Aug. –   *Acta synodi.*[38] Mansi, 16. 658–
      6 Sept.   78; Delalande, pp. 248–59.

(154) 871, 6 Sept.   *Epistola synodalis* to Hadrian.[38]
                    PL 126. 635–41; Mansi, 16. 678–
                    82; Delalande, pp. 259–61.

(155) 871, c. 6 Sept.   HR, letter to Hadrian.[38] *PL*
                    126. 641–48; Mansi, 16. 682–88;
                    Delalande, pp. 261–64.

(156) 871, c. 6 Sept.   CB, letter to Hadrian.[38] *PL*
                    124. 876–81; Delalande, pp. 264–
                    67.

(157) 871, 26 Dec.   Hadrian, letter to Council of
                    Douzy.[39] MGH *Epp.* 6, no. 34,
                    pp. 738–40 (JE, 2945).

(158) 871, 26 Dec.   Hadrian, letter to CB, regar-
                    ding Bishop Actard and deposi-
                    tion of HL.[39] Ibid., no. 35,
                    pp. 741–43 (JE, 2946).

(159) 872, Feb.–Mar.   Council of Douzy, response to
                    (157).[39] Mansi, 16. 569–71.

(160) 872, Feb.–Mar.   CB, response to (158).[39] Dela-
                    lande, pp. 267–74. Also, but
                    excised, at *PL* 124. 881–96.

(161) 872, Feb.–Mar.   CB, covering letter for (160)[39]
                    PL 124. 896; Delalande, p. 274.

(162) 872, c. June   Hadrian, letter to CB.[39] MGH
                    Epp. 6, no. 36, pp. 743–46 (JE,
                    2951).

(163) 876, 5 Jan.   John VIII, letter to HR, con-
                    firming deposition of HL and
                    calling for election of new
                    bishop of Laon.[40] *Epistolae*
                    collectae, no. 4, MGH *Epp.* 7.
                    316–17.

(164) 876, 28 Mar.   Laon clergy and people, letter
                    to HR, requesting ordination
                    of Hedenulfus as bishop.[40] MGH
                    Form., pp. 553–54.

(165) 876, 28 Mar –   HR, letter to CB, regarding or-
      877, Apr.   dination of Hedenulfus.[40]
                    Flodoard, 3. 18. 510.

(166) 876, 28 Mar. –   HR, second letter to CB, regar-
      877, Apr.   ding ordination of Hedenulfus[40]
                    Ibid.

(167) 877, c. Feb.-Apr.   HR, letter to Odo of Beauvais,
                            concerning ordination of
                            Hedenulfus.[40] Ibid., 23. 530-
                            31.
(168) 877, 16 Mar. -   HR, letter to clergy of Laon,
      1 Apr.   regarding ordination of
                            Hedenulfus.[40] *PL* 126. 271-76.
(169) 873 - before   HR, letter to Isembert, con-
      878, Aug.   cerning troubles of HL.[41]
                            Flodoard, 3. 26. 545.
(170) 878, before   HR, letter to Ottulfus of
      12 Aug.   Troyes, concerning directive
                            of John VIII regarding HL.[42]
                            Ibid., 23. 533.
(171) 878, 12 Aug.   HL, *Reclamatio*. MGH *Epp*. 6,
                            no. 101, pp. 94-95.
(172) 877, c. Feb. -   HR, justification of ordination
      878, Aug.   of Hedenulfus.[40]
(173) 878, 11 Aug. -   Assembly at Troyes.[43]
      10 Sept.
(174) 871, mid -   *Narratio eorum, quae post data*
      878, end of   *55 capitula peracta sunt ab*
                            utroque Hincmaro.[43] Mansi, 16.
                            856-64.
(175) 878, Sept.- end of   HR, apologia directed to accu-
                            sations made against him.[43]
                            Flodoard, 3. 21, 515 and 29.
                            554.
(176) 878, Sept.-end   HR, letter to Hildebold of
                            Soissons et al., concerning
                            dispositions regarding HL and
                            Hedenulfus.[43] Ibid., 23. 532.
(177) 879, end of   HR, letter to Abbot Hugo, an-
                            nouncing death of HL and re-
                            questing prayers for him.[44]
                            Ibid., 24. 537.

(178) 869, 24 Apr.   "John of Cambrai," letter to
                            HL.[45] *Analecta Bollandiana*
                            27:385-86.

Appendix II

The Villa of Poilly

The problem of the **villa** of Poilly runs through the career of Hincmar of Laon like a red thread. Although the **villa** is first mentioned in 868 by the bishop himself, who places the origin of the troubles connected with it back to the year 860 (Mansi, 16. 597b), certain aspects of the situation of Count Nortmannus still remained to be considered at the Council of Douzy in 871 (*PL* 126. 637c-d); and during the intervening period the original problem of right of possession became complicated with other elements, including charges involving violence, although the property question appears to have been settled by late October 870. The great difficulty that this case presents for the historian is caused by the status of those involved and the nature of their involvement; for no one was blameless, it would seem, with respect to Poilly. The resultant tendentious presentation of facts has led to the sort of obfuscation that usually accompanies an attempt to show things in their best light. What follows can be considered only as a reasonable interpretation of those facts, and the proofs presented cannot be regarded as conclusive.

Certain basic facts concerning the **villa** and its status, both real and alleged, are presented from the sources. Poilly, which was originally the property of the church of Laon, had been withdrawn from that church at some unknown time and had been given in benefice to royal vassals. Around 860, at the request of Hincmar of Laon, the king agreed to restore Poilly to the church of Laon; but the price was a private agreement, negotiated by the king's allies, Conrad and Rudolf of the Welf family, that the bishop permit the present tenant, Count Nortmannus, to retain Poilly. Hence the bishop received a royal precept that recognized the proprietary rights

of his church over the **villa**; and Poilly was recognized
as having the status, not of a portion of the royal
fisc, but of an ecclesiastical property held in precarial tenure by Nortmannus.

In 868 Hincmar of Laon complained that Nortmannus had
no right to Poilly, and he wrote to Hadrian II, who returned letters commanding that the land be restored
under threat of excommunication. On the basis of this
reply, and feeling that nothing would come from the king,
the younger Hincmar occupied the property by force, in
the process ejecting Nortmannus's pregnant wife. Force
played a part again later on as well; for when he finally did gain Poilly, Hincmar appears to have coerced
Nortmannus himself. But earlier, when the question was
raised, the count denied the charge, and asserted that
his right came from the king. During the course of the
quarrel, Hincmar of Laon admitted the agreement he had
made with Conrad and Rudolf to that effect, signing letters which were given to Charles and Hincmar of Reims;
and the bishop also finally received the **villa**, a part
of which he ultimately beneficed to the son of Nortmannus, as is mentioned in the letter written by Hincmar
of Reims to Hadrian II in October 870 (*PL* 126. 185c).

These are the bare bones of evidence. But the sources, anxious as always to present their principles well,
make it difficult to deduce the sequence of events and
sometimes even the events themselves. In the following
reconstruction, two matters are of central importance:
(1) the restitution itself (and the whole possession of
the **villa**, legal or illegal, during these years) and (2)
the agreement with Conrad and Rudolf (and hence the
status of the **villa** during this time).

The significance of Hincmar's concession to the Welfs
is clear and is fully indicated in the *Responsa episcoporum ad libellum proclamationis Caroli regis*, ch. 5,
(Mansi, 16. 649-50), where it is noted that not only had
the bishop violated the canons in making this concession
without the knowledge of his clergy and of other bishops
(particularly, of course, his metropolitan), but also in
so doing he had created a dangerous precedent. This is
surely hyperbole; but an even more striking fact is that

the bishop had apparently given written acknowledgment
of his action. In so doing, he not only placed himself
in a potentially dangerous position (as the future would
in fact reveal), but he also entirely vitiated the case
raised by him against Charles to Hadrian II. Furthermore, Hincmar had written the pope regarding the **villa**
on two occasions, and he had had no qualms about showing
the letters he received to the king, odd behavior for
one who had himself conceded the property to Charles.
In this strange situation, if we drop the possibility
that Bishop Hincmar was a total idiot (and perhaps we
should not), we are left with three alternatives: (1)
that the concession in fact did not occur, (2) that it
was really other than it is made to appear, and (3)
that the bishop thought no one knew of it.

We may begin a discussion of the supposed concession
with a consideration of the letters that purportedly
contain the admission. These were apparently sent to
Charles the Bald and Hincmar of Reims, but the time when
they were executed is quite unclear. They are mentioned
prominently at Douzy (Mansi, 16. 579d, 649-50; *PL* 126.
585), but these references are, of course, quite late.
The earliest definite mention occurs in the letter written by the archbishop to Hadrian in October 870 (*PL* 126.
185b; cf. also ibid., 504b-c, to his nephew during the
following month), although it is possible that the archbishop is referring to them at HR Opusculum, ch. 43 (*PL*
126. 441c) and probable that he is referring to the
situation at ch. 40 (*PL* 126. 438b). Thus the admission
must have been made prior to the last months of 870 and
probably prior to June 870. But it appears that by mid-
870 Hincmar of Laon was in possession of Poilly (see the
words of the king at *PL* 126. 495-96) and that he had
held it, with the property pertaining to it, since approximately January 870 (*PL* 124. 1030c-d); the king's
word *"reciperes"* (*PL* 126. 496a) probably, although not
certainly, meaning "retain". The circumstance of this
conversation with the bishop was a hearing concerning
new complaints with regard to land held by a tenant of
Nortmannus, which Hincmar had also taken on the assumption that it belonged to Poilly.

An attempt to date the letters of admission may help
to clear up the above, but the likelihood is not great.
That they must date from a time later than 868 is clear,
since Hincmar of Reims, when he received the first letter from Hadrian II and confronted Nortmannus with it,
apparently did not know of the agreement (*PL* 126. 585-
86). This incident led the count to cite Charles as the
person who had authorized his occupancy; and, as it occurred in the presence of the king and many bishops and
since the archbishop would naturally have wished to
learn of the matter as quickly as possible, it is not unlikely that the time was December 868 and the place
Quierzy. Since the context of the archbishop's threat
shows that Nortmannus was then in possession of Poilly
and there is no murmur in the sources of any trouble
prior to this, we may assume that Hincmar of Laon had
not yet attacked the count's wife.

A fair terminus ad quem for the letters may be found
in the good relations that existed between Charles and
the bishop from September 869 until about May 870 at any
rate. But the notion of a concession made by the bishop
was long in the air, for at HR Opusculum, ch. 40 (*PL*
126. 438c) the archbishop asserts, in denial of his
nephew's contention that he had been responsible for his
situation--that is, for those things "*de tuis hominibus,
et de hominibus suis ad Laudunum directis, et de eo quod
te commendavit Conrado,*" (ibid., 438b)--and that the
king had contradicted the charge *coram plurimis epis-
copis apud Pistas* necessarily referring to the assembly
held there in July 869. It may have been then that the
situation came to the knowledge of many (as Hincmar of
Reims says at *PL* 126. 504b and 185b); but it is likely
that this occurred still earlier, since the language of
HR Opusculum, ch. 40, concerning what the bishop thinks,
is very much like that in the letter (at Mansi, 16.
617b-c) written by the archbishop to Charles in June,
which may have aided in getting the young Hincmar released from Servais. Probably the many who knew were
those who attended the Council of Verberie in April 869;
but the stormy scene at and aftermath of that council
indicated that, if there was evidence, there was no admission. Thus it would seem likely that the admission

was one of the conditions laid down for the bishop's return into the royal good graces and that it was made and
presumably written up in July or, perhaps, August 869.

When did Hincmar hold the **villa** of Poilly and what were
the times when he ejected the family of Nortmannus? We
are told that this had happened twice prior to June 870,
since the count intended to complain (about both incidents) at Attigny (*PL* 126. 502a-b). We may doubt this,
however, as the two incidents appear to have been entirely
separate and there is no indication of royal anger in the
sources, whereas there almost surely would be if the incident of the count's wife had occurred just prior to
Attigny. If it had occurred long before Attigny, it would
have been a notable topic at Verberie. In fact, the archbishop does not mention the matter at all until he does so
in a private letter to his nephew; and no other sources
mention it until 871, when it appears as one of the topics
the council at Douzy did not have time to consider (*Epistola synodalis* at *PL* 126. 637c-d). The order of topics
in the letter of November 870 indicates that the attack on
Nortmannus followed the summer of 869 and preceded the
oath at Attigny (see *PL* 126. 502a, 503d-504d), while the
incident does not seem to have been pressed until Douzy,
an indication that after late 870 it was considered closed.
We may note in passing that the attack also is not mentioned in HR Opusculum.

The following hypothetical chronology may then be
drawn. Having received the papal letters and been rebuffed by Charles upon their presentation to him, the
bishop treated the papal orders as a mandate for action;
then possibly the troops were sent by Charles for the purpose of restoring Poilly to Nortmannus. At Verberie the
bishop presented his case, which was rejected by the
bishops, as was the anathema. If Poilly was not given
back to Nortmannus before then, it presumably was restored thereafter. Violence against the count's wife
would better account for the anger of the *proceres* at
Verberie than would the anathema alone (*PL* 126. 315c).
Hence the bishop sent his second letter to Rome and also
the letter to Charles that eventually led to his imprison-
onment. The Conrad-Rudolf agreement was probably formulated at Verberie to permit the king to avoid blame
for having beneficed Nortmannus; thus the new letter to

Hadrian stressed the role of the king, and of the archbishop, in taking the goods of the kingdom. The subsequent reconciliation between Bishop Hincmar and King
Charles resulted in the latter's agreeing to restore the
villa at last, and Hincmar occupied it after his return
from Lorraine in January 870 (*PL* 124. 1029-31, especially 1030d), presumably this time ejecting Nortmannus himself. The problems connected with the contested properties were probably settled at Servais in September 870
(*PL* 126. 506-7); at any rate, prior to October (when
they are mentioned in a letter to the pope as having
been resolved; see *PL* 126. 185b-d).

It seems likely that the letters of admission were
part of the price of settlement and were then presumably
exacted from the bishop to protect against any renewal
of his charges to the pope. A priori they are appropriate to either September 870 (when Charles would definitely have received the second papal letter) or to the
latter part of 869 (when the bishop, then on good terms
with the king, might have been anxious to remove the
pressure from his monarch). The earlier date is more
likely, because of the apparent reference at HR Opusculum, ch. 43 (*PL* 126. 441c), and Hadrian II's reference
to Charles's lies about Hincmar (presumably concerning
Poilly, which was the subject of the earlier papal correspondence; and, further, Charles would not be likely
to go too far into questions that involved Lothar II).
Since the papal letter must date from 869 (see Reg. HL,
nos. 63-65), it is likely that the written admission
was given as a guarantee against what the pope might
continue to assert both in general and as evidence of
Charles's character; hence, written late in 869, it was
probably a prerequisite to the restoration of the **villa**.

On the historicity of the actual agreement made by
Bishop Hincmar with the two Welfs, it is far more difficult to make a judgment; but one tends to regard this
as dubious simply out of commonsense. Granted that such
agreements were frequently hard to prove during the
ninth century, yet this was no small matter. Involving
agents of the king, the king himself, and eventually the
pope as well, the assumption of historicity requires
that Hincmar of Laon himself had either forgotten the

agreement or was so insane or stupid as to think there
was no chance of its being discovered. Further, in November 870, he again mentions Nortmannus in terms calling
for his punishment as a violator of church property (*PL*
124. 1036b), although he had, as his uncle was quick to
point out (*PL* 126. 504b), already signed statements that
effectively precluded such a claim. A clue may be provided by the passage in which the archbishop argues that
he was not responsible for the royal policy (HR Opusculum, ch. 40, at *PL* 126. 438), which, when taken with
the plea made by Nortmannus to the archbishop (*PL* 126.
586a), clearly indicates Charles's own danger as mentioned above. Thus it seems likely that the agreement
did not in fact occur, but had been first asserted by
royal witnesses and had then been put into writing by
the bishop himself, in an attempt to eliminate at a critical time at least this area of possible papal interference. It was, if not quite fair, at least quite
effective.

Notes

Chapter I

1. See Vogel, *Die Normannen und das fränkische Reich*, and more recently, Musset, *Les invasions*, 2, chs. 3 and 7. Also, cf. d'Haenens, *Les invasions normande en Belgique*.

2. On the serious attacks of the mid-ninth century, see the many articles of Lot, especially "Godfried et Sidroc;" "Sidroc sur la Loire;" "La grande invasion normande." For Oscelle, see Lair, "Les Normands."

3. BML, 1435d. See especially Calmette, *La diplomatie carolingienne*, pp. 52 ff. On Louis the German, see Zatschek, "Ludwig der Deutsche."

4. Reg. HL, no. 4.

5. BML, 1435k; Calmette, *La diplomatie carolingienne*, p. 53.

6. *Ann. Bert.*, p. 79.

7. On Judith, see Cabaniss, "Judith Augusta and Her Time."

8. On the Treaty of Verdun, see Classen, "Die Verträge;" Ganshof, "On the Genesis;" Mayer, *Der Vertrag von Verdun*. Pepin died in 838.

9. On the "rule of concord," see Doizé, "Le gouvernement."

10. *Annales sancti Benigni Divionensis*, MGH SS 13. 39. The standard source for the early portion of the reign of CB, covering the years to 851, is Lot and

Halphen, *Le règne de Charles le Chauve*, 1. The only
full biography is that of Zumthor, *Charles le Chauve*,
a brief popular work.

11. According to Nithard, *Historiae*, 3, ch. 6, in
Rau, 1:111. There are several portraits of CB. For
the type, see the first bible of CB (Paris BN lat. 1,
fol. 423); reproduced in Zumthor, *Charles le Chauve*,
p. 85.

12. See Thompson, *Literacy of the Laity*, p. 32.

13. The passage quoted here is my own translation
from the Latin source. *Ann Bert.*, pp. 44-45.

14. Russell, in *Late Ancient and Medieval Population*, pp. 94-95, estimates the population of Carolingian Gaul to have been just over 5 million.

15. At least these terms were used by Louis the
Pious to describe them; Astronomer, *Vita Hludowici*,
2, ch. 61, in Rau, 1:372.

16. Auzias, *L'Aquitaine carolingienne*, p. 299. In
857 Pepin II called upon the Normans for aid in his
contest with CB; Lot, "La grande invasion normande," p.
725. For a good recent account of some of the problems
of Aquitanian history in the latter half of the ninth
century, see Oexele, "Bischof Ebroin von Poitiers."

17. Dhondt, *Etudes sur la naissance*, pp. 82 ff. The
studies of Merlet, such as his *Guerres d'indépendence
de la Bretagne*, should be read with care. For a chart
of the Breton dukes, see Kienast, *Der Herzogstitel*,
p. 141.

18. *Annales regni francorum*, in Rau, 1:72.

19. For convenient discussions of this class, see
Poupardin, *Le royaume de Provence*, pp. 377 ff., and
Dhondt, *Etudes sur la naissance*, pp. 315 ff.

20. Lot, "Les tributs au Normands." See also the discussion of Joranson, *Danegeld in France*, pp. 33, 42-43.

21. MGH *Cap.* 2. 427.

22. MGH *Cap.* 2, no. 247, pp. 427-41.

23. Calmette, *La diplomatie carolingienne,* pp. 59 ff.

24. See Mohr, "Die Krise des kirchlichen Einheits-programmes."

25. MGH *AA* 9. 552-612; Griffe, *La Gaule chrétienne à l'époque romain,*" 2:113-17.

26. On Charlemagne's ecclesiastical reforms, Lesne, *La hiérarchie épiscopale,* remains essential. See also Ganshof, "The Church and the Royal Power;" Delaruelle, "Charlemagne et l'église;" Büttner, "Mission und Kirchenorganisation."

27. See Delaruelle, "En relisant le "De institutione regia" de Jonas d'Orléans."

28. Lesne, *La hiérarchie épiscopale,* p. 198.

29. See ch. 4 below.

30. Boussinesq and Laurent, *Histoire de Reims,* 1:49 ff.

31. *Dictionnaire d'archéologie chrétienne et de liturgie,* 14 2:2213.

32. Ibid.

33. Boussinesq and Laurent, *Histoire de Reims,* 1:57.

34. Vercauteren, *Etude sur les civitates,* pp. 36 ff.

35. *Dictionnaire d'archéologie chrétienne et de liturgie,* 14^2:2224.

36. Wallace-Hadrill, *The Long-Haired Kings,* pp. 151 ff.

37. See Duchesne, *Fastes épiscopaux*, 3:9.

38. Duchesne, *Fastes épiscopaux*, 3:81.

39. Ibid., pp. 88-141.

40. Boussinesq and Laurent, in *Histoire de Reims*, 1:307, provide a reconstruction of the church.

41. Ibid., pp. 144 ff.

42. Duchesne, *Fastes épiscopaux*, 3:12 ff.

43. On Ebbo of Reims, see *Dictionnaire de biographie française*, 12:1087-89; McKeon, "Archbishop Ebbo of Reims."

44. CB himself was responsible for much of the loss, according to HR; *Vita sancti Remigii*, ch. 28, in MGH *SS rer. merov.* 3. 328.

45. The request was made at Ver in December 844. MGH *Cap.* 2. 385.

46. HR, *De praedestinatione II*, ch. 36, in *PL* 125. 382; MGH *Epp.* 8. 180. The principal biographical accounts are those of C. F. J. von Noorden, *Hinkmar Erzbischof von Rheims*, and Schrörs, *Hinkmar, Erzbischof von Reims*. See also Gess, *Merkwürdigkeiten aus dem Leben und den Schriften Hinkmars*; Pritchard, *Hincmar, Archbishop of Rheims*; Diez, *De Hincmari vita et ingenio*; Loupot, *Vie de Hincmar*; Vidieu, *Hincmar de Reims*; Lee, "Hincmar;" and Manitius, *Lateinischen Literatur des Mittelalters*, 1:339-54.

47. For nobility, see Loup de Ferrières, *Correspondence*, no. 43 (ed. Levillain, p. 180); for family, see Flodoard, 3. 26. 545.

48. Flodoard 3. 26. 545.

49. Ibid., p. 475.

50. On the abbot Hilduin, see Lot, "De quelques personnages," pp. 461-63. On the literary production at Reims under Hincmar, see Carey, "Scriptorium of Reims."

51. Flodoard, 3. 1. 475.

52. MGH *Epp.* 8[1]. 202.

53. Flodoard, 3. 1. 475.

54. Ibid., p. 474.

55. Ibid., p. 475.

56. HR, *De divortio Hlotharii regis,* interr. ii, resp. (*PL* 125. 641). On the poor relations that existed between Hincmar and Ebbo's initial champion, Lothar I, for several years, see Lesne, "Hincmar et l'empereur Lothaire."

57. Tessier, 1, no. 57, pp. 162, 163.

58. See Calmette, *La diplomatie carolingienne*, pp. 191-94.

59. MGH *Epp.* 8[1], no. 126, p. 64.

60. MGH *Cap.* 2, no. 269, pp. 295-97.

61. Reg. HL, no. 4.

62. MGH *Epp.* 8[1], no. 126, p. 64.

63. Cf. n. 43 above.

64. See Vercauteren, *Etude sur les civitates*, p. 238, and cf. Longnon, *Atlas historique*, p. 120; Duchesne, *Fastes épiscopaux*, 3:25.

65. *PL* 126. 334b. To HR, arguing later, this made his nephew the equivalent of a corebishop; PL 126. 340c-d. This information is also given by the archbishop in the *Vita sancti Remigii*, ch. 16, in MGH *SS rer. merov.* 3.

300-6. Krusch, "Reimser-Remigius Fälschungen," pp. 550
ff., found the passage suspect, since it appeared to
fit so well the argument against HL. But Jones et al.
("Authenticity of the Testamentum sancti Remigii," pp.
367-68), observe that the evidence indicates that
Archbishop Hincmar, regardless of his motives and
intents, is probably providing accurate information.

66. MGH *Conc.*, pp. 87-99.

67. Vercauteren, *Etude sur les civitates*, pp. 328-
29.

68. On the ninth century episcopal school of Laon,
see Jeauneau, "Les écoles de Laon et d'Auxerre au IXe
siècle," pp. 496-509. See also the studies of Contreni,
especially "Formation of Laon's Cathedral Library."

69. See Carey, "Scriptorium of Reims."

70. Flodoard, 3. 26. 545.

71. Beck, "Selection of Bishops Suffragan to
Hincmar of Reims," p. 277 and n. 9.

72. HR Epp. no. 198, p. 212. Pardulus was vidâme
of the church of Reims and abbot of Montier-en-Der.

73. See ch. 5 below.

74. Or possibly early 858. His last certain mention occurs in an act dated 6 February 858 (Tessier,
1:499-501), but a forgery dated 24 January 858 speaks
of him as living (ibid., 2:575-80). See Beck, "Selection of Bishops Suffragan to Hincmar of Reims," p. 280
and n. 15.

75. The relationship between nephew and maternal
uncle was extremely close among the Germans and Franks.
Regarding literary treatments of the theme, see Bell,
The Sister's Son in the Medieval German Epic. On HL,
see Dupin, *Bibliothèque,* 9:131-72; *Histoire litteraire
de la France,* 5:522-27; Ceillier, *Histoire générale,*
12:635-37; Cellot, *Vita Hincmari junioris,* in Mansi,

16. 688-724; Le Long, *Histoire du diocèse de Laon*, pp. 118-21; Gess, *Merkwürdigkeiten*, pp. 271-331; Noorden, *Hinkmar*, ch. 5; Schrörs, *Hinkmar*, pp. 259 ff., 315-53; Vidieu, *Hincmar*, pp. 82-114; Delius, *Hinkmar, Bischof von Laon*, and "Papst Hadrian II."

76. *PL* 126. 545a.

77. Estimated, since he was raised at Reims, i.e., presumably following 845; *PL* 126. 488c.

78. *PL* 126. 540b.

79. *PL* 126. 503c.

80. Especially *PL* 126. 379-80c.

81. Following HR, at *PL*, 126. 483-84. Cf. the possible reference at Eriugena, *Carmina*, x, in MGH *Poet. lat.* 3. 542.

82. See *PL* 126. 448b ff.; cf. ibid. 383b.

83. *PL* 126. 455c-d; cf. ibid. 488c.

84. Thus, *PL* 126. 487-88.

85. MGH *Cap.* 2. 276; MGH *Epp.* 8[1]. 55.

86. *PL* 126. 292b-c.

87. On the ordination, see *PL* 126. 292c-293a. In general, Andrieu, "Le sacre épiscopal d'après Hincmar de Reims." See MGH *Form.*, p. 556, for an example of the examination of a bishop, and Mansi, 15. 861-66, for one conducted by HR.

88. *PL* 126. 292c. An example at MGH *Form.*, p. 555.

89. *PL* 126. 292c, 412d, 544b-c. Devisse, in *Hincmar et la loi*, p. 56, suggests that the canonical collection exists in Paris lat. 12445. See also Conrat, "Hinkmariana." The archbishop apparently gave his nephew other books as well at various times; see *PL* 126. 316d.

90. Following HR, in the instructions given for ordination, at *PL* 126. 186d-188d.

91. *PL* 124. 1029a.

92. *PL* 126. 495d; cf. *PL* 124. 1029c ff.

93. *PL* 124. 1031d. The time was probably c. 864-65. Cf. *Ann. Bert.*, p. 105.

94. *PL* 124. 1032a.

95. See Quierzy: March 858 (Reg. HL, no. 4; n. 62 above) and December 858 (n. 60 above); Metz, 859 (MGH *Cap.* 2. 442); Savonnières, 859 (MGH *Cap.* 2. 450); Tusey, 860 (*PL* 124. 1039b, 1040a; *PL* 126. 496d; cf. ch. 6 below); Pîtres-Soissons, 862 (Mansi, 15. 636, 663; *PL* 126. 510c, 602a; Havet, "Questions mérovingiennes," p. 240; cf. ch. 4 below); Verberie, 863 (Tessier, 2:85; cf. ch. 4 below); Soissons, 866 (Mansi, 15. 731, 734, 737; cf. ch. 4 below); Troyes, 867 (Mansi, 15. 796; cf. ch. 4 below).

96. Thus, *PL* 126. 645.

97. See appendix 2 below.

98. See ch. 4 below.

99. Cf. n. 82 above, and *Carmina Scottorum*, iii, in MGH *Poet. lat.* 3. 686.

100. *PL* 126. 295-96.

101. *PL* 126. 463c, 642c.

102. Ibid.; cf. *PL* 126. 467a.

103. *PL* 126. 424c-d, 486a, 544b-c, 642c. Flodoard indicates that HR sent his nephew letters of admonition, intending to guide his behavior (also at MGH *Epp.* 8[1] nos. 119, 123, pp. 58, 59; Reg. HL, nos. 5, 6); the passage at *PL* 126. 488c-d may be drawn from one of these.

104. One his uncle would use against him; see *PL* 126.

455d, and cf. 463a-b, 499a. See also the statement at Mansi, 15. 664e.

105. *PL* 126. 449a; cf. col. 463a-b.

106. *PL* 126. 642c-643a.

Chapter II

1. See Lesne, *Histoire de la propriété ecclésias-tique,* 2.

2. Ganshof, "The Church and the Royal Power," p. 218.

3. Ganshof, "The Church and the Royal Power," pp. 219-20.

4. On the *divisio,* see Ganshof, *Feudalism,* pp. 18-19; but cf. discussion of Goffart, *The Le Mans Forgeries,* pp. 11, 13 ff. On the tithe, Lesne, "La dîme des biens ecclésiastiques," remains useful.

5. Ganshof, "The Church and the Royal Power," p. 221. The time of institution is not certain. See the discussions of Constable, "Nona et Decima," pp. 225 ff.; Lesne, "La dîme des biens ecclésiastiques," p. 495 and n. 2; and Boyd, *Tithes and Parishes,* ch. 2.

6. MGH *Cap.* I, no. 138, pp. 275-80.

7. See Goffart, *The Le Mans Forgeries,* pp. 14 ff. Herlihy, "Church Property on the European Continent," indicates a great increase in the land claimed by the church in the late eighth century and the first half of the ninth. pp. 87 ff.

8. Thus HR, at MGH *Epp.* 8[1], no. 126, p. 64. Cf. ch. 1 above.

9. MGH *Cap.,* I, no. 227, pp. 113-16, for the six

capitula presented, *capitula* 4 and 5 especially (pp. 114-16).

10.   MGH *Cap.* 2, no. 291, pp. 383-87; see especially *capitulum* 12 (pp. 385-87).

11.   MGH *Cap.* 2, no. 292, pp. 387-88.

12.   MGH *Cap.* 2, no. 293, pp. 390-421.   The proposed legislation consisted of eighty-three *capitula*, of which *capitula* 1 to 24 were issued at councils held prior to Meaux, *capitula* 25 to 82 at Meaux, and *capitulum* 83 at Paris.   For a discussion of the date, see de Clercq, *La législation religieuse franque*, 2:120-22.

13.   MGH *Cap.* 2, no. 257, pp. 261-62.

14.   Thus, see *PL* 126. 122-32, in connection with which cf. ch. 7 below.   On the theme in the sermon and apocalypse literature of the time, see Lesne, *Histoire de la propriété ecclésiastique*, 2:236 ff.   A paradigm sermon by HR was presented at Quierzy in 857.   See n. 37 below.   On Carolingian sermon literature, see Linsenmayer, *Geschichte der Predigt*, pp. 14 ff.

15.   *Capitulare missorum*, ch. 5, in MGH *Cap.* 2. 268.

16.   *Capitulare missorum*, ch. 11, in MGH *Cap.* 2. 270.

17.   *PL* 124. 1027a-b.

18.   See *PL* 126. 495d; cf. *PL* 124. 1029c ff.

19.   See *PL* 126. 495-96.   For Nortmannus as count, see Mansi, 15. 679d; as friend of HL, Mansi, 15. 650c.

20.   See *PL* 126. 643a-b.

21.   *PL* 125. 1035c.

22.   *PL* 126. 637d. This is not the same man whom the

bishop excommunicated; see ch. 4 below. For a Count
Amalbertus see Flodoard, 3. 26. 546-47.

23. *PL* 125. 1035c. Cf. the letters sent by Charles
to the archbishop regarding such charges, which are
mentioned at *PL* 126. 570b, and likely in reference to
these cases, although they may postdate the assembly at
Pîtres.

24. *PL* 125. 1035e-1037a.

25. Ibid. On the *advocatus*, see Laprat, "Avoués,
avoueries ecclésiastiques;" Balon, *Jus medii aevi* 1:17
ff.

26. *PL* 124. 1025-26, 125. 1037a-b. Archbishop Hincmar
refers clearly to the double charge at *PL* 126. 94-95.

27. *PL* 125. 1037b; cf. *PL* 126. 642a-b, though the
archbishop's remarks are some three years later. On the
vicedominus, see Ganshof, *Frankish Institutions*, p. 48;
Balon, *Jus medii aevi*, 2, ch. 2.

28. *PL* 125. 1035c.

29. Charles arrived at Pîtres about 15 August; *Ann.
Bert.*, p. 150.

30. *PL* 124. 1027a-b.

31. *PL* 124. 1025-28; Reg. HL, no. 24. For the
date, see *PL* 124. 1025c.

32. Council of Hippo, ann. 393, canons 9-11, Dionysius Exiguus, *Codex canonum*, in *PL* 67. 189a-b.

33. *PL* 124. 1027-28. The bishop invoked the
exceptio spolii, concerning which see ch. 5 below. For
two other examples, see *PI*, pp. 184, 201.

34. The treatise, known by the title "Quaterniones,"
forms the first and longest part of a set of three
treatises entitled *Pro ecclesiae libertatum defensione*;
see Reg. HL, no. 25.

35.   See the implied statement of *PL* 125. 1049-50;
explicit at col. 1059c-d, with which cf. the use of disas-
sociation by the archbishop in quite other circumstances,
thus *PL* 126. 631a-b.

36.   *PL* 125. 1038b.   The argument relies on *Codex
Theodosianus*, 16. 2.8, 16, 26, 29-31, 34-35   (see *PL*
125. 1038-39); Ansegis, *Capitularium collectio*, 1, ch.
87, in MGH *Cap.* 1. 405; *Codex Africanus*, ch. 13 in *PL*
67. 188d.

37.   *PL* 125. 1042d.   At cols. 1042-43 the archbishop
cites Pseudo-Urban (*PI*, p. 144), drawing for this and for
much of what follows from the *Collectio de raptoribus*,
MGH *Cap.* 2, no. 266, p. 289.   This work had been written
by him for presentation at the assembly held at Quierzy
in February 857; see V. Krause, "Hincmar von Reims."   In
the *Quaterniones*, other Pseudo-Isidorian material from
the *Collectio* or elsewhere includes Pseudo-Stephen and
Pseudo-Lucius (*PI*, pp. 184, 178, 179); see *PL* 125. 1043a-c.
The sentiments here expressed had great significance for
HL.

38.   *PL* 125. 1044b-1045a.   The conciliar support is
drawn from the councils of Hippo (cf. n. 32 above) and
Carthage, ann. 407, canon 9 (*PI*, p. 298).   The archbishop
cites *Codex Theodosianus*, 16. 2.12, 23, and 41 on clerical
immunity (*PL* 125. 1045b-1046a), and Pseudo-Stephen (*PI*,
pp. 181-82) on the necessary qualifications of accusers
(*PL* 125. 1047-48).

39.   *PL* 125. 1043c-d, supported by the councils of
Antioch, canons **24, 25** (*PI*, pp. 272-73); Gangres, canons 7,
8 (*PI*, p. 265); Chalcedon, canon 25 (*PI*, p. 287), and 1
Toledo, canon 11 (*PI*, pp. 350-51).

40.   *PL* 125. 1050b-c.   These benefices may be passed
on to the vassal's children.

41.   *PL* 125. 1050-51.   Public judgment is of great injury to the church under any circumstances.   Thus, the
hearing must be private, the judgment by *judices electi*,
the procedure careful and thorough (cols. 1051-52).

42.   *PL* 125. 1054-55. Cf. the archbishop's use of an

exceptio spolii regulation drawn from Leo of Bourges (at col. 1047c); he refers it to Pope Leo I, as also at *PL* 124. 886d.

43. See *PL* 125. 1054b-c.

44. *PL* 125. 1057c-d.

45. *PL* 126. 95c-d; but cf. heading of the *Extemporalis admonitio*, at Mansi, 16. 781a-b.

46. *PL* 126. 95d. The *Rotula*, the second part of the *Pro ecclesiae libertatum defensione*, is at *PL* 125. 1060-65. See Reg. HL, no. 25.

47. Perhaps implied at *PL* 126. 95c-d.

48. *Codex Africanus*, canon. 19, 15, 104 (*PL* 67. 189, 190, 216); *Codex Theodosianus*, 16. 2.12; Ansegis, *Capitularium collectio*, I, chs. 8, 28, 38 (MGH *Cap.* I. 398, 400).

49. *PL* 125. 1061b. Following the letter of Innocent I to Victricius of Rouen (especially at ch. 3, in *PI*, pp. 529-30), a *causa maior* should go to Rome; cf. *PL* 125. 1061c.

50. *PL* 125. 1061-62.

51. Ibid. On the primate of the province, see ch. 5 below.

52. *PL* 125. 1068a-c.

53. *PL* 125. 1064b-c.

54. *PL* 125. 1064c.

55. Perhaps a hint at *PL* 126. 643b.

56. Ibid.; Mansi, 16. 781a. Cf. *PL* 125. 1064c-1065b.

57. The *Extemporalis admonitio* (*PL* 125. 1065-70). *Ann. Bert.*, ann. 868, p. 150; Mansi, 16. 781a. See, for

the announced subject, *PL* 125. 1065-66. The references
are to Ansegis, *Capitularium collectio*, 1, chs. 8, 28,
38, 77 (MGH *Cap*. 1. 398, 400, 405).

58. *PL* 125. 1066a-1068a cites the assemblies of
Coulaines (MGH *Cap*. 2, no. 245; see ch. 1, at p. 255),
Beauvais, Meersen (ann. 851), Soissons (ann. 853),
Quierzy and Brienne (ann. 858), Coblence (ann. 860)(MGH
Cap. 2, no. 242, pp. 154-55).

59. This according to *Ann. Bert.*, p. 150. But cf. *PL*
126. 95a. The letters of CB mentioned at *PL* 126. 570 may
be directives to hold this synod. But see the discussion
at Reg. HL, no. 28.

60. *Ann. Bert.*, pp. 150-51.

61. *PL* 126. 94-95a. The archbishop's ambivalence
seems to appear here.

62. *PL* 126. 95a-b. Odo of Beauvais was sent to
Charles to report on the synod. He probably carried
this letter from the archbishop and the apologia of HL
(Reg. HL, nos. 27, 26); see the subheading to the latter
at *PL* 124. 1027-28.

63. On the mission of Celsanus, see *PL* 126. 643a;
Mansi, 16. 651a-b. On all, Reg. HL, no. 17.

64. Reg. HL, no. 29. See Imbart de la Tour, *Les
élections épiscopales*, p. 29.

65. *Ann. Bert.*, p. 151; Mansi, 16. 578e, 651b.

66. The letters sent to King Charles and Archbishop
Hincmar may be found at Hadrian *Epp.*, nos. 14, 15, pp.
715-17 (JE, 2911, 2910). The letter to HL may be indicated at *PL* 126. 495c. See McKeon, "Toward a Reestablishment," pp. 172-73, 175-76.

67. MGH *Epp*. 6. 716, 717.

68. Thus the implication of *PL* 126. 643a. But cf.
n. 61 above.

69. He had been ill for some time; see *PL* 126. 606b
referring to June 869. At Attigny in mid-870 he was
suffering from rheumatism; Mansi, 16. 856e, and ch. 5
below.

70. *PL* 126. 585-86. The incident may not have
occurred at Quierzy. See appendix 2 below.

71. *PL* 126. 570-71.

72. Mansi, 16. 579d.

73. Mansi, 16. 579d-e; *PL* 126. 571a-b. Charles was
at Compiègne by Christmas (*Ann. Bert.*, p. 152) and into
January (Tessier, 2, no. 318).

74. *PL* 126. 571a-b.

75. Thus the recital of HR (*PL* 126. 571a-b), confirming his testimony in *Ann. Bert.*, p. 152; cf. *PL* 126.
499-500. On Odo of Beauvais, who was an important
figure in the late ninth-century church and will be
encountered frequently in the following pages, see
Grierson, "Eudes Ier." Grierson's belief that Odo was
archchaplain to Charles from 860 (ibid., p. 192) is
questioned by Tessier, *Diplomatique royale français*, p.
57, n. 1.

76. Mentioned at Mansi, 16. 617c.

77. Synopsized by Flodoard, 3. 23. 530. The fragment at Mansi, 16. 617d is probably from the same letter.

78. See Reg. HL, no. 37.

79. *Ann. Bert.*, p. 152; *PL* 126. 512b, 515b. See
Tessier, 2, no. 319, dated 30 January.

80. *Ann. Bert.*, p. 152.

81. *PL* 126. 605c; cf. col. 512b.

82. Inferred from *PL* 126. 603c. Cf. letter to Odo
quoted at Mansi, 16. 617e-618e.

83. *PL* 126. 511d-512. On the institution of the
interdict, see Krehbiel, *The Interdict,* ch. 1. For the
diocesan synod, see Feine, *Kirchliche Rechtsgeschichte,*
pp. 213 ff.

84. HR, at *PL* 126. 531c, says more than twenty. The
diploma for Saint-Vaast, which may date from this
council, has forty-three names, including those of
twenty-six bishops (ed. Drival,*Cartulaire de l'abbaye
de Saint-Vaast*, pp. 30-31; but see Reg. HL, no. 17), and
that for Charroux shows twenty-nine bishops present
(Mansi, 16. 552). A confected letter addressed to HL
by Bishop John of Cambrai, dated 24 April 869, is
extant; see Reg. HL, no. 178. On the likely circumstances of its origin, see Poncelet, "Les documents de
Claude Despretz."

85. *PL* 126. 526b, 500b. For a possible indication
that the excommunication of January 869 was discussed,
see *PL* 126. 526b.

86. *PL* 126. 531c; cf. *PL* 124. 992b. On this point,
see chs. 4 and 5 below.

87. See *PL* 126. 315c; cf. col. 566c. The *placitum*
was called for 1 May; *Ann. Bert.*, pp. 152-53.

88. *PL* 126. 315b-c.

89. Reg. HL, no. 41.

90. *PL* 126. 601-2, 604d. See the rather lame
explanation of these letters given by HR; Mansi, 16.
604-8. The archbishop admittedly wrote letters for
King Charles; see *PL* 126. 438c.

91. This would seem likely from the failure of his
name to appear on the Charroux diploma (Mansi, 16. 552),
but on the dubious quality of that document, see Reg.
HL, n. 17. Further, HR states that the bishop did not
appeal "*regulariter*" from Verberie (*PL* 126. 531c), which
presumably signifies that charges brought against him
remained unheard. HL, at *PL* 124, 992b, strengthens this
implication. The passage at *PL* 126. 313-14 may refer

to the bishop's exit, in which case secular force or connivance may already have been at work.

92. On this letter, see Reg. HL, no. 44.

93. Mansi, 16. 579-80, 653-54; CB, *Epistolae*, no. 7, passim (*PL* 124. 876-81).

94. *PL* 126. 185c ff., 643c-d.

95. Mansi, 16. 616d-e. For date and location of citation, see Reg. HL, no. 45.

96. *PL* 126. 604c.

97. Mansi, 16. 616d-e. The archbishop was apparently ill during this period; see *PL* 126. 606e.

98. Thus the archbishop's implication at *PL* 126. 500b.

99. *PL* 126. 512b-c; cf. cols. 532-33. I do not find, with Morrison, *Two Kingdoms*, n. 33, pp. 176-77 that this latter passage indicates the imprisonment was ordered by king and bishops; clearly, no synodal proceeding led to it. Cf. also HR, at *PL* 126. 500b.

100. Mansi, 16. 667a-b.

101. *PL* 126. 512c, 515c.

102. Ibid.

103. Mansi, 16. 857a; Reg. HL, no. 50.

104. In general, see the implication of *PL* 126. 554-55. On Teutlandus, see Mansi, 15. 983a; *PL* 126. 595a; but cf. wording of the same passage at Mansi, 16. 608d. Cf. *PL* 124. 1039b.

105. See *PL* 126. 512d, 572-74. The refusal of the viaticum was seen by the archbishop as a direct contravention of 1 Nicaea, canon 13 (Alberigo, *Conciliorum oecumenicorum decreta*, p. 11); see *PL* 126. 574a-b.

106. *PL* 126. 515d.

107. *PL* 126. 511d, 515a. Portions of the petition appear at *PL* 126. 511-12, 515-16.

108. Mansi, 16. 606b.

109. *PL* 126. 616b.

110. Mansi, 16. 857b-c. See Reg. HL, nos. 54-56.

111. *PL* 126. 511-14.

112. *PL* 126. 512-13.

113. See especially *PL* 126. 513d-514a.

114. *PL* 126. 514a-d.   The interdict had been in force for about five days; see *PL* 126. 613c.

115. The letter is at *PL* 126. 515-26; Reg. HL, no. 55.

116. *PL* 126. 517c-d.

117. *PL* 126. 523b-c.

118. *PL* 126. 524b.

119. *PL* 126. 525b-526a.

120. See Krehbiel, *The Interdict*, ch. 1 and especially p. 17.   Conran, *The Interdict*, p. 23, states that HR condemned not the interdict but what the author considered its abuse by his nephew.

121. *PL* 126. 529d.

122. *PL* 126. 531b-c.

123. *PL* 126. 526-31.

124. *PL* 126. 529b.

125. *PL* 126. 527c-d.

126. *PL* 126. 527-28, 529a.

127. *PL* 126. 529d-531c.

128. Judging from the fact that Charles had left Servais before that day, when he is found at Bèzu (Tessier, 2, no. 325, pp. 216-17), from the statement of HR that a council was awaited to deal with the matter (*PL* 126. 532-33) and from the hypothesis that the bishop accompanied the king to Pîtres. See Reg. HL, no. 60.

129. The letter is at *PL* 126. 531-33. On the date, see Reg. HL, no. 59.

130. On the chronology, see Reg. HL, no. 66. The date of Hincmar's appearance is indicated by two collections compiled in July; see Reg. HL, nos. 61, 62. That both Hincmars were at Pîtres may be indicated by *PL* 126. 534a, 438c, but this was not necessarily before a conciliar session; cf. de Clercq, *La legislation religieuse franque*, 2:280. The undated privilege for the monastery of Saint-Pierre-le-Vif is signed by twelve bishops, including Archbishop Hincmar but not the bishop of Laon (Quantain, *Cartulaire général de l'Yonne*, 1:98).

131. For the oath as presented by the archbishop, see *PL* 126. 575-76. On problems connected with it, see Reg. HL, nos. 60, 96. On the influence of Aeneas and Wenilon, see *PL* 126. 577a. The date is uncertain, and the sequence of events given by HR at *PL* 126. 313d-314d is of little help; see discussion at Reg. HL, nos. 60-62, 66. De Clercq, *La législation religieuse franque*, 2:282, suggests that the council effected the bishop's release. But Hincmar was at Laon by 8 July, and the oath preceded this; see HR *Libellus*, chs. 10-11 (*PL* 126. 575-81.

132. See appendix 2 below for discussion of the interpretation of such passages as *PL* 126. 585c, and Mansi, 16. 579c-d, 649c, 650a. All basically refer to the letter of HL mentioned at *PL* 126. 441c.

Chapter III

1. *PL* 125. 629, 672.

2. On the ordeal of water, see Esmein, *Les ordalies dans l'église gallicane*; Grelewski, "La réaction contre les ordalies;" Ganshop, "La preuve dans le droit franq." Hincmar of Reims explained and defended the institution in a letter at *PL* 126. 161-71.

3. On the events connected with the divorce and its political ramifications, see especially Parisot, *La royaume de Lorraine*, pp. 142-324; Calmette, *La diplomatie carolingienne*, pp. 69 ff.; Hefele-Leclercq, *Histoire des conciles*, 4^1:365 ff. Convenient shorter accounts may be found in Dupraz, "Deux preceptes de Lothaire II," pp. 204-24, and Lot, *Naissance de la France*, pp. 375-79. Regarding the effects of the situation in a broader context, see Hlawitschka, *Lotharingien und das Reich*, pp. 17 ff.; Haller, *Nikolaus I. und Pseudosidor*, pp. 4-15, 35 ff. passim.

4. *Ann Bert.*, ann. 855, p. 71.

5. For Louis, see Hartmann, *Geschichte Italiens im Mittelalter*, 3^1:231 ff.

6. *Ann. Bert.*, ann. 856, p. 73. See Poupardin, *Le royaume de Provence*, ch. 1. On Gerard of Vienne, see especially Louis, *Girart, comte de Vienne*, 1; Levillain, "Girart, comte de Vienne."

7. See Parisot, *Le royaume de Lorraine*, pp. 92 ff.

8. Ibid., pp. 86 ff.

9. Regino, *Chronicon*, ann. 859, in Rau, 3:188.

10. Benedict II, *Epistola*, in MGH *Epp*. 5. 612-14 (JE, 2669). See Poupardin, *Le Royaume de Provence*, pp. 42 ff.

11. See Parisot, *Le royaume de Lorraine*, p. 86.

12. Ibid., p. 147.

13. On the legal issues arising in connection with the divorce, see Esmein, *La mariage en droit canonique*, 1:9 ff.; Daudet, *Etudes sur l'histoire de la juridiction matrimoniale*, 1:94-122. For a convenient catalog of sources relating to Gunthar and his career, see Oediger, *Die Regesten der Erzbischöfe von Köln im Mittelalter*, 1, nos. 163-226, pp. 53-77.

14. *PL* 125. 629. It was also alleged that Hubert had made her pregnant, and that Theutberga had been rendered sterile by an abortion; cf. Nicholas *Epp.*, no. 46, pp. 322-25 (JE, 2870).

15. BML, 1282b.

16. On the invasion, see ch. 1 above.

17. An account of the first assembly at Aachen may be found in MGH *Cap.* 2, no. 305, pp. 463-66, as drawn from the *De divortio Hlotharii regis* of Hincmar of Reims; the passage is at *PL* 125. 629-641. For the alleged offense, see *PL* 125. 689-707. On Gunthar's violation of the confessional, see ibid., 641-645.

18. MGH *Cap.* 2, no. 306, pp. 466-68.

19. See *PL* 125. 645 ff.; MGH *Epp.* 8[1]. 74 ff.

20. For the request, *PL* 125. 627. The treatise is at *PL* 125. 619-772. A summary is given by Parisot, *Le royaume de Lorraine*, pp. 173-76. On the dissidents, see M. Sdralek, *Hincmars von Rheims kanonistisches Gutachten*, p. 127.

21. *PL* 125. 746-47.

22. But cf. Parisot, *Le royaume de Lorraine*, pp. 171 ff.

23. Halphen, *Charlemagne*, p. 344.

24. On this period, see Calmette, *La diplomatie carolingienne*, pp. 74 ff.

25. *Ann. Bert.*, ann. 860, 861, 862, pp. 84, 87, 88. Poupardin, *Le royaume de Provence*, pp. 26 ff.

26. *Ann. Bert.*, ann. 862, p. 87; *Gesta episcoporum Cameracensium*, MGH *SS* 8. 418; MGH *Cap.* 2. 160; Nicholas *Epp.*, no. 15, pp. 281-82 (JE, 2731). On Judith, see also ch. 7 below.

27. BML, 1293a.

28. Mansi, 15. 611-30.

29. See the dissident report, ibid., cols. 617-25.

30. Among the large literature on the development of the papacy during this period, see Haller, *Das Papsttum*, 2:7 ff.

31. For Nicholas I, Rocquain, *La papauté au moyen âge*, pp. 4-74, remains useful; as do the studies of Roy, "Principes du pape Nicolas Ier" and *Saint Nicolas Ier*. See also Mann, *Lives of the Popes in the Early Middle Ages*, 3:1-148. Norwood, "Political Pretensions of Pope Nicholas I," is a useful short treatment. See also Congar, "S. Nicolas Ier," and *L'ecclésiologie du haut moyen âge*, pp. 206 ff. Arquillière, *L'augustinisme politique*, pp. 189 ff., suggests that Nicholas presented not a new program but a new force.

32. Congar, *L'ecclésiologie du haut moyen âge*, pp. 207 ff.

33. See ch. 4 below.

34. Parisot, *Le royaume de Lorraine*, pp. 195-96.

35. *Ann. Bert.*, ann. 862, pp. 93-94.

36. Nicholas *Epp.*, nos. 3-6, pp. 268-72 (JE, 2702, 2701, 2699, 2698).

37. Ibid., nos. 10, 57, pp. 275-76, 355-62 (JE, 2725, 2723); cf. ibid., no. 106, pp. 618-19 (JE, 2697).

38. Parisot, *Le royaume de Lorraine*, p. 217.

39. Poupardin, *Le royaume de Provence*, p. 32.

40. Parisot, *Le royaume de Lorraine*, pp. 217-18.

41. *Ann. Bert.*, ann. 863, p. 98; cf. Nicholas *Epp.*, no. 53, pp. 340-51 (JE, 2886), at p. 343.

42. *Ann Bert.*, p. 99.

43. Ibid., pp. 99 ff.

44. *Ann. Bert.*, ann. 864, pp. 105 ff. See Parisot, *Le royaume de Lorraine*, pp. 241 ff.

45. See H. Fuhrmann, "Eine im Original erhaltene Propagandaschrift des Erzbischofs Gunthar von Köln;" the letter of the council of Pavia is edited at pp. 38-51.

46. See *Epistolae ad divortium Lotharii II regis pertinentes*, nos. 6 and 8, in MGH *Epp.* 6. 217, 219-22; Nicholas Epp., nos. 18-26, 29-32, pp. 284-93, 295-301 (JE, 2750, 2749, 2751-53, 2766, 2755, 2758, 2764, 2767, 2768).

47. Cf. ch. 4 below.

48. See Parisot, *Le royaume de Lorraine*, pp. 265ff.

49. MGH *Cap.*, 2 no. 244, pp. 165-67. Chaume, *Les origines du duché de Bourgogne*, 1:242-43, indicates the implicit threat to the realm of Lothar that seems a reasonable conclusion from ch. 7. See also Parisot, *Le royaume de Lorraine*, pp. 272 ff.; cf. n. 61 below.

50. *Ann. Bert.*, ann. 865, pp. 118 ff.; Calmette, *La diplomatie carolingienne*, p. 99.

51. Calmette, *La diplomatie carolingienne*, p. 101ff.

52. Parisot, *Le royaume de Lorraine*, pp. 288ff.

53. Nicholas *Epp.*, nos. 45-48, pp. 319-32 (JE, 2870-72).

54. Ibid., nos. 51-53, pp. 334-51 (JE, 2884-86).

55. Ibid., no. 50, p. 334 (JE, 2878). The latest extant letter of the pope to the German prelates is dated 31 October; ibid., no. 53, pp. 340-51 (JE, 2886).

56. Duchesne, *Liber pontificalis*, 2:167.

57. On Hadrian II, see especially, H. Grotz, *Erbe wider Willen*; Amann, *L'époque carolingienne*, pp. 395-412.

58. For Lothar's letter, see *Epistolae ad divortium Lotharii II regis pertinentes*, no. 18, MGH *Epp.* 6. 238-40. Hadrian's responses may be found at Hadrian *Epp.*, nos. 1, 4, pp. 695-97, 701 (JE, 2892, 2897). Lothar's uncles were also informed; ibid., nos. 6, 7, pp. 702-7 (JE, 2895, 2902).

59. See Parisot, *Le royaume de Lorraine*, pp. 313-15.

60. MGH *Cap.* 2, no. 245, pp. 167-68. An inscription in the Laon codex from which this source was edited identifies the time as the twenty-ninth year of the reign of Charles, and as the first indiction, i.e., 868 (p. 167), but the date has been the subject of controversy, since no mention of the meeting is made in the annals, since Lothar and Louis the German were reconciled shortly after the meeting, and due to difficulties in the itineraries of the two monarchs (see the chart in Parisot, *Le royaume de Lorraine*, p. 298n.). This latter problem is discussed by Calmette (*La diplomatie carolingienne*, pp. 195-200), whose argument is followed here. The first two criticisms of the date 868 do not seem to me to be significant. It is unlikely that such a meeting would have found mention in the widely circulated annals. But the majority of scholars have opted for 867 and have identified the meeting with that mentioned at *Ann. Bert.*, p. 136, and MGH *Epp.* 8[1].

205. Thus, see Noorden, *Hinkmar*, p. 223, n. 1; BML, p.
565; Dümmler, *Geschichte des ostfränkischen Reiches*,
2²:160 and n. 2; Parisot, *Le royaume de Lorraine*, p. 297
and n. 4; Zatschek, *Wie das erste Reich der Deutschen
entstand*, p. 123; Tessier, 2:156, n. 1; Brühl,
"Königspfalz und Bischofsstadt," p. 239; Oexele, "Die
Karolinger und die Stadt des heiligen Arnulf," p. 353;
Devisse, "Essai sur l'histoire d'une expression qui a
fait fortune," pp. 193-94 and n. 4. Other scholars besides Calmette whose choice is 868 are: Schrörs,
Hinkmar, p. 304, n. 4; Grotz, *Erbe wider Willen*, p. 97,
n. 27, and p. 199 and n. 27. C. de Clercq, *La
législation religieuse franque*, 2:267, feels the choice
between the two yet uncertain.

61. Parisot, *Le royaume de Lorraine*, p. 315.

62. MGH *Cap.* 2. 167.

63. *Ann. Bert.*, p. 153.

64. On Engelberga, see Pochettino, "L'imperatrice
Angilberga;" von Pölnitz-Kehr, "Kaiserin Angilberga;"
Odegaard, "Empress Engilberge." See also ch. 9 below.

65. For the speech, see Mansi, 16. 890-96, and
edited by Maasen, "Eine Rede des Papstes Hadrian II.
vom Jahre 869," pp. 532-54. Maasen's attribution of
the speech to Hadrian himself was challenged by Lapôtre,
"Hadrian II et les fausses décrétales," who argued for
Bishop Formosus (later pope). Lapôtre's view was
accepted by Parisot, *Le royaume de Lorraine*, p. 320, n.
2, but not by Dümmler, *Geschichte des ostfränkischen
Reiches*, 2:238, n. 1. See also Schrörs, "Eine
vermeintliche Konzilrede des Papstes Hadrian II."

66. *Ann. Bert.*, p. 157.

67. Ibid., p. 156.

68. *PL* 126. 533-34. The whole question should take
into account the remarks at *Ann. Bert.*, p. 153, concerning Charles's refusal to give a firm guarantee of
respect for Lotharingian autonomy.

69.   Reg. HL, no. 70.

70.   *Ann. Bert.*, p. 157.

71.   Ibid. See below, ns. 76ff.

72.   MGH *Cap.* 2, nos. 276, 302, pp. 338-41, 456-58; see Sprengler, "Die Gebete der Krönungsordines Hincmars von Reims," pp. 245-53. On the incident, see especially Péré, "Le sacre et le couronnement des rois de France," pp. 6-9; Oppenheimer, *Legend of the Sainte Ampoule*, pp. 169-77; Lemarignier, "Autour de la royauté française," pp. 6-7; Schramm, *Der König von Frankreich*, 1:145-50, 2:16-17; Schlesinger, "Karolingisches Königswahlen," pp. 114 ff. Of related if not direct interest is Michels, "La date du couronnement de Charles le Chauve." Friend, "Two Manuscripts of the School of St. Denis," relates the coronation theme of Paris lat. 1141 to the coronation of 869.

73.   MGH *Cap.* 2, no. 302, pp. 456-58.

74.   See Reg. HL, no. 74, and ch. 5 below for other events at Gondreville.

75.   The extant letters of this group may be found at Hadrian *Epp.*, nos. 16-18, pp. 717-21 (JE, 2917-19); the undated no. 19 (pp. 721-23; JE, 2921) also probably belongs to this group.

76.   *PL* 126. 611.

77.   *Ann. Bert.*, p. 169.

78.   At least, following the evidence of the *Annales Fuldenses*, ann. 870, in Rau, 3:76.

79.   See n. 6 above, and cf. ch. 7 below.

80.   See Tessier, 2, nos. 330, 334, 337, 342, 348, pp. 228-35, 238-40, 244-48, 263-65, 274-76.

81.   Ibid., pp. 232-35.

82. Thus, e.g., *PL* 124. 875-76.

83. On the complex problem of determining the
identity of this and other Hilduins, see Lot, "De
quelques personnages," especially pp. 465-66, 476ff.,
with which cf. the disagreement of Calmette, "Les abbés
Hilduin au IXe siècle," and Lot's "Les abbés Hilduin au
IXe siècle. Réponse à M. J. Calmette."

84. Duchesne, *Fastes épiscopaux*, 3:43. See
Heydenreich, *Die Metropolitangewalt der Erzbischöfe von
Trier*, pp. 67-69.

85. Cf. Parisot, *Le royaume de Lorraine*, pp. 364-65,
which favors a later date.

86. On Richilde, see Poupardin, *Le royaume de
Provence*, pp. 41 ff. Cf. the genealogical chart in
Hlawitschka, *Die Anfänge des Hauses Habsburg-Lotharingen*,
p. 41.

87. *Ann. Bert.*, p. 167.

88. Ibid., p. 169.

89. Duchesne, *Fastes épiscopaux*, 3:183-84; Oediger,
Die Regesten der Erzbischöfe von Köln im Mittelalter,
1, nos. 227-76, pp. 77-92.

90. See the protest of Hincmar of Reims and five of
his archiepiscopal colleagues, at *PL* 126. 262-64 (and in
Flodoard, 3. 21. 511-13).

91. *Ann. Bert.*, p. 169. On all, Parisot, *Le royaume
de Lorraine*, pp. 350ff.; Calmette, *La diplomatie
carolingienne*, p. 123.

92. *Ann. Bert.*, p. 169.

93. The pact of Aachen may be found at MGH *Cap.*, 2,
no. 250, pp. 191-92; it is given by Hincmar of Reims at
Ann. Bert., p. 169. For the earlier agreement at Metz,
see MGH *Cap.* 2, no. 245, pp. 167-68, and n. 61 above.

94. *Ann. Bert.*, p. 169.

95. The king is found at Saint-Denis on 5 April; Tessier, 2:236.

96. *Ann. Bert.*, p. 169.

97. Ibid., pp. 169-70.

98. Ibid., p. 171.

99. The treaty was to have been signed on 1 August, but was postponed due to an injury suffered by Louis; *Ann. Bert.*, p. 171. For the terms see, MGH *Cap.* 2, no. 251, pp. 193-95, and *Ann. Bert.*, pp. 171-74. Compare the discussion at Parisot, *Le royaume de Lorraine* pp. 365-78, with Vanderkindere, *Formation territoriale des principautés belge*, pp. 16-19. See also the brief discussion of Thompson, *Dissolution of the Carolingian Fisc*, pp. 52 ff. The interpretation of a passage is subject of dispute between Hoyoux, "La clause ardennaise." The southeast parts of the division are clearly shown in Chaume, *Les origines du duché de Bourgogne*, 1:251. For a general discussion of the treaties between the Carolingian monarchs, see Ganshof, "Treaties of the Carolingians," pp. 36ff.

100. Thus, see *PL* 126. 179.

101. *PL* 125. 611-12.

102. *PL* 126. 175-76; cf. n. 108 below.

103. *Ann. Bert.*, p. 177. On the mission see Schieffer, *Die päpstlichen Legaten in Frankreich*, pp. 111-14. The papal letters may be found at Hadrian *Epp.*, pp. 724-30 (JE, 2926-29). See also Bertolini, "La dottrina gelasiana," pp. 749 ff.

104. MGH *Epp.* 6. 729.

105. *PL* 126. 174.

106. *PL* 126. 174-86, of 20-25 October; see Reg. HL,

no. 114. On this important letter, see Amann, *L'époque carolingienne*, pp. 402ff.; David, *La souveraineté*, pp. 121ff.; Knabe, *Die gelasianische Zweitgewaltentheorie*, pp. 81ff.; Lemarignier, "Autour de la royauté française," p. 7; Halphen, *Charlemagne*, p. 353; Grotz, *Erbe wider Willen*, pp. 252-68.

107. *PL* 126. 176.

108. *PL* 126. 177. Compare the words directed by the archbishop to the pope, at col. 177, with those of Hincmar of Laon to his uncle the previous May (*PL* 124. 589).

109. *PL* 126. 179.

110. *PL* 126. 181.

Chapter IV

1. On Rothad, see Schrörs, *Hinkmar*, pp. 237-70; Hefele-Leclercq, *Histoire des conciles*, 4^1:343 ff. The bishop signed the deposition of Ebbo in 833 (HR, *De praedestinatione II*, in *PL* 125. 390c; MGH *Epp.* 8^1. 182) and was present at his reinstatement seven years later (Ebbo, *Apologeticus,* MGH *Conc.* 2^2. 804-5; but cf. *Narratio clericorum Remensium,* ibid., 808-9). For Rothad at Hincmar's ordination, see MGH *Epp.* 8^1. 209. Hincmar was ordained by Archbishop Wenilon of Sens, as Andrieu notes ("Le sacre épiscopal d'après Hincmar de Reims," p. 30 and n. 2), correcting Lesne, *La hiérarchie épiscopale*, pp. 209, 218.

2. At first in connection with Gottschalk, see, e.g., MGH *Epp.* 8^1. no. 169, p. 160. For later reports of maladministration, see ibid., pp. 7, 40-41.

3. The suggestion of Nicholas I; MGH *Epp.* 6. 381-82, 389.

4. MGH *Epp.* 8^1. 53. The main offender, according to Hincmar of Reims, was bishop Prudentius of Troyes; HR,

De ecclesiis et capellis, ed. Gundlach, p. 102. The
question of the nature and origin of the proprietary
church system is much disputed. The two principle views
are represented by Stutz in *Geschichte des kirchlichen
Benefizialwesens* and "Leben und Pfründe," and by Dopsch
in *Wirtschaftliche und soziale Grundlagen der
europäischen Kulturentwicklung*, 2:230 ff. Feine, a
student of Stutz, concurs with his view; see Feine,
"Ursprung, Wesen und Bedeutung des Eigenkirchentums."
Both positions may be found in English: in Stutz's
essay, "The Proprietary Church as an Element of Mediaeval Germanic Ecclesiastical Law," and in the translation of Dopsch, *Economic and Social Foundations of
European Civilization*, pp. 241 ff. See also Imbart de
la Tour, "Private Churches in Ancient France." Various
legislative efforts were made to reform the practice
during the earlier years of the ninth century; see Jedin,
Handbook of Church History, 3:261, n. 3. For a convenient bibliography, see Boyd, *Tithes and Parishes*, pp.
252-54, supplemented by Feine, *Kirchliche Rechtsgeschichte*, pp. 170-72.

5. See HR, *De ecclesiis et capellis*, in the
editions by Gundlach and Gaudenzi. These two editions
are discussed in Gietl, "Hincmars collectio de ecclesiis
et capellis," pp. 572-73. The preface and opening
section may also be found in MGH *Epp.* 8[1]. 52-55. See
also the recent treatment in Lemarignier, "Quelques
remarques sur l'organisation ecclésiastique," pp. 478-79.

6. On complaints regarding Rothad, see HR *Epp.*, nos.
31, 128, pp. 10, 67. For Adeloldus, who lost his congregation, see ibid., nos. 108, 112, pp. 52-53, 56.
Rothad was not present at Quierzy, where the renewed
oath of fidelity to CB was taken (ibid., no. 110, p. 55;
cf. ch. 1 above). HR later accused the bishop of having
sided with Louis the German during his invasion (ibid.,
p. 149). This is implicitly contradicted by CB (MGH
Cap. 2. 451); but cf. Rothad, *Libellus proclamationis*,
(in Mansi, 15. 684. For the provincial council of 861,
see *Ann. Bert.*, pp. 86-87.

7. For the council, see De Clercq, *La législation
religieuse franque*, 2:244 ff. The actual deposition

occurred in a rump session at Soissons (Mansi, 15. 681-85; but cf. MGH *Epp.* 8[1]. 148ff., and *Ann Bert.*, pp. 91-92). For Rothad's plea, see *Libellus proclamationis*, in Mansi, 15. 682. See also Pseudo-Julius and Pseudo-Victor, in *PI*, pp. 459 and 128; cf. HR *Epp.*, pp. 139-54. The exact date of the council is uncertain, but it was probably held between June and September. On appeal to Rome according to the Pseudo-Isidore, see ch. 5 below.

8. HR *Epp.*, nos. 160, 169, pp. 135, 147, 149; Nicholas *Epp.*, no. 57, p. 357, (JE, 2714).

9. Duchesne, *Fastes épiscopaux*, 3:113; HR *Epp.*, nos. 160, 169, pp. 135, 149. The Lotharingian bishops also tried to compel Hincmar of Reims to attend the council of Metz; see their letter, at *PL* 121. 381-82, and Hincmar's comments at HR *Epp.*, pp. 120-21. On the incident, see Parisot, *Le royaume de Lorraine*, p. 220, n. 1, and ch. 3, n. 26, above.

10. Nicholas *Epp.*, nos. 55, 56, pp. 353-55 (JE, 2712-13), commanding restoration within thirty days. HR later alleged that he had never seen the letter (HR *Epp.*, p. 145).

11. On Odo's journey, see MGH *Epp*, 8[1]. 122-23. For Nicholas's response, see Nicholas *Epp.*, no. 57, pp. 355-62 (JE, 2723). For the insistence upon immediate restoration of office and goods, see Schrörs, "Die pseudo-isidorianische Exceptio spolii bei Papst Nikolaus I.," especially pp. 281 ff, This period also saw Hincmar's first extensive exposition of his metropolitan doctrines (HR *Epp.*, no. 160, pp. 122-40); see discussion of the editor, Perels, in "Eine Denkschrift Hinkmars von Reims im Prozess Rothads von Soissons," pp. 43-72.

12. On the policies and tactics of Nicholas, see ch. 3, n. 31, above.

13. MGH *Epp.* 6. 360. The pope also wrote to CB, in Nicholas *Epp.*, no. 60, pp. 369-72 (JE, 2722).

14. HR *Epp.*, no. 165, p. 143; cf. no. 169, p. 148. Nicholas *Epp.*, nos. 62, 64, pp. 374, 376 (JE, 2738, 2739).

15. For the council of Verberie, see *Ann. Bert.*, p. 103; MGH *Epp.*, 8[1]. 144.

16. *Ann. Bert.*, p. 112. For the date of his arrival, see Mansi, 15. 685; MGH *Epp.* 6. 381-82. It is likely that Rothad carried with him a copy of the Pseudo-Isidore. Thus, see Perels, *Papst Nikolaus I.*, p. 112; Haller, *Nikolaus I. und Pseudoisidor*, pp. 173 ff.; Congar, *L'ecclésiologie du haut moyen âge*, p. 175. For the view that the false decretals arrived in Rome only during the pontificate of Hadrian II, see Ertl, "Dictatoren frühmittelalterlicher Papstbriefe," pp. 105 ff.

17. Rothad, *Libellus proclamationis* (Mansi, 15. 681-85); Nicholas *Epp.*, nos. 66a, 67, pp. 379-82 (JE, 2782).

18. *Ann. Bert.*, p. 118.

19. Nicholas *Epp.*, nos. 68-72, pp. 382-401 (JE, 2781, 2783-86).

20. Ibid., no. 71, pp. 392-400 (JE, 2785).

21. See, e.g., Congar, *L'ecclésiologie du haut moyen âge*, p. 228.

22. MGH *Epp.* 6. 367-68 (JE, 2664).

23. Nicholas *Epp.*, no. 59, pp. 365-67 (JE, 2720).

24. McKeon, "Archbishop Ebbo of Reims," p. 444.

25. At least fourteen, according to the *Narratio clericorum Remensium*, MGH *Conc.*, 2. 813; the *acta* of Soissons mention thirteen (Mansi, 16. 983). HR alleges there were only nine (HR *Epp.*, p. 189).

26. For the council of Soissons (ann. 853), see Mansi, 16. 978 ff.; Hefele-Leclercq, *Histoire des*

conciles, 4[1]. 192 ff. The problem of the clerics is discussed by Saltet, *Les réordinations*, pp. 125 ff., and Schebler, *Die Reordinationen*, 2[2]: 172 ff. See also Hampe, "Zum Streite Hincmars von Reims."

27. HR *Epp.*, nos. 198, 199, pp. 212, 218. In connection with this affair, probably about 852, Hincmar fabricated portions of an earlier letter to demonstrate the analogy between his situation vis-à-vis Ebbo and that of his eight-century predecessor Tilpin with regard to Abel. See Lesne, "La lettre interpolée d'Hadrien I à Tilpin."

28. HR *De praedestinatione II*, ch. 2 (*PL* 125. 85c). Wulfad's absence from the council, allegedly due to illness, was a factor in the reversal of his sentence. On Wulfad, see Schrörs, *Hinkmar*, pp. 273 ff.

29. Thus, Paris Mazarine 561, fol. 219[V], has a list of over thirty volumes that belonged to him. See G. Becker, *Catalogi bibliothecarum antiqui*, no. 21; L. Brix, "Note sur la bibliothèque de Wulfad de Reims;" Cappuyns, *Jean Scot Erigène*, pp. 165-66, and "Les 'Bibli Vulfadi' et Jean Scot Erigène." Eriugena dedicated the *De divisione natura* to Wulfad; *PL* 122. 1022a.

30. MGH *Epp.* 8[1]. 185-87. Cf. Flodoard, 3. 24. 535; and MGH *Epp.* 8[1], nos. 101-3, p. 50.

31. *Carmina Scottorum*, 7. 3 (MGH *Poet. lat.* 3. 690); *Ann. Bert.*, p. 130. Cf. ch. 7 below.

32. Bouquet, *Recueil*, 7. 549, 642, n. b; ibid., 8. 551. CB, *Epistolae*, no. 3, in *PL* 124. 867-69. MGH *Cap.* 2. 154.

33. For his office, see *PL* 124. 867-69; MGH *Poet. lat.* 3. 519, n. 4. Among the important assemblies he attended was that at Coblence (ann. 860); MGH *Cap.* 2. 154.

34. Nicholas *Epp.*, nos. 73, 74, pp. 402-7; JE, nos. ----, 2802). The alternative was that the council be called by Archbishop Remi of Lyons, an earlier opponent

of Hincmar. On word of the case reaching Rome, see ibid., p. 403, and cf. Mansi, 15. 729. On all the following, see Lot, "Une année du règne de Charles le Chauve."

35. MGH *Epp.* 6. 406; cf. HR *Epp.*, pp. 212-13.

36. For Wulfad as tutor, see *PL* 124. 868. Rudolf was archbishop from 840-41 to 866; see Duchesne, *Fastes épiscopaux*, 2:31. According to HR he had presided over the synod at Bourges (c. 841), which had reviewed the circumstances of Ebbo's deposition (MGH *Epp.* 8[1]. 192).

37. *PL* 124. 868. On the situation, see Auzias, *L'Aquitaine carolingienne*, pp. 328 ff; for Wulfad, see ibid., pp. 354 ff.

38. Rudolf died before the council met (*PL* 124. 868). Lot, "Une année du règne de Charles le Chauve," p. 410, makes the date of his death 21 June. For Charles's accident, see *Ann. Bert.*, pp. 117-18. Cf. MGH *Cap.* 2. 453-55; Mansi, 15. 726-28; ch. 7 below.

39. *PL* 124. 867-69.

40. Nicholas *Epp.*, no. 77, pp. 411-23 (JE, 2811).

41. For the Council of Soissons (ann. 866), see Mansi, 15. 703 ff.; Hefele-Leclercq, *Histoire des conciles*, 4[1]:392 ff.

42. The synodal letter, signed by thirty-five prelates, may be that at Mansi, 15. 728-32.

43. Nicholas *Epp.*, pp. 414-22 (JE, 2822). However, he congratulated Wulfad's success; ibid., pp. 431-32.

44. Ibid., pp. 415-16, 417-18. The criticisms also involve a comparison of the *acta* with the account of the clerics, which is, perhaps, the *Narratio clericorum Remensium* in MGH *Conc.*, 2[2]. 807-13. Cf. the similar but different letter to Hincmar of Reims at MGH *Epp.* 6. 422-31.

45. Immediately following Soissons; *Ann. Bert.*, p. 130.

46. For the council of Troyes, see Mansi, 15. 789 ff.; Hefele-Leclercq, *Histoire des conciles*, 4^1: 413 ff.

47. See the synodal letter at Mansi, 15. 791-96. The one remaining bishop was Rothad.

48. CB, *Epistolae*, no. 5, in *PL* 124. 870-75; see especially ibid, 873-74. Cf. Hampe, "Zum Streite Hincmars von Reims," pp. 180-91.

49. Duchesne, *Liber pontificalis*, 2:167.

50. Hadrian *Epp.*, no. 3, pp. 699-700 (JE, 2894).

51. These appointments are discussed by H. G. J. Beck, "Selection of Bishops Suffragan to Hincmar of Reims."

52. *PL* 125. 645. Cf. ch. 3 above.

53. The suggestion of Dümmler, *Geschichte des ostfränkischen Reiches*, 2:234; but cf. Parisot, *Le royaume de Lorraine*, p. 290, n. 4. In 862 the Lotharingian prelates had argued against the bishop's right to hold his office, but their true target had been HR (*PL* 121. 382).

54. Cf. ch. 1 above.

55. *PL* 126. 295 ff.

56. *PL* 126. 295-96.

57. Mansi, 16. 614 c.

58. *PL* 126. 510 c.

59. Duchesne, *Fastes épiscopaux*, 3:139.

60. *PL* 126. 294.

61. Ibid. See U. Stutz, *Geschichte des kirchlichen Benefizialwesens*, 1:186; Lesne, *Histoire de la propriété ecclésiastique*, 2:67 ff.

62. *PL* 126. 294c.

63. Ibid., 294-95.

64. See Reg. HL, n. 5, on the date. On the provost, see Balon, *Jus medii aevi*, I:43 ff.

65. Reg. HL, no. 9.

66. *PL* 126. 294-95.

67. *PL* 126. 298b-299, 449-50. For the dating, see Reg. HL, no. 13.

68. See n. 9 above; Nicholas *Epp.*, nos. 13-15, pp. 279-82 (JE, 2730-32). On the delay, see ibid., p. 312; *Gesta episcoporum Cameracensium*, in MGH *SS* 7. 418. On the incident, see Beck, "Selection of Bishops Suffragan to Hincmar of Reims," pp. 283 ff.

69. HR *Epp.*, no. 182, p. 172, on the basis of *PL* 126. 297, 569.

70. MGH *Epp.* 8[1]. 173.

71. *PL* 126. 569-70, 297-98.

72. MGH *Epp.* 8[1]. 206. 214 ff., 224-25.

73. Ibid., 6. 429 ff., in response to an earlier complaint of Hincmar's; cf. *Ann. Bert.*, p. 138.

74. MGH *Epp.* 8[1]. 206. For the charge against Hincmar of Laon, see *PL* 126. 310a.

75. For the documents, see HR *Epp.*, nos. 185-88, 198-200, pp. 187-201, 204-25. The manuscript is Laon bibliothèque municipale, 407; see Lot, "Une année du règne de Charles le Chauve," 412-14 and n. 1, 417 n. 1. On the ascription, see Tessier, 2:150, n. 2.

76. *PL* 126. 298d-299a.

77. *PL* 126. 438c, 534a.

78. Reg. HL, no. 61 On the large collection, see
Fuhrmann, *Einfluss und Verbreitung der pseudoisidorischen Fälschungen*, 3, 629 ff. A version of these signed
sentences is extant in Paris lat. 12445. On this manuscript, see Conrat, "Hinkmariana"; Mor, "Un manoscritto
canonistico francese del secolo IX"; Devisse, *Hincmar et
la loi*, especially pp. 39 ff.; Fuhrmann, *op. cit.*, pp.
655 ff., 705 ff. See also Reg. HL, n. 21.

79. So HR, at *PL* 126. 577b.

80. *PL* 126. 577c-d.

81. *PL* 126. 577d-578b.

82. *PL* 126. 577b, 559b. The signatures were probably added later; see Reg. HL, n. 21.

83. *PL* 126. 607a. The bishop presented the collection at the council of Attigny (*PL* 126. 604b), although
HR had seen it previously (*PL* 126. 301a, 302a-b). It was
the basis for the *Pittaciolus*; see Reg. HL, n. 21.

84. *PL* 126. 301a; Mansi, 16. 856d. See also *PL* 126.
441c. Probably the affair of the monk whom the bishop
excommunicated dates from this period and, more specifically, between the return from Metz and the assembly at
Gondreville. See *PL* 126. 315-16; cf. ibid., 533-34.

85. *Ann. Bert.*, p. 156.

86. MGH *Cap.* 2, no. 302, pp. 456-58.

87. *PL* 124. 1033d.

88. Flodoard, 3. 21. 516; but cf. HR, at *PL* 126.
262-64. Parisot, in *Le royaume de Lorraine*, at p. 364,
finds the first account more likely, and his interpretation has been followed here. The ordination was not ac-

cepted by either Louis the German or Hadrian II; cf. ch. 9 below.

89. Cf. ch. 3 above.

90. *PL* 126. 290a-b. That the archbishop was hurt is plain from his comments in a letter, written shortly afterward to his nephew, which is given at *PL* 126. 290-91 and forms the preface to HR Opusculum. See Reg. HL, no. 77.

91. *PL* 126. 290b, 299c.

92. *PL* 126. 290b-c; see also HR Libellus, ch. 29 (*PL* 126. 615-17).

93. *PL* 126. 290c-d, 300d-301b.

94. *PL* 126. 301c.

95. This famous collection, various versions of which are extant in a number of manuscripts, is printed in one form at *PL* 124. 1001-26, and its metrical title also in MGH *Poet. lat.* 3. 416. But this is not the version discussed by HR, nor is it the fullest version. On the collection, see Fournier and Le Bras, *Histoire des collections canoniques*, 1:215-16. A fuller version, contained in Salzburg Saint Peter's 9. 32, fol. 172-94, is analyzed by Phillips, "Der Codex Salisburgensis S. Petri IX. 32," at pp. 46 ff. The version in Metz Bibliothèque Municipale 351, fol. 78v-102v, is treated by Meyer, "Ueber Hincmars von Laon Auslese aus Pseudo-Isidore, Ingilram, und aus Schreiben des Papstes Nicolaus I." On the manuscript, see also Prost, "Caractère et signification de quatre pièces liturgiques composées à Metz." Most recently, the indispensable studies of Fuhrmann, "Zur Überlieferung des Pittaciolus Bischofs Hinkmars von Laon," and *Einfluss und Verbreitung der pseudoisidorischen Fälschungen*, 3:628-9. See also Reg. HL, n. 21.

96. *PL* 126. 441c. The popes are Leo I, Gregory I, and Nicholas.

97. The bishop cites Pseudo-Alexander, ch. 18;
Pseudo-Sixtus I, ch. 6; Pseudo-Hyginus, ch. 6; Pseudo-
Anicetius, ch. 2; Pseudo-Victor, ch 6; Pseudo-Calixtus,
ch. 13; Pseudo-Sixtus III; *Cap. Ang.*, chs. 1, 14. (*PI*,
pp. 104, 108-9, 114-15, 121, 128-29, 139, 561-65, 758-
59, 761.) The texts of these fragments may be found in
PL 124. 1001-5, 993-95, 1015-20. The article of Meyer
in n. 95 above conveniently locates the citations; cf.
also his remarks (ibid., p. 220) on the version of the
work at *PL* 124.

98. Pseudo-Lucius, ch. 3; Pseudo-Julius, ch. 6; the
Nicene canons (nos. 19 and 20) as given by Pseudo-Felix,
with other portions of the letter, at chs. 12-13;
Pseudo-Damasus, ch. 8; *Cap. Ang.*, ch. 11; Gelasius to
the emperor Anastasius. (*PI*, pp. 176, 459-60, 488, 489,
502-3, 761, 643.) These segments may be found at *PL*
124. 995-98, 1006-7, 1021.

99. Pseudo-Eusebius, ch. 12; Pseudo-Zephyrinus, chs.
11-12; *Cap. Ang.*, ch. 5. (*PI*, pp. 237-38, 133, 758-59.)
See *PL* 124. 1006-7, 1014.

100. Pseudo-Julius, chs. 11, 12, 12-15, 16-17, 18-20;
Pseudo-Felix, chs. 12, 16; Celestine I, chs. 1, 2;
Gregory I to Theoctista; Leo I. (*PI*, pp. 464-67, 470,
471-74 [with omissions], 561-62 [with omissions], 745
[and at MGH *Epp*. 2. 296, 294], 615.) See *PL* 124. 1007-
14, 1021-22. At *PL* 126. 367c, 581c, HR criticizes his
nephew's use of the Gregorian letter, saying that he had
truncated it and perverted the sense of the passage (referring to *PL* 124. 1021d, with which cf. MGH *Epp*. 2. 296.

101. At *PL* 124. 1022-26; Nicholas *Epp*., no. 88, pp.
454-87 (JE, 2796). For some comments of HR regarding
this letter, see, e.g., *PL* 126. 382-83.

102. *PL* 124. 1001-2.

103. *PL* 126. 534-37.

104. *PL* 126. 301d.

105. *PL* 126. 534d; also ibid., 329d.

106.   See *PL* 126. 617b-c.

107.   *Ann. Bert.* p. 138.

108.   Contained in HR Opusculum, ch. 4, at *PL* 126.
299-300c;quoted also in HR Libellus, ch. 30, at *PL* 126.
617-18.   On the unsubstantiated charges, ch. *PL* 126.
291d. The date of the archbishop's request is uncertain;
see Reg. HL, nos. 89, 90.

109.   The letter is at the preface to the HR Opusculum,
at *PL* 126. 290-93; the request, ibid., 290c-d.

110.   *PL* 126. 290d-291d.

111.   See Reg. HL, no. 89; the letter probably appears
in the HR Opusculum, ch. 4; see *PL* 126. 299d ff.   It is
also used in HR Libellus, ch. 30; see *PL* 126. 617c ff.

Chapter V

1.   *PL* 126. 279-80; Reg. HL, no. 80.

2.   The fullest account is at *PL* 126. 442b-444c.

3.   Thus, see *PL* 125. 1017a-1036b.

4.   *PL* 126. 443c-444a.

5.   *PL* 126. 444a-b, largely reiterating the letter of
13 February to HL; cf. n. 1 above.

6.   *PL* 126. 279c. Another example of the charge,
said to be common rumor, is at *PL* 126. 486a. The bishop
denies the charge at *PL* 124. 981a.

7.   *PL* 126. 280b.

8.   *PL* 124. 979-86; Reg. HL, no. 81.   For Heddo, see
PL 126. 442a-b.

9.   *PL* 124. 979a-b.

10. *PL* 124. 980a-c.

11. *PL* 124. 984-86. HR later said that his nephew
would find out about the procedure in this case when he
told the archbishop the same regarding Amalbertus (*PL*
126. 449-50). This seems an odd remark for a man who
accused the bishop of indulging in puerile arguments (cf.
n. 59 below).

12. *PL* 124. 980b.

13. *PL* 124. 981c ff. The bishop here presents a
small treatise on proper procedure, stressing the harm
to the priestly order if improper accusations are permitted to be bandied about, and the need for credible
witnesses; he cites Pseudo-Calixtus, ch. 3; Pseudo-
Eleutherius, ch. 4; Pseudo-Felix II, chs. 9-16; and
Pseudo-Damasus (*PI*, pp. 136, 127, 489-90, 519-20). The
tone of the letter is reminiscent, on the one hand, of
HR, in *Pro ecclesiae libertatum defensione* and, on the
other, of the archbishop's letter to his nephew remon-
strating with him for the unsubstantiated charges made
to Wenilon of Rouen (ch. 4 above and *PL* 126. 290-93).

14. *PL* 124. 983-84d. The authorities are Pseudo-
Hadrian I (cf. the attribution of HL, which presumably
refers to Benedictus Levita, *Capitularium collectio*,
add. 4, ch. 20 [*PL* 97. 891-92]; the same regulation
appears at *Cap. Ang.*, ch. 11, p. 761) and Pseudo-Damasus,
chs. 8-9 (*PI*, pp. 502-3).

15. *PL* 126. 280c.

16. *PL* 126. 554-55.

17. *PL* 126. 281a. Witgarius, it may be observed, was
one of the aides of Louis the German at Metz in 868.

18. *PL* 126. 280-81; Reg. HL, no. 82.

19. *PL* 124. 985-86; Reg. HL, no. 83.

20. He was still there in early May; *PL* 124. 986-87.

21.   Cf. ch. 1 above.

22.   On Follembray and its neighboring *villae*, see also Imbart de la Tour, *Les origines religieuses de la France*, pp. 166 ff.

23.   *PL* 126. 538a.

24.   Thus HR, at *PL* 126. 542a-b.

25.   *PL* 126. 538b. Virtually all of these dates must be calculated on the basis of internal evidence.

26.   *PL* 126. 538d. The date may be fixed by the fact that Bishop Pardulus was still alive.

27.   For Bishop Pardulus, see ch. 1 above.

28.   *PL* 126. 538-39. Perhaps at the time the arch-bishop of Reims dominated the inquiry.

29.   *PL* 126. 539a-b. At some point, also, the chapel was burned.

30.   *PL* 126. 539b.

31.   *PL* 126. 539a-b, for the grant. The relationship, *PL* 126. 540b; cf. Flodoard, 3. 26. 546-47.

32.   *PL* 126. 539c. This lasted for a period of four years; see *PL* 126. 556d. On the vicar, see Imbart de la Tour, *Les origines religieuses de la France*, p. 247.   On the *mancipium*, see Balon, *Jus medii aevi*, 1:88 ff.; Dubled, "'Mancipium' au moyen age.'"

33.   See ch. 4 above.

34.   *PL* 126. 543d.

35.   *PL* 126. 556-57.

36.   *PL* 126. 557a.

37.   *PL* 126. 537-38.

38. *PL* 126. 544c.

39. *PL* 124. 987 ff.; cf. *PL* 126. 539-40.

40. *PL* 126. 537-45; Reg. HL, no. 85.

41. *PL* 126. 540a-b.

42. *PL* 126. 540d. The reference is to the council of Orange, ann. 429, canon 10 (*PI*, pp. 328-29).

43. *PL* 126. 540-41. The archbishop here cites 3 Toledo (ann. 589), canon 19; Antioch, canon 25; Orleans (ann. 511), canon 10; and canon 9 of the council of Pîtres, held in 869. (*PI*, pp. 360-61, 272-73, 337-38; MGH *Cap.* 2. 335-36).

44. *PL* 126. 541. On the requirement that the priest at a private church be free, see Astronomer, *Vita Hludowici*, ch. 28 in Rau, 1:302. HL had alleged that Senatus's status barred his elevation; *PL* 124. 988c. ff.

45. *PL* 126. 541-42.

46. *PL* 126. 542d-543d.

47. *PL* 126. 543-44b.

48. Cf. n. 38 above.

49. *PL* 124. 985-94; Reg. HL, no. 86.

50. *PL* 124. 985d, again reflecting his view that the archbishop had engineered his imprisonment. HR, on 11 May, seems almost to imply that the charge is true, and states that the experience was a beneficial one, in some respects at least (*PL* 126. 549-53). Some of these arguments appear later; thus, HR, late in 870 (*PL* 126. 500b; cf. Mansi, 16. 667c.) But the archbishop always explicitly denies any role in the episode (thus, *PL* 126. 438).

51. *PL* 124. 987b.

52. *PL* 124. 987c.

53. *PL* 124. 988-89. The reference is to Ansegis, *Capitularium collectio*, lib. 1, ch. 82 (MGH *Cap*. 1. 406).

54. *PL* 124. 989c ff.

55. *PL* 124. 992a-994. The remainder of the letter is a diatribe against those who ignored his own rights of procedure and appeal.

56. *PL* 126. 545-66; Reg. HL, no. 87. The letter is in large measure a disquisition on the metropolitan privilege, in which, for example, the archbishop opposes HL's charges of impropriety and prejudicial judgment in the Follembray matter by distinguishing between a judicial proceeding and a metropolitan correction.

57. Thus, i.e., *PL* 126. 557a. A treatise on lying follows (*PL* 126. 557-58).

58. *PL* 126. 554-55.

59. *PL* 126. 558c-559b. HR likens this situation to that of the signed collection of the previous year.

60. For the number of provinces, see, e.g., Mansi, 16. 580b,654a; *PL* 126. 582. On the council, see McKeon, "Le concile d'Attigny (870)."

61. *PL* 124. 998.

62. See Reg. HL, no. 174.

63. *PL* 126. 501d; see ch. 4 above.

64. Mansi, 16. 856b.

65. Mansi, 16. 856c-e. On the "rotula prolixissima", see *PL* 126. 501d. On this and other material that HL presented, which the archbishop considered particularly irrelevant, see HR Libellus, ch. 13 (*PL* 126. 582-83).

66. Quoted in the *Narratio*, at Mansi, 16. 856-57. The gambit of presenting his complaints as requests for

episcopal advice was apparently a favorite of the elder Hincmar, who used it again at Douzy, where he asserted that he had done so also at Verberie and Gondreville (HR Libellus, [*PL* 126. 566c]).

67. Mansi, 16. 857-58.

68. Mansi, 16. 858-63.

69. See the observations of Morrison, *Two Kingdoms*, p. 77, n. 29, on the need to modify the first notion.

70. Ibid. But Morrison does consider HL to have been a papal monarchist (ibid., p. 83). Actually, he seems to have been more an opportunist than a theoretician.

71. Thus, e.g., Ignatius to Magnesians, ch. 13 (ed. Lake, in *Apostolic Fathers*, 1:208-10); Cyprian, *Epistolae*, nos. 59, 66.8 (ed. Hartel, in *Opera omnia*, 3:666-91, 732-33). See Baus, *From the Apostolic Community to Constantine*, p. 346.

72. Thus, Cyprian, *Epistolae*, nos. 14, 20, 31, 53, 55 (Hartel, op. cit., 509-16, 527-29, 57-64, 620, 24-48). See also Eusebius, *Ecclesiastical History*, passim, especially 5. 16, 10 (ed. Lake, 1:476), 23 (ibid., 1:502-4); 6. 33, 37, 43 (ibid., 2:86, 90, 112).

73. Thus see Cyprian, *Epistolae*, nos. 14, 33 (Hartel, op. cit., pp. 509-13, 66-68); Dionysius of Alexandria to Philemon, at Eusebius, *Ecclesiastical History*, bk. 7 ch. 7 (Lake, op. cit., 2:144). For a clear and concise statement of ecclesiastical unity mediated through the episcopacy, see Cyprian, *De catholicae ecclesiae unitate*, ch. 5 (ed. Hartel, in *Opera omnia*, 3:213-14). Cf. Athanasius, *De synodis*, chs. 9, 10 (ed. Opitz, in *Athanasius Werke*, 2:236-38); Sozomen, *Historia ecclesiastica*, 1. 20, 3. 12 (ed. Bidez and Hansen, pp. 41-42, 115-17); Theodoret, *Historia ecclesiastica*, 2. 13 (ed. Palmentier and Scheidweiler, pp. 123-25). The association of ecclesiastical unity and finality of conciliar judgment is explicitly made in Optatus, *Adversus Parmenianem*, 1, ch. 25 (ed. Ziwsa, p. 27).

74. In spite of the disclaimers of imperial influence upon the church, Eusebius provides evidence of its cooptation by the empire; see, e.g., *Vita Constantini*, 3. 5 (ed. Heikel, p. 79).   Also, *Codex Theodosianus*, 16. 2.1.2, 2.4 (ed. Mommsen, pp. 835-36).

75. Council of Nicaea, canon 5, at *PI*, p. 259.

76. Ullmann, *Growth of Papal Government*.

77. De Ghellinck, *La littérature latine au moyen âge*, I. Munier, *Les sources patristiques*.

78. Ganshof, "The Church and the Royal Power," p. 210.

79. On the ninth century councils, see Hefele-Leclercq, *Histoire des conciles*, 4[2]; De Clercq, *La législation religieuse franque*. See also Hinschius, *System des katholischen Kirchenrechts*, 3:325-668; Barion, *Das fränkisch-deutsche Synodalrecht* and *Die National-synode*. The sources are given by Werminghoff, "Verzeichnis der Akten fränkischer Synoden."

80. See ch. 4 above. On the Pseudo-Isidorian decretals, see Fuhrmann, *Einfluss und Verbreitung der pseudo-isidorischen Fälschungen*. For comprehensive bibliographies of earlier literature, see Seckel, "Pseudo-isidor," pp. 265-67; and Seckel "Die erste Zeile Pseudo-isidors," pp. 11-15, n. 3.

81. For the quarrel between HR and HL and the uses made of the Pseudo-Isidore in its course, see Fuhrmann, *Einfluss und Verbreitung der pseudoisidorischen Fälschungen*, 1:219-24, 3:625 ff. In the following pages, the Pseudo-Isidore will at times be used to fill out the thought of the bishop of Laon.

82. Thus, in various sources, Benedictus Levita, *Capitularium collectio*, 1, no. 116 (*PL* 97. 715); HR, at MGH *Cap.* 2. 428-41, passim, especially ch. 15 (pp. 438-41). On the collection of Benedictus, see Baix, "Benedictus Levita."

83. Even the size, frequency, and importance of the
assemblies held during the reign of CB stand as indices
of proof of this. See also the statements of, e.g.,
Meaux-Paris (MGH *Cap.* 2. 396-97), typical of the perennial expressions regarding the need for episcopal consultation for the good of the realm. See Morrison, *Two
Kingdoms*, pp. 39 ff.

84. HR Opusculum, ch. 6, cols. 310-13. Cf. ch. 2, at
col. 298; HR Libellus, ch. 9, cols. 574-75. For valuable discussion of the ecclesiology of HR, see Congar,
"Structures et régime de l'église," and *L'ecclésiologie
du haut moyen âge*, pp. 166 ff.; Morrison, *Tradition and
Authority*, pp. 240-51.

85. Thus, HR Opusculum, ch. 27, col. 393.

86. Literally, in the case of HL, who, says the
archbishop, is really equivalent to a corebishop (*PL* 126.
503). On the problem of the corebishop in the ninth
century, see Gottlob, *Der abendländische Chorepiskopat*.
But, more generally, see the letter of record concerning
the trial of Rothad of Soissons; HR *Epp.*, no. 160, pp.
122-40, especially 135 ff.

87. HR Opusculum, chs. 16-17, cols. 334-350; MGH *Epp.*
8[1]. 129 ff., where the reasons are given full exposition.
For ninth-century equivalence of the terms "metropolitan"
and "archbishop," see Prou, *La Gaule mérovingienne*, p.
122; Ganshof, "The Church and the Royal Power," p. 210.
On the question of primacy, see Fuhrmann, "Studien zur
geschichte mittelalterlicher Patriarchate." The issue
arose most directly in Archbishop Hincmar's quarrel with
Ansegis of Sens; see Fliche, "La primatie des Gaules."

88. MGH *Epp.* 8[1]. 135-37. Cf. HR Libellus, *praefatio*,
col. 567; and ch. 9, cols. 574-75.

89. HR Opusculum, ch. 6, cols. 310-13; cf. *PL* 126.
501. See the discussion at Lesne, *La hiérarchie épiscopale*, pp. 146 ff. Also, the metropolitan may "correct"
a suffragan informally through conversation with a
cleric, as at *PL* 126. 597.

90.   This "corrective" process is quite different
from a formal procedure. See *PL* 126. 561, and cf. *De
divortio Hlotharii regis*, q. iii., at *PL* 125. 748 ff.
For the metropolitan function in general, see HR
Opusculum, ch. 5, especially cols. 304-8.   See Lesne,
La hiérarchie épiscopale, pp. 71 ff.

91.   HR Opusculum, ch. 6, col. 313.   Cf. *ibid.*, ch.
24, at col. 416 ff.   On the importance of the canons,
see below, passim, especially ns. 132-33.

92.   See HR Opusculum, ch. 35.   The real meaning of
the maxims regarding mutuality does not concern mutuality of decision, for the metropolitan has care of the
province; rather, it refers to the right of suffragan
bishops to hear his sentences (cols. 422-23).   At the
provincial council, the metropolitan receives the
"*consilium et consensus*" of his suffragans (*PL* 126. 427).
See also the role of HR at Douzy in 871, in ch. 8 below,
and at Soissons in 853, in Mansi, 14. 983, with which
cf. MGH *Epp.* 8[1]. 188, and Nicholas *Epp.*, no. 79 (JE,
2822). pp. 414-22, especially 415.   HR used the argument
against the bishop of Laon in 870; see HR Opusculum, ch.
5, col. 309.

93.   See MGH *Epp.* 8[1]. no. 160, p. 127; cf. HR Opusculum, ch. 36, col. 428.   The whole is implied in the
episcopal oath of obedience promised in the province of
Reims to the metropolitan; see HR Opusculum, *praefatio*,
col. 292, and ch. 1 above.   According to HR, violation
of such an oath is in itself grounds for deposition; see
HR Libellus, ch. 34, cols. 627-28.

94.   See HR Opusculum, ch. 2, cols. 295-96, and cf.
ch. 7, cols. 313-15; cf. particular instances of violation at HR Libellus, chs. 1, 10, cols. 568, 575-76).   On
the numerous occasions when he uses this argument, the
archbishop refers to Antioch, canon 13; thus, against
Rothad, at MGH *Epp.* 8[1]. 135-36.

95.   The petition must be presented in proper, written form (Mansi, 14. 983), in the presence of the other
bishops (MGH *Epp.* 8[1]. 146 ff., 154 ff.), and with the
accused present, unless he has failed to respond to

three calls (HR Libellus, ch. 35, at *PL* 126. 628-29).
Witnesses are generally required (HR Libellus, ch. 24,
col. 606), and ordinarily one is not sufficient (ibid.,
ch. 25, at cols. 607). They must be credible (ibid.,
cf. also ch. 30, cols. 619-20). The judgment, especially if the accused has not appeared, may be made on the
basis of signed writings alone (*PL* 126. 628), and shall
issue from the whole synod (as at Douzy, where the prelates heard the testimony and rendered judgment; see
ch. 9 below), or from elected judges (cf. following
note).

96. See Mansi, 14. 984; MGH *Epp.* 8[1]. 159.

97. HR Libellus ch. 9, cols. 574-75; see ch. 2
above. Cf. discussion at *De divortio Hlotharii regis*, q.
i. (*PL* 125. 746).

98. HL, at *PL* 124. 1054 (regarding the archbishop's
interpretation of Pseudo-Calixtus); cf. *PL* 124. 1055-56.

99. HL, at *PL* 124. 1029, and as reported by HR, at
PL 126. 495. Cf. also the doctrine of Rothad and Prudentius of Troyes, as expressed in HR, *De ecclesiis et
capellis*, passim; see ch. 4 above.

100. Thus Pseudo-Aniticius, at *PI*, pp. 120-22; *Cap.
Ang.*, no. 43, p. 765. See HL, at *PL* 124. 1054-55, com-
menting upon the correct interpretation of Pseudo-
Calixtus, as at *PI*, pp. 137-43; the bishop's citation is
at pp. 139-40, found at *PL* 124. 994-95.

101. Pseudo-Stephen, at *PI*, p. 185; Pseudo-Felix I,
passim, especially *PI*, p. 201; *Cap. Ang.*, ch. 26, p. 763.

102. HL, at *PL* 124. 1059. Cf. Pseudo-Marcellus II, at
PI, p. 227.

103. See n. 76 above.

104. Soissons, ann. 866. See HR, at MGH *Epp.* 8[1]. 174-
177, 182-85; cf. Mansi, 15. 725-26. On the episcopal
endorsement, see Mansi 15. 728. On the exception, see
n. 105.

105.   Regarding Rothad, for example, HR stated to
Nicholas I the principle that the sentence of a unanimous synod must stand, and that Rothad was wrong in
appealing to the Lotharingian bishops (ch. 4 above, and
MGH *Epp*. 8[1]. 135-36).   The only permissible appeal is
to the pope (loc.cit.; cf. ibid.,146, and *PL* 126. 576).

106.   The synod is complete, and hence synodal, only
due to the metropolitan presence; see HR Opusculum, ch.
2, at col. 297.

107.   *PL* 126. 393.   This follows from the notion of
the province as the *synodus*, i.e., the governmental entity of the church.   See also the argument against HL's
interpretation of mutuality, at *PL* 126. 595-96.

108.   *PL* 126. 393.

109.   MGH *Epp*. 8[1]. 135-36.

110.   Council of Sardica, canons 3-5, at *PI*, p. 267.

111.   Innocent I, *Epistolae*, no. 1, to Victricius of
Rouen, in *PL* 20. 468-81, especially col. 473; cf. no. 29,
at *PL* 20. 582-88; cf. HR Opusculum, ch. 12. Cf. Leo I,
Epistolae, no. 6, at *PL* 54. 616-20, specifically ch. 5,
at col. 619.

112.   On the precedence of Nicaea, see HR Opusculum,
ch. 23.   Sardica was not a general council, but rather
an explication of Nicaea (*PL* 126. 361), and hence did
not issue immutable rules (*PL* 126. 363 ff.; cf. col.
428).   For the *assensus*, see *PL* 126. 448.   On the possibility of deposing a pope deviating from the rules,
see n. 132, and ch. 8 below.   The principle that the
canons are uniquely determinative is absolutely fundamental to the entire ecclesiology of HR, and appears in
numerous contexts.   Since the canons are promulgated by
divine inspiration (*PL* 126. 567), which is imparted not
to one but to a group (cf. n. 126 below), the canons
alone are truly legislative enactments (cf. ns. 135-36
below).   The metropolitan privilege then, having been
established by the council of Nicaea (*PL* 126. 580), was
issued by the Holy Spirit (thus, *PL* 126. 316-24), so

opposing it is equivalent to opposing God (*PL* 126. 580-81),i.e., to schism (ibid., and cf. n. 130 below). Thus, the bishop of Laon was wrong in signing his canonical collections, not only since he had signed an oath to his metropolitan, but also since the canons do permit the metropolitan to raise such a sentence as the Laon interdict (*PL* 126. 427-34).

113. See *praefatio*, p. 18; implicit at *Cap. Ang.*, ch. 26, p. 764. Cf. HL, at *PL* 124. 984. The popes did not disapprove of these sentiments; see Nicholas *Epp.*, nos. 66a, 118, pp. 379-81, 637. See Hartmann, *Der Primat des römischen Bischofs*.

114. Thus, e.g., Pseudo-Julius, at *PI*, p. 195; Pseudo-Victor, at *PI*, p. 128. Of course, similar pronouncements existed, too, in real decretals. See also HL, at *PL* 124. 1052, 1059. Also, at *PL* 124. 1066, the bishop attempts to place the equal status accorded by ordination in the position of a governmental role, relegating the differences imposed by "dignitas" to a place of slight importance.

115. Passim. E.g., Pseudo-Athanasius, at *PI*, p. 479; *Cap. Ang.*, ch. 2, pp. 757-58.

116. *Praefatio*, at *PI*, p. 17. On the Pseudo-Isidore's use of patristic sources, see Munier, *Les sources patristiques*, p. 32.

117. See Reg. HL, ns. 5, 7, 21.

118. HR Opusculum, ch. 20, cols. 353-65. The whole chapter is concerned with types of councils.

119. *PL* 126. 361. For HR's theory of the universal council, see Bacht, "Hinkmar von Reims."

120. Matt. 16:18-19: "And I tell you, you are Peter, and on this rock I will build my church, and the powers of death shall not prevail against it. I will give to you the keys of the kingdom of heaven, and whatever you bind on earth shall be bound in heaven, and whatever you

loose on earth shall be loosed in heaven." Cf. MGH *Epp.* 8[1]. 132.

121.   Matt. 18:19-20:   "Again I say to you, if two or three of you agree on earth about anything they ask, it will be done for them by my Father in heaven.   For where two or three are gathered in my name, there am I in the midst of them."   Cf. use in *De divortio, Hlotharii regis,* q. iii, at *PL* 125. 750.

122.   On the *assensus ecclesiae,* see Morrison, *Two Kingdoms,* pp. 91 ff.

123.   Thus, i.e., to HL, at HR Opusculum, ch. 36, cols. 427-434, especially at HR Libellus,ch. 35, col. 630; if HL had won over all the bishops, their *consensus* would still have been schismatic.   Cf. HR Libellus, ch. 11, cols. 580-81.

124.   See Gregory I, *Registrum epistolarum,* at MGH *Epp.* I. 25.

125.   HR *Epp.,* no. 160, p. 139, and many other places. Cf. n. 116 above.

126.   In his *Responsio cur in suae scripto posuerit mysticam Nicaenam synodum* (*PL* 125. 1197-200), the archbishop explains certain of the mystical significations of the great council.

127.   HR Opusculum, ch. 25, col. 388.

128.   See the letter to Hadrian II, at *PL* 124. 895-96. For HR as the author, see Devisse, *Hincmar et la loi,* p. 85.

129.   HR Opusculum, ch. 25, cols. 384-391.

130.   Ibid., ch. 20, cols. 353-365. Cf. n. 116 above.

131.   MGH *Epp.* 8[1]. 129 ff.

132.   See *PL* 124. 893; Kirn, "Aequitatis judicium."

133. *De divortio, praefatio,* at MGH *Epp.* 8[1]., no. 134, pp. 76 ff.; HR *Epp.,* no. 160a, pp. 132, 135; HR Opusculum, ch. 20, col. 361.

134. *PL* 124. 893. Christ gave the keys to all, although to Peter specifically, for these purposes; see MGH *Epp.* 8[1]. 132. Cf. Congar, "Structures et régime de l'église," p.13.

135. In HR Opusculum, ch. 20, cols. 361, 363 ff., HR had denied ecumenical (or general) status to Sardica; cf. n. 116 above. He had also denied the notion that Sardica was an extension or reaffirmation of Nicaea (the effective implication of attributing the Sardican canons to Nicaea), alleging that there would have been no need to have reaffirmed the decrees previously enacted. HL had distinguished between types of Sardican decrees and had bolstered his argument by referring to three papal witnesses (*PL* 124. 1047; see ch. 7 below).

136. HR Libellus, col. 633; MGH *Epp.* 8[1]. no. 169, p. 146. Cf. ch. 4 above.

137. See the *acta* of Douzy, ann. 871, ch. 4, at Mansi, 16. 662-64; ch. 8 below.

Chapter VI

1. Cf. ch. 2 above.

2. See appendix 2 below and *PL* 124. 1029c-d, 1030d.

3. For Charles's arrival, see *Ann. Bert.,* p. 169. On the chronology, see McKeon, "Le concile d'Attigny."

4. *PL* 126. 495c. On the *mansus,* see, e.g., Dubled, "Encore la question du manse;" Herlihy, "The Carolingian *Mansus.*"

5. *PL* 124. 1030b.

6. *PL* 126. 495-96, 504b.

7. For the bishop's account, see *PL* 124. 1029-30.

8. See, e.g., *PL* 126. 502a.

9. *PL* 125. 999a. For the denial by HR, see *PL* 126. 623d, 625d.

10. *PL* 124. 998c-999. HL later complained that the requisite copy of the gospels was not present when he swore to Charles; see the discussion of David, "Le serment du sacre du IXe au XVe siècle," pp. 77-78. The debate regarding the significance of the royal oath is summarized by Odegaard, "The Concept of Royal Power." See also his *Vassi and Fideles*, p. 67.

11. *PL* 124. 999b-c.

12. *PL* 124. 999c-d.

13. *PL* 126. 624c-d.

14. *PL* 126. 625b-c, 502c-d, and, largely on the basis of this latter citation, Mansi, 16. 860d-861e, which includes texts that are only mentioned at other sources.

15. *PL* 124. 998c.

16. *PL* 126. 502a-b.

17. *PL* 124. 1031b-d; cf. cols. 999b, 1036a. See HR, at *PL* 126. 505a, 583c (where the prelates are named), and Mansi, 16. 862a.

18. Prefaced, at *PL* 124. 1032b, by "*cum canones decernant ut per episcopos judices causa finiatur*," the citations are to Benedictus Levita, *Capitularium collectio*, 2, col. 390 (*PL* 97. 796), and Pseudo-Stephen, ch. 5 (*PI*, p. 184).

19. *PL* 124. 1033a-b.

20. Cf. ch. 2 above.

21. He was with the king at Aachen; *PL* 124. 1033c, and cf. col. 1032d.

22. *PL* 124. 1033-34b.

23. *PL* 124. 1034b-d.

24. Reg. HL, nos. 63-65. The letters are not extant, but portions of one can be reconstructed on the basis of a later letter from Charles to the pope; see *PL* 124. 876b-d, 877c, 878a, 878c-d, 879d-880a. See McKeon,"Toward a Reestablishment of the Correspondence of Pope Hadrian II," pp. 173, 178 ff.

25. *PL* 126. 186b-c.

26. See *PL* 124. 999a-b, 1036a-b; *PL* 126. 502a.

27. *PL* 124. 1027d; *PL* 126. 494d.

28. Mansi, 16. 580c.

29. *PL* 124. 1035b.

30. Mansi 16. 861-62; *PL* 126. 505a. Schubert ("Per murum dimiserunt eum," p. 85) saw a reference to Hincmar's flight in the strange frontispiece scene in the San Paolo Bible, which shows Saint Paul fleeing from Damascus; Gaehde, ("Turonian Sources," p. 389, n. 125) who had originally tended toward this interpretation, now views the scene as a current topos. On this Bible, produced between the latter months of 866 and October 869, see Kantorowicz, "Carolingian King in the Bible of San Paolo"; Schade, "Studien zu der Karolingischen Bilderbibel aus St. Paul vor den Mauern zu Rom"; Gaehde, "Bible of San Paolo fuori le mura in Rome."

31. Cf. n. 16 above.

32. For this theme, see *PL* 124. 1036 ff.

33. HR, at MGH *Epp.*, 8^1, no. 123, p. 59 (=Flodoard, 3. 22. 519). The same, of course, could be said of the archbishop.

34. Well-deserved, that is, in the sense that by his expectation the bishop acknowledged that some act of his

would have angered his uncle and the king. Even his
likening himself to Athanasius, through his reference
(at *PL* 124. 1035b) to Pseudo-Julius (ch. 14, at *PI*, p.
471), where the author justifies the patriarch's flight,
reflects Hincmar's situation in ways perhaps not intended by him, for Athanasius was charged at Tyre with,
among other things, misuse of his episcopal office
through excessive harshness. In HR Libellus, ch. 14
(*PL* 126. 584-85), HR expounds reasons for rejecting the
analogy; actually, it is rather apt, at least as regards
circumstances, since both Athanasius and Bishop Hincmar
faced hostile and prejudiced tribunals, both could
reasonably fear imprisonment, and both appealed to Rome.

35.   Cf. ch. 3 above.

36.   Reg. HL, no. 99.

37.   *PL* 124. 1035b; *PL* 126. 494d, 584c-d. See Reg.
HL, no. 98. But for the bishop's denial that his uncle
was present, see *PL* 124. 1036a.

38.   *PL* 124. 1000d. See Reg. HL, nos. 100, 101.

39.   See ch. 4 above; and for the same argument used
against Hincmar of Laon, see *PL* 126. 587b-c, 625d.

40.   *PL* 126. 506c-d, 587a.

41.   See chs. 4 and 5 above. Hincmar of Laon alleged,
of course, that he had appealed from both Verberie and
Attigny; *PL* 124. 1000b.

42.   Reg. HL, no. 103. The letter is given by the
bishop, in evidence of the archbishop's failure to follow the conditions agreed upon at Attigny (*PL* 124.
1000a-d); it is given by Hincmar of Reims (Mansi, 16.
862; *PL* 126. 505-6, and in abbreviated form at col.
586c-d) as evidence of his nephew's failure to abide by
the oath of obedience he had taken at the synod (thus,
see *PL* 126. 588c). Here, then, the polarity between the
two is encapsulated.

43.   Mansi, 16. 862e; *PL* 126. 506a.

44. Reg. HL, no. 104.

45. Mansi, 16. 580c.

46. The message is cited by Charles (Mansi, 16. 580d-e). For Bertharius, see *PL* 126. 506b. On date and source, see Reg. HL, no. 105.

47. Presumably the restoration concerned the property about which the bishop complained to his uncle in mid-July; see *PL* 126. 494d; cf. *PL* 124. 1030c. Regarding the pledges, see *PL* 124. 1031a.

48. *PL* 126. 507d.

49. *PL* 126. 494d. That Flotharius had been sent prior to Bertharius's journey appears likely from *PL* 124. 1030b.

50. Cf. ns. 6 and 7 above. Hincmar of Laon alleged that Abbot Ansegis read the precept before the assembly; *PL* 124. 1030b-c, 1038d.

51. See Reg. HL, no. 106.

52. *PL* 126. 495a.

53. Cf. ch. 3 above.

54. Reg. HL, no. 107.

55. *PL* 126. 495b-c.

56. *PL* 126. 589d. The reason for this, the archbishop says, was to assure that witnesses would see that Hincmar of Laon had, in fact, sent him the schedule containing the Tusey *capitula*.

57. Cf. n. 6 above.

58. *PL* 126. 496a-c.

59. The *capitula* of Tusey may be found at Mansi, 15. 557-61.

60. *PL* 124. 1030d.

61. *Capitulum* 1, at Mansi, 15. 558-59.

62. *Capitulum* 4, ibid., 559-60.

63. Ibid., 560-61. Among the names are those of both Hincmars; cf. below, ns. 64, 68.

64. *PL* 126. 589-90, from a later date. For the immediate reply, see Reg. HL, no. 109.

65. *PL* 126. 496-98. That the bishop attended either the provincial council or else some less formal meeting with his uncle in August may be indicated by *PL* 126. 587b.

66. Reg. HL, no. 116, and below, ns. 87 ff.

67. *PL* 124. 1039a-b.

68. *PL* 124. 1039b-c. On Hartgarius as a scribe, see Contreni, "Formation of Laon's Cathedral Library," pp. 935-36.

69. *PL* 124. 1040a-1041c. The letter to which the bishop refers is at *PL* 126. 122-32. He gives quotations to demonstrate (though incorrectly) the agreement of letter and *capitula* (*PL* 124. 1040b-1041b). The archbishop had told Bertharius that excommunications imposed on this basis would be invalid; this led Bishop Hincmar to reflect that such an attitude was not surprising, since the archbishop held even a papal excommunication as nothing (*PL* 124. 1041c.). On the eventual reply to this charge, see *PL* 126. 607-11.

70. The whole problem is discussed in McKeon, "Carolingian Councils of Savonnières (859) and Tusey (860)."

71. Reg. HL, no. 111.

72. *PL* 126. 506d-507b, 591b-592a.

73. See Mansi, 16. 580-81, and HR, at *PL* 126. 587a-b

74. Cf. ch. 2 above, and the schedule the bishop himself had read at Pîtres two years earlier (Reg. HL, no. 24).

75. Thus, HR, at *PL* 126. 505a, 592-93, with references to canon 9 of the third Council of Carthage and to canon 10 of the eleventh council of that city. See discussion of Lesne, *La hiérarchie épiscopale*, p. 135 and n. 5, p. 137 and n. 4.

76. See ch. 2 above, and *PL* 124. 1032b, 1034d.

77. See the evidence of Charles the Bald, at Mansi, 16. 579d, as well as col. 654b. The hearing, of course, had initially been interrupted by the king himself. See *PL* 124. 1034c-d, confirmed by Archbishop Hincmar, at *PL* 126. 505a; cf. n. 23 above.

78. *PL* 124. 1034d.

79. See appendix 2 below. Noorden, *Hinkmar*, p. 285, considered that the bishop had bribed the judges at Servais; Schrörs notes that the sources contain nothing to indicate this (*Hinkmar*, p. 340, n. 133), which does not, of course, rule out the possibility.

80. *PL* 126. 185b-c.

81. Cf. ch. 3 above.

82. Reg. HL, no. 108.

83. Reg. HL, no. 115.

84. *PL* 126. 185b-c.

85. The wording of the papal letter, as quoted by HR (see *PL* 126. 185), is strikingly similar to the language used by the bishop of Laon in the message received by the archbishop on 18 July. See especially *PL* 126. 495a-b.

86. *PL* 126. 185-86. The letter was carried to Rome by Ansegis. Amann, *L'époque carolingienne*, pp. 406-7, placed his embarkation at mid-October; but see Reg. HL, no. 114.

87. Reg. HL, no. 116.

88. *PL* 124. 1027-42.

89. *PL* 124. 1042-52.

90. *PL* 124. 1042-43. The reference is to the letter of Pseudo-Marcus to Athanasius and the Egyptian bishops, chs. 1-2 (*PI*, pp. 453-54). For the archbishop's criticism, see especially HR Opusculum, chs. 20-21, cols. 353-66.

91. *PL* 124. 1044-46. The lists in question are at *PI*, pp. 467, 485 ff.

92. *PL* 124. 1046-47.

93. *PL* 124. 1047-48, in opposition to the archbishop's arguments at HR Opusculum, ch. 20, col. 363.

94. *PL* 126. 363-64.

95. *PL* 124. 1048-49.

96. *PL* 124. 1053-54.

97. Pseudo-Calixtus, chs. 14-15 (*PI*, pp. 139-40). cited by HL in *Pittaciolus*, at *PL* 124. 1005 (and cf. cols. 994-95).

98. See *PL* 126. 393-97.

99. *PL* 124. 1054-55.

100. *PL* 124. 1055-59. The Pseudo-Isidorian references are to Pseudo-Calixtus, ch. 13; Pseudo-Lucius, ch. 3; Pseudo-Anicius, ch. 4 (*PI*, pp. 139, 176, 121). The conciliar authorities are Antioch, canon 9; Milevis (ann. 402), canon 22; Sardica, canons 16 and 17 (*PI*, pp. 271,

319, 269); and Nicaea I, canon 5 (Alberigo, *Conciliorum oecumenicorum decreta*, p. 7).

101. *PL* 124. 1061 ff.

102. Reg. HL, no. 117.

103. Thus, see *PL* 126. 498c, and the description given by Flodoard, 3. 22. 520.

104. See, thus, the tone of *PL* 124. 1064 ff.

Chapter VII

1. See Parisot, *Le royaume de Lorraine*, pp. 336 ff.

2. The eldest child, a daughter named Judith, was married in 856, at the age of twelve, to the old king Aethelwulf of Kent (*Ann. Bert.*, p. 73; marriage and coronation *ordo*, MGH *Cap*. 2. 425-27. See Schramm, "Ordines Studien," p. 8; Brühl, "Fränkischer Krönungs-brauch."), and, at his death in 858, to his son Aethel-bald (*Ann. Bert.*, p. 76). When Aethelbald died two years later, Judith returned to the continent and was immured by King Charles at Senlis. She escaped in 862 (with the aid of her brother) and eloped with Baldwin, a *fidelis* of Lothar II (ibid., pp. 87-88). Through the mediation of Pope Nicholas I, Charles eventually accepted the marriage (see Nicholas *Epp.*, nos. 7-8, pp. 272-75 [JE, 2703-4]) and made Baldwin count of Flanders (see *Ann. Bert.*, pp. 95, 98, 103-4; Sproemberg, *Die Entstehung der grafschaft Flandern*. Baldwin appears later as a partisan of Carloman; see n. 14 below. On Judith, see also Sproemberg, "Judith, Königin von England."

3. For the date of Louis's birth, 11 November 846, cf. *Annales Vedastini*, ann. 879, in Rau, p. 44, with Bouquet, 9. 403. On Charles the Younger, see chapter 4 above. On Lothar, whom CB had made an oblate, see *Annales Floriacenses*, MGH *SS* 2. 254; also Ado of Vienne mentions his death (*Chronicon*, MGH *SS* 2. 323), but the

year was actually 865. Lothar is often not even mentioned among Charles's children; thus, *Annales Einsidlinenses*, (MGH *SS* 3. 140), and *Domus Carolingica genealogia*, pt. 4 (MGH *SS* 2. 323).

4. *Ann. Bert.*, p. 129; MGH *Cap.* 2, no. 301, pp.
453-55. See Schramm, *Der König von Frankreich*, 1:23.

5. Judging from the fact of his having four older
siblings and from the year he received the tonsure. On
Carloman, see especially MGH *Poet. lat.* 3. 267 ff.;
Amann, *L'époque carolingienne*, pp. 402-11; G. Drioux,
"Carloman," in *Dictionnaire d'histoire et de géographie
ecclésiastiques*, 11:1062-65; Grotz, *Erbe Wider Willen*,
pp. 243-47, 268-69.

6. *Annales Mettenses*, ann. 870 (Bouquet, 7. 198);
Ann. Bert., p. 70; PL 126. 277d, 594a-b.

7. See MGH *Cap.* 2. 313; *Ann. Bert.*, ann. 866, 870,
pp. 130, 171, and Tessier, 2:252-54 (Saint-Médard);
ibid., pp. 168-70, 225-26, 237-38 (Saint-Amand, Saint-
Arnoul, Saint-Riquier); MGH *SS* 13. 80 (Saint-Germain);
Folcuinus, *Gesta abbatum Lobiensium*, MGH *SS* 4. 61
(Lobbes).

8. Cf. ch. 4 above; *Carmina Scottorum* 7. 3 (MGH
Poet. lat. 3. 690).

9. See their letter, at *Epistolae variorum*, no.
25[2], (MGH *Epp.* 6. 179-80).

10. At least according to Hariulf, the twelfth-
century compiler of the chronicle of Saint-Riquier; see
Chronique de Saint-Riquier, 3, ch. 19, pp. 135-39. The
editor remarks (at p.xlv) that the abbatial eulogies in
the work have no value. See also *Carmina Centulensia*
105 (MGH *Poet. lat.* 3. 336-37).

11. In 868 he led troops against Viking invaders;
Ann. Bert., p. 151.

12. See ch. 3 above.

13. Thus, the continual statements of HR in the *Ann. Bert.*, passim.

14. The rebels also included Conrad, count of Paris and father of the future King Odo, and Harduinus; cf. n. 32 below.

15. That he was surprised is indicated by the presence of his name on the list of attendants at the session of 16 June; Mansi, 16. 860c.

16. *Ann. Bert.*, p. 171. This was, then, presumably the reason for the assembly's adjournment; cf. chs. 4 and 5 above.

17. *Ann. Bert.*, p. 177. Cf. chs. 3 and 6 above.

18. *Ann. Bert.*, p. 177. Lesne, *Histoire de la propriété ecclésiastique*, 4:210, considers the illuminated bible at Paris lat. 2 to be connected with this event; see also the discussion of Guilman, "Illuminations of the Second Bible of Charles the Bald."

19. For the dates of this itinerary, see Reg. HL, nos. 114-15.

20. *Ann. Bert.*, pp. 177-78.

21. See Poupardin, *Le royaume de Provence*, pp. 37 ff.

22. See Kremers, "Ado von Vienne."

23. Cf. ch. 2 above.

24. Parisot, *Le royaume de Lorraine*, p. 393, notes the unlikelihood that Gerard reasonably expected to establish an independent rule.

25. See Halphen, *Charlemagne*, pp. 409-13. On the war in Italy against the Arabs, see Lokys, *Die Kämpf der Araber*; also the brief treatment in Musset, *Les invasions*, pp. 147 ff.

26. *Ann. Bert.*, pp. 177-78.

27. Ibid., p. 178.

28. Ibid.; see Poupardin, *Le royaume de Provence*, pp. 39-40 and n. 6.

29. *Ann. Bert.*, pp. 178-79.

30. Flodoard, 3. 23. 530; Reg. HL, no. 118.

31. Flodoard, 3. 26. 543. The archbishop's attitude seems apparent in this synopsis and in the synopsis of a letter to CB (ibid., ch. 18, p. 508).

32. Two letters to Carloman are synopsized by Flodoard, 3. 18, 26. 508-9, 543. See also, for example, the letters to Counts Engelramnus and Harduinus, ibid., 26. 543, 544. See Reg. HL, nos. 120, 123-26. Engelramnus may have been the official who was discharged by reason of Richilde's hostility; see *Ann. Bert.*, p. 199. His connections are uncertain. See, e.g., Vanderkindere, "Le capitulaire de Servais," pp. 100 ff.; Grierson, "Translation of the Relics of St. Amalberga," pp. 308-9.

33. *Ann. Bert.*, p. 179.

34. *PL* 126. 598a-b for the location.

35. *Ann. Bert.*, pp. 179-80. He appears to have been offered the opportunity to return to imprisonment, now at Saint-Médard; see Flodoard, 3. 18. 508. Hincmar of Reims alleged that Carloman had made impossible demands; *Ann. Bert.*, p. 179. We do not know what his demands were.

36. Mansi 16. 605-6. For the date of the council, see Reg. HL, no. 127.

37. A fragment of the letter to Archbishop Remi and the other prelates of Lyons is at *PL* 126. 279-80; its ending is given at Mansi, 16. 605-6. See Reg. HL, no. 129.

38. *PL* 126. 594b-c.

39. Mansi, 16. 606b-c. Charles appears to contradict the archbishop when he refers to Hincmar of Laon as having been at Compiègne in February (ibid., 580e); and, in fact, the archbishop contradicts himself (*PL* 126. 587b). See Reg. HL, no. 128.

40. *PL* 126. 594c.

41. *PL* 126. 594c-d.

42. *PL* 124. 1069-72.

43. *PL* 126. 595a-b.

44. *PL* 126. 596-97, 599b-c.

45. *PL* 126. 598a-599b. The latter demand was the requested alteration (cf. n. 42 above). Hincmar of Reims later denied that Heddo had relayed any such request (Mansi, 16. 606e-608c.

46. *PL* 126. 599b-c.

47. *PL* 126. 597b-d.

48. *PL* 126. 596-97. It was not that the absence of this one signature deprived the conciliar sentence of its efficacy; the first council of Nicaea expressly allows the passage of a judgment lacking the agreement of two or three members of a provincial council (Alberigo, *Conciliorum oecumenicorum decreta*, canon 6, p. 8). HR cited this canon in regard to John of Cambrai (*PL* 126. 298a; see also HR, *De divortio Hlotharii regis*, q. iii, at *PL* 125. 750c).

49. Since there was a total of ten suffragans in the province, of whom HL and the "others," i.e., at least two, who according to HR had sent in their agreement (*PL* 126. 594c-d), were absent.

50. *Ann. Bert.*, p. 179.

51. Ibid., pp. 180-81. Charles the Bald is mentioned as being at Senlis with a number of his *fideles*,

at *PL* 126. 587b. The gathering of such a force, at about
this time, is indicated at *Ann. Bert.*, p. 181.   The
calling of the larger council is indicated at the same
place; cf. Flodoard, 3. 22. 519-20, where reference is
made to the deacon Bertharius, *"quem metropolitani atque
comprovincialis sinodi iudicium appellantem,"* a designation which for HR signifies a larger rather than provincial council; cf. ch. 5 above.   Also, the implication of
the letter from Archbishop Hincmar to Bishop Adventius
of Metz (Flodoard, 3. 23. 528), which Schrörs has dated
to c. mid-871 (Reg. HR, no. 312, and p. 577, n. 105).
Finally, the papal letters sent on 13 July (n. 53 below) seem to indicate that such an assembly was in the
offing.   The army, though, could not legally be summoned
during Lent except in a serious emergency; cf. the
charge against Louis the Pious in 833, at MGH *Cap.* 2.
54.

52.   MGH *Epp.* 6. 735-36.

53.   Hadrian *Epp.*, nos. 31-33, pp. 735-38 (JE, 2940-
42).

54.   This is the opinion of Noorden, *Hinkmar*, p. 286;
cf. Schrörs, *Hinkmar*, p. 341, n. 138.   The letter of 14
May, given by the archbishop at HR Libellus, *praefatio*,
pp. 566-67, is interpreted by Schrörs as a call to the
council of Douzy (Reg. HR, no. 307).   This is unlikely,
because of the early date, the existence of another
letter, dated 5 July, with specific reference to that
villa (*PL* 126. 567b; Flodoard, 3, ch. 22, p. 520), and
the fact that the first letter appears to have been addressed to the bishops of the province of Reims only;
see *PL* 126. 566d. That other bishops were present at
Servais appears from the king's remark at Mansi, 16. 580e.

55.   Synopsized by Flodoard, 3. 22. 519-20. Presumably, then, the deacon's appeal had been made to HR between 14 May and 10 June, since the summons of the
earlier date contains no mention of it; see *PL* 126. 566c-d.

56.   See ch. 9, n. 5 below.

57.   A form of this collection may be found at *PL* 124.

993-1002. Actually, the source says it was *delivered* on
16 June. On the likelihood of its having existed in a
fuller form than we possess, see Reg. HL, no. 140.

58. *PI*, pp. 484-91. The bishop, at *PL* 124. 998-99,
cites ch. 20 (*PI*, p. 488).

59. For this passage in the context of the council
at Attigny, see ch. 6 above. That the bishop knew of
these letters is another indication of the easy access
to information between Reims and Laon.

60. These arguments appear in fragments of the
letter quoted by the archbishop in HR Libellus, ch. 23
(Mansi, 16. 614b-c). Cf. ch. 4, ns. 58, 59 above.

61. HR Libellus, ch. 32 (Mansi, 16. 633-35); this
passage may be found in the extant document, at *PL* 124.
998c-1002a.

62. The letter exists only as a fragment, as preserved by Flodoard, 3. 22. 527-28; it can also be found
at *PL* 126. 509-11. The date is hypothesized; for the
arguments, see Reg. HL, no. 143.

63. *PL* 126. 510c.

64. *PL* 126. 510-11.

65. The abbot's arrival may be dated approximately
by the fact that Hincmar of Reims notified his nephew of
the papal letters on 5 July; see ch. 8 below.

66. Hadrian *Epp.*, no. 29 (MGH *Epp.* 6. 734 [JE,
2936]). The letter is dated 25 March. For conflicting
interpretations of it, see Mansi, 16. 666b-c.

67. Hadrian *Epp.*, no. 30 (MGH *Epp.* 6. 734-35; JE,
2938). Amann, *L'époque carolingienne*, p. 407, n. 1,
refers to these letters as "deux textes de grande
importance pour l'étude du droit des metropolitains."

68. *PL* 126. 567b.

69. *Ann. Bert.*, p. 181. According to CB, he, too, had summoned the bishop to the council (Mansi, 16. 581); but cf. HL, *Reclamatio* (MGH *Epp.* 7. 94). On the authenticity of the summons, see Reg. HL, no. 144.

70. The bishop had attended Charles at Servais (Mansi, 16. 580; *PL* 126. 587).

71. HR attempts to relate the alleged royal summons to the case he himself was preparing (*Ann. Bert.*, p. 181), but the king's charges are patently distinct; see ch. 8 below.

72. *Ann. Bert.*, p. 182.

73. *Annales Fuldenses*, in Rau, 3:80; BML, 1484b, 1485c.

74. *Ann. Bert.*, p. 181.

Chapter VIII

1. The councils of the Carolingian period are recorded in MGH *Conc.*, vol. 2, *Concilia aevi karolini (742-842)*, and in Mansi, vols. 12-18. They are also treated in Hefele-Leclercq, *Histoire des conciles*, vols. 3 and 4. See also ch. 5 above.

2. Cf. Morrison, *Two Kingdoms*, p. 13.

3. For these records, see Reg. HL, nos. 146-56. On Douzy, see also Hefele-Leclercq, *Histoire des conciles*, 4:620-35.

4. See ch. 7 above, ns. 54, 55.

5. Mansi, 16. 581d-e.

6. Mansi, 16. 581b.

7. Mansi, 16. 658b.

8. See Mansi, 16. 671a, for the third call; and cf. col. 581d-e. See *PL* 126. 628-31 on the triple call.

9. See Mansi, 16. 671-75, 677-78, for the two differing name lists.

10. Ansegis had just been created archbishop; see Duchesne, *Fastes épiscopaux*, 2:418, and cf. ch. 7 above.

11. They demanded recognition of Willibert as archbishop of Cologne, according to a letter of CB to Hadrian published in *Concilia antiqua Galliae, Supplementa*, ed. Delalande, 4:273, col. 2. This version, edited from Paris lat. 1594, here contains material deleted in the other extant form of the letter; see n. 94 below.

12. Mansi, 16. 659e-660a.

13. *PL* 126. 566c.

14. HR, *Schedula sive Libellus expostulationis Hincmari metropolitanis Remensis* (*PL* 126. 566-634); see Reg. HL, no. 148.

15. On the dates, see Reg. HL, n. 38.

16. HR Libellus, preface, cols. 566-68.

17. Ibid., col. 567c-d. This statement of nonpersonal involvement is repeated in various forms a number of times in the documents that make up the records of the synod; thus, Hincmar of Reims, (*PL* 126. 631a; cf. col. 646a), and the bishops of the synod, speaking through their representatives, (Mansi, 16. 658-59). The *Acta synodi*, which appear at Mansi 16. 658-78, were, like the other records, written by or under the strong influence of the archbishop of Reims; this is evident in the *Acta* by the use of the phrase "*rex surgens*" (ch. 4, col. 662e), which is found in other Hincmarian reports (cf. the Council of Soissons, ann. 853, at Mansi, 14. 985b; cf. also n. 60 below). The purpose of the disclaimer was to avoid the charge of prejudice, which following Pseudo-Isidore should cause a suspension in the proceedings and allow immediate appeal to Rome. See Pseudo-

Victor, ch. 6, (*PI*, p. 128); Pseudo-Sixtus II, ch. 3
(*PI*, pp. 190-91); Pseudo-Julius, ch. 12 (*PI*, p. 468).

18.   *PL* 126. 568-607.

19.   *PL* 126. 607-28.

20.   See *PL* 126. 631b.

21.   *PL*, 126. 631-32. The references are to the letters of Leo to Anastasius of Thessalonica (Leo I,
Epistolae, no. 84, at *PL* 54. 921-22) and of Celestine I
to Cyril of Alexandria (Celestine I, *Epistolae*, no. 11,
at *PL* 50. 459-64).

22.   *PL* 126. 633a.

23.   The bishop's failure to appear was also made a
contravention of papal command; see *PL* 126. 631b.

24.   They are mentioned briefly at *Acta synodi*, ch. 7
(Mansi, 16. 670a and c), and by certain of the bishops,
notably Adventius of Metz, Gislebertus of Chartres, and
Eugenoldus of Poitiers, in their judgments, ibid., ch. 9
(cols. 673-74).

25.   CB, *Petitio proclamationis adversus Hincmarum
Laudunensem episcopum*, in Mansi, 16. 578-81; Reg. HL, no.
147.   Nortmannus was also prepared to make charges;
Mansi, 16. 679e and cf. *PL* 126. 637d.

26.   CB, *Petitio*, ch. 4, at Mansi, 15. 578-80.

27.   Ibid., ch. 5, cols. 580-81. The king omits mention of Hincmar of Laon's attendance on him at Senlis in
April, of which we learn from the archbishop (*PL* 126.
587b).

28.   CB, *Petitio*, ch. 6, at Mansi, 16. 581.

29.   Mansi, 16. 581d-e.

30.   See Reg. HL, no. 147.

31.   *Acta synodi*, ch. 1, at Mansi, 16. 658-60.

32.   Mansi, 16. 658-59. See n. 22 above, and cf.
Mansi, 16. 661b.

33.   Both charges are later made by HL to Pope John
VIII. See HL, *Reclamatio* (MGH *Epp*. 7. 94-95). HR is
at pains to make Douzy appear the continuation of
Attigny; *PL* 126. 566-67 and Mansi, 16. 662b.

34.   *Acta synodi*, ch. 4, Mansi, 16. 662e-664a.

35.   HL, *Reclamatio*, MGH *Epp*. 7. 94-95.

36.   *Acta synodi*, ch. 2, Mansi, 16. 660.

37.   Ibid., ch. 3, cols. 660-61.

38.   HL, *Reclamatio*, MGH *Epp*. 7. 94; see also Mansi,
16. 662a-b.

39.   A wish he states quite frankly; Mansi, 16. 581a.

40.   *Ann. Bert*. p. 182. The importance of this meeting is indicated by Hincmar of Reims in a later message
sent to the pope in the name of the king (at *PL* 124.
880b-c). The concern evidenced in this passage for responsible administration of government and assessment of the
needs of royal subjects is particularly striking in that
it issues from the same source as had in October 870 informed Hadrian that, contrary to papal assertions of
rights, needs, and propriety, it was the opinion of many
in the north that peace would follow from the treaty of
Meersen, but "*si ipsa firmitas exsecuta non fuerit,
praelia et seditiones . . . inter eos exsurgent, et
maxima strages populi ac perditio animarum inde pro-
veniet, quod postea emendari non potuerit*" (*PL* 126.
176b-c).

41.   Cf. Mansi, 16. 581d-e, with *Acta synodi*, ch. 8,
ibid., col. 671.

42.   *Responsa episcoporum*, Mansi, 16. 643-58; Reg. HL,
no. 150. The influence of the archbishop of Reims is

particularly apparent in ch. 2 (Mansi, 16. 643-45),
which is largely drawn from his treatise *De cavendis
vitiis et virtutibus exercendis*, ch. 3 (*PL* 125. 882-88).

43. *Acta synodi*, ch. 4 (Mansi, 16. 662a).

44. For the following, see ibid., cols. 662-64.

45. Pseudo-Felix, ch. 10. (*PI*, pp. 201-202).

46. Mansi 16. 662e.

47. *Acta synodi*, ch. 5 (Mansi 16. 664-65).

48. *PI*, p. 272.

49. Specifically, Council of Antioch canon 25 (*PI*,
pp. 272-73), which was read to the council immediately
afterward (see Mansi 16. 665b-d) and which also called for
synodal adjudication in such cases. Hincmar of Laon is
also stated (Mansi, 16. 665b) to have violated the
thirty-second canon of the "Codex Africanus" (canon 49
of the third Council of Carthage, ann. 397; Dionysius
Exiguus, *Collectio canonum*, (at *PL* 67. 192c). On the later
history of the unfortunate treasure, see Flodoard, 3. 27.
549.

50. *Acta synodi*, ch. 6, Mansi, 16. 665e.

51. Mansi, 16. 666.

52. Mansi, 16. 666-67.

53. Ibid., ch. 7, col. 669b, once more a justification of the proceedings. Cf. HR *Libellus*, ch. 35, *PL*
126. 628c.

54. Mansi, 16. 668a-670d.

55. Mansi, 16. 670d-e.

56. *Acta synodi*, ch. 8, Mansi, 16. 671.

57. Ibid., ch. 9, cols. 671-75.

58. Only Adalardus of Rouen based his judgment on the violation of law involved in having yielded Poilly without the knowledge of the bishop's metropolitan, co-bishops, or cathedral clergy (Mansi, 16. 672b-c).

59. See n. 24 above.

60. Another favorite phrase at Douzy; it or its equivalent may be found appended to the judgment of each bishop (e.g., *PL* 126. 631b-c) in the sentence of deposition (cols. 635c-d), and in the synodal letter (col. 638a).

61. For the sentence, see *PL* 126. 634-35.

62. See Reg. HL, nos. 154-56.

63. It may be found at *PL* 126. 635-41.

64. *PL* 126. 636a. Thus, by placing emphasis upon his election, denying any imputation of blame to CB or HR. Cf. the archbishop, in his own letter to the pope, col. 644a-b.

65. *PL* 126. 636c, thus involving Hadrian, on the basis of his letter of 25 March, in the act of deposition. See ch. 7 above.

66. *PL* 126. 636c-d.

67. *PL* 126. 638c-d. See the Council of Sardica, canons 4 and 5 (*PI*, p. 267).

68. See *PL* 126. 638c-d. The canonical references are to letters of Boniface I to Hilary of Narbonne, (*PI*, p. 556), and the African council, ann. 419, to Celestine I (Dionysius Exiguus, *Collectio canonum*, at *PL* 67. 227-30; see col. 229b).

69. *PL* 126. 638c-d. The references are to Gregory I, *Registrum epistolarum*, 5, no. 3, and 3, no. 8 (MGH *Epp.* 1. 282-83, 168-69).

70. *PL* 126. 639d-640c. This final definition should be

made based upon the documents carried by Actard; an interpolation then reads "[Q]*uod et de Rothado faceremus, si legatis nostris facultas transeundi Alpes in illis temporibus concederetur.* . . ." (col. 640c).

71. *PL* 126. 641-48. See also the letter to Anastasius, synopsized by Flodoard, 3. 24. 536, dated by Schrörs to the beginning of September 871 (Reg. HR, no. 316).

72. Hincmar recalls the letter sent to him by Rome in 868 (MGH *Epp*. 6. 710-12; JE, 2905) concerning Actard (see *PL* 126. 641c). Archbishop Herardus of Tours probably died on 30 June 871; see Duchesne, *Fastes épiscopaux*, 2:308, 365.

73. *PL* 126. 642d-643c; cf. the letter HR sent to Hadrian the previous year, *PL* 126. 185b-c.

74. See n. 64 above.

75. *PL* 126. 646a.

76. *PL* 126. 646b-648c.

77. Each of his acts as recounted by the archbishop involves a clear violation of a specific canon.

78. CB, *Epistolae*, no. 7 (*PL* 124. 876-81).

79. See Reg. HL, no. 156.

80. *PL* 124. 876b.

81. *PL* 126. 876-77.

82. *PL* 126. 879-880.

83. *PL* 126. 880c-d.

84. *PL* 126. 881a-b.

85. See the arguments in McKeon, "Toward a Reestablishment of the Correspondence of Pope Hadrian II."

86. *PL* 124. 877b ff.

87. See Lâpotre, *De Anastasio*, pp. 260 *et seq.*

88. *Epistola synodalis* (*PL* 126. 636c).

89. Hadrian *Epp.* nos. 34, 35, pp. 738-43 (*JE*, 2945-46).

90. Ibid., no. 34, pp. 738-40.

91. Ibid., no. 35, pp. 740-42.

92. The fragment of this letter may be found at *Mansi*, 16. 569-71. The letter is in Paris lat. 1594, folio 196-227^V, where twelve chapters are to be found; it is still apparently incomplete, and is largely ruined past folio 211 (*capitulum* 8).

93. *Mansi*, 16. 570b ff. The same figure is found in the other Frankish letters.

94. CB *Epistolae*, no. 8 (*PL* 124. 881-96). The edition in Migne is incomplete. P. Delalande edited the complete letter in the supplement to Sirmond, *Concilia antiqua Galliae*, 4:267-74, from the manuscript cited in note 92 above. Camus mentions the excision in his review of the manuscript, "Notice d'un manuscrit de la Bibliothèque Nationale n. 1594," and cites the marginal note, but he neglects the significance of the whole. The letter stands at folio 174-95. A note is found at folio 191^V, in the left margin: "[A]b *isto signo ad sequens signum, quae hic posita sunt, non fuerunt missa in epistola Romam directa.*" Above this note is the sign, and in the text a bracket; another bracket appears at folio 194 with the same sign in the right-hand margin. The missing portion comes between paragraphs at *PL* 124. 895c. It relates that HL, after his deposition, was aided by the bishops of Louis the German, who refused their consent to the deposition and demanded, as a condition to their consent, that Charles (who was then with Louis at a "near-by place," [i.e., Maestricht]) consent to the ordination of Willibert as archbishop of Cologne. The letter proceeds to a discussion of the uncanonical

aspects of this, particularliy in view of Hincmar's
crimes. The passage thus informs us that Hincmar
received support from Louis's bishops (actually to be
inferred from other sources as well, and at all events
no real indication of personal support) and, also, that
the eastern bishops presumably never consented, since
Willibert did not receive the pallium until 874. See
Parisot, *Le royaume de Lorraine*, pp. 357 ff. The suffragans of Cologne had petitioned the pope for Willibert
(*ibid.*, p. 360). It may be assumed, perhaps, that the
excision in Charles's letter was occasioned by a desire
to avoid any connection between the two issues, which
might thus prejudice the pope against Charles's man
Hilduin as a candidate for the see of Cologne.

95. *PL* 124. 883d.

96. *PL* 124. 883-84, following the Council of Valence,
ann. 374, canon 4, (*PI*, p. 324).

97. *PL* 124. 885b-d.

98. *PL* 124. 886b-c.

99. *PL* 124. 886d-889d; see especially cols. 886d,
888a-b, 889b-d.

100. *PL* 124. 894a-c.

101. *PL* 124. 895a-c; see especially col. 895c.

102. *PL* 124. 895-96. For the reference, see Gregory
I, *Registrum epistolarum*, 1, no. 24, at MGH *Epp*. 1. 36,
and various other places. The fifth ecumenical council,
held under the emperor Justinian against the Three Chapters, resulted in the imprisonment and coercion of Pope
Vigilius; still, it seems less likely that this is the
threat intended than that the reference is meant to remind the reader of later western reaction, when many of
the great sees refused communion with the papacy and a
schism opened, which in a number of cases lasted for
some years. Perhaps due to this, Gregory I did not always mention the council; see, e.g., *Registrum epistolarum*, 5, no. 59 (MGH *Epp*. 1. 372).

103. CB, *Epistolae*, no. 9 (*PL* 124. 896). The long letter had been sent on a quaternion, which was rarely done with royal correspondence.

104. MGH *Epp.* 6. 743.

105. Hadrian *Epp.*, no. 36, pp. 743-46 (JE, 2951). For the date, see McKeon, "Toward a Reestablishment of the Correspondence of Pope Hadrian II."

106. MGH *Epp.* 6. 745-46.

107. Ibid., p. 746.

108. Ibid., p. 745.

Chapter IX

1. BML, no. 1246b, e, f.

2. *Ann. Bert.*, p. 182.

3. BML, no. 1251b.

4. See ch. 7 above.

5. *Ann. Bert.*, p. 182; *Annales Fuldenses*, in Rau, 3:82; Flodoard, 3. 18. 508.

6. *Ann. Bert.*, p. 182.

7. Ibid., pp. 182-84.

8. See Odegaard, "Empress Engelberge." It seems clear that events in Italy during the latter months of 871 had caused perhaps disproportionate concern to both pope and emperor. In the first months of 872, the empress held a strange pair of interviews with Louis the German and with Charles (on this see also Calmette, *La diplomatie carolingienne*, pp. 136-41); and on 18 May Louis II had himself recrowned by the pope (*Ann. Bert.*, pp. 184 ff.).

9.   See ch. 8 above.

10.   The exact date is unknown; JE, p. 375.

11.   The biography of Pope John VIII by Lapôtre, *L'Europe et le Saint Siège*, remains essential. See also Mann, *The Popes during the Carolingian Empire*, 3:231-352.

12.   The implication at *Ann. Bert.*, p. 189.

13.   Ibid., pp. 189-90.   We possess only the chapter headings of this synod, which was composed of bishops from the provinces of Reims and Sens (Carloman's province); see Mansi, 17. 282.   According to Flodoard, (3. 18. 508-9), it was a national council, and the call was relayed by Hincmar of Reims.

14.   *Ann. Bert.*, p. 190.   See also Heiricus, *Annales breves*, in MGH *SS* 13. 80; *Annales Lemovicenses*, in MGH *SS* 2. 251; cf. *Annales Xantenses*, in Rau, 2:368.   The archbishop of Reims asserts that Carloman's followers had actually pressed his claim.   That the prince's eyes may have been removed prior to the council may appear from the *Catalogus I abbatum Epternacensium*, which states (at MGH *SS* 13. 739) that Carloman died eight years after the death of Lothar II and seven years after he was blinded; this is repeated in *Series regum et abbatum* (ibid., 742).   Regino, *Chronicon* (in Rau, 3:230-32), places the whole of his account of Carloman under the year 870.   *Ann. Bert.* (p. 190) attributes the decision: (1) to a desire to mitigate the death penalty and thus allow the prince time to realize the seriousness of his deeds and to come to repentence; (2) to a decision made by all the bishops present.   While this may be true, it is worthwhile to note (bearing in mind the strong bias of the annalist Meginhardus) the comment in *Annales Fuldenses*, that places the onus on Charles, calling him a tyrant (p. 88).

15.   *Ann. Bert.*, pp. 192-93.   On Adalard in this incident, see Lot, "Note sur le sénéschal Alard," p. 603. But identities are in doubt.   Cf. Hlawitschka, *Die Anfänge des Hauses Habsburg-Lothringen*, pp. 162-63.

16. *Ann. Bert.*, p. 194.

17. The presentation of the abbey of Echternach appears in both *Catalogi abbatum Epternacensium* (MGH *SS* 13. 739, 741), and in the *Series regum et abbatum* (ibid., 742). The same sources indicate the prince's death.

18. BML, no. 1275a.

19. See the discussion by Lapôtre, *L'Europe et le Saint-Siège*, pp. 209 ff.

20. *Ann. Bert.*, p. 199.

21. Ibid., p. 200; *Annales Fuldenses*, in Rau 3:98. Charles was definitely anointed, as is observed by Poupardin, "L'onction impériale," pp. 123-24. On aspects of Charles's imperial period, see Schramm, *Kaiser, Könige und Päpste*, 2:119 ff.

22. The problem of the basically intermittent, non-continuous Carolingian defense against the Arabs is discussed by Engreen, "Pope John VIII and the Arabs."

23. Thus, John VIII, *Epistolae collectae*, no. 22 (MGH *Epp.* 7. 19-21; JE, 3062).

24. See, e.g., John VIII, *Registrum epistolarum*, no. 56 (MGH *Epp.* 7. 51-52; JE, 3099). For John's turn to Charles, see Partner, *Lands of St. Peter*, pp. 68 ff.

25. MGH *Cap.* 2, no. 220, pp. 98-100. See Calmette, *La diplomatie carolingienne*, pp. 201-204.

26. *Ann. Bert.*, pp. 198-99. A leader of the revolt was the former chamberlain **Engelramnus**, who had lost his office due to the influence of Richilde, in favor of her brother Boso. This must have occurred in the period following early 871 (Flodoard, 3. 26. 543). On **Engelramnus** also, cf. ch. 7 above.

27. *Ann. Bert.*, p. 199; *Annales Fuldenses*, in Rau, 3:98.

28.   John VIII, *Registrum epistolarum*, nos. 5-8 (MGH *Epp*. 7. 317-26; JE, 3037-40).

29.   See Halphen, *Charlemagne*, p. 377.

30.   On the Council of Ponthion held during June and July 876, see MGH *Cap*. 2, no. 279, pp. 347-53; also Mansi, 17. 307-18.   See also Schieffer, *Die päpstlichen Legaten in Frankreich*, pp. 16-25.

31.   *Ann. Bert.*, pp. 201 ff.   At p. 204, HR testifies to the widespread indignation felt by the prelates, who were constrained by Charles's presence to accept the establishment of the vicariate.   It must, of course, be recalled that HR himself was its foremost opponent, and he wrote the treatise *De jure metropolitanorum* (*PL* 126. 189-210) against it.   On the event, see Fliche, "La primatie des archevêques de Sens," and "La primatie des Gaules," pp. 329-35.

32.   *Ann. Bert.*, p. 206.

33.   BML, 1519b.

34.   *Ann. Bert.*, pp. 206-7; *Annales Fuldenses*, in Rau, 3:100-4.

35.   BML, 1547i.

36.   Hartmann, *Geschichte Italiens im Mittelalter*, 3:21 ff.

37.   *Ann. Bert.*, p. 213.   See Joranson, *Danegeld in France*, pp. 93-110; and Lot, "Les tributs au Normands."

38.   For the assembly at Quierzy, see MGH *Cap*. 2, nos. 281-82, pp. 355-63.   The old work of Bourgeois, *Le capitulaire de Kiersy-sur-Oise*, which is in fact a much broader study than its title would indicate, must be used with care.

39.   *Ann. Bert.*, p. 216.   Among the leaders of the widespread revolt were Boso himself and Hugh the Abbot. The old study by Bourgeois, "Hugues l'Abbé," contains

many errors. See also Oexele, "Bischof Ebroin von Poitiers," pp. 191 ff.

40. *Ann. Bert.*, p. 217.

41. See Dhondt, "Election et hérédité sous les Carolingiens," pp. 921-22.

42. *Ann. Bert.*, p. 219; MGH *Cap.* 2, no. 283, pp. 363-65. See Sprengler, "Die Gebete der Krönungsordines Hincmars von Reims," pp. 254 ff.; Schramm, *Kaiser, Könige und Päpste*, 2:142 ff., 209-10.

43. See ch. 8 above.

44. See Berza, "Sur le voyage en France du pape Jean VIII (878)."

45. Of the immense number of sources for Troyes, the most important documents may be found in Mansi, 17. 93-94, 345-58, and app. 2, cols. 187-88. See also *PL* 126. 795 ff. A number of papal letters are particularly significant: JE, 3137-40, 3147, 3150-51, 3154, 3157, 3159, 3162, 3169, 3170-3240. Cf. JE, 3158, 3205. For chronology of the council as it pertains to the present subject, cf. Reg. HL, no. 173.

46. Mansi, 17. 349-50; *Acta synodalia de Formoso episcopo*, ed. Dümmler, in *Auxilius und Vigilius*, pp. 159-61.

47. The assembly was postponed several times on this account; see *Ann. Bert.*, p. 223.

48. Hartmann, *Geschichte Italiens im Mittelalter*, 3^2:60-61.

49. Cf. ch. 8, n. 98.

50. HL, *Reclamatio* (MGH *Epp.* 7. 94-95).

51. On the reaction of the eastern prelates who were requested to affirm the decision of Douzy, see ch. 8 above; and for Hincmar's episcopal supporters in the west, see n. 67 below.

52.   Boso at this time was regent for Louis the Stammerer in Aquitaine; see Poupardin, *Le royaume de Provence*, pp. 65 ff.

53.   The approximate date may be calculated from HL, *Reclamatio* (MGH *Epp.* 7. 95).

54.   The bishop was imprisoned in 873, i.e., a few months after Carloman was deposed; he was blinded, he says, almost two years later.   Boso is blamed in the *Annales Vedastini* (in Rau, 2:292).   On CB as instigator, see Schrörs, *Hinkmar*, p. 424; Dümmler, *Geschichte des ostfränkischen Reiches*, 3^2:87.   I agree with Marlot that no evidence indicates HR was responsible; *Histoire de la ville, cité et université de Reims*, 2:459 n. 3.

55.   John VIII, *Epistolae collectae*, no. 4 (MGH *Epp.* 7. 316-17; JE, 3034).

56.   According to a note at the end of the letter (p. 317 and n. 2); see Lohrmann, *Das Register Papst Johannes VIII.*, p. 242.

57.   See *PL* 126. 270 or, better, MGH *Form.*, pp. 553-54.   This document, which has long been assumed to be the decree of election, may well be, rather, a *petitio supplex*; see Andrieu, "Le sacre épiscopal d'après Hincmar de Reims," p. 26n.   For Hedenulphus at an earlier time, see *PL* 126. 539a.   Presumably the strict adherence to canonical regulation here covers the actual selection of the candidate by HR.

58.   With many varied complaints being raised, one by the supporters of HL would not be surprising.   As it must have been, under any circumstances, nearly or over three months since the election of Hedenulphus, there was additional opportunity to raise the matter.   On the possibility of the legates having brought oral instructions to Ponthion, see Beck, "Selection of Bishops Suffragan to Hincmar of Reims," p. 296, n. 62.

59.   Two are synopsized by Flodoard, 3. 18. 510.   On the date, see Reg. HL, nos. 165-66.

60. See the letter of announcement to Laon sent by the archbishop, at *PL* 126. 271-76; for the date, see Reg. HL, no. 168. Seven bishops were present: Odo of Beauvais, Ragenelmus of Noyon, John of Cambrai, Willebert of Châlons, Hildebert of Soissons, Geroldus of Amiens, and Hadebertus of Senlis. The first five have been frequently mentioned in the preceding pages. Of the last two, Geroldus, who was then serving as representative for bishop Hilmeradus, had signed the sentence at Douzy; Mansi, 16. 677d-e.

61. According to the words of denial from the archbishop (Flodoard, 3. 21. 515 and 3. 29, 554). In each case a passage follows relating to HL and to Carloman. The charge that HR did not respect the decretals is a familiar one from the complaints made by the bishop of Laon against his uncle; the other charge, which was probably exaggerated by the archbishop's detractors and was an almost natural outgrowth of his metropolitan theory, is implicit in the letter sent to Hadrian II in the name of King Charles (Reg. HL, no. 160), and might well have represented an attitude that was receiving impetus from the vicarial appointment of Ansegis.

62. *Ann. Bert.*, p. 229.

63. Ibid., p. 228.

64. This seems a likely interpretation of the letter sent by HR to Bishop Ottolfus of Troyes; Flodoard, 3. 23. 533. See Reg. HL, no. 170.

65. HL, *Reclamatio*; see Reg. HL, no. 171.

66. Clearly a bargain had been made. Also discussed by the two rulers was the problem of two rebels: Hugh the son of Lothar II and Immo (*Ann. Bert.*, p. 228). The first announcement made by the pope concerned their excommunication, an action that benefited both Louis the Stammerer and HR (ibid.).

67. Ibid., p. 229. The *Annales Vedastini* (Rau, 2:292) state, however, that HL *"inculpabilem reddidit atque iubente apostolico missas celebravit"*; and considering

that John had also put himself in an awkward position by effectively negating to some degree the election he himself had approved, he now may well have had some feelings concerning the possibility of injustices perpetrated against the bishop. On the fulfillment of the order, see Flodoard, 3. 23. 532, and Reg. HL, no. 174.

68. Flodoard, 3. 24. 537.

Notes

Appendix I

1. Nos. 1-4. (4) Attendance of HL at Quierzy is attested by his signature. The oath is given in MGH *Cap.*, 2, no. 269, pp. 295-97; Hincmar's name is found at p. 296. The date of the oath, 21 March 858, provides the dates for the other entries here. (2) Oath of obedience is at *PL* 126. 292c; subscribed profession of faith and obedience at ibid., 316a. (3) is mentioned at *PL* 126. 292c, 421d, 544b-c, 558b-c. (1) is self-evident.

2. Nos. 5-6. The synopsis of Flodoard states that (5) was written to HL "in ordinationis ipsius initio," hence the date. The work may still be extant, in the first portion (to folio 163) of Paris lat. 12445; see suggestion and discussion at Devisse, *Hincmar et la loi*, p. 54. The entry at (6) is dated to 858-59 by Schrörs, *Hinkmar*, at Reg. HR, no. 127. In toto the entry seems to be a composite, made by Flodoard in synopsis, of letters written over a period of time; lines 7-10 are appropriate to 858. In and following late 858 HL was with CB in Bourgogne (MGH *Epp.* 8^1. 64).

3. The precept (7) is mentioned inter alia at *PL* 126. 495d. Its date is indicated by HL, writing early in 869, as nearly nine years earlier; Mansi, 16. 579b. See (34) in n. 13 below.

4. No. 8. The letter, written with reference to the assembly held at Savonnières on November 862, itself refers to the impending Council of Metz, which it fixes for 15 March 863 (*PL* 121. 382). The order to hold this council was given by Pope Nicholas in letters dated 23 November 862 (JE, 2698-99, 2701-2); but due to the death of King Charles of Provence on 24 January 863, the original date was not kept and the synod was held in mid-June (*Ann. Bert.*, p. 98). Hence the letter of the Lotharingian met-

ropolitans must fall between the time of receipt of the
papal command and the arrival of news of Charles's death.

5.   No. 9.   Delivered to HR by Hadulfus (*PL* 126.
290c), thus not possibly later than early 870, when
Hadulfus was excommunicated by HL [see (82), (83), (86),
(87) below].   On the basis of the list of HL's collections given at *PL* 126. 441c, where this collection heads
a list that is almost surely in chronological order, it
is likely about contemporary with the event, considering
particularly that this is an occurrence of the sort
that the archbishop would have demanded his nephew justify or retract.   In this list, the Aguilcourt collection
is placed before the collection on the excommunication
of Amalbertus, which in turn precedes the *Pittaciolus*
and must likely date from 866 or earlier; see n. 21 below.   Hence the Aguilcourt incident and collection may
well date from c. 865.   This receives support from the
fact that HR was not present at the time of the incident,
and administration of the diocese had been left in the
hands of a delegate (*PL* 126. 293b-c), a fact that could
be in accord with the circumstances following the meeting at Tusey on 19 February 865 (MGH *Cap*. 2, no. 244, pp.
166-67) and HR's role thereafter (see *Annales Fuldenses*);
the archbishop was not present at the meeting at Ven-
dresse on 3 August 865 (MGH *Cap*., 2, no. 307, pp. 468-
69).

6.   Nos. 10-12.   (11) is dated; see it in the context
of the whole issue at *PL* 126. 569c-d.   Since the ordination had originally been scheduled for 7 July, and considering HR's great desire now to get a new bishop for
Cambrai (cf. *PL* 126. 499c), (10) can reasonably be placed
in June.   (12) is mentioned at HR Opusculum, ch. 2, (*PL*
126. 298b), with the indication that HL still had not
given his consent.

7.   Nos. 13, 52.   Dating for (13) appears from several sources.   From *PL* 126. 365b, we know it to have preceded the *Pittaciolus* of 869 (see n. 21 below), while
the collection is placed second in a list furnished by
the archbishop at *PL* 126. 441c.   The date of the incident
and the contemporaneity of the collection are clearly
implied at *PL* 126. 298c, which indicates that the inci-

dent preceded the ordination of John of Cambrai. The
same passage informs us that, from that time up to the
imprisonment of HL at Servais, the archbishop had written
three times requesting that his nephew raise the sentence; thus, the dating for (52).

8. No. 14. For the date of this letter, see MGH
Epp. 8[1]. 205, no. 1.

9. Nos. 15-19. The series (15)-(19) is dated in
relation to the meeting at Pîtres, which is known to have
been held during August 868 [see (23) below]. (15) is
mentioned at Mansi, 16. 755d-e. The summons followed a
complaint made to CB in the presence of HL and other
fideles (ibid., 755b); presumably (and particularly as
it involved a tenant of the bishop) it was made near
Laon. CB left Saint-Denis for Servais about 26 May (*Ann.
Bert.*, p. 143), and was at Quierzy on 29 May (Tessier,
2, no. 309), following which he remained at Attigny
(where he held a *placitum*) and in the Laonnais. During
these stays he issued the summons to HL (*Ann. Bert.*, p.
150). It seems likely then that the complaint was made
at the Attigny *placitum*; and, according to HL, the summons was issued immediately afterward, with the *mallus*
also held a short time later (Mansi 16. 779c). (16)
would then fall between the time when the summons was
issued and the court met; it is mentioned at Mansi 16.
755e, 779d. (17) and (18) must follow soon after the
mallus and the results of HL's nonappearance. (16) is
mentioned at Mansi, 16. 684b. (17), mentioned ibid. and
at 578e, was roughly contemporaneous with (18), almost
certainly antedated the meeting at Pîtres, and surely
was sent by September. Hence, the mention of this letter
at Mansi 16. 684b just prior to (18) would indicate
its chronological precedence; HR also says, ibid., that
it was sent unnecessarily, thus implying a date before
Pîtres, the resolutions and the council that accompanied
it [see especially (27) in n. 11 below.] A more explicit example of what HR regarded as overanticipating is
the letter HL sent to Rome with Walco and Berno [see (44)
and n. 18 below]. On HL's having taken this action without first having seen what HR could do for him, see *PL*
126. 314a. The testimony of the bishops at Douzy in
Responsa episcoporum, ch. 6, at Mansi, 16. 651a, refers to

the Celsanus letter as having been sent prior to the complaint made in a Reims provincial synod; but this, of
course, does not include Pîtres. That the appeal followed Pîtres may be indicated from HL's contemporary notice
of appeal given in the *Schedula*, at *PL* 124. 1028a-b (if
he is to be considered trustworthy on this point); cf.
(24) and n. 11 below. CB received the papal response in
early December (*Ann. Bert.*, p. 151), indicating the likelihood that HL's letter may have been sent prior to
Pîtres, but also the possibility that it may have been
sent later. Finally, in the papal response, Hadrian sets
the terminus ad quem for HL's visit to Rome at the following August (MGH *Epp.* 6. 715-17), perhaps indicating
that he received the letter from the bishop after 1
August 868 and, perhaps too, that he received it near
that date and was allowing an even year; cf. (20) and
(21) and n. 10 below. (19), which is clearly later than
(18) and prior to Pîtres, is mentioned at Mansi, 16.
755b, 684b. Cf. Schrörs, *Hinkmar*, p. 574, n. 91.

10. Nos. 20-22. See n. 9 above, which suggests an
early date. On the other hand, the papal letters need
only have been sent early enough to have been presented
by HL at Quierzy on or around 5 December 868, the last
day the bishop was known to have been there [Mansi 15.
861-66; cf. (30) and n. 13 below]. On the presentation
at Quierzy, see *Ann. Bert.*, p. 151; Mansi, 16. 578e,
651a-b. The above pertains to the two letters that are
extant: those sent for HR and CB [(20) and (21)]. (22)
is natural to assume and is also implied at Mansi, 16.
579b and, perhaps, at *Ann. Bert.*, p. 151 and *PL* 126. 495c
as well.

11. Nos. 23-27. For (23) a terminus a quo is provided by the *Ann. Bert.*, p. 150, which state that the
king came to Pîtres in mid-August. (24) is the last
document attributed to Pîtres. According to its instruction, it was delivered to the bishops at Pîtres on
30 August (*PL* 124. 1025c). For the possibility that
this *Schedula* may have been read or reread at Verberie
the next year, see (43) in n. 17 below. (25) consists of
three parts: *Quaterniones, Rotula,* and *Admonitio extemporalis,* each of which must be assigned to a different
time. The *Quaterniones* (*PL* 125. 1035-60) were written

between the time of HL's letter to his metropolitan in
July [cf. (18)] and the time of the assembly at which
they were offered to CB (*PL* 126. 315c) and were rejected
by him, either because they were too long (thus HR at
Mansi, 16. 785c) or because Charles was unwilling to
hear arguments against episcopal trials in matters of
this sort being handled by himself (the introductory
comment to the *Admonitio*, at Mansi, 16. 781a-b). This
seems to have occurred prior to 30 August (ibid.). The
same source states that the *Rotula* (*PL* 125. 1060-65)
was prepared as a substitute for the *Quaterniones* (ibid.,
and see *PL* 126. 95c-d) and was apparently given to
Charles by HR along with the *Admonitio* (*PL* 125. 1065-70),
probably at Pîtres. Although Mansi, 16. 785e, seems to
indicate a later time, this is probably later only within the context of the assembly, perhaps on 30 or 31
August. HL read the *Quaterniones* (*PL* 124. 1037-38). The
attempts of HR were not unsuccessful; and that the question of the complaints against HL was handled in the province of Reims is reported to the king in (27). That
both the trial and the letter date from September appears from the reference the archbishop makes to a sanction he intends to impose "*in die missa sancti Remigii*,"
that is, 1 October (*PL* 126. 97b). That both may have
been early in September may be indicated by HR's reference to the *Quaterniones* as having offered "*nuper*" at
Pîtres (*PL* 126. 95c, which reads "*super*," cf. Mansi, 16.
785e). (26) may be contemporary with this trial. According to the introduction at *PL* 124. 1027-28, it was given
to the king by Odo of Beauvais; and HR mentions Odo in a
similar intermediary capacity at *PL* 126. 94d.

12. No. 28. A date following Pîtres seems most
likely. In addition to its appropriateness to the
situation, the mention, which is found at *PL* 126.
570b, immediately precedes the call issued by the
king for HL to appear at Ponthion, where none of our
sources place CB until 27 September, when he confirmed
an agreement, made between his *fidelis* Gotbertus and
Bishop Erchanraus of Châlons (Tessier, 2, no. 316, p.
199). The *Ann. Bert.* state that after Pîtres CB went
to Orville for the hunt and that by 1 December he was at
Quierzy (p. 151), hence the dating for these letters. On
the other hand, if one disregards the order, or the ap-

parent reference in the context of *PL* 126. 570b (see above, this note; the reference here is to HR Libellus ch. 4, at cols. 570-72)--and indeed the whole interpretation of this tendentious passage is extremely difficult--then (28) may antedate Pîtres and may refer, for example, to the earlier complaints of Ariulfus and Amalbertus. The situation of Amalbertus at least was similar to that of the son of Liudo, and by the testimony of HR, both of these complaints were properly handled by the king (Mansi, 16. 755b).

13. Nos. 29-31, 34-36, 67, 113. The meeting at Quierzy (30) provides the dates for (29)-(31), (34)-(36), (67), and (113). The examination of the bishop-elect occurred on 3 December (Mansi, 15. 861; Schrörs, *Hinkmar*, p. 575, n. 93, has 3 November accidentally), and the ordination two days later (Mansi, 15. 864). On the presence of HL, see Mansi, 15. 861; *Ann. Bert.*, p. 151; CB, *Petitio*, ch. 4, at Mansi, 16. 578. As Bishop Erchanraus was last seen on 27 September (see Duchesne, *Fastes épiscopaux*, 3:98) and since two elections of Willebert were required because he was a royal nominee and HR had not been consulted beforehand and hence has no representative at the first election (Mansi, 15. 862), the date for (29), which sent Odo as *visitator* for the election, is justified. (34) is quoted at length at Mansi, 16. 579a-b, thus showing that this letter followed the incident of the papal epistles at Quierzy in early December 868; but the tone of HL's statement is not defiant, but rather conciliatory, hence it surely must be different from and earlier than the letter that was interpreted by the king as planning flight to Lothar II (cf. (45) and n. 16 below). That letter probably followed CB's sending of a force to Laon in January 869 (*Ann. Bert.*, p. 152) and the declaration of anathema by HL; thus, the fragment cited at *PL* 126. 571c-d should probably be included in it. Cf. (48) and n. 22 below, which may be contemporaneous. (67) is mentioned in a letter of CB, at *PL* 124. 880a, with reference to a responding letter of remonstrance sent by Hadrian. See McKeon, "Toward a Reestablishment." (35), mentioned at Mansi, 16. 617c, involves a request that Odo advise HL; hence it probably relates to January, when Odo was sent to Laon (see *Ann. Bert.*, p. 152; HR Libellus, ch. 4, at *PL* 126. 571b); its

location as the first in a series of descriptions of
three letters indicates an early date. (36), at Mansi,
16. 617d, requests Odo's intercession with CB in favor
of HL. Schrörs, *Hinkmar*, at Reg. HR, no. 230, and p.
576, n. 98, gives a date of March-April 868. Contrary
to Schrörs, at Reg. HR, no. 247, at p. 575, n. 93, (31),
which is synopsized by Flodoard at 3. 23. 530 and is
entered by Schrörs only with a date of 869, seems likely
to date from December 868; the implied reference to
Celsanus ("...*de presbitero, qui epistolam papae Romam
detulerat, ...*"; ibid.) indicates an early date, as does
HR's consternation, which would surely have been dis-
pelled once a synodal determination had been approved,
as it had been by March. For (113) see app. 2 below.

14. No. 32. For the date, see Schrörs, *Hinkmar*, p.
575, n. 93. Cf. Reg. HR, nos. 219 and 221.

15. No. 33. The chronology is extremely difficult;
and tendentious reporting appears to account for the
discrepancies between the major accounts of *Ann. Bert.*,
HR Libellus, ch. 4, and CB, *Petitio*, ch. 3. The mention
of these letters by CB at Mansi, 16. 579d, immediately
precedes: (1) Charles's mention of rumors of the bishop's desertion to Lothar II (which he says are supported by HL's own letter; see Mansi, 16. 579d-e), and (2)
an account of the *missi* sent to Laon. HR, at *PL* 126.
571a (a reference also connected with the synod of Douzy
in 871), has a similar account with a quotation from the
letter, for which see (45) and n. 16 below. But the *Ann.
Bert.*, at p. 152, describe the sending of troops as an
act of anger caused by HL's having left Quierzy and by
his refusal to respond to the royal summonses. This account seems likely; with credible information concerning
HL's impending defection, Charles would not leave the
bishop free only to capture him for the same reason a
long while later; while HL, in turn, would be unlikely
to appear at Verberie, from which indeed he left freely.
Two possible alternatives are: (1) a synod in the province of Reims in about February, at which the bishop
gave an oath of fidelity; or (2) a shift in the chronology to place the *missi* and anathema after Verberie.
There is no explicit indication of the first alternative
in the sources, and the *Ann. Bert.* contain a clear con-

tradiction. The second alternative requires a tortuous
interpretation of the sources and leaves it difficult to
account for the topic of excommunication, which loomed
so large at Verberie (see *PL* 126. 526b), while giving
little time prior to Servais for a long series of correspondence and a number of acts; furthermore, with HL
present at Verberie, the king could not well allege that
the bishop had refused his calls (as at Mansi, 16. 579d).
I conclude that the *Ann. Bert.* must be followed in the
main; the other accounts, which are after all basically
briefs in a trial, are in this respect apologiae for the
king's hasty act of violence in January. With respect
to the present letters then, the dates range from an uncertain terminus a quo to c. January 869, before the
council was called.

16. Nos. 37-38, 45-49. (45) is mentioned particularly
at *PL* 126. 571a; Mansi, 16. 579e. As HL had been able
to leave the council at Verberie (see *PL* 126. 511-12), it
would seem that prior to May Charles did not have any
particular reason to believe the bishop anticipated leaving the kingdom. The correspondence between CB and HR
at about this time--most notably Schrörs, Reg. HR, no.
232--seems, from the fragments we possess, to be concerned with appeal [see (48) below]; and if this is true,
it is likely that another letter was sent by HL during
May. The sequence then would take the form: Verberie,
letter of appeal to CB, CB's refusal, letter mentioning
HL's "intention" to go over to Lothar II. On the other
hand, the letter announcing HL's "intention" may well be
identical with the present one, since we have only fragments of these works, since the quotations from the "intention" letter do not necessarily indicate such an intention (thus *PL* 126. 571a, and cf. 604c-d), and since no
explicit mention exists of a second letter written by HL
to the king. At any rate, letter or letters must follow
Verberie, since CB in May sent a letter to HR for response [see (46)]; yet both king and archbishop were present at Verberie in late April. (46) is mentioned in HR
Libellus, ch. 24, at Mansi, 16. 616d, in a letter of HR.
The archbishop here refers to Charles's request that he
come to the king at Servais and bring the reply along;
CB was at Pîtres on 1 May (*Ann. Bert.*, p. 151-52), while
the last letter in this series (48) probably dates from
the last week in May. Assuming time for Charles to have

received HL's letter, the present letter may be dated
late in the second week of May. (47) is mentioned in HR
Libellus, ch. 24, at Mansi, 16. 616d; while (48), at Mansi,
16. 616-17, contains the citations to (46) and (47). From
the context of (48), it appears that HR did not know of
either seizure or interdict; hence the letter must ande-
date receipt of this news on 31 May (see n. 19 below). HL
later felt that it was by this letter that the archbishop
persuaded CB to have him imprisoned; see HL's version of
the letter at HR Libellus, ch. 23 (*PL* 126. 601-2) and the
references in ch. 24 (*PL* 126. 605c ff.). In these passages
HL also implies, perhaps, that the letter sent by HR to
Charles preceded Verberie, since he makes reference not to
Servais but to Senlis. Schrörs, Reg. HR, no. 232, dates
(48) at May 869, and says with regard to the date that it
speaks for itself (p. 576, n. 99). But, in addition to
what was said above, HR's reference to his impending journey to the king "...*nunc Kalend. Jun. ad Codiciacum* (Coucy-
le Château [Aisne]), *et in crastino ubi vos esse audiero*"
(Mansi, 16. 616d) would indicate a date at least past mid-
May. (49) is the letter requested by Charles, which upon
the arrival of HR at Servais, was given to CB, and then
in turn to HL for reply; it is mentioned at *PL* 126. 606b.
(38) is an entry in Flodoard, 3. 23. 530. Schrörs (Reg.
HR, no. 264) gives a date of 869-70; but 870 does not seem
appropriate, since during the portion of the year when HL
was at odds with the king, his uncle was not even concerned with supporting him. The reference may be to early
869 [cf. (35) above], but it seems more likely to indicate
May; and the letter may be (56), which appears at Reg. HR,
no. 232. (37) is the letter referred to in (38).

17. Nos. 39-43. (39) is mentioned at *PL* 126. 512b. CB
commanded the council prior to his journey to Cosne (*Ann.
Bert.*, p. 152), and a diploma for the Abbot Hugh is dated
there on 30 January (Tessier, 2, no. 319, p. 203). (40) is
mentioned at *PL* 126. 605c, clearly after HL's receipt of
the summons but before the council. (41) is Reg. HR, no.
231; fragments at Mansi, 16. 617-18 (HR Libellus, ch. 24)
show both that (41) preceded Verberie and that HR had already received (40). On the date see also Grierson,
"Eudes Ier," p. 181. Cf. HL's interpretation of this
letter, given at *PL* 126. 602a. For (42), the date is

given at *PL* 126. 511-12, 512c, 515a, 515c, all HR's
transcriptions of (42). In spite of the paucity of
existing information concerning the Verberie synod, its
dates and the date of (43) may be fixed with at least
some confidence. The synod was called for 24 April
(*Ann. Bert.*, p. 152; *PL* 126. 512b, 515b), while CB had
also called a *placitum* at Verberie for 1 May (*Ann. Bert.*,
152-53); here are two likely limits, although the synod
may not have continued until the end of April. A diploma
confirming royal donations to the monastery of **Charroux**
is dated at the council on 30 April (Mansi, 16. 551-52);
but this, like the diploma it affirms (Tessier, 2, no.
236 bis, pp. 25-26), is of dubious authenticity. Tessier
questions it (at p. 25) on, among other grounds, its
style and the reference to CB as though he were emperor.
The name of HL does not appear on this diploma but is
included on another confirming certain villas to the
monastery of Saint-Vaast in Arras (Mansi, 16. 565-68),
which is based upon a royal diploma issued 30 October
867 (Tessier, 2, no. 304) for which Charles required
synodal confirmation. However, the date of our diploma
fails: it is assigned by De Clercq (*La législation
religieuse franque*, 2:380-81) to spring 868, a time when
no council was being held at Verberie; by Werminghoff
("Verzeichnis der Akten fränkischer Synoden," *Neues
Archiv* 26:643) to 870?; and by Tessier (2, no. 214) to
869. Tessier notes, however, that it is suspect, although he says this does not necessarily affect the original diploma of CB; and suspect it is--containing, e.g.,
the name of Bishop Erchanraus of Châlons, who had been
dead for about six months; this is among the reasons for
De Clercq's dating. HL's name occurs at Mansi, 16. 568,
and his presence is sufficiently attested by other
sources, e.g., at *PL* 126. 526b, 315c; *PL* 124. 1000.

18. Nos. 44, 63, 65. For (44) the year is certain;
see McKeon, "Toward a Reestablishment of the Correspondence of Pope Hadrian II." The context of the letter,
as known from the fragments and references at Mansi, 16.
579-80, 653c-d, and *PL* 124. 876 ff., does not seem to indicate that HL had reported his imprisonment and would
thus argue for an early date. For (63)-(65) see McKeon,
op. cit.

19. Nos. 50, 51, 53-59. This entry contains letters
pertaining to the imprisonment of HL. 28 May, the date
he left for Servais (*PL* 126. 512b), provides one terminus. (51) was written at Laon following a meeting held on
30 May (*PL* 126. 512c, 515d); it was received by HR on
the following day (*PL* 126. 511d, 515a). (50) is referred to at Mansi, 16. 857a, in the same sentence with the
Laon letter. (53) is synopsized at Flodoard, 3. 23. 530.
Schrörs, at Reg. HR, no. 250, gives a date of 869 and
makes (53) follow Reg. HR, no. 247 [see (36) and n. 13
above]; but the reference, in no. 250, to "*his, quae
obiciebantur Hincmaro*" and to Odo as having to be informed are appropriate to Servais, while the archbishop's writing here "*de correctione suae epistolae, quam
illi pridem miserat,*" which precedes the mention of HL,
is best explained if the present letter were written
just after HR had learned of the imprisonment and prior
to his journey to Servais, where he met Odo (*PL* 126.
606b). After this journey the archbishop returned, leaving Servais probably on 3 June (on the basis of HR
Libellus, ch. 24, at Mansi, 16. 616e, compared with *PL*
126. 606c). Since he was notified of the interdict on
31 May (see above, this note) and left Reims presumably
on 1 June (Mansi, 16. 616e), (54), (55), and (56), with
their canonical citations, must have been drawn up following his return to Reims. Their preparation prior to
his departure for Servais would have been unnecessary
(except to record the incident, in which case there
would have been no rush), since the archbishop would see
both Charles and HL at Servais (Mansi, 16. 618d-e); and,
indeed, we know that these letters were not delivered in
person but by messengers (Mansi, 16. 857c). At Mansi, 16.
857c, HR states that he sent these letters to HL, to CB,
and to the Laon faithful. The first (*PL* 126. 515-26)
and third (*PL* 126. 511-14) are clearly contemporaneous;
and we may assume that the similar letter to Charles,
which is mentioned at Mansi, 16. 857c-d, also dates from
the same time. Schrörs, at Reg. HR, nos. 234-36 and p.
576, n. 100, dates the letters at the beginning of June;
but mid-June is more probable. Apart from HR's absence
from Reims until 4 or 5 June and the time needed for re-
daction of the letters, apparent references to their delivery are at *PL* 126. 529d and *PL* 126. 533d. These references occur in a letter dated 24 June written by the

archbishop after the return of his messengers from
Servais, [(57) and below, this note]. Given the gravity
of the situation, it is unlikely that HR would have long
delayed this letter after his *missi* had returned or that
they would have been dilatory in returning. (57) is
dated, albeit "VIII. Kal. Jun." (*PL* 126. 531c and Mansi,
16. 826d). Schrörs (*Hinkmar*, p. 576, no. 100), in correcting this, has given the date as 25 June. (58), which
exists as a fragment given by HR at HR Libellus, ch. 24
(*PL* 126. 617b-c) is dated by Schrörs (Reg. HR no. 233)
to May or June. Either date is possible, as also is an
earlier date; but the context of the fragment, as well
as its position in the list of letters that occupies a
large part of this chapter indicates that this letter
followed the bishop's imprisonment and hence dates from
June 869. (59) may be assumed to follow HL's failure
to lift the sentence after receiving the letter of 24
June; see the indication at *PL* 126. 533d. This letter
refers to the bishop's contumacy and to the need for HR
to consult with other bishops regarding a permanent
disposition of the problem. The language of (58) is
sufficiently similar to that of (59) to allow both to be
dated around the same time, and (58) may well have been
instrumental in gaining HL's release. This letter also
refers to the bishop's charges that his uncle was responsible for inducing CB to have him imprisoned, charges
that HR says Charles denied at Pîtres (*PL* 126. 438c). A
terminus non post quem is provided by the fact that the
letters, or at any rate that to HL, were written while
HR believed the bishop still to be at Servais (see *PL*
126. 532-33); Charles is known to have left by 28 June,
when at Bèzu he issued a diploma for the monastery of
Saint-Lucien (Tessier, 2, no. 325, pp. 216-17).

20. Nos. 60, 66. (60) is given in HR Libellus, ch.
10, at *PL* 126. 575-76. The date may be ascertained as
follows. The oath was sworn and subscribed outside the
province of Reims, at the suggestion of Aeneas of Paris
and Wenilon of Rouen (*PL* 126. 577a). The order of topics
in HR Libellus, ch. 10, places this oath immediately
after an account of the Laon interdict (ibid., chs. 5-9).
According to HR (at *PL* 126. 315b), the oath preceded the
sending of HL's second letter to Hadrian, and the reply
to this letter was sent from Rome during 869 [see (63)

and (64) below]. HL had probably returned to Laon by 8
July 869; see (61) below. Hence, a likely date for the
oath is sometime between c. 27 June and c. 5 July. (66)
is bounded by two diplomas issued at Pîtres by CB, dated
28 June and 21 July (Tessier, 2, nos. 325, 326, pp. 217,
223). HR, at *PL* 126. 534a, may give a reference to HL's
presence at Pîtres, as may the oath to the king. If the
bishop was present, no official record of his presence
exists; but the only list of names, contained on a privilege for Saint-Pierre of Le Mans, is suspect (Tessier,
2, no. 325 bis; the whole of the synodal diploma, with
the signatures, is edited by Quantain in *Cartulaire
général de l'Yonne*, 1:97, n. 49). HL may have accompanied the king and returned to Laon prior to the end
of the meeting; see (62).

   21.   Nos. 61, 62, 68, 69, 75, 76, 91, 103, 116, 117.
(75) was presented to Hincmar of Reims at Gondreville
(*PL* 126. 501c, 534c, 441d; Mansi, 16. 856b); hence it
was completed by November 869 (Reg. HL, no. 74). The
Pittaciolus which was edited in *PL* 124. 1001-26 is
a different version from that received by the archbishop
at Gondreville. In the former, when HL quotes a passage
from the letter of Gregory I to Theoctista (*PL* 124. 1021-
22), he commits several errors, for which HR later criticized him on two occasions: in HR Opusculum, ch. 22
(*PL* 126. 367c) and in HR Libellus, ch. 12 (*PL* 126. 581).
The archbishop states that this criticism applied as
well to the larger collection compiled by his nephew.
The passage in question begins "*Si qui vero sunt, qui
dicunt, quia compulsus quispiam necessitate, si anathema-
tizaverit, . . . ,*" and HR's criticism begins after this
passage, which he gives in full. But at *PL* 124. 1021d,
the passage runs, "...*necessitate, si anathematizatus
fuerit... .*" Since HR, in two places where he is anxious to attack his nephew, does not mention the deviation and each time is clearly quoting the passage as it
appears in HL's collections (for no work of the archbishop prior to 881 containing this same quotation fails
to omit the word *vero*; cf. Narratio at *Mansi* 16. 859b-
d; HR Libellus, ch. 34, [*PL* 126. 627-28]; and *De causa
Teutfridi*, [*PL* 125. 1114c-d], with the later citations
in *Quae exsequi debeat episcopus* [July 881] [*PL* 125.
1092b] and the letter of the same approximate date [*PL*

126. 228a]), it may be concluded that this variant was
not in the version of *Pittaciolus* presented to him. The
Pittaciolus in Paris lat. 5095, **at folio 75^V, follows**
the version cited by HR, as does the enlarged *Pittaciolus* in Metz Stadtbibliothek 351, folios 97^V-98; the
former dates from 882-92 and is of Laon provenance, as
indicated at folio 1. That a larger collection (62) had
preceded and formed the basis for (75) is stated by the
bishop at the end of the work (*PL* 124. 1026b). HR couples this larger collection with the *Pittaciolus* (thus,
PL 126. 500d-1d); he calls it a "*libellus monstruosus*"
(*PL* 126. 501c, 583a) and states that he answered both it
and the *Pittaciolus* in HR Opusculum (*PL* 126. 501c,
582d). Consequently, he must have received it prior to
June 870, when HR Opusculum was presented to HL (see
Reg. HL, no. 91). This collection was signed by HL and
by his clergy (see *PL* 126. 582d, and cf. col. 511b). In
HR Libellus, ch. 11 (*PL* 126. 578a) the archbishop gives
the formula of subscription without any date; in HR
Opusculum, ch. 36 (*PL* 126. 428c) the same formula is
given, with the addition "[A]ctum Lauduno VIII Idus
Julias." Presumably, then, the year must be 869. But
the large collection was presented at Attigny (*PL* 126.
604b, 501d; and see the statement at *PL* 126. 583a: "*Sed
et praefatus suum monstruosum libellum, a se et ea suis
subscriptum, in eadem synodo* [Attigny; cf. *PL* 126. 582d]
protulit, quem ibidem accipiens, hactenus servo.") **Fur**ther, nowhere in HR Opusculum does the archbishop
indicate that he had seen the formula; even the full quotation at *PL* 126. 428c is cited as hearsay. To have
lied about having answered the "monstrous" collection in
HR Opusculum is absurd, for the statement to this
effect is made not only publicly but also in a private
letter to his nephew (Reg. HL, no. 112), who would know
whether or not the statement were true. Again, HR speaks
too specifically for a figurative meaning to be assumed.
Finally, (91) does answer a larger collection than the
Pittaciolus, as a glance at ch. 24 (*PL* 126. 377-78)
makes clear. Here HR cites a number of sentences from
the *Cap. Ang.*, in demonstration of their discordance.
These total eight: Cor Par 44 (*PI*, p. 765), Cor Par Sal
1 (*PI*, p. 766), Cor 13 (*PI*, p. 768), Cor 14 (ibid.), Cor
Par 19 (*PI*, p. 762), Cor Par 23 (*PI*, p. 763), Cor Par 49
(*PI*, p. 766), Cor Par Sal 24 (*PI*, p. 763). But the

Pittaciolus in its form as published at *PL* 124. 1001-26
contains only two citations. Both are repeated (at
least in part) in this collection (thus, cf. *PL* 124. 1006
with col. 1020, and col. 1014 with col. 1020), and neither is among those cited by HR in the above list; *Pittaciolus* citations are Cor Par 11 (*PI*, p. 761) and Cor
Par Sal 4 (*PI*, p. 758-59). Further, at *PL* 126. 377c-d,
the archbishop paraphrases a passage that appears in the
collection he is discussing; it is drawn from either
Pseudo-Julius, ch. 12 (*PI*, pp. 468-69) or Pseudo-Felix
II, ch. 13 (*PI*, p. 487), neither of which appears in the
Migne *Pittaciolus*. What else is known about this collection? Other contents are indicated at *PL* 126. 577-
78; *Cap. Ang.* Cor Par Sal 51 (*PI*, p. 766), Cor Par 17
(*PI*, p. 762), Cor Par 44 (*PI*, p. 765), and the encycli-
cal of Leo I, ch. 5 (at *PI*, p. 615). At *PL* 126. 604b
the archbishop mentions that the work included *Breviary
of Alaric* 10. 5. 1. The identity of all these citations
with the contents of the "monstrous" collection is definite; the conclusions must then be that HR had seen
this collection prior to completion of HR Opusculum
and that at that time it lacked a signature.

Since the formula at *PL* 126. 578a is the same as that
at *PL* 126. 428c, and the collection may be surely dated
prior to 23 August (see the reference at *PL* 126. 501b to
a letter of admonition sent following compilation of the
collection, which clearly alludes to the letter of 23
August 869 [*PL* 126. 533-34]; cf. the summary in Flodoard,
3. 22. 519 in virtually the same language), it may be
that the large collection was promulgated on 8 July.
There is no certain basis for such an assumption, unless
there was only one signed collection; but there appear
to have been two. In HR Opusculum, ch. 4 (*PL* 126. 301a-
b) HR names three works that he requested from HL at
Gondreville: a collection made against himself and his
writings concerning the interdict, writings on the same
subject subscribed by HL and his priests, and writings
that HL said dissolved the force of the archbishop's own
statements. Here the archbishop is not certain, it would
seem, of the actual number of documents; but Wenilon of
Rouen delivered the *Pittaciolus* to HR on the same day.
In subsequent requests it is clear that the collection
is the *Pittaciolus* and that what remained to be delivered

were the subscribed document and the other (thus, see *PL*
126. 302a-b; cf. col. 316b). If the subscribed document
referred to is the collection answered in HR Opusculum,
then HR already had it, although without the subscrip-
tions, or else he would receive it within the next seven
months. If he had it already, he would presumably not
request it, unless he did not know that his unsigned collection was the same. But when at Gondreville HL was
asked for the writings, he sent the *Pittaciolus* and said
that, as he did not have the other writings with him, he
would send them later (*PL* 126. 301c-d). If the signed
collection were among those requested, the bishop would
surely have said that HR already possessed it, unless
either he did not know or the archbishop did not have the
collection. But since HR answered the collection in HR
Opusculum, he did have it; and since he never saw the
signature, he did not get the signed collection from HL
(see also *PL* 126. 301-2; on this Reg. HL, no. 98. The
passage does stand in HR Opusculum). This, in combination with HL's answer to the request, indicates the existence of another signed work, probably that mentioned at
PL 126. 428c and dated 8 July. Thus too, of course, there
is no indication that HR ever saw the full, dated, formula.

This formula is extant today in Paris lat. 12445, folio
166[v]. Fournier and Le Bras, *Histoire des collections canoniques*, 1:223-24 and n. 1, and Devisse, *Hincmar et la loi*,
p. 56, connect this manuscript, respectively, with the collection referred to in HR Libellus and the schedule mentioned in HR Opusculum, and both presumably mean a single
work. That there were two, and that one is a large collection, has been shown. The other work is connected with
Paris lat. 12445. The first part of this manuscript, to folio 163, consists of various canon law texts; at folios 163-
66[v] appears the complete *Cap. Ang.*, nos. 35-42 (*PI*, pp. 764-
65), and a portion of ch. 43, to the word *concilio* (*PI*, p.
765). Here the text breaks off; it is crossed out in the
same ink. At the top of the page, again in this ink, appears the formula given by HR, exactly as it appears at
PL 126. 428c; it extends across the top of the page and
is preceded by a monogram in the lefthand corner. This
same monogram appears in the right-hand margin just

below line 13. The crossbar has its upper-right-hand
terminus in the base of the monogram.

Devisse, *loc.cit.*, suggests that these *capitula* initiate the schedule, which was completed on succeeding
folios. But this seems unlikely. It is hard to tell
what the *capitula* form, or what their relationship is to
the *Cap. Ang.* written before. Why should the compiler
have begun again, and why in the middle? Why was the
passage then barred? Not only is the hand different,
but the *capitula* at folio 166^V, col. 2, are peculiar,
and even at variance with the complete *Cap. Ang.* standing just prior. *Cap.* 40, at folio 166^V, col. 2, lines
18-21, reads "*sententia non a suo*"; the same *capitulum*,
at folio 165^V, col. 1, line 17 has "*a non suo*"; strange-
ly, it is the addition which follows other texts (see
PI, p. 764). But the inversion is not important; it
occurs, too, in the phrase as it appears in Pseudo-
Zepherinus, ch. 5 (*PI*, p. 131-32). More important is
the full quotation at folio 166^V, col. 2: "*sententia
non a suo iudice distingat*." The texts invariably have,
rather, "*constringat*". Thus, Pseudo-Zepherinus, *loc.
cit.*; Pseudo-Fabian, ch. 29 (*PI*, p. 168); Pseudo-Julius,
ch. 18 (*PI*, p. 473); Pseudo-Sixtus III (*PI*, p. 563).
Finally, HL himself quotes the passage correctly, as
drawn from Pseudo-Sixtus, in the *Pittaciolus* (at *PL*
124. 1017d). Two conclusions follow. First, the *capitula* at folio 166^V, col. 2, could neither be the basis
for either the signed collection or the *Pittaciolus*,
nor is it likely that HL was responsible for the additions. Second, the subscription and monogram that appear at folio 166^V apply to the *Cap. Ang.* at folios 163-
66^V (thus, Fournier and Le Bras, *loc.cit.*), and not to
anything following. Thus the subscribed *Cap. Ang.* was
promulgated on 8 July 869 (Reg. HL, no. 61); and the
signed collection (Reg. HL, no. 62), while in compilation prior to 23 August 869, did not have signatures
added until a later time.

Both (68) and (69) are mentioned numerous times (see
PL 126. 504b, of November 870; CB at Douzy, in the
Petitio at [Mansi 16. 579a-c]; *Responsa episcoporum*,
ch. 5 [Mansi 16. 649-50]. On 869 as the year, see HR
Opusculum, ch. 40 (*PL* 126. 438); and cf. *PL* 126. 441c,

which indicates that this collection preceded the *Pittaciolus* and was in the possession of HR prior to November 869. On the dating more specifically, see app. 2.

(76), a short pro tempore answer to the *Pittaciolus*, was sent to HL on the day after Wenilon of Rouen had given that collection to HR (*PL* 126. 534c). On Gondreville, cf. (74) and n. 24 below. (91) is stated in several places to have been presented to HL at Attigny (thus, HL, writing in November 870, at *PL* 126. 501c; *Narratio*, at Mansi, 16. 856b) and, consequently, on 16 June; cf. (96) and n. 27 below. The date given here is quite arbitrary, as HR Opusculum appears to have been written in a series of bulk insertions. It consists of (1) a recounting of deeds, (2) a mélange of letters, written particularly during the first months of 870, (3) a treatise that forms the body of the work, and (4) a consideration of recent and rumoured events. That the whole was rewritten later is clear. In addition to internal anachronisms, the chapter index (*PL* 126. 282-86) is intended for a third person, while the *Narratio* at Mansi, 16. 856 indicates the later addition of letters appended to the front of the work and is itself a continuation that included later letters (see especially Mansi, at the cutoff, 16. 863-64). It is not unlikely that the purpose of these additions and revisions was, at a time yet far removed, to make up a dossier for later use, perhaps at Douzy the next year (an indication of such a dossier is in the *acta* of that synod, ch. 7 [Mansi, 16. 670a]) or later (see [175] and n. 43). (116) is dated by HR at HR Libellus, ch. 25 (*PL* 126. 607b), and at *PL* 126. 498d. (117) is for the most part an answer to (116) and may be assumed to follow soon after it. See *PL* 126. 498d.

22. Nos. 70, 73, 79. (70) is dated at *PL* 126. 534c. For the date of (73) see *Ann. Bert.*, pp. 157, 158. On (79) see Flodoard, 3. 21. 516 and Parisot, *Le royaume de Lorraine*, p. 364.

23. Nos. 71-72. See McKeon, "Toward a Reestablishment of the Correspondence of Pope Hadrian II."

24. Nos. 74, 77-78, 89-90. (74) provides the ter-

minus a quo for this series. The summons to Gondreville
for 11 November 869 is mentioned at *Ann. Bert.*, p. 167. A
diploma for the monastery of Saint-Évre in Toul is dated
from Gondreville on 24 November (BML, 1762; Tessier, 2,
230); A. Giry considered it of doubtful authenticity (see
Parisot, *Le royaume de Lorraine*, p. 353, n. 4), but cf.
Tessier, 2:231. For (77), the long quotation at HR Libellus, ch. 29 (*PL* 126. 615-16), the only citation made by
Schrörs (Reg. HR, no. 243) states (at *PL* 126. 615d) that a
letter was written on this subject after the encounter at
Gondreville. The quotation is found again in expanded form
at HR Opusculum, *praefatio* (*PL* 126. 290-93); this is quite
possibly the letter itself (cf. the remarks at [91] and n.
21 above), in which case the word "[n]uper" (*PL* 126. 290a),
gives the approximate date. (78) is mentioned at *PL* 126.
611-12; (89) and (90) are mentioned in HR Libellus, ch. 30
(*PL* 126. 617b-c). (89) is quoted by HR at *PL* 126. 617c-618c
and also in HR Opusculum, ch. 4 (*PL* 126. 299-300c). The
same chapter, at cols. 300d ff., mentions, and perhaps is,
(90); see especially col. 302a.

    25. Nos. 80-87, 92-93. (80) is dated (*PL* 126. 280b).
(81) must predate 28 March [the date of (83)], on the
basis of HR Opusculum, ch. 43 (*PL* 126. 442a-b), where
HR mentions (81) as having been sent him "nuperrime" and
makes no mention of (83). Cf. (91) and n. 21 above.
(82) is dated (*PL* 126. 281c). (83) is dated (*PL* 124.
986c). (84) is indicated at *PL* 126. 540b ff., where HR
chides his nephew for having cited inappropriate canons.
The date for (85) appears at *PL* 126. 545d, for (86) at
PL 124. 994b, and for (87) at *PL* 126. 566a. (92) was
presented by HL at Attigny (Mansi, 16. 856c-d, 659d) in
mid-June (see [96] and n. 27 below). The terminus a quo
is furnished by the closing of the Follembray church on
4 February (*PL* 126. 538a), but the preparation of (92)
probably dates from the period after HR's first letter
(of 27 April) on the subject [(85), and see above, this
note]. (93) is indicated by references at HR Opusculum,
ch. 43 (*PL* 126. 440-53) to a letter of HL that is not
found in the extant correspondence.

    26. (88) is quoted in HR Opusculum, ch. 51 (*PL* 126.
487-88); it is clearly among those letters that the archbishop admitted writing for CB (see HR Libellus, ch. 24,

at *PL* 126. 604c-d; HR Opusculum, ch. 40, at *PL* 126. 438d). The import of the message is quite similar to HR Opusculum, ch. 16 (*PL* 126. 334-40) and to the language of the letter sent on 11 May 870 (87); see, e.g., *PL* 126. 555a. On the other hand, the answer is appropriate to the repudiation of HR by HL in the case of the excommunicated monk (see HR Opusculum, ch. 9, at *PL* 126. 315-16), which probably occurred between August and November 869.

27. Nos. 94, 96-101, 103. See McKeon, "Le concile d'Attigny."

28. Nos. 102, 104-106. (102) is indicated by the king in *Petitio*, ch. 5 (Mansi, 16. 580b), and in *Responsa episcoporum*, ch. 10, (Mansi, 16. 654b). (104) was written after the letter of 2 July (Reg. HL, no. 103), according to HR (at *PL* 126. 506a-b). It is presumably earlier than HL's letter to his uncle of 18 July (Reg. HL, no. 107), since mention is made there of a message sent by CB to HL through Bertharius (*PL* 126. 495a), and the present letter was sent to CB through Bertharius (Mansi, 16. 580c). The message from CB is (105). HR provides clear indication that these transactions long preceded the journey to Meersen (see *PL* 126. 506b, which is strengthened by the statement, ibid., that this reply was given to Bertharius, thus implying that it was given immediately). CB's reference, at Mansi, 16. 580e, to the secular trial at Servais (see Reg. HL, no. 111) as "*sequentis mensis Septembris*" is apparently contradicted, ibid., by the statement immediately following his reply, that "*tunc ipse venire non voluit.*" From HR (*PL* 126. 506b) it appears that the king did not return from the meetings with his brother until about 1 September. (106) is referred to by HL as quoted by HR (*PL* 126. 495a), seems to have been shown to the bishop following the return of Bertharius, and is of course slightly earlier than the message and letter delivered to HR on 18 July (107). Tessier, 2:235, dates this document at the beginning of 870.

29. Nos. 107, 109. (107), which is apparently a desperate verbal message, was delivered to HR by the provost Heddo on 18 July (*PL* 126. 494c). Heddo also

carried the canons attributed to the council of Tusey;
see *PL* 126. 496c, and HR Libellus, ch. 18, (*PL* 126.
589-91). On the problem of these canons, see McKeon,
"Carolingian Councils of Savonnières (859) and Tusey
(860)." This letter was delivered at Ponthion (HR
Libellus, ch. 18, at *PL* 126. 589d) and indicates thus
an appropriate time for the termination of the Council
at Attigny, since the *indiculus* (106) was probably
issued there and probably at the very end of Charles's
stay, when it had become apparent that HL was not going
to return. (109) is the response to (107), and its
approximate date may be inferred from HR's reference,
at *PL* 126. 496b, to CB's absence on journey to meet
with his brother at Meersen. The dating to the beginning of August, by Schrörs, *Hinkmar*, p. 579, n.
114, depends upon the time of Louis the German's accident at Flamersheim, which delayed the meeting from
the scheduled 1 August until 8 August (*Ann. Bert.*, p.
171). *BML*, 1479f dates the accident in July, in which
case Charles might have gotten word prior to leaving
Ponthion; but if it occurred in the last days of July,
the king would have already left for the meeting as
originally scheduled and hence this letter must be
dated earlier. The late response, under either circumstance, may be credited to the press of business at
Ponthion.

30. Nos. 108, 110, 114, 115. (108) and (110) are
bare but not unlikely hypothesis, a condition which
accompanies much study of the correspondence involving Pope Hadrian; McKeon, "Toward a Reestablishment of
the Correspondence of Pope Hadrian II." (108), a
letter or a message, either from or concerning HL, is
implied by HR in his letter written to the pope between 20 and 25 October 870 (114), in the passage at
PL 126. 185-86. If sent by HL, it probably dates from
the period following the letter of 2 July to which HR
did not reply (*PL* 126. 506a; Mansi, 16. 862e); thus
the bishop did not hear from his uncle until the end
of July; and, meanwhile, Flotharius had given over the
disputed property to Nortmannus's vassal, while Charles
apparently was adamant (see [105]). HL did threaten a

new appeal (*PL* 126. 495c). The possibility of (110)
also appears at *PL* 126. 185-86 in the course of a somewhat confusing discussion of various letters and messages that HR had received from Hadrian. A response to
(108), (110) would have been delivered by the papal legates at Reims on 19 October (*PL* 126. 174c). It is possible but highly unlikely that the legates requested
HL's attendance at Rome on their own initiative. The
fact that the legates carried letters from the pope
dated 27 June by no means indicates that Hadrian could
not have received word of HL's predicament and hence
instructed his representatives, for the papal correspondence during the summer of 870 became extremely confused
and spread over a long **period**. According to the *Ann.
Bert.* (p. 177), the legates, supported by some of
Charles's *fideles*, also requested (and in this case obtained) the release of Prince Carloman, whose present
troubles like those of Hincmar of Laon were related to
the Council of Attigny. (114) followed receipt of the
letters in October. However, the dating given by
Schrörs (*Reg. HR*, no. 287 and p. 579, n. 115), October-
November 870, should be modified and made precise on
the basis of the chronology for that month as the archbishop gives it. According to the *Ann. Bert.* (p. 177),
the papal legates arrived at Saint-Denis on 9 October
and went to Reims following the release of Carloman,
while Charles remained for eight days before leaving for
the campaign in the south. At *PL* 126. 174c, HR states
that he received the letters from the legates on 19 October, and we must take it as highly probable that they were
delivered on the first day of the stay. Consequently,
since Abbot Ansegis, who served as royal *missus* to Rome
bearing the response, accompanied the royal party to
Lyons (*Ann. Bert.*, p. 178), the letter must have been completed by 26 October and earlier if the archbishop did
not receive the papal correspondence immediately. (115)
Paris lat. 1594, folio 204, says that HR delegated
Ansegis to carry a written record of HL's offenses to
Rome.

31. (111) is dated, by CB, at *Petitio*, ch. 5 (Mansi
16. 580e), and by HR at *PL* 126. 506b.

32. Nos. 112, 122. (122) follows the dating by Schrörs;

the context gives no further hint. (112) is dated by
Schrörs (Reg. HR, no. 285 and p. 579, n. 114) to the end
of July, but this is on the basis of the papal letters of
June, concerning which there was no meeting until October
(see *Ann. Bert.*, p. 177) and which HR surely did not have
or know of during the summer of 870. The letter is appropriate to two occasions in 870 when HR had summoned
bishops for response to papal letters. It might be connected with the Council at Attigny (and cf. the allegations of HL that he was lured there on precisely this
pretext; *PL* 124. 1035d, 998d, with which must be con-
trasted HR in Libellus, ch. 27, at *PL* 126. 611-12), in
which case the likely date is March-April 870. Or the
call may be that to Reims in October 870, in which case
it would have been sent between 9-10 and 19-20 October.
HL was at Reims at this time for a week (*PL* 126. 506c,
587b). Cf. with this letter, Schrörs, Reg. HR, nos. 283,
289.

33. Nos. 118-121, 123-130, 133-135, 137. (118) follows the escape of Carloman from the royal party at Lyons
in November 870 (*Ann. Bert.*, p. 178). (119) informs and
asks advice of Odo, and may be dated fairly closely by
reference to (120), a similar notice, which mentions the
approach of Christmas. HR here expresses his concern
that a council might not be appropriate, as he does also
in (121). (123)-(126) all follow the decision to hold a
meeting between the opposing sides, which was done in
January 871 (*Ann. Bert.*, p. 179). (127) may be dated
from HR's letter of 31 January (128) to HL and from the
fact that Heddo came to HR on 1 February, but without the
requested letter of consent (*PL* 126. 594c). (128) is
dated, at HR Libellus, ch. 20 (Mansi, 16. 608b-c), the
location of the letter. For (129) see Schrörs, Reg. HR,
no. 304. (130) may be dated by HR's statement (*PL* 126.
594c) that this letter followed (128) by more than 30
days. (133) falls between (130) and (134), i.e., between
early March and 19 April. The date for (134) is given
at Mansi, 16. 608c, the letter at cols. 606e-8c. (135),
mentioned at *PL* 126. 595a-b, is stated to have followed
the interview of 5 May with Teutlandus, and presumably
antedated the first conciliar call For (137) I have
followed the dating of Schrörs (Reg. HR, no. 312 and p.
577 n. 105).

34. Nos. 131-132. See McKeon, "Toward a Reestablishment of the Correspondence of Hadrian II."

35. (136) is dated at *PL* 126. 567a.

36. Nos. 138-139. (138) is mentioned at *PL* 126. 566c-d. The date for (139) is given in HR Libellus, *praefatio* (*PL* 126. 566c).

37. No. 140. The proofs that the scattered reference here connected belonged to one letter are no more than likely hypothesis, counterbalanced by the fact that, if the hypothesis is correct, then either there were covering letters with the *rotula* which are now lost or else the *rotula* itself is incomplete. The date 16 June is given at HR Libellus, *praefatio*, and at chs. 32 and 23 (*PL* 126. 567a, 623c, 601d, the latter reading "4 Kal. Julias"; cf. the same passage in the edition of Mansi, 16. 614b, for "16 Kal. Julias"). This may be identified with the collection compiled by HL and printed at *PL* 124. 993-1002, on the basis of the passage from HR Libellus, ch. 32, at Mansi, 16. 633-35, which is dated (*PL* 126. 567a) and is almost entirely a quotation of HL (from *PL* 124. 998c-1002a). At HR Libellus, ch. 21 (*PL* 126. 595b), the reference to *"memorata rotula sua"* appears to be that mentioned at *PL* 126. 567a. Ibid., ch. 22 (*PL* 126. 597-601), the archbishop makes no distinction between the writing mentioned in the previous chapter, while at col. 599a he again refers to *"sua rotula"*. The quotation, ibid., ch. 23 (*PL* 126. 601-2), is preceded by a date, certainly 16 June (see above, this note). On a citation at *PL* 126. 509d, see (136). Cf. (142) at n. 38.

38. Nos. 141-156. In (143) the reference to Wulfad and Rothad (*PL* 126. 510c, as well as other references) would perhaps indicate that this is a reply to a letter of HL's that we no longer have (142); however, (142) may be identical with (140). The angry tone is appropriate to an answer to the *rotula* of 16 June, and not to an earlier date; but the facts that no mention of HL's charges concerning Rothad occur in HR Libellus, which reviews the correspondence through 5 July, and that at *PL* 126. 567b the order makes HR's letter of 5 July fol-

low immediately after the *rotula* of 16 June, indicate a
date later than 5 July, as do the scornful references to
the metropolitan's former disobedience to papal orders.
(141) is given, with the date, at *PL* 126. 567b. (144),
cited at CB, *Petitio*, ch. 6 (Mansi, 16. 581b) and in the
acta of Douzy, ch. 4 (Mansi, 16. 662-63), would seem to be
posterior to HR's summons (141) and probably written in
support of it, perhaps as a result of (142). For (145) see,
e.g., Mansi, 16. 671a. (149) is mentioned in the *acta* of
Douzy, ch. 1 (Mansi, 16. 658b) as being offered to the delegates from the council at the time of the first additional
summons on 11 August (see below). Possibly it is connected
with the letter of HL hypothesized under (142). The council at Douzy (146) was called for 5 August (HR Libellus,
praefatio, at *PL* 126. 567b). Terminus ad quem is provided
by (154), which is dated (*PL* 126. 641b); this provides,
too, the approximate dates for (155) and (156). (147) was
read to the council on about 6 August, following the third
summons to HL (*acta*, ch. 8, at Mansi, 16. 671b). The king
requested (150) at the end of his *Petitio* (Mansi, 16. 581d-
e), and the bishops asked for a delay for the compilation
of their collection (*Responsa episcoporum*, ch. 1, at Mansi,
16. 643d-e). Since HL was condemned on 14 August, (150)
must have been drawn up between 6 and 13 August. (148)
was presented to the council between 6 and 9 August; this
appears from the facts that the third summons "regulariter"
(145) was issued by 6 August (Mansi,16. 671b) and that HL
made his first appearance before the synod on 10 August
(*acta*, ch. 2, at Mansi, 16. 660, with ch. 3 at col. 660e
[first order to reply, the following day], col. 661a [de-
ferred until the next day, Sunday], and ch. 4 at col. 662a
[appearance on 14 August]). The reference in HR Libellus,
praefatio (*PL* 126. 566c) to HR having warned the bishop
on 10 June "*de his quae in hac schedula breviter collecta
sequuntur*" indicates that by this time a primitive form,
at least, of the Libellus had been prepared. (153) was
sent to Hadrian II with the synodal letter (see Mansi, 16.
682a). (152) is mentioned at *PL* 126. 637d as having been
presented before the synod.

39. Nos. 157-162. See also McKeon "Toward a Reestablishment of the Correspondence of Pope Hadrian II."
(157) (JE, 2945) is dated at MGH *Epp.* 6. 740. (158)

(JE, 2946) is substantially the same letter. (159)-(161) are the replies to (157) and (158). I have followed the dating of Schrörs, *Reg. HR*, no. 325 and p. 580, n. 120. The fragment of (159) at Mansi, 16. 569-71, may be supplemented by the complete letter as it stands (in badly damaged condition) in Paris lat. 1594, folios 196-227^V. For (160) and (161), Tessier, 2, nos. 358 and 359, pp. 296, 297, gives January-February, 872. (159) is clearly contemporaneous. (162) (JE, 2951) is the papal response to nos. (159)-(161) and is dated accordingly.

40. Nos. 163-168, 172. The date for (163) is given in a marginal note at MGH *Epp.*, 7. 317, line 37. (164) may be found also at *PL* 126. 270; the date appears at col. 270d. On the dates for (165) and (166), see Beck, "Selection of Bishops Suffragan to Hincmar of Reims," pp. 296-97 and nos. 61, 63. (167) can be dated by reference to (168), on which see Beck, ibid. For (172) see Flodoard, 3. 21. 515.

41. No. 169. The terminus a quo for (169) is fixed following HL in his *Reclamatio,* (171), where the bishop's imprisonment seems to date from the year 873 (MGH *Epp.* 7. 95); the terminus ad quem is fixed by the synod of Troyes (173).

42. (170) is dated in 878-879 by Schrörs, *Reg. HR*, no. 453 and p. 586, n. 161, but it seems appropriately related to the Council of Troyes (173).

43. Nos. 171, 173-176. For (173), the date of opening is fixed in the synopsis of the *acta*, at Mansi, 17. 345d, and the closing at *Ann. Bert.*, p. 229. The anathema against Formosus of Porto, dated 14 September, is of doubtful authenticity; see Hefele-Leclercq, *Histoire des conciles*, 4:677-78. Following the synopsis, at Mansi, 17. 347a, (171) was presented at the third session of the synod, which was held on 12 August, according to *Ann. Bert.* p. 224. After the presentation of the *Reclamatio*, HR received a delay for the presentation of his response to the charges made by his nephew. Flodoard, 3. 29. 554, states that the archbishop gave an answer pro tempore to the various accusations made against him and later sent a fuller response to the pope. Thus the date for (175),

which follows Schrörs (Reg. HR, no. 440). (174) may have
been among the writings sent, as perhaps too a revised
version of the HR Opusculum; on all this, cf. (91) and n.
21 above. Schrörs, Reg. HR, no. 460 and p. 580, n. 124,
gives (176) a date of September-end 879; but 878 seems
more likely. However, the fact that Bishop Gislebertus
of Chartres, one of the addressees of the letter, is
last mentioned at Troyes (Duchesne, *Fastes épiscopaux*,
2:426), does not necessarily substantiate this dating,
since for a number of years following Troyes there were
no large assemblies of the northern bishops.

44. No. 177. See Schrörs, Reg. HR, no. 464, and p.
587 n. 165.

45. No. 178. A confected letter attributed to John,
ed. Poncelet, "Une lettre de S. Jean évêque de Cambrai à
Hincmar de Laon," pp. 385-86. Poncelet remarks (p. 389)
that at the supposed time the letter was written both
bishops were at Verberie.

Bibliography

Primary Sources

Acta synodalia de Formoso episcopo. In *Auxilius und Vigilius*, edited by E. Dümmler, pp. 157-61. Leipzig, 1866.

Ado. *Chronicon*. In MGH *SS* 2. 315-26.

Alberigo, J., ed. *Conciliorum oecumenicorum decreta*. Freiburg, 1962.

Annales Bertiniani--Annales de Saint-Bertin. Edited by F. Grat, et al. Paris, 1964.

Annales Einsidlinenses. In MGH *SS* 3. 145-49.

Annales Floriacenses. In MGH *SS* 2. 254-55.

Annales Fuldenses. In Rau, 3:20-177.

Annales Lemovicenses. In MGH *SS* 2. 251-52.

Annales Mettenses. Bouquet, 7. 184-203.

Annales regni Francorum. In Rau, 1:9-135.

Annales sancti Benigni Divionensis. In MGH *SS* 5. 37-50.

Annales Vedastini. In Rau, 2:289-337.

Annales Xantenses. In Rau, 2:339-71.

Ansegis. *Capitularium collectio*. In MGH *Cap.* 1. 394-450.

Astronomer [pseud.]. *Vita Hludowici*. In Rau, 1:257-381.

Athanasius. *De synodis*. In *Athanasius Werke*, edited by Hans-Georg Opitz. 3 vols. Berlin, 1934-40.

Benedict III. *Epistola*. In MGH *Epp.* 5. 612-14.

Benedictus Levita. *Capitularium collectio*. In *PL* 97. 697-912.

Böhmer, J. F. and Mühlbacher, M., eds. *Die Regesten des Kaiserreichs unter den Karolingern, 751-918*. 2d. rev. ed., ed. J. Lechner. Innsbruck, 1908.

Bouquet, M., et al., eds. *Recueil des historiens des Gaules et de la France*. 24 vols. Paris, 1738-1904.

Carmina Centulensia. In MGH *Poet. lat.* 3. 265-368.

Carmina scottorum latina et graecanica. In MGH *Poet. lat.* 3. 685-701.

Catalogi abbatum Epternacensium.   In MGH *SS* 13. 737-42.

Celestine I. *Epistolae.*   In *PL* 50. 417-558.

Charles the Bald. *Epistolae.*   In *PL* 124. 861-96.

Chronique de Saint-Riquier.   Edited by F. Lot. 3 vols. Paris, 1894.

Codex Theodosianus.   Edited by Theodore Mommsen. Berlin, 1905.

Cyprian. *De catholicae ecclesiae unitate.*   In *Opera omnia,* edited by G. Hartel, 3:209-33.   3 vols. Vienna, 1871.

Cyprian. *Epistolae.*   In *Opera omnia,* ed. G. Hartel, 3: 465-842.   3 vols.   Vienna, 1871.

Concilia antiqua Galliae cum epistolis pontificum, principum constitutionibus et aliis Gallicanae rei ecclesiasticae monumentis.   Vol. 4, *Supplementa.* Edited by P. Delalande.   Paris, 1666.

Dionysius Exiguus. *Collectio canonum.*   In *PL* 67. 39-346.

Domus Carolingica genealogia, pt. 4.   In MGH *SS* 2. 308-12.

Drival, E. van., ed. *Cartulaire de l'abbaye de Saint-Vaast d'Arras.*   Arras, 1875.

Duchesne, L., ed. *Le liber pontificalis.*   2 vols. Paris, 1886-92.

Ebbo. *Apologeticus.*   In MGH *Conc.* 2, pt. 2, pp. 794-806.

Epistolae ad divortium Lotharii II regis pertinentes. In MGH *Epp.* 6. 207-40.

Epistolae variorum inde a saeculo nono medio usque ad mortem Karoli II. (Calvi) imperatoris collectae. In MGH *Epp.* 6. 127-206.

Eriugena, Johannes Scotus. *Carmina.*   In MGH *Poet. lat.* 3. 518-56.

Eriugena, Johannes Scotus. *De divisione naturae.*   In *PL* 122. 441-1022.

Eusebius. *The Ecclesiastical History.* Edited by K. Lake. 2 vols. Cambridge, Mass., 1964-65.

Eusebius. *Vita Constantini.*   Edited by I. A. Heikel. Leipzig, 1902.

Flodoard. *Historia ecclesiae Remensis.*   In MGH *SS* 13. 409-599.

Folcuinus. *Gesta abbatum Lobiensium.*   In MGH *SS* 4. 52-74.

Gesta episcoporum Cameracensium.   In MGH *SS* 7. 393-525.

Gregory I. *Registrum epistolarum.* In MGH *Epp.* 1.

Hadrian II. *Epistolae.* In MGH *Epp.* 6. 695-765.

Havet, J., ed. *Les Chartes de Saint-Calais.* In *Oeuvres de Julien Havet. I. Questions mérovingiennes*, pp. 103-90. Paris, 1896.

Havet, J. "Questions mérovingiennes, IV. Les chartes de Saint-Calais," *Bibliothèque de l'Ecole des chartes* 48 (1887):209-47.

Heiricus. *Annales breves.* In MGH *SS* 13. 80.

Hincmar of Laon, *Epistolae et opuscula.* In *PL* 124. 979-1072.

Hincmar of Reims, *Opera.* In *PL* 125 and 126. 9-648.
Particular works:
Annales Bertiniani, as above (ann. 861-882).
Collectio de raptoribus. In MGH *Cap.* 1. 287-89.
De cavendis vitiis et virtutibus exercendis. In *PL* 125. 857-930.
De divortio Lotharii regis et Tetbergae reginae. In *PL* 125. 623-772.
De ecclesiis et capellis. Edited by W. Gundlach. *Zeitschrift für Kirchengeschichte* 10(1889):93-144.
-----. Edited by J. Gaudenzi. *Bibliotheca juridica medii aevi. Scripta anecdota glossatorum* 2 (1901): 7-23.
De jure metropolitanorum. In *PL* 126. 189-210.
De praedestinatio Dei et libero arbitrio dissertatio posterior. In *PL* 125. 65-474.
Epistolae. In *PL* 126. 9-280.
-----. In Mansi, 16. 809-55.
-----. In MGH *Epp.* 8.
Opuscula et epistolae quae spectant ad causam Hincmari Laudunensis. In *PL* 126. 279-648.
Responsio cur in suae scripto posuerit mysticam Nicaenam synodum. In *PL* 125. 1197-1200.
Vita sancti Remigii. In MGH *SS rer. merov.* 3. 239-341.

Hinschius, P., ed. *Decretales Pseudo-Isidorianae et Capitula Angilramni.* Leipzig, 1863.

Ignatius. *Letter to the Magnesians.* In *Apostolic Fathers*, edited by K. Lake, vol. 1. 2 vols. New York, 1925.

Jaffé, P., et al., eds. *Regesta pontificum Romanorum.* Vol. 1. 2d ed. Leipzig, 1881.

John VIII. *Epistolae collectae.* In MGH *Epp.* 7. 313-29.

John VIII. *Registrum epistolarum.* In MGH *Epp.* 7. 1-312.

Leo I. *Epistolae.* In *PL* 54.

Lupus of Ferrières. *Epistolae.* Edited by L. Levillain. 2 vols. Paris, 1927-35.

Mansi, J. D., et al., eds. *Sacrorum conciliorum nova et amplissima collectio.* Florence and Venice, 1759-.

Migne, J. P., ed. *Patrologiae Latinae cursus completus.* Paris, 1844-.

Monumenta Germaniae historica. Edited by G. Pertz et al.
    Auctores antiquissimi. 17 vols. Berlin, 1877-1919.
    Capitularia regum Francorum. 2 vols. Hanover, 1883-97.
    Concilia. 2 vols. Hanover, 1893-1924.
    Epistolae. 8 vols. Berlin, 1887-1939.
    Formulae merovingici et karolini aevi. Hanover, 1886.
    Poetae latini. 6 vols. Berlin, 1880-1951.
    Scriptores. 32 vols. Hanover, 1826-1934.
    Scriptores rerum merovingicarum. 7 vols. Hanover, 1884-1920.

Narratio clericorum Remensium. In MGH *Conc.* 2, pt. 2, pp. 806-14.

Nicholas I. *Epistolae.* In MGH *Epp.* 6. 257-690.

Nicholas I. *Sermo.* In Mansi, 15. 685-87.

Nithard. *Historiarum libri IV.* In Rau, 1:385-461.

Notitia provinciarum. In MGH *AA* 9. 552-612.

Oediger, F. W., ed. *Die Regesten der Erzbischöfe von Köln im Mittelalter.* 3 vols. Vol. 1, *313-1099.* Publikation der Gesellschaft für Rheinische Geschichtskunde, no. 21. Bonn, 1954-61.

Optatus. *Adversus Parmenianem.* Edited by C. Ziwsa. Prague, 1893.

Quantain, M., ed. *Cartulaire général de l'Yonne.* 2 vols. Auxerre, 1854-60.

Rau, R., ed. *Quellen zur Karolingischen Reichsgeschichte.* 3 vols. Darmstadt, 1956.

Regino. *Chronicon.* In Rau, 3. 179-319.

Rothad. *Libellus proclamationis.* In Mansi, 15. 681-85.

Series regum et abbatum. In MGH *SS* 13. 742.

Sirmond, J. *Concilia antiqua Galliae.* 3 vols. Paris, 1629.

Sozomen. *Historia ecclesiastica.* Edited by J. Bidez and G. C. Hansen. Berlin, 1960.

Tessier, G., et al., eds. *Recueil des actes de Charles II le Chauve.* 3 vols. Paris, 1943-55.

Theodoret. *Historia ecclesiastica*. Edited by L. Parmentier and F. Scheidweiler. Berlin, 1954.

Secondary Sources

Amann, E. *L'époque carolingienne*. Histoire de l'église, no. 6. Paris, 1937.

Andrieu, M. "Le sacre épiscopal d'après Hincmar de Reims," *Revue d'histoire ecclésiastique* 48 (1953): 22-73.

Arquillière, H.-X. *L'augustinisme politique*. 2d. ed. Paris, 1955.

Auzias, L. *L'Aquitaine carolingienne*. Toulouse-Paris, 1937.

Bacht, H. "Hincmar von Reims: Ein Beitrag zur Theologie des Allgemeinen Konzils." In *Unio Christianorum: Festschrift für Erzbischof Dr. Lorenz Jaeger*, pp. 223-42. Paderborn, 1962.

Baix, F. "Benedictus Levita," *Dictionnaire de droit canonique*, 2:400-6. Paris, 1937.

Balon, J. *Jus medii aevi*. Vol. 1, *La structure et la gestion du domaine de l'église au môyen-age dans l'Europe des Francs*. 2d. ed. Namur, 1963.

Barion, H. *Das fränkisch-deutsche Synodalrecht im Frühmittelalter*. Kanonistische Studien und Texte, vols. 5 and 6. Bonn, 1931.

Barion, H. *Die Nationalsynode im fränkisch-deutschen Synodalrecht des Frühmittelalters*. Königsberg, 1934.

Baus, K. *From the Apostolic Community to Constantine*. New York, 1965.

Beck, H. G. J. "Canonical Election to Suffragan Bishoprics according to Hincmar of Reims," *Catholic Historical Review* 43 (1957):137-59.

Beck, H. G. J. "The Selection of Bishops Suffragan to Hincmar of Reims, 845-882," *Catholic Historical Review* 45 (1959):273-308.

Becker, G. *Catalogi bibliothecarum antiqui*. Bonn, 1895.

Bell, C. H. *The Sister's Son in the Medieval German Epic: A Study in the Survival of Matriliny*. University of California Publications in Modern Philology, vol. 10., no. 2. Berkeley, 1922.

Bertolini, O. "La dottrina gelasiana dei due poteri nella polemica per la successione nel regno di Lorena (869-870)," *Mélanges E. Tisserant* 4 (Studi e Testi, 234 [1964]):35-58.

Berza, M. "Sur le voyage en France du pape Jean VIII (878)," *Revue historique du Sud-est européen* 18 (1941):68-86.

Betz, Karl-Ulrich. *Hinkmar von Reims, Nikolaus I., Pseudo-Isidor. Fränkisches Landeskirchentum und römischer Machtanspruch im 9. Jahrhundert.* Bonn, 1965.

Bourgeois, E. "Hugues l'Abbé," *Annales de la Faculté des lettres de Caen* 1 (1885):61-72, 97-130.

Bourgeois, E. *Le capitulaire de Kiersy-sur-Oise (877). Etude sur l'état et le régime politique de la société carolingienne à la fin du IXe siècle d'après la législation de Charles le Chauve.* Paris, 1885.

Boussinesq, G., and Laurent, G. *Histoire de Reims depuis les origines jusqu'à nos jours, I: Reims ancien.* Reims, 1933.

Boyd, C. E. *Tithes and Parishes in Medieval Italy.* New York, 1952.

Brühl, C. "Fränkischer Krönungsbrauch und das Problem der 'Festkrönungen,'" *Historische Zeitschrift* 194 (1962):265-326.

Brühl, C. "Hinkmariana," *Deutsches Archiv* 20 (1964):48-77.

Brühl, C. "Königspfalz und Bischofsstadt in fränkischer Zeit," *Rheinische Vierteljahrsblättern* 23 (1958):161-274.

Brix, L. "Note sur la bibliothèque de Wulfad de Reims," *Revue des études augustiniennes* 14 (1968):139-41.

Büttner, H. "Mission und Kirchenorganisation des Frankenreiches bis zum Tode Karls des Grossen," *Karlswerk* 1:454-87.

Cabaniss, A. "Judith Augusta and Her Time," *Studies in English* 10 (1969):67-109.

Calmette, J. *La diplomatie carolingienne du traité de Verdun à la mort de Charles le Chauve.* Paris, 1901.

Calmette, J. "Les abbés Hilduin au IXe siècle," *Bibliothèque de l'Ecole des Chartes* 65 (1904):530-36.

Camus, A. G. "Notice d'un manuscrit de la Bibliothèque Nationale n. 1594, droit canon E, contenant plusiers pièces historiques du IXe siècle." In *Notices et extraits des manuscrits*, an. 7, tom. 5 (1799), pp. 79-85.

Cappuyns, M. *Jean Scot Erigène*. Paris, 1933.

Cappuyns, M. "Les 'Bibli Vulfadi' et Jean Scot Erigène," *Recherches de théologie ancienne et médiévale* 33 (1966):137-39.

Carey, M. "The Scriptorium of Reims during the Archbishopric of Hincmar," *Classical and Mediaeval Studies in Honor of Edward Kennard Rand*, pp. 41-60. New York, 1938.

Cellot, L. *Vita Hincmari Junioris*. In Mansi, 16. 688-724.

Ceillier, R. *Histoire générale des auteurs sacrés et ecclésiastiques*. 16 vols. 2d ed. Paris, 1858-69.

Chaume, M. *Les origines du duché de Bourgogne*. Vol. 1. 2 vols. Dijon, 1925-27.

Classen, P. "Die Verträge von Verdun und von Coulaines 843 als politische Grundlagen des westfränkischen Reiches," *Historische Zeitschrift* 196 (1963):1-35.

Clercq, C. de. *La législation religieuse franque*. Vol. 2, *De Louis le Pieux à la fin du IXe siècle (814-900)*. Antwerp, 1958.

Congar, Y. M.-J. *L'ecclésiologie du haut moyen âge. De Saint Gregoire le Grand à la désunion entre Byzance et Rome*. Paris, 1968.

Congar, Y. M.-J. "S. Nicolas Ier (+867). Ses positions ecclésiologiques," *Rivista di storia della chiesa in Italia* 21 (1967):393-410.

Congar, Y. M.-J. "Structures et régime de l'église d'après Hincmar de Reims." *Communio. Commentarii Internationales de Ecclesia et Theologia* 1:5-18. Granada, 1968.

Conran, E. J. *The Interdict*. Washington, D.C., 1930.

Conrat, M. "Hinkmariana im Cod. Paris. Sang. 12445," *Neues Archiv* 35 (1910):769-75.

Constable, G. "'Nona et Decima.' An Aspect of Carolingian Economy," *Speculum* 35 (1960):224-50.

Contreni, J. J. "A propos de quelques manuscrits de l'école de Laon au IXe siècle: Découvertes et problèmes," *Le Moyen Age* 78 (1972):5-39.

Contreni, J. J.   "The Formation of Laon's Cathedral
    Library in the Ninth Century," *Studi Medievali,*
    3d ser., 13 (1972):919-39.
Daudet, P.   *Etudes sur l'histoire de la juridiction ma-
    trimoniale.   Les origines carolingiennes de la com-
    pétence exclusive de l'église (France et Germanie).*
    2 vols. Paris, 1933.
David, M.   *La souveraineté et les limites juridiques du
    pouvoir monarchique du IXe au XVe siècle.*   Paris,
    1954.
David, M.   "Le serment du sacre du IXe au XVe siècle.
    Contribution a l'étude des limites juridiques de la
    souveraineté," *Revue du moyen âge latine* 6 (1950):5-
    272.
Delaruelle, E.   "Charlemagne et l'église," *Revue d'his-
    toire de l'église de France* 39 (1953):165-99.
Delaruelle, E.   "En relisant le 'De institutione regia'
    de Jonas d'Orléans," *Mélanges d'histoire du moyen
    âge dédiés a la mémoire de Louis Halphen,* pp. 185-92.
    Paris, 1951.
Delius, W.   *Hinkmar, Bischof von Laon.*   Ph.D. disserta-
    tion.   Halle, 1924.
Delius, W.   "Papst Hadrian II. (867-872) und die beiden
    Hinkmare."   In *Antwort aus der Geschichte.   Beobach-
    tungen und Erwägungen zum geschichtlichen Bild der
    Kirche.   Walter Dress zum 65. Geburtstag,* pp. 49-
    65.   Berlin, 1969.
Devisse, J.   "Essai sur l'histoire d'une expression qui
    a fait fortune: 'Consilium et auxilium' au IXe
    siècle," *Le Moyen Age* 74 (1968):179-205.
Devisse, J.   *Hincmar et la loi.*   Université de Dakar,
    Faculté des Lettres et Sciences Humaines, Section
    d'histoire, no. 5 Dakar, 1962.
Dhondt, J.   "Election et hérédité sous les Carolingiens
    et les premiers Capétiens," *Revue belge de philo-
    logie et d'histoire* 18 (1939):913-53.
Dhondt, J.   *Etudes sur la naissance des principautés
    territoriales en France (IXe-Xe siècle).*   Bruges,
    1948.
Dictionnaire d'archéologie chrétienne et de liturgie.
    Edited by F. Cabrol.   15 vols.   Paris, 1907-53.

Dictionnaire de biographie française. Edited by J. Balteau et al. Paris, 1933-.

Dictionnaire d'histoire et de géographie ecclésiastiques. 18 vols. to date. Paris, 1912-.

Diez, C. *De Hincmari vita et ingenio.* Sens, 1859.

Dinkler-von Schubert, E. "'Per murum dimiserunt eum.' Zur Ikonographie von Acta IX, 25 und 2. Cor. XI, 33." In *Studien zur Buchmalerei und Goldschmiedekunst des Mittelalters. Festschrift für Karl Herman Usener zum 60. Geburtstag,* pp. 70-92. Marburg, 1967.

Doizé, J. "Le gouvernement confraternel des fils de Louis le Pieux et l'unité de l'empire (843-855)," *Le Moyen Age* 11 (1898):253-85.

Dopsch, A. *The Economic and Social Foundations of European Civilization.* Translated by M. G. Beard and N. Marshall. New York, 1937.

Dopsch, A. *Wirtschaftliche und soziale Grundlagen der europäischen Kulturentwicklung aus der Zeit von Cäsar bis auf Karl den Grossen.* Vienna, 1924.

Drioux, G. "Carloman," *Dictionnaire d'histoire et de géographie ecclésiastiques* 11:1062-65.

Dubled, H. "Encore la question du manse," *Revue du moyen âge latine* 5 (1949):203-10.

Dubled, H. "'Mancipium' au moyen âge," *Revue belge de philologie et d'histoire* 5 (1949):51-56.

Duchesne, L. *Fastes épiscopaux de l'ancienne Gaule.* 3 vols. Paris, 1907-15.

Dümmler, E. *Geschichte des ostfränkischen Reiches.* 5 vols. 2d ed. Leipzig, 1887-88.

Dupin, L. E. *Nouvelle bibliothèque des auteurs ecclésiastiques.* 19 vols. Paris, 1691-1715. Vol. 9 (1697).

Dupraz, L. "Deux préceptes de Lothaire II (867 et 868) ou les vestiges diplomatiques d'un divorce manqué," *Zeitschrift für Schweizerische Kirchengeschichte* 59 (1965):193-236.

Engreen, F. E. "Pope John VIII and the Arabs," *Speculum* 20 (1945):318-30.

Ertl, N. "Dictatoren frühmittelalterlicher Papstbriefe," *Archiv für Urkundenforschung* 15 (1938):56-133.

Esmein, A. *La mariage en droit canonique.* 2 vols. 2d ed. Paris, 1929.

Esmein, A. *Les ordalies dans l'église gallicane au IXe siècle. Hincmar de Reims et ses contemporains.* Paris, 1898.

Feine, H. E. *Kirchliche Rechtsgeschichte. Die Katholische Kirche.* 5th ed. Cologne, 1972.

Feine, H. E. "Ursprung, Wesen und Bedeutung des Eigenkirchentums," *Mitteilungen des Instituts für oesterreichische Geschichtsforschung* 58 (1950):195-208.

Fliche, A. "La primatie des archevêques de Sens," *Bulletin de la Société archéologique de Sens, 1929-1930* (1933):54-70.

Fliche, A. "La primatie des Gaules depuis l'époque carolingienne jusqu'à la fin de la querelle des investitures (876-1121)," *Revue historique* 173 (1934): 329-42.

Fournier, P., and Le Bras, G. *Histoire des collections canoniques en occident.* 2 vols. Paris, 1931-32.

Friend, A. M. "Two Manuscripts of the School of St. Denis," *Speculum* 1 (1926):59-70.

Fuhrmann, H. "Eine im Original erhaltene Propagandaschrift des Erzbischofs Gunthar von Köln," *Archiv für Diplomatik, Schriftsgeschichte, Siegel- und Wappenkunde* 4 (1958):1-51.

Fuhrmann, H. *Einfluss und Verbreitung der pseudoisidorischen Fälschungen.* 3 vols. Schriften der MGH, no. 24. Stuttgart, 1972-74.

Fuhrmann, H. "Studien zur Geschichte mittelalterlicher Patriarchate," *Zeitschrift der Savigny-Stiftung für Rechtsgeschichte, Kanonistische Abteilung* 40 (1954): 1-84.

Fuhrmann, H. "Studien zur Geschichte mittelalterlicher Patriarchate," *Zeitschrift der Savigny-Stiftung für Rechtsgeschichte, Kanonistische Abteilung* 40 (1954): 1-84.

Fuhrmann, H. "Zur Überlieferung des Pittaciolus Bischof Hinkmars von Laon (869)," *Deutsches Archiv* 27 (1971): 517-24.

Gaehde, J. E. "The Bible of San Paolo fuori le mura in Rome: Its Date and Its Relation to Charles the Bald," *Gesta* 5 (1966):9-21.

Gaehde, J. E. "The Turonian Sources of the Bible of San Paolo Fuori Le Mura in Rome," *Frühmittelalterliche Studien* 5 (1971):359-400.

Ganshof, F. L. *The Carolingians and the Frankish Monarchy*. Translated by J. Sondheimer. Ithaca, 1971.

Ganshof, F. L. "The Church and the Royal Power in the Frankish Monarchy under Pippin III and Charlemagne." In *The Carolingians and the Frankish Monarchy*, pp. 205-39. Ithaca, 1971.

Ganshof, F. L. *Feudalism*. New York, 1964.

Ganshof, F. L. *Frankish Institutions under Charlemagne*. Providence, R.I., 1969.

Ganshof, F. L. "La preuve dans le droit franc." In *Recueils de la Société Jean Bodin, 17. La preuve, 2. Moyen Age et Temps Modernes*, pp. 71-98. Brussels, 1965.

Ganshof, F. L. "On the Genesis and Significance of the Treaty of Verdun." In *The Carolingians and the Frankish Monarchy*, pp. 289-302. Ithaca, 1971.

Ganshof, F. L. "The Treaties of the Carolingians," *Medieval and Renaissance Studies* 3 (1968):23-52.

Gess, W. F. *Merkwürdigkeiten aus dem Leben und den Schriften Hinkmars, Erzbischofs von Rheims*. Göttingen, 1806.

J. de Ghellinck. *La littérature latine au moyen âge*. Paris, 1939.

Gietl, A. M. "Hincmars collectio de ecclesiis et capellis," *Historisches Jahrbuch* 15 (1894):556-73.

Goffart, W. *The Le Mans Forgeries. A Chapter from the History of Church Property in the Ninth Century*. Cambridge, Mass., 1966.

Gorissen, P. "Encore la clause ardennaise du traité de Meersen," *Le Moyen Age* 55 (1949):1-4.

Gottlob, T. *Der abendländische Chorepiskopat*. Bonn, 1928.

Grelewski, S. "La reáction contre les ordalies en France depuis le IXe siècle jusqu'au décret de Gratien. Agobard, archevêque de Lyon et Yves, évêque de Chartres." Ph.D. dissertation, Strassburg, 1924.

Grierson, P. "Eudes Ier, évêque de Beauvais," *Le Moyen Age* 45 (1935):161-98.

Grierson, P. "The Translation of the Relics of St. Amalberga," *Revue Bénédictine* 51 (1939):292-315.

Griffe, E. *La Gaule chrétienne à l'époque romain*. Vol. 2, *L'église des Gaules au Ve siècle*. Paris, 1966.

Grotz, H. *Erbe wider Willen. Hadrian II. (867-872) und seine zeit*. Vienna, 1970.

Guilman, J. "The Illuminations of the Second Bible of
    Charles the Bald," *Speculum* 41 (1966):246-60.
Haenens, A. d'. *Les invasions normandes en Belgique au
    IXe siècle: Le phénomène et sa répercussion dans
    l'historiographie médiévale.* Recueil de travaux
    d'histoire et de philologie, 4th ser., no. 38. Lou-
    vain-Paris: Université de Louvain, 1967.
Haller, J. *Das Papsttum.* 2 vols. 2d ed. Stuttgart,
    1950.
Haller, J. *Nikolaus I. und Pseudoisidor.* Stuttgart,
    1936.
Halphen, L. *Charlemagne et l'empire carolingien.* 2d
    ed. Paris, 1968.
Hampe, K. "Zum Streite Hincmars von Reims mit seinem
    Vorgänger Ebo und dessen Anhängern," *Neues Archiv*
    23 (1898):180-95.
Hartmann, G. *Der Primat des römischen Bischofs bei
    Pseudo-Isidor.* Stuttgart, 1930.
Hartmann, L. M. *Geschichte Italiens im Mittelalter.
    Italien und die Fränkische Herrschaft.* Vol. 3, 3
    vols. Gotha, 1908.
Hefele, K., and Leclercq, H. *Histoire des conciles.*
    Vol. 4. Paris, 1911.
Herlihy, D. "The Carolingian *Mansus*," *Economic History
    Review* 33 (1960-61):79-89.
Herlihy, D. "Church Property on the European Continent,
    701-1200," *Speculum* 36 (1961):81-105.
Heydenreich, J. *Die Metropolitangewalt der Erzbischöfe
    von Trier bis auf Baldwin.* Marburg, 1938.
Hinschius, P. *System des katholischen Kirchenrechts.*
    Vol. 3. Berlin, 1883.
Histoire littéraire de la France. Vol. 5. Paris, 1866.
Hlawitschka, E. *Die Anfänge des Hauses Habsburg-Loth-
    ringen; genealogische Untersuchungen zur Geschichte
    Lothringens und des Reiches im 9., 10. und 11.
    Jahrhundert.* Saarbrücken, 1969.
Hlawitschka, E. *Lotharingien und das Reich an der
    Schwelle d. deutschen Geschichte.* Stuttgart, 1968.
Hoyoux, J. "La clause ardennaise du traité de Meersen,"
    Le Moyen Age 53 (1947):1-13.
Imbart de la Tour, P. *Les élections épiscopales dans
    l'église de France du IXe au XIIe siècle.* Paris,
    1891.

Imbart de la Tour, P. *Les origines religieuses de la France. Les paroisses rurales du IVe au XIe siècle.* Paris, 1900.

Imbart de la Tour, P. "Private Churches in Ancient France." In *Early Medieval Society*, edited by S. Thrupp, pp. 58-66. New York, 1967.

Jeauneau, E. "Les écoles de Laon et d'Auxerre au IXe siècle." In *La scuola nell' occidente Latino dell' alto medioevo*, 2:495-522. Settimane di studio del Centro Italiano di Studi sull' alto medioevo, no. 19. Spoleto, 1972.

Jones, A. H. M.; Grierson, P.; and Crooy, J. A. "The Authenticity of the Testamentum sancti Remigii," *Revue belge de Philologie et d'Histoire* 35 (1957): 356-73.

Joranson, E. *The Danegeld in France.* Rock Island, Illinois, 1923.

Kantorowicz, E. "The Carolingian King in the Bible of San Paolo fuori le mura." In *Late Classical and Medieval Studies in Honor of Albert Mathias Friend, Jr.*, pp. 287-300. Princeton, 1955.

Kienast, W. *Der Herzogstitel in Frankreich und Deutschland (9. bis 12. Jahrhundert).* Munich, 1968.

Kirn, P. "Aequitatis judicium von Leo dem Grossen bis zu Hinkmar von Reims," *Zeitschrift für Rechtsgeschichte, germanistische Abteilung* 52 (1932):53-64.

Knabe, L. *Die gelasianische Zweitgewaltentheorie bis zum Ende des Investiturstreits.* Berlin, 1936.

Krause, V. "Hincmar von Reims der Verfasser der sog. Collectio de raptoribus im Capitular von Quierzy 857," *Neues Archiv* 18 (1893);303-8.

Krehbiel, E. B. *The Interdict. Its History and Its Operation.* Washington, 1909.

Kremers, W. *Ado von Vienne. Sein Leben und seine Schriften.* Bonn, 1911.

Krusch, B. "Reimser-Remigius Fälschungen," *Neues Archiv* 20 (1895):511-68.

Lair, J. "Les Normands dans l'île d'Oscelle," *Mémoires de la Société historique et archéologique de Pontoise et du Vexin* 20 (1897):9-40.

Lapôtre, A. *De Anastasio Bibliothecario.* Paris, 1885.

Lapôtre, A. "Hadrien II et les fausses décrétales," *Revue des questions historiques* 27 (1880):377-431.

Lapôtre, A.   *L'Europe et le Saint-Siège à l'époque carolingienne.* Vol. 1, *Le pape Jean VIII.* Paris, 1895.

Laprat, R.   "Avoués, avoueries ecclésiastiques," *Dictionnaire d'histoire et de géographie ecclésiastiques* 5:1222-28.

Lee, G. C.   "Hincmar, an Introduction to the Study of
the Revolution of the Organization of the Church in
the Ninth Century," *Papers of the American Society
of Church History,* no. 8. New York, 1897.

Le Long, N.   *Histoire ecclésiastique et civile du diocèse de Laon.* Chalons, 1783.

Lemarignier, J.-Fr.   "Autour de la royauté française du
IXe au XIIIe siècle," *Bibliothèque de l'Ecole des
Chartes* 113 (1955):1-36.

Lemarignier, J.-Fr.   "Quelques remarques sur l'organisation ecclésiastique en Gaule du VIIe à la fin du IXe
siècle," *Settimane de studio del Centro Italiano di
Studi sull' alto medioevo* 13 (Spoleto, 1965):451-86.

Lesne, E.   "Hincmar et l'empereur Lothaire," *Revue des
questions historique* 78 (1905):5-58.

Lesne, E.   *Histoire de la propriété ecclésiastique en
France.* 4 vols. Paris, 1905-43.

Lesne, E.   "La dîme des biens ecclésiastiques aux IXe et
Xe siecles," *Revue d'histoire ecclésiastique* 13
(1912):477-503, 659-73; 14 (1913):97-112, 489-509.

Lesne, E.   *La hiérarchie épiscopale. Provinces, métro-
politains, primats en Gaule et Germanie depuis la
réforme de Saint Boniface jusqu'à la mort d'Hincmar
(742-882).* Paris, 1905.

Lesne, E.   "La lettre interpolée d'Hadrien I à Tilpin et
l'église de Reims en IXe siècle," *Le Moyen Age* 26
(1913):325-48, 389-413.

Levillain, L.   "Girart, comte de Vienne," *Le Moyen Age*
55 (1949):225-45.

Linsenmayer, A.   *Geschichte der Predigt in Deutschland.*
Munich, 1866.

Lohrmann, D.   *Das Register Papst Johannes VIII. (872-
882): Neue Studien zur Abschrift Reg. Vat. 1, zum
verlorenen Originalregister und zum Diktat der
Briefe.* Bibliothek des Deutschen Historischen Instituts in Rom, no. 30. Tübingen, 1968.

Lokys, G.   *Die Kämpfe der Araber mit den Karolingern bis
zum Tode Ludwigs II.* Heidelberg, 1906.

Longnon, A. *Atlas historique de la France depuis César jusqu'à nos jours. Texte explicatif des planches.* Paris, 1907.

Lot, F. "De quelques personnages du IXe siècle qui ont porté le nom de Hilduin." In *Recueil*, 2:461-94.

Lot, F. "Godfried et Sidroc sur la Seine (852-853)." In *Recueil*, 2:686-90.

Lot, F. "La grande invasion normande de 856-862." In *Recueil*, 2:713-70.

Lot, F. "Les abbés Hilduin au IXe siècle. Réponse à M. J. Calmette." In *Recueil*, 2:500-3.

Lot, F. "Les tributs au Normands et l'église de France au IXe siècle." In *Recueil*, 3:699-719.

Lot, F. *Naissance de la France.* 2d ed. Paris, 1970.

Lot, F. "Note sur le sénéschal Alard." In *Recueil*, 2:591-611.

Lot, F. *Recueil des travaux historiques.* 3 vols. to date. Geneva, 1968-. (Elsewhere referred to as *Recueil.*)

Lot, F. "Sidroc sur la Loire. Les Normands en Bretagne, en Aquitaine, en Gascogne (853-857)." In *Recueil*, 2:691-704.

Lot, F. "Une année du règne de Charles le Chauve." In *Recueil*, 2:415-60.

Lot, F., and Halphen, L. *Le règne de Charles le Chauve,* 1(840-51). Bibliothèque de l'Ecole des Hautes Etudes, sciences historiques et philologiques, no. 175. Paris, 1909.

Louis, R. *Girart, comte de Vienne.* 3 vols. Auxerre, 1946-1947.

Loupot [l'abbé]. *Vie de Hincmar.* Travaux de l'Académie impériale de Reims, Vol. 46 [1867], nos. 3, 4. Reims, 1870.

Maasen, F. "Eine Rede des Papstes Hadrian II. vom Jahre 869. Die erste umfassende Benutzung der Falschen Decretalen zur Begründung der Machtfülle des römanischen Stuhles," *Sitzungsberichte der Kaiserl. Akademie der Wissenschaften, Phil.-hist. Kl.* 72 (1872): 521-54.

Manitius, M. *Geschichte der lateinischen Literatur des Mittelalters.* Vol. 1. Munich, 1911.

Mann, H. K. *The Popes during the Carolingian Empire, 858-891.* Vol. 3. The Lives of the Popes in the Early Middle Ages. 16 vols. 2d ed. London, 1925.

Marlot, G. *Histoire de la ville, cité et université de Reims metropolitaine de la Gaule Belgique*. Reims, 1843-46.

Mayer, T., ed. *Der Vertrag von Verdun 843*. Leipzig, 1943.

McKeon, P. R. "Archbishop Ebbo of Reims (816-51)," *Church History* 43 (1974):437-47.

McKeon, P. R. "The Carolingian Councils of Savonnières (859) and Tusey (860) and Their Background. A Study in the Ecclesiastical and Political History of the Ninth Century," *Revue Bénédictine* 84 (1974):75-110.

McKeon, P. R. "Le concile d'Attigny (870)," *Le Moyen Age* 80 (1970):401-25.

McKeon, P. R. "Toward a Reestablishment of the Correspondence of Pope Hadrian II: The Letters Exchanged between Rome and the Kingdom of Charles the Bald regarding Hincmar of Laon," *Revue Bénédictine* 81 (1971):169-85.

Merlet, R. *Guerres d'indépendence de la Bretagne sous Charles le Chauve*. Vannes, 1891.

Merlet, R. "L'émancipation de l'église de Bretagne et la concile de Tours (848-851)," *Le Moyen Age* 11 (1898):1-30.

Meyer, W. "Über Hincmars von Laon Auslese aus Pseudo-Isidor, Ingilram, und aus Schreiben des Papstes Nicolaus I.," *Nachrichten von der kgl. Gesellschaft der Wissenschaften zu Göttingen, philol.-hist. Kl.* (1912):219-27.

Michels, Th. "La date du couronnement de Charles le Chauve (9 Sept., 869) et le culte de St. Gorgon à Metz," *Revue Bénédictine* 51 (1939):288-91.

Mohr, W. "Die Krise des kirchlichen Einheitsprogrammes im Jahre 858," *Archivum Latinitatis medii aevi*, 25 (1955):189-213.

Mor, C. G. "Un manoscritto canonistico francese del secolo IX," *Rendiconti dell' Istituto Lombardo* 76 (1942-43):188-202.

Morrison, K. F. *Tradition and Authority in the Western Church 300-1140*. Princeton, 1969.

Morrison, K. F. *The Two Kingdoms. Ecclesiology in Carolingian Political Thought*. Princeton, 1964.

Munier, Ch. *Les sources patristiques du droit de l'église du VIIIe au XIIIe siècle*. Strassburg, 1957.

Musset, L. *Les invasions, II. Le second assaut contre l'Europe chrétienne (VIIe-XIe siècles)*. Paris, 1965.

Noorden, C. F. J. von. *Hinkmar Erzbischof von Rheims*. Bonn, 1863.

Norwood, F. A. "The Political Pretensions of Pope Nicholas I," *Church History* 15 (1946):271-85.

Odegaard, C. E. "The Concept of Royal Power in the Carolingian Oaths," *Speculum* 20 (1945):279-89.

Odegaard, C. E. "The Empress Engelberge," *Speculum* 26 (1951):77-103.

Odegaard, C. E. *Vassi and Fideles in the Carolingian Empire*. Cambridge, Mass., 1945.

Oexele, O. G. "Bischof Ebroin von Poitiers und seinen Verwandten," *Frühmittelalterliche Studien* 3 (1969): 138-210.

Oexele, O. G. "Die Karolinger und die Stadt des Heiligen Arnulf," *Frühmittelalterliche Studien* 1 (1967): 250-364.

Oppenheimer, F. *The Legend of the Sainte Ampoule*. London, 1955.

Parisot, R. *Le royaume de Lorraine sous les Carolingiens (843-923)*. Paris, 1899.

Partner, P. *The Lands of St. Peter*. Berkeley, 1972.

Péré, G. *Le sacre et le couronnement des rois de France*. Bagnères-de-Bigorre, 1921.

Perels, E. "Eine Denkschrift, Hinkmars von Reims im Prozess Rothads von Soissons," *Neues Archiv* 44 (1922):43-100.

Perels, E. *Papst Nikolaus I. und Anastasius Bibliothecarius*. Berlin, 1920.

Phillips, G. "Der Codex Salisburgensis S. Petri IX. 32. Ein Beitrag zur Geschichte der vorgratianischen Rechtsquellen," *Sitzungsberichte der Akademie der Wissenschaften in Wien* 44 (1863):437-510.

Pochettino, G. "L'imperatrice Angilberga (850-890)," *Archivio storico lombardico* 48 (1921):39-149.

Pölnitz-Kehr, G. von. "Kaiserin Angilberga. Ein Exkurs zur Diplomatik Kaiser Ludwigs II. von Italien," *Historisches Jahrbuch* 60 (1940):429-40.

Poncelet, A. "Les documents de Claude Despretz," *Analecta Bollandiana* 29 (1910):241-57.

Poncelet, A. "Une lettre de S. Jean évêque de Cambrai à Hincmar de Laon," *Analecta Bollandiana* 27 (1908): 384-90.

Poupardin, R.   "L'onction impériale," *Le Moyen Age* 18 (1905):113-26.

Poupardin, R.   *Le royaume de Provence sous les Carolingiens (855-933?)*.   Bibliothèque de l'Ecole des Hautes Etudes, sciences historiques et philosophiques, no. 131.   Paris, 1901.

Prichard, J. C.   *The Life and Times of Hincmar, Archbishop of Rheims*.   Oxford, 1849.

Prost, A.   "Caractère et signification de quatre pièces liturgiques composées à Metz en Latin et in Grec au IXe siècle," *Mémoires de la Société Nationale des Antiquaires de France* 35 (1879):149-320.

M. Prou.   *La Gaule mérovingienne*.   Paris, 1897.

Rocquain, F.   *La papauté au moyen âge*.   Paris, 1881.

Roy, J.   "Principes du pape Nicolas Ier sur les rapports des deux puissances."   *Etudes d'histoire du moyen âge dediées à Gabriel Monad*, pp. 95-105.   Paris, 1896.

Roy, J.   *Saint Nicolas Ier*.   Paris, 1899.

Russell, J. C.   *Late Ancient and Medieval Population*.   Transactions of the American Philosophical Society, n.s., vol. 48, no. 3.   Philadelphia, 1958.

Saltet, L.   *Les réordinations*.   Paris, 1907.

Schade, H. S.   "Studien zu der Karolingischen Bilderbibel aus St. Paul vor den Mauern zu Rom," *Wallraf-Richartz-Jahrbuch* 21 (1959):12-18.

Schebler, A.   *Die Reordinationen in der "altkatholischen" Kirche*.   Stuttgart, 1936.

Schieffer, Th.   *Die päpstlichen Legaten in Frankreich vom Vertrage von Meersen (870) bis zum Schisma von 1130*.   Historische Studien, no. 263.   Berlin, 1935.

Schlesinger, W.   "Karolingische Königswahlen," *Beiträge* 1 (Göttingen, 1963):88-138.

Schramm, P. E.   *Der König von Frankreich*.   2 vols.   2d ed.   Darmstadt, 1960.

Schramm, P. E.   *Kaiser, Könige und Päpste, II.   Beiträge zur Allgemeinen Geschichte.   Vom Tode Karls des Grossen (814) bis zum Anfang des 10. Jahrhunderts*.   Stuttgart, 1968.

Schramm, P. E.   "Ordines Studien, II.   Die Krönung bei den Westfranken und den Franzosen," *Archiv für Urkundenforschung* 15 (1938):3-55.

Schrörs, H.   "Die pseudo-isidorianische Exceptio spolii bei Papst Nikolaus I.," *Historisches Jahrbuch* 26 (1905):275-98.

Schrörs, H. "Eine vermeintliche Konzilrede des Papstes Hadrian II.," *Historisches Jahrbuch* 22 (1901):23-36, 257-75.

Schrörs, H. *Hinkmar, Erzbischof von Reims*. Freiburg im Breisgau, 1884.

Schrörs, H. *Registrum Hincmari [Remensis]*. In *Hinkmar, Erzbischof von Reims*, pp. 512-88.

Sdralek, M. *Hinkmars von Rheims kanonistisches Gutachten über die Ehescheidung des Königs Lothar II*. Freiburg im Breisgau. 1881.

Seckel, E. "Die erste Zeile Pseudoisidors, die Hadriana-Rezension 'In nomine domini incipit praefatio libri huius' und die Geschichte der invokationen in den Rechtsquellen. Aus dem Nachlass mit Ergänzungen hg. von H. Fuhrmann." *Sitzungsberichte der deutschen Akademie der Wissenschaften zu Berlin, Klasse für Philosophie, Geschichte, Staats--, Rechts-- und Wirtschaftswissenschaften,* 1959, Heft. 4.

Seckel, E. "Pseudoisidor." In *Realencyclopädie für protestantische theologie,* 16 (1905):265-307. Leipzig, 1896-1913.

Sprengler, A. "Die Gebete der Krönungsordines Hinkmars von Reims für Karl den Kahlen als König von Lothringen und für Ludwig den Stammler," *Zeitschrift für Kirchengeschichte* 63 (1950-51):245-67.

Sproemberg, H. *Die Entstehung der Grafschaft Flandern. Teil I, Die ursprüngliche Graftschaft Flandern (864-892)*. Berlin, 1935.

Sproemberg, H. "Judith, Königin von England, Gräfin von Flandern," *Revue belge de philologie et d'histoire* 15 (1936):397-428, 915-50.

Stutz, U. *Geschichte des kirchlichen Benefizialwesens von seinen Anfängen bis auf Alexander III.* Vol. 1 Berlin, 1895.

Stutz, U. "Leben und Pfründe," *Zeitschrift der Savigny-Stiftung für Rechtsgeschichte, Germanistische Abteilung* 20 (1899):213-47.

Stutz, U. "The Proprietary Church as an Element of Medieval Germanic Ecclesiastical Law." In *Medieval Germany, 911-1250,* edited by G. Barraclough, 2:35-70. 2 vols. New York, 1961.

Tessier, G. *Diplomatique royale française*. Paris, 1962.

Thompson, J. W. *The Dissolution of the Carolingian Fisc in the Ninth Century*. University of California Publications in History, no. 23. Berkeley, 1935.

Thompson, J. W. *The Literacy of the Laity in the Middle Ages*. Berkeley, 1939.

Ullmann, W. *The Carolingian Renaissance and the Idea of Kingship*. London, 1969.

Ullmann, W. *The Growth of Papal Government in the Middle Ages*. 3d ed. London, 1970.

Vanderkindere, L. *Formation territoriale des principautés belge au moyen âge*. 2d ed. Brussels, 1902.

Vanderkindere, L. "Le capitulaire de Servais et les origines du comté de Flandre." In *Choix d'études historiques*, pp. 93-140. Brussels, 1909.

Vercauteren, F. *Etude sur les civitates de la Belgique seconde*. Académie royal de Belgique. Classe des lettres et des sciences morales et politiques. Mémoires. 2d ser. Vol. 33. Brussels, 1934.

Vidieu [l'abbé]. *Hincmar de Reims. Etude sur le IXe siècle*. Paris, 1875.

Vogel, W. *Die Normannen und das fränkische Reich bis zur Gründung der Normandie* (799-911). Heidelberger Abhandlungen, no. 14. Heidelberg, 1906.

Wallace-Hadrill, J. M. *The Long-Haired Kings*. London, 1962.

Werminghoff, A. "Verzeichnis der Akten fränkischer Synoden von 843-918," *Neues Archiv* 26 (1901):611-78.

Zatschek, H. "Ludwig der Deutsche." In *Der Vertrag von Verdun*, edited by Mayer, pp. 31-65.

Zumthor, P. *Charles le Chauve*. Portraits de l'histoire, no. 9. N.p., 1957.

Index

Aachen (royal residence), 10, 39, 44, 70; councils at (860), 41-42; council at (862), 43; meeting at (870), 52-53

Actard (bishop of Nantes), 102, 148, 151-54

Adalard (count), 158

Adalgis (duke of Benevento), 156

Adelelmus (count), 123

Adeloldus (priest), 58

Ado (archbishop of Vienne), 51-52, 122

Adventius (bishop of Metz), 42, 48, 52, 133

Aeneas (bishop of Paris), 16, 37, 87

Aequitas, 153

Aguilcourt (villa), 66-67, 71, 73, 81, 83, 86

Amalbertus (vassal of Laon), 22

Amalbertus (excommunicated by Hincmar of Laon), 67,

69-70, 226 n.11

Anastasius (papal librarian), 151

Andernach, 160

Angers, 158

Anicius (pope), 118

Ansegis (archbishop of Sens), 122, 129, 131, 133, 159

Ansgarius (royal vassal), 99, 109, 110

Antioch, council at (341), 69, 144

Appeal, 24, 46, 58-59, 72, 94-95, 116-17

Aquitaine, 5, 7, 10, 63

Arabs, 39, 49, 122, 156, 158, 160

Arsenius (papal legate), 46, 60, 67

Ariulfus (vassal of Laon), 22

Athanasius, 95

Attigny (royal residence),

3, 6, 9, 50, 98, 157, 159; meeting at (865), 60; *placitum* at (870), 53-54, 100-6, 113, 116, 118, 183; council at (870), 85-88, 121, 127-29, 132, 134, 137

Attolus (bishop of Laon), 66

Ausoldus (priest), 66

Baldwin (count of Flanders), 121, 124, 247 n.2

Bari, 122, 156

Beauvais, council at (845), 10, 20

Benedict III (pope), 40, 61-62

Benevento, 49

Berno (vassal of Laon), 32

Bertha (wife of Gerard of Vienne), 123

Bertharius (provost of Laon), 66, 108-10, 113, 127, 134

Bertricus (vassal of Reims), 76-77

Bertulfus (archbishop-designate of Trier), 52, 70, 133

Besançon, 156-57

Boniface (saint), 91

Boniface (pope), 118

Boso (count), 40, 159-60, 167, 266 n.39, 268 n.54

Boulogne, 9, 14

Bourges, 7

Brienne, 3

Brittany, 5

Burgundy, 3, 12, 51

Calixtus (pope), 118

Cambrai, 9, 58, 67

Canons, 59, 72, 82, 90-93, 95-98, 108, 117-18, 134, 147

Carloman (son of Charles the Bald), 62, 120-31, 150-51, 156-58, 162-63

Carloman (son of Louis the German), 142, 158

Celestine (pope), 136

Celsanus (cleric of Laon), 28, 30

Charlemagne, 5, 7, 13, 19, 27, 82, 84, 88, 91

Charles Martel, 17

Charles (king of Aquitaine), 63, 120

Charles (king of Provence), 40, 43, 45, 122

Charles (son of Louis the German), 142, 158

Charles the Bald, realm of, 4-6, 11, 14; agrees to restore church property, 20-21; meets Louis the German at Metz (868), 48; crowned king of Lotharingia, 50; marries Richilde, 52; crowned emperor, 158; death of, 161

Church property, 15, 17-21, 25, 76-77, 93

Clarentius (priest), 32, 77-78, 116

Clergy, trial of, 24-28, 71-72, 77, 93, 114

Clovis, 9, 12

Cologne, succession to see of, 46-47, 52, 70

Compiègne (royal residence), 9, 29, 53; council at (871), 124

Conrad (uncle of Charles the Bald), 15, 179-80, 182-83

Corbie (monastery), 158

Cosne, 30

Council, provincial, 24, 71-72, 83, 90-94, 96, 112, 118; supra-provincial, 89-90, 95-98

Danegeld, 6, 160

Decretals, 60-61, 72, 96, 98, 118, 134

Diocesan synod, 81-84, 89

Douzy (villa), council at (871), 130-51, 156, 161-62

Ebbo (archbishop of Reims), 9-10, 57, 62-64

Echternach (monastery), 158

Egilo (archbishop of Sens), 68

Eiricus (count), 33

Eligius (vassal of Laon), 110

Engelberga (empress), 49, 157, 159

Engelramnus (count), 123, 250 n.32, 255 n.26

Epernay, assembly at (846), 20

Episcopate, 7, 57-59, 85-86, 89-94

Ermintrude (queen), 52, 59, 120-21, 143

Eutramnus (vassal of Reims), 76

Exceptio spolii, 72, 108, 142, 153, 217 n.11

Excommunication, 29, 35-36

Fagenulfus (priest), 143

Felix (pope), 117, 142

Flotharius (*missus*), 109

Follembray (villa), 79-84, 86

Fontenoy, 160

Formosus (bishop, later pope), 211 n.65

Frankfurt, 53, 110

Frotarius (archbishop of Bordeaux), 87, 101

Gelasius (pope), 61, 150

Gennobaudis (bishop of Laon), 12

Gerard (count), 40, 51, 122-23

Gondreville, assembly at (869), 51-52, 54, 70-72, 86, 134-35

Goslinus (count), 123

Gottschalk (monk), 215 n.2

Gregory I (pope), 14, 91, 153

Grivo (vassal of Laon), 104-5

Gunthar (archbishop of Cologne), 41, 43, 46, 49, 58

Hadrian II (pope), 28, 32, 36, 38; and divorce of Lothar II, 47-49; on succession in Lotharingia, 51, 54-55, 99, 105, 114, 122; and Carloman, 126-27; and council of Douzy, 146-155; favors Charles the Bald as emperor, 155

Hadulfus (priest), 77-78, 83-84

Haimeradus (priest), 79, 86, 134

Hardwic (archbishop of Besançon), 51, 106-8, 111-12, 122, 146

Hartgarius (deacon), 112

Heddo (cleric), 76, 110-11,

124-25

Hedenulfus (bishop of Laon), 162-63

Heiric of Auxerre, 13

Hildeboldus (cleric), 33

Hildegarius (bishop of Meaux), 120

Hilduin (abbot of Saint Denis), 10-11

Hilduin (archbishop-designate of Cologne), 52, 58

Hincmar of Laon, early life, 14-16; advocates divorce of Lothar II, 42, 65; and Aguilcourt, 66-67; excommunicates Amalbertus, 67; and election of John of Cambrai, 67; at Pîtres (868), 23-24; appeals to pope, 28, 32, 106; places diocese under interdict, 30; at Verberie (869), 31; imprisoned, 32-37, 83; signs canon law collection, 69; at coronation of Charles the Bald, 50, 70; excommunicates monk, 224 n.84; at Gondreville (869), 70-74; and Nivinus, 75-77; and Follembray, 78-84; at Attigny (870), 85-87, 100-6; and Tusey *capitula*, 110-13; and Carlo-

man, 127; at Douzy (871), 140-46; blinded, 162; restored to priesthood, 164; on council of Nicaea, 117-18; ecclesiological theories, 65, 71-72, 91-98, 116-18, 128

Hincmar of Reims, early life, 10-12; opposes divorce of Lothar II, 42-43; and Rothad, 58-61; and Nicholas I, 59-64; and Wulfad, 62-64; crowns Charles the Bald at Metz, 50; on appeal, 94, 98; on council of Nicaea, 95, 97, 117; on jurisdiction over clergy, 25-27; on papal primacy, 97-98; on private churches, 57-58; on property of church, 25-27; on provincial council, 92-93, 96; on rights of metropolitans, 34-36, 91-98

Hosius of Cordova, 117

Hubert (count), 40

Hugh (abbot, 267 n.39

Hugh (son of Lothar II), 162

Humerus (vassal of Reims), 76

Imbetausius (archbishop of Reims), 9

Innocent (pope), 95

Irminonus (priest), 143

Italy, 39, 48-49, 54, 156, 161

John VIII (pope), 157-64

John (bishop of Cambrai), 67, 103

John of Cervia (legate), 45

John of Scot, 13, 16, 121

Jouvincourt (villa), 66

Jouy, 6

Judith (daughter of Charles the Bald), 43, 247 n.2

Judith (empress), 4, 16

Langres, 62

Leo I (pope), 61, 69, 136

Leo IV (pope), 62

Liudo (vassal of Laon), 23

Lothar I (emperor), 3-4, 6-7, 10, 39-40, 42, 44, 122, 159

Lothar II (king), 3, 38, 65; divorce of, 39-50

Lothar (son of Charles the Bald), 120

Lotharingia, 39-40, 48-51, 55-56, 70, 114-5, 120-22, 130

Louis the Pious (emperor), 3, 9-11, 19-20, 61

Louis the German (king), 41, 46, 130-31, 156, 158; invades west Francia (858) 3, 6, 12; and succession in Lotharingia, 48-54, 120; invades west Francia (876), 159

Louis II (emperor), 39, 44-45, 49, 51, 122, 156-58

Louis (son of Louis the German), 142, 160

Louis the Stammerer (king), 120, 160-61, 164

Lucius (pope), 118

Maestricht, meeting at (871), 131 156-57, 261 n.94

Mainz, 158

Mark (pope), 117

Meaux-Paris, council at (844-45), 11, 20

Metropolitans, 24-25, 34-36, 58-59, 71-72, 77, 89-98, 113, 118, 134

Metz, 70; council at (863), 44-45; meeting at (868), 48-49; Charles the Bald crowned at, 50

Monte-Cassino, council at (869), 49

Nicaea, council at (325), 61, 95, 97, 117-18, 134

Nicholas I (pope), 68, 132; and divorce of Lothar II, 43-47; on Rothad, 59-61; on Wulfad, 63-64; on papal primacy, 44, 60-61

Nivinus (vassal of Reims), 75-76

Nortmannus (count), 22, 28-29, 100, 105-6, 114-15, 134, 137, 148, 179-83, 185

Odo (bishop of Beauvais), 29-31, 53, 59, 61, 87, 111, 128, 201 n.75

Ordeal, 39

Orville, 157

Oscelle, 3

Ottericus (priest), 79

Ottolfus (cleric), 33

Pardulus (bishop of Laon), 13-14, 66, 79, 104, 143, 192 n.72

Pepin of Herstal, 17

Pepin the Short, 18-19, 79

Pepin I (king of Aquitaine), 3, 187 n.8

Pepin II (king of Aquitaine), 188 n.16

Pîtres (villa), *placitum* at (868), 23-28, 31; *placitum* at (869), 37, 69, 182; council at (862), 58

Poilly (villa), 22, 28-29, 37, 100, 106, 109, 114, 138, 179-85

Ponthion (royal residence), 9, 110-12, 157; council at (876), 159, 163

Provence, 40, 51

Prudentius (bishop of Troyes), 5, 215 n.4

Pseudo-Isidorian decretals, 58, 61, 65, 71, 73, 85, 89, 91, 93-96, 108, 117, 132, 218 n.16

Quierzy (villa), 9; assembly at (March, 858), 3, 12; council at (November, (858), 6, 58; assembly at (868), 28, 182; assembly at (876), 160

Radoaldus (legate), 45

Ragenardus (vassal of Laon), 103

Rainelmus (bishop of Noyon), 103, 141

Remi (archbishop of Reims), 9, 12, 129

Remi (archbishop of Lyons), 40, 51, 106-8, 111, 122, 219-20 n.34

Richilde (queen), 52, 121

Rome, council at (864), 60; primacy of, 44, 59-61, 72, 89-90, 94-97, 116, 118

Rothad (bishop of Soissons), 57-61, 66, 68, 73, 80, 91, 103, 107, 128-29

Rudolf (archbishop of Bourges), 63

Rudolf (count), 15, 179-80, 183

Saint Alban's (monastery), 158

Saint-Denis (monastery), 10, 30, 53-54, 114-15, 122, 126, 162

Samoussy (royal residence), 68

Sardica, council at (343), 59, 95, 98, 117, 142, 147

Senatus (cleric), 80-84

Senlis, 23, 50, 104, 121, 125, 156-57

Servais (villa), 9, 15, 32-33, 36-37, 49, 69, 77, 83, 107, 113, 128, 145, 157, 182; council at (871), 127

Simeon (bishop of Laon), 13

Sylvester (pope), 117

Tardenois, 13

Teutlandus (deacon), 32-33, 112, 125

Theodore (bishop of Cambrai), 58

Theodoricus (papal *missus*), 162

Theutberga (queen), 39-40,

43, 46, 52

Theutgard (archbishop of Trier), 45-46, 52

Toul, 51

Tours, 7

Trier, 52; succession to see of, 46-47, 52, 70

Trisingus (priest), 148-49

Troyes, council at (867), 64; council at (878), 160, 163-64

Tusey (villa), council at (860), 111-14, 116; assembly at (865), 46

Ver (royal residence), council at (844), 20

Verberie (royal residence), 9, 30; council at (863), 60; council at (869), 31, 36, 105, 134, 182-83

Verdun, 50, 130; treaty of (843), 4-5, 7, 10, 20, 58

Vikings, 3, 5, 13, 153, 158-60, 188 n.16

Walco (vassal of Laon), 32

Waldrada (mistress of

Lothar II), 40, 43, 46-47, 120, 162

Waltonus (archbishop-designate of Trier), 52

Wenilon (bishop of Laon), 79

Wenilon (archbishop of Rouen), 16, 37, 70, 86, 135

Willebert (bishop of Châlons), 28-29

Willibert (archbishop-designate of Cologne), 52, 261 n.94

Witgarius (bishop of Augsburg), 78

Wulfad (archbishop of Bourges), 57, 62-64, 68, 91, 121, 128-29

Yütz (royal residence), council at (844), 20